15th Workshop on Innovative Use of NLP for Building Educational Applications 2020

Online
10 July 2020

ISBN: 978-1-7138-1382-8

15th Workshop on Innovative Use of NLP for Building Educational Applications 2020

Online
10 July 2020

ACL 2020

**Innovative Use of NLP for
Building Educational Applications**

Proceedings of the 15th Workshop

July 10, 2020

Gold Sponsors

Silver Sponsors

Introduction

When we sent out our call for papers this year, we never imagined that the *Workshop on Innovative Use of NLP for Building Educational Applications* would be held virtually. While the circumstances are far from ideal, this will be an interesting experiment. We are pleased to host a set of innovative papers – even if virtually! Our papers this year include topics related to automated writing and speech and content evaluation, writing analytics, text revision analysis, building dialog resources, tracking writing proficient, neural models for writing evaluation tasks, and educational applications for languages other than English.

This year we received a total of 49 submissions and accepted 8 papers as oral presentations and 13 as poster presentations, for an overall acceptance rate of 43 percent. Each paper was reviewed by three members of the Program Committee who were believed to be most appropriate for each paper. We continue to have a strong policy to deal with conflicts of interest. First, we continue to make a concerted effort to resolve conflicts of interest - specifically, we do not assign papers to a reviewer if the paper has an author from their institution. Second, organizing committee members recuse themselves from discussions about papers if there is a conflict of interest.

Papers are accepted on the basis of several factors, including the relevance to a core educational problem space, the novelty of the approach or domain, and the strength of the research. The accepted papers were highly diverse – an indicator of the growing variety of foci in this field. We continue to believe that the workshop framework designed to introduce work in progress and new ideas is important and we hope that the breadth and variety of research accepted for this workshop is represented.

The BEA15 workshop has presentations on automated writing evaluation, readability, dialog, speech and grammatical error correction, annotation and resources, and educational research that serves languages other than English.

Automated Writing Evaluation
González-López et al's *Assisting Undergraduate Students in Writing Spanish Methodology Sections* discusses a method that provides feedback to students with regard to how they have improved the methodology section of a paper; Ghosh et al's *An Exploratory Study of Argumentative Writing by Young Students: A Transformer-based Approach* uses a transformer-based architecture (e.g., BERT) fine-tuned on a large corpus of critique essays from the college task to conduct a computational exploration of argument critique writing by young students; Afrin et al's *Annotation and Classification of Evidence and Reasoning Revisions in Argumentative Writing* introduces an annotation scheme to capture the nature of sentence-level revisions of evidence use and reasoning and apply it to 5th- and 6th-grade students' argumentative essays. They show that reliable manual annotation can be achieved and that revision annotations correlate with a holistic assessment of essay improvement in line with the feedback provided. They explore the feasibility of automatically classifying revisions according to their scheme; Wang et al's *Automated Scoring of Clinical Expressive Language Evaluation Tasks* present a dataset consisting of non-clinically elicited responses for three related sentence formulation tasks, and propose an approach for automatically evaluating their appropriateness. They use neural machine translation to generate correct-incorrect sentence pairs in order to create synthetic data to increase the amount and diversity of training data for their scoring model and show how transfer learning improves scoring accuracy,

Automated Content Evaluation & Vocabulary Analysis
Riordan et al's *An Empirical Investigation of Neural Methods for Content Scoring of Science Explanations* presents an empirical investigation of feature-based models, recurrent neural network models, and pre-trained transformer models on scoring content in real-world formative assessment data. They demonstrate that recent neural methods can rival or exceed the performance of feature-based methods and provide evidence that different classes of neural models take advantage of different

learning cues, and that pre-trained transformer models may be more robust to spurious, dataset-specific learning cues, better reflecting scoring rubrics.; Cahill et al's *Context-based Automated Scoring of Complex Mathematical Responses* proposes a method for automatically scoring responses that contain both text and algebraic expressions. Their method not only achieves high agreement with human raters, but also links explicitly to the scoring rubric; Ehara's *Interpreting Neural CWI Classifiers' Weights as Vocabulary Size* studies Complex Word Identification (CWI) – a task for the identification of words that are challenging for second-language learners to read. The paper analyzes neural CWI classifiers and shows that some of their parameters can be interpreted as vocabulary size.

Writing Analytics and Feedback

Davidson et al's *Tracking the Evolution of Written Language Competence in L2 Spanish Learners* presents an NLP-based approach for tracking the evolution of written language competence in L2 Spanish learners using a wide range of linguistic features automatically extracted from students' written productions. The authors explore the connection between the most predictive features and the teaching curriculum, finding that their set of linguistic features often reflect the explicit instructions that students receive during each course; Hellman et al's *Multiple Instance Learning for Content Feedback Localization without Annotation* considers automated essay scoring as a Multiple Instance Learning (MIL) task. The authors show that such models can both predict content scores and localize content by leveraging their sentence-level score predictions; Kerz et al's *Becoming Linguistically Mature: Modeling English and German Children's Writing Development Across School Grades* employs a novel approach to advancing our understanding of the development of writing in English and German children across school grades using classification tasks. Their experiments show that RNN classifiers trained on complexity contours achieve higher classification accuracy than one trained on text-average complexity scores; Mayfield and Black's *Should You Fine-Tune BERT for Automated Essay Scoring?* investigates whether, in automated essay scoring research, transformer-based models are an appropriate technological choice. The authors conclude with a review of promising areas for research on student essays where the unique characteristics of transformers may provide benefits over classical methods to justify the costs; Mathias and Bhattacharyya's *Can Neural Networks Automatically Score Essay Traits?* shows how a deep-learning based system can outperform both feature-based machine learning systems and string kernel-based systems when scoring essay traits.

Readability & Item Difficulty/Selection

Deutsch et al's *Linguistic Features for Readability Assessment* combines linguistically-motivated machine learning and deep learning methods to improve overall readability model performance; Xue et al's *Predicting the Difficulty and Response Time of Multiple Choice Questions Using Transfer Learning* investigates whether transfer learning can improve the prediction of the difficulty and response time parameters for 18,000 multiple-choice questions from a high-stakes medical exam. The results indicate that, for their sample, transfer learning can improve the prediction of item difficulty; Gao et al's *Distractor Analysis and Selection for Multiple-Choice Cloze Questions for Second-Language Learners* considers the problem of automatically suggesting distractors for multiple-choice cloze questions designed for second-language learners. Based on their analyses, they train models to automatically select distractors, and measure the importance of model components quantitatively.

Evaluation, Resources, Speech & Dialog

Loukina et al's *Using PRMSE to Evaluate Automated Scoring Systems in the Presence of Label Noise* discusses the effect that noisy labels have on system evaluation and propose the use of a new educational measurement metric (PRMSE) to help address this issue; Raina et al's *Complementary Systems for Off-topic Spoken Response Detection* examines one form of spoken language assessment; whether the response from the candidate is relevant to the prompt provided. The work focuses on the scenario when the prompt, and associated responses have not been seen in the training data, enabling the system to be applied to new test scripts without the need to collect data or retrain the model; Maxwell-Smith et al's *Applications of Natural Language Processing in Bilingual Language Teaching: An Indonesian-*

English Case Study discusses methodological considerations for using automated speech recognition to build a corpus of teacher speech in an Indonesian language classroom; Stasaki et al's *Construction of a Large Open Access Dialogue Dataset for Tutoring* proposes a novel asynchronous method for collecting tutoring dialogue via crowdworkers that is both amenable to the needs of deep learning algorithms and reflective of pedagogical concerns. The CIMA dataset produced from this work is publicly available.

Grammatical Error Correction
Omilianchuk et al's *GECToR – Grammatical Error Correction: Tag, Not Rewrite* presents a simple and efficient GEC sequence tagger using a transformer encoder; White & Rozovskaya's *A Comparative Study of Synthetic Data Generation Methods for Grammatical Error Correction* compares techniques for generating synthetic data utilized by the two highest scoring submissions to the restricted and low-resource tracks in the BEA-2019 Shared Task on Grammatical Error Correction.

We wish to thank everyone who showed interest and submitted a paper, all of the authors for their contributions, the members of the Program Committee for their thoughtful reviews, and everyone who is attending this workshop, virtually! We would especially like to thank our Gold Level sponsor, the National Board of Medical Examiners.

Finally, our special thanks go to the emergency reviewers who stepped in to provide their expertise and help ensure the highest level of feedback: we acknowledge the help of Beata Beigman Klebanov, Christopher Bryant, Andrew Caines, Mariano Felice, Yoko Futagi, Ananya Ganesh, Anastassia Loukina, and Marek Rei.

Jill Burstein, Educational Testing Service
Ekaterina Kochmar, University of Cambridge
Nitin Madnani, Educational Testing Services
Claudia Leacock, Grammarly
Ildikó Pilán, University of Oslo
Helen Yannakoudakis, King's College London
Torsten Zesch, University of Duisburg-Essen

Organizers:

Jill Burstein, Educational Testing Service
Ekaterina Kochmar, University of Cambridge
Nitin Madnani, Educational Testing Services
Claudia Leacock, Grammarly
Ildikó Pilán, University of Oslo
Helen Yannakoudakis, King's College London
Torsten Zesch, University of Duisburg-Essen

Program Committee:

Tazin Afrin, University of Pittsburgh
David Alfter, University of Gothenburg
Dimitris Alikaniotis, Grammarly
Fernando Alva-Manchego, University of Sheffield
Rajendra Banjade, Audible (Amazon)
Timo Baumann, Universität Hamburg
Lee Becker, Pearson
Beata Beigman Klebanov, Educational Testing Service
Lisa Beinbron, University of Amsterdam
Maria Berger, German Research Center for Artificial Intelligence
Kay Berkling, DHBW Cooperative State University Karlsruhe
Delphine Bernhard, Université de Strasbourg, France
Sameer Bhatnagar, Polytechnique Montreal
Serge Bibauw, KU Leuven; UCLouvain; Universidad Central del Ecuador
Joachim Bingel, University of Copenhagen
Kristy Boyer, University of Florida
Chris Brew, Facebook AI
Ted Briscoe, University of Cambridge
Chris Brockett, Microsoft Research AI
Julian Brooke, University of British Columbia
Christopher Bryant, University of Cambridge
Jill Burstein, Educational Testing Service
Aoife Cahill, Educational Testing Service
Andrew Caines, University of Cambridge
Guanliang Chen, Monash University
Mei-Hua Chen, Department of Foreign Languages and Literature
Martin Chodorow, City University of New York
Leshem Choshen, Hebrew University of Jerusalem
Mark Core, University of Southern California
Luis Fernando D'Haro, Universidad Politécnica de Madrid
Vidas Daudaravicius, UAB VTeX
Orphée De Clercq, LT3, Ghent University
Kordula De Kuthy, Tübingen University
Iria del Río Gayo, University of Lisbon
Carrie Demmans Epp, University of Alberta
Ann Devitt, Trinity College, Dublin

Yo Ehara, Shizuoka Institute of Science and Technology
Noureddine Elouazizi, Faculty of Science
Keelan Evanini, Educational Testing Service
Mariano Felice, University of Cambridge
Michael Flor Educational Testing Service
Thomas François, Université catholique de Louvain
Jennifer-Carmen Frey, Eurac Research
Yoko Futagi, Educational Testing Service
Michael Gamon, Microsoft Research
Ananya Ganesh, University of Massachusetts Amherst
Dipesh Gautam, University of Memphis
Sian Gooding, University of Cambridge
Cyril Goutte, National Research Council Canada
Roman Grundkiewicz, University of Edinburgh
Masato Hagiwara, Octanove Labs LLC
Jiangang Hao, Educational Testing Service
Homa Hashemi, Microsoft
Trude Heift, Simon Fraser University
Heiko Holz, LEAD Graduate School and Research Network
Andrea Horbach, University Duisburg-Essen
Renfen Hu, Beijing Normal University
Chung-Chi, Huang Frostburg State University
Yi-Ting Huang, Academia Sinica
Radu Tudor Ionescu, University of Bucharest
Lifeng Jin, Ohio State University
Marcin Junczys-Dowmunt, Microsoft
Tomoyuki Kajiwara, Osaka University
Elma Kerz, RWTH Aachen University
Fazel Keshtkar, St. John's University
Mamoru Komachi, Tokyo Metropolitan University
Lun-Wei Ku, Academia Sinica
Kristopher Kyle, University of Oregon
Ji-Ung Lee, UKP Lab, TU Darmstadt
Lung-Hao Lee, National Central University
John Lee, City University of Hong Kong
Chee Wee (Ben) Leong, Educational Testing Service
Chen Liang, Facebook
Diane Litman, University of Pittsburgh
Zitao Liu, TAL Education Group
Peter Ljunglöf, University of Gothenburg; Chalmers University of Technology
Anastassia Loukina, Educational Testing Service
Lieve Macken, Ghent University
Nabin Maharjan, Audible (Amazon)
Montse Maritxalar, University of the Basque Country
James Martin, University of Colorado Boulder
Irina Maslowski
Sandeep Mathias, IIT Bombay
Noboru Matsuda, North Carolina State University
Julie Medero, Harvey Mudd College
Detmar Meurers, University of Tübingen

Michael Mohler, Language Computer Corporation
Natawut Monaikul, University of Illinois at Chicago
Farah Nadeem, University of Wahington
Courtney Napoles, Grammarly
Diane Napolitano, Refinitiv
Hwee Tou Ng, National University of Singapore
Huy Nguyen, LingoChamp
Rodney Nielsen, University of North Texas
Yoo Rhee Oh, Electronics and Telecommunications Research Institute (ETRI)
Robert Östling, Department of linguistics, Stockholm university
Ulrike Pado, HFT Stuttgart
Patti Price, PPRICE Speech and Language Technology
Long Qin, Singsound Inc
Mengyang Qiu, University at Buffalo
Martí Quixal, Universität Tübingen
Vipul Raheja, Grammarly
Zahra Rahimi Pandora Media
Taraka Rama, University of North Texas
Vikram Ramanarayanan, Educational Testing Service; University of California, San Francisco
Hanumant Redkar, IIT Bombay
Marek Rei, University of Cambridge
Robert Reynolds, Brigham Young University
Brian Riordan, Educational Testing Service
Andrew Rosenberg, Google
Alla Rozovskaya, City University of New York
C. Anton Rytting, University of Maryland
Keisuke Sakaguchi, Allen Institute for Artificial Intelligence
Katira Soleymanzadeh, EGE University
Swapna Somasundaran, Educational Testing Service
Helmer Strik, Radboud University Nijmegen
Jan Švec, University of West Bohemia
Anaïs Tack, UCLouvain and KU Leuven
Alexandra Uitdenbogerd, RMIT University
Sowmya Vajjala, National Research Council, Canada
Piper Vasicek, Brigham Young University
Giulia Venturi, Institute for Computational Linguistics
Tatiana Vodolazova, University of Alicante
Elena Volodina, University of Gothenburg, Sweden
Yiyi Wang, UIUC; Boston College
Shuting Wang, Facebook
Zarah Weiss, University of Tübingen
Michael White, The Ohio State University; Facebook AI
Alistair Willis, Open University, UK
Wei Xu, Ohio State University
Kevin Yancey, Duolingo
Victoria Yaneva, NBME; University of Wolverhampton
Seid Muhie Yimam, University of Hamburg
Marcos Zampieri, Rochester Institute of Technology
Klaus Zechner, Educational Testing Service
Fabian Zehner, DIPF, Leibniz Institute for Research and Information in Education
Haoran Zhang, University of Pittsburgh

Table of Contents

Conference Program

Linguistic Features for Readability Assessment

Tovly Deutsch   Masoud Jasbi   Stuart Shieber
Harvard University
tdeutsch@college.harvard.edu, masoud_jasbi@fas.harvard.edu
shieber@seas.harvard.edu

Abstract

Readability assessment aims to automatically classify text by the level appropriate for learning readers. Traditional approaches to this task utilize a variety of linguistically motivated features paired with simple machine learning models. More recent methods have improved performance by discarding these features and utilizing deep learning models. However, it is unknown whether augmenting deep learning models with linguistically motivated features would improve performance further. This paper combines these two approaches with the goal of improving overall model performance and addressing this question. Evaluating on two large readability corpora, we find that, given sufficient training data, augmenting deep learning models with linguistically motivated features does not improve state-of-the-art performance. Our results provide preliminary evidence for the hypothesis that the state-of-the-art deep learning models represent linguistic features of the text related to readability. Future research on the nature of representations formed in these models can shed light on the learned features and their relations to linguistically motivated ones hypothesized in traditional approaches.

1   Introduction

Readability assessment poses the task of identifying the appropriate reading level for text. Such labeling is useful for a variety of groups including learning readers and second language learners. Readability assessment systems generally involve analyzing a corpus of documents labeled by editors and authors for reader level. Traditionally, these documents are transformed into a number of linguistic features that are fed into simple models like SVMs and MLPs (Schwarm and Ostendorf, 2005; Vajjala and Meurers, 2012).

More recently, readability assessment models utilize deep neural networks and attention mechanisms (Martinc et al., 2019). While such models achieve state-of-the-art performance on readability assessment corpora, they struggle to generalize across corpora and fail to achieve perfect classification. Often, model performance is improved by gathering additional data. However, readability annotations are time-consuming and expensive given lengthy documents and the need for qualified annotators. A different approach to improving model performance involves fusing the traditional and modern paradigms of linguistic features and deep learning. By incorporating the inductive bias provided by linguistic features into deep learning models, we may be able to reduce the limitations posed by the small size of readability datasets.

In this paper, we evaluate the joint use of linguistic features and deep learning models. We achieve this fusion by simply taking the output of deep learning models as features themselves. Then, these outputs are joined with linguistic features to be further fed into some other model like an SVM. We select linguistic features based on a broad psycholinguistically-motivated composition by Vajjala Balakrishna (2015). Transformers and Hierarchical attention networks were selected as the deep learning models because of their state-of-art performance in readability assessment. Models were evaluated on two of the largest available corpora for readability assessment: WeeBit and Newsela. We also evaluate with different sized training sets to investigate the use of linguistic features in data-poor contexts. Our results find that, given sufficient training data, the linguistic features do not provide a substantial benefit over deep learning methods.

The rest of this paper is organized as follows. Related research is described in section 2. Section 3 details our preprocessing, features, and model construction. Section 4 presents model evaluations on

1

Proceedings of the 15th Workshop on Innovative Use of NLP for Building Educational Applications, pages 1–17
July 10, 2020. ©2020 Association for Computational Linguistics

two corpora. Section 5 discusses the implications of our results.

We provide a publicly available version of the code used for our experiments.[1]

2   Related Work

Work on readability assessment has involved progress on three core components: corpora, features, and models. While early work utilized small corpora, limited feature sets, and simple models, modern research has experimented with a broad set of features and deep learning techniques.

Labeled corpora can be difficult to assemble given the time and qualifications needed to assign a text a readability level. The size of readability corpora expanded significantly with the introduction of the WeeklyReader corpus by Schwarm and Ostendorf (2005). Composed of articles from an educational magazine, the WeeklyReader corpus contains roughly 2,400 articles. The WeeklyReader corpus was then built upon by Vajjala and Meurers (2012) by adding data from the BBC Bitesize website to form the WeeBit corpus. This WeeBit corpus is larger, containing roughly 6,000 documents, while also spanning a greater range of readability levels. Within these corpora, topic and readability are highly correlated. Thus, Xia et al. (2016) constructed the Newsela corpus in which each article is represented at multiple reading levels thereby diminishing this correlation.

Early work on readability assessment, such as that of Flesch (1948), extracted simple textual features like character count. More recently, Schwarm and Ostendorf (2005) analyzed a broader set of features including out-of-vocabulary scores and syntactic features such as average parse tree height. Vajjala and Meurers (2012) assembled perhaps the broadest class of features. They incorporated measures shown by Lu (2010) to correlate well with second language acquisition measures, as well as psycholinguistically relevant features from the Celex Lexical database and MRC Psycholinguistic Database (Baayen et al., 1995; Wilson, 1988).

Traditional feature formulas, like the Flesch formula, relied on linear models. Later work progressed to more complex related models like SVMs (Schwarm and Ostendorf, 2005). Most recently, state-of-art-performance has been achieved on readability assessment with deep neural network incor-

porating attention mechanisms. These approaches ignore linguistic features entirely and instead feed the raw embeddings of input words, relying on the model itself to extract any relevant features. Specifically, Martinc et al. (2019) found that a pretrained transformer model achieved state-of-the-art performance on the WeeBit corpus while a hierarchical attention network (HAN) achieved state-of-the-art performance on the Newsela corpus.

Deep learning approaches generally exclude any specific linguistic features. In general, a "featureless" approach is sensible given the hypothesis that, with enough data, training, and model complexity, a model should learn any linguistic features that researchers might attempt to precompute. However, precomputed linguistic features may be useful in data-poor contexts where data acquisition is expensive and error-prone. For this reason, in this paper we attempt to incorporate linguistic features with deep learning methods in order to improve readability assessment.

3   Methodology

3.1   Corpora

3.1.1   WeeBit

The WeeBit corpus was assembled by Vajjala and Meurers (2012) by combining documents from the WeeklyReader educational magazine and the BBC Bitesize educational website. They selected classes to assemble a broad range of readability levels intended for readers aged 7 to 16. To avoid classification bias, they undersampled classes in order to equalize the number of documents in each class to 625. We term this downsampled corpus "WeeBit downsampled". Following the methodologies of Xia et al. (2016) and Martinc et al. (2019), we applied additional preprocessing to the WeeBit corpus in order to remove extraneous material.

3.1.2   Newsela

The Newsela corpus (Xia et al., 2016) consists of 1,911 news articles each re-written up to 4 times in simplified manners for readers at different reading levels. This simplification process means that, for any given topic, there exist examples of material on that topic suited for multiple reading levels. This overlap in topic should make the corpus more challenging to label than the WeeBit corpus. In a similar manner to the WeeBit corpus, the Newsela corpus is labeled with grade levels ranging from grade 2 to grade 12. As with WeeBit, these labels

---

[1]`https://github.com/TovlyDeutsch/Linguistic-Features-for-Readability`

can either be treated as classes or transformed into numeric labels for regression.

3.1.3 Labeling Approaches

Often, readability classes within a corpus are treated as unrelated. These approaches use raw labels as distinct unordered classes. However, readability labels are ordinal, ranging from lower to higher readability. Some work has addressed this issue such as the readability models of Flor et al. (2013) which predict grade levels via linear regression. To test different approaches to acknowledging this ordinality, we devised three methods for labeling the documents: "classification", "age regression", and "ordered class regression".

The classification approach uses the classes originally given. This approach does not suppose any ordinality of the classes. Avoiding such ordinality may be desirable for the sake of simplicity.

"Age regression" applies the mean of the age ranges given by the constituent datasets. For instance, in this approach Level 2 documents from Weekly Reader would be given the label of 7.5 as they are intended for readers of ages 7-8. The advantage of age regression over standard classification is that it provides more precise information about the magnitude of readability differences.

Finally, "ordered class regression" assigns the classes equidistant integers ordered by difficulty. The least difficult class would be labeled "0", the second least difficult class would be labeled "1" and so on. As with age regression, this labeling results in a regression rather than classification problem. This method retains the advantage of age regression in demonstrating ordinality. However, ordered regression labeling removes information about the relative differences in difficulty between the classes, instead asserting that they are equidistant in difficulty. The motivation behind this loss of information is that such age differences between classes may not directly translate into differences of difficulty. For instance, the readability difference between documents intended for 7 or 8 year-olds may be much greater than between documents intended for 15 or 16 year-olds because reading development is likely accelerated in younger years.

For final model inferences, we used the classification approach for comparison to previous work. For intermediary CNN models, all three approaches were tested. As the different approaches with CNN models produced insubstantial differences, other model types were restricted to the simple classification approach.

3.2 Features

Motivated by the success in using linguistic features for modeling readability, we considered a large range of textual analyses relevant to readability. In addition to utilizing features posed in the existing readability research, we investigated formulating new features with a focus on syntactic ambiguity and syntactic diversity. This challenging aspect of language appeared to be underutilized in existing readability literature.

3.2.1 Existing Features

To capture a variety of features, we utilized existing linguistic feature computation software[2] developed by Vajjala Balakrishna (2015) based on 86 feature descriptions in existing readability literature. Given the large number of features, in this section we will focus on the categories of features and their psycholinguistic motivations (where available) and properties. The full list of features used can be found in appendix A.

Traditional Features The most basic features involve what Vajjala and Meurers (2012) refer to as "traditional features" for their use in long-standing readability formulae. They include characters per word, syllables per word, and traditional formulas based on such features like the Flesch-Kincaid formula (Kincaid et al., 1975).

Another set of feature types consists of counts and ratios of part-of-speech tags, extracted using the Stanford parser (Klein and Manning, 2003). In addition to basic parts of speech like nouns, some features include phrase level constituent counts like noun phrases and verb phrases. All of these counts are normalized by either the number of word tokens or number of sentences to make them comparable across documents of differing lengths. These counts are not provided with any psycholinguistic motivation for their use; however, it is not an unreasonable hypothesis that the relative usage of these constituents varies across reading levels. Empirically, these features were shown to have some predictive power for readability. In addition to parts of speech counts, we also utilized word type counts as a simple baseline feature, that is, counting the number of instances of each possible word

---

in the vocabulary. These counts are also divided by document length to generate proportions.

Becoming more abstract than parts of speech, some features count complex syntactic constituent like clauses and subordinated clauses. Specifically, Lu (2010) found ratios involving sentences, clauses, and t-units[3] that correlated with second language learners' abilities to read a document. For many of the multi-word syntactic constituents previously described, such as noun phrases and clauses, features were also constructed of their mean lengths. Finally, properties of the syntactic trees themselves were analyzed such as their mean heights.

Moving beyond basic features from syntactic parses, Vajjala Balakrishna (2015) also incorporated "word characteristic" features from linguistic databases. A significant source was the Celex Lexical Database Baayen et al. (1995) which "consists of information on the orthography, phonology, morphology, syntax and frequency for more than 50,000 English lemmas". The database appears to have a focus on morphological data such as whether a word may be considered a loan word and whether it contains affixes. It also contains syntactic properties that may not be apparent from a syntactic parse, e.g. whether a noun is countable. The MRC Psycholinguistic Database Wilson (1988) was also used with a focus on its age of acquisition ratings for words, an clear indicator of the appropriateness of a document's vocabulary.

3.2.2 Novel Syntactic Features

We investigated additional syntactic features that may be relevant for readability but whose qualities were not targeted by existing features. These features were used in tandem with the existing linguistic features described previously; future work could utilize these novel feature independently to investigate their particular effect on readability information extraction. For generating syntactic parses, we used the PCFG (probabilistic context-free grammar) parser (Klein and Manning, 2003) from the Stanford Parser package.

Syntactic Ambiguity   Sentences can have multiple grammatical syntactic parses. Therefore, syntactic parsers produce multiple parses annotated with parse likelihood. It may seem sensible to use the number of parses generated as a measure of

ambiguity. However, this measure is extremely sensitive to sentence length as longer sentences tend to have more possible syntactic parses. Instead, if this list of probabilities is viewed as a distribution, the standard deviation of this distribution is likely to correlate with perceptions of syntactic ambiguity.

Definition 3.1. PD_x

The parse deviation, $PD_x(s)$, of sentence s is the standard deviation of the distribution of the x most probable parse log probabilities for s. If s has less than x valid parses, the distribution is taken from all the valid parses.

For large values of x, $PD_x(s)$ can be significantly sensitive to sentence length: longer sentences are likely to have more valid syntactic parses and thus create low probability tails that increase standard deviation. To reduce this sensitivity, an alternative involves measuring the difference between the largest and mean parse probability.

Definition 3.2. PDM_x

$PDM_x(s)$ is the difference between the largest parse log probability and the mean of the log probabilities of the x most probable parses for a sentence s. If s has less than x valid parses, the mean is taken over all the valid parses.

As a compromise between parse investigation and the noise of implausible parses, we selected PDM_{10}, PD_{10}, and PD_2 as features to use in the models of this paper.

Part-of-Speech Divergence   To capture the grammatical makeup of a sentence or document, we can count the usage of each part of speech ("POS"), phrase, or clause. The counts can be collected into a distribution. Then, the standard deviation of this distribution, $POSD_{dev}$, measures a sentence's grammatical heterogeneity.

Definition 3.3. $POSD_{dev}$

$POSD_{dev}(d)$ is the standard deviation of the distribution of POS counts for document d.

Similarly, we may want to measure how this grammatical makeup differs from the composition of the document as a whole, a concept that might be termed syntactic uniqueness. To capture this concept, we measure the Kullback-Leibler divergence (Kullback and Leibler, 1951) between the sentence POS count distribution and the document POS count distribution.

Definition 3.4. POS_{div}

---

[3]Defined by Vajjala and Meurers (2012) to be "one main clause plus any subordinate clause or non-clausal structure that is attached to or embedded in it".

Let $P(s)$ be the distribution of POS counts for sentence s in document d. Let Q be the distribution of POS counts for document d. Let $|d|$ be the number of sentences in d.

$$POS_{div}(d) = \sum_{s \in d} \frac{D_{KL}(P(s) \;\|\; Q)}{|d|}$$

3.3 Models

A large range of model complexities were evaluated in order to ascertain the performance improvements, or lack thereof, of additional model complexity. In this section we will describe the specific construction and usage of these models for the experiments conducted in this paper, ordered roughly by model complexity.

SVMs, Linear Models, and Logistic Regression
We used the Scikit-Learn library (Pedregosa et al., 2011) for constructing SVM models. Hyperparameter optimization was performed using the guidelines suggested by Hsu et al. (2003). From the Scikit-Learn library, we also utilized the linear support vector classifier (an SVM with a linear kernel) and logistic regression classifier. As simplicity was the aim for these evaluations, no hyperparameter optimization was performed. The logistic regression classifier was trained using the stochastic average gradient descent ("sag") optimizer.

CNN Convolutional neural networks were selected for their demonstrated performance on sentence classification (Kim, 2014). The CNN model used in this paper is based on the one described by Kim (2014) and implemented using the Keras (Chollet and others, 2015), Tensorflow (Abadi et al., 2015), and Magpie libraries.

Transformer The transformer (Vaswani et al., 2017) is a neural-network-based model that has achieved state-of-the-art results on a wide array of natural language tasks including readability assessment (Martinc et al., 2019). Transformers utilize the mechanism of attention which allows the model to attend to specific parts of the input when constructing the output. Although they are formulated as sequence-to-sequence models, they can be modified to complete a variety of NLP tasks by placing an additional linear layer at the end of the network and training that layer to produce the desired output. This approach often achieves state-of-the-art results when combined with pretraining. In this paper, we use the BERT (Devlin

et al., 2019) transformer-based model that is pretrained on BooksCorpus (800M words) (Zhu et al., 2015) and English Wikipedia. The model is then fine-tuned on a specific readability corpus such as WeeBit. The pretrained BERT model is sourced from the Huggingface transformers library (Wolf et al., 2019) and is composed of 12 hidden layers each of size 768 and 12 self-attention heads. The fine-tuning step utilizes an implementation by Martinc et al. (2019). Among the pretrained transformers in the Huggingface library, there are transformers that can accept sequences of size 128, 256, and 512. The 128 sized model was chosen based on the finding by Martinc et al. (2019) that it achieved the highest performance on the WeeBit and Newsela corpora. Documents that exceeded the input sequence size were truncated.

HAN The Hierarchical attention network involves feeding the input through two bidirectional RNNs each accompanied by a separate attention mechanism. One attention mechanism attends to the different words within each sentence while the second mechanism attends to the sentences within the document. These hierarchical attention mechanisms are thought to better mimic the structure of documents and consequently produce superior classification results. The implementation of the model used in this paper is identical to the original architecture described by Yang et al. (2016) and was provided by the authors of Martinc et al. (2019) based on code by Nguyen (2020).

3.4 Incorporating Linguistic Features with Neural Models

The neural network models thus far described take either the raw text or word vector embeddings of the text as input. They make no use of linguistic features such as those described in section 3.2. We hypothesized that combining these linguistic features with the deep neural models may improve their performance on readability assessment. Although these models theoretically represent similar features to those prescribed by the linguistic features, we hypothesized that the amount of data and model complexity may be insufficient to capture them. This can be evidenced in certain models failure to generalize across readability corpora. Martinc et al. (2019) found that the BERT model performed well on the WeeBit corpus, achieving a weighted F1 score of 0.8401, but performed poorly on the Newsela corpus only achieving an F1 score of 0.5759. They posit that this disparity occurred "because BERT is pretrained as a language model, [therefore] it tends to rely more on semantic than structural differences during the classification phase and therefore performs better on problems with distinct semantic differences between readability classes". Similarly a HAN was able to achieve better performance than BERT on the Newsela but performed substantially worse on the WeeBit corpus. Thus, under some evaluations the models have deficiencies and fail to generalize. Given these deficiencies, we hypothesized that the inductive bias provided by linguistic features may improve generalizability and overall model performance.

In order to weave together the linguistic features and neural models, we take the simple approach of using the single numerical output of a neural model as a feature itself, joined with linguistic features, and then fed into one of the simpler non-neural models such as SVMs. SVMs were chosen as the final classification model for their simplicity and frequent use in integrating numerical features. The output of the neural model could be any of the label approaches such as grade classes or age regressions described in section 3.1. While all these labeling approaches were tested for CNNs, insubstantial differences in final inferences led us to restrict intermediary results to simple classification for other model types.

3.5 Training and Evaluation Details

All experiments involved 5-fold cross validation. All neural-network-based models were trained with the Adam optimizer (Kingma and Ba, 2015) with learning rates of $10^{-3}, 10^{-4}$, and 2^{-5} for the CNN, HAN, and transformer respectively. The HAN and CNN models were trained for 20 and 30 epochs. The transformer models were fine-tuned for 3 epochs.

All results are reported as either a weighted F1 or macro F1 score. To calculate weighted F1, first the F1 score is calculated for each class independently, as if each class was a case of binary classification. Then, these F1 score are combined in a weighted mean in which each class is weighted by the number of samples in that class. Thus, the weighted F1 score treats each sample equally but prioritizes the most common classes. The macro F1 is similar to the weighted F1 score in that F1 scores are first calculated for each class independently. However, for the macro F1 score, the class F1 scores are com-

Features	Weighted F1
HAN	0.8024
SVM with HAN and linguistic features	0.8014
SVM with HAN	0.7931
SVM with linguistic features and Flesch Features	0.7694
SVM with transformer and linguistic features	0.7678
SVM with transformer, Flesch features, and linguistic features	0.7627
SVM with Linguistic features	0.7582
SVM with CNN age regression and linguistic features	0.7281
SVM with CNN ordered classes regression and linguistic features	0.7231
SVM with transformer and Flesch features	0.7186
Transformer	0.5435
CNN	0.3379

Table 1: Top 10 performing model results, transformer, and CNN on the Newsela corpus

bined in a mean without any weighting. Therefore, the macro F1 score treats each class equally but does not treat each sample equally, deprioritizing samples from large classes and prioritizing samples from small classes.

4 Results

In this section we report the experimental results of incorporating linguistic features into readability assessment models. The two corpora, WeeBit and Newsela, are analyzed individually and then compared. Our results demonstrate that, given sufficient data, linguistic features provide little to no benefit compared to independent deep learning models. While the corpus experiment results demonstrate a portion of the approaches tested, the full results are available in appendix B

4.1 Newsela Experiments

For the Newsela corpus, while linguistic features were able to improve the performance of some models, the top performers did not utilize linguistic features. The results from the top performing models are presented in table 1.

While the HAN performance was not surpassed by models with linguistic features, the transformer models were. This improvement indicates that linguistic features capture readability information that transformers cannot capture or have insufficient data to learn. The outsize effect of adding the linguistic features to the transformer models, resulting in a weighted F1 score improvement of 0.22, may reveal what types of information they address. Martinc et al. (2019) hypothesize that a pretrained language model "tends to rely more on semantic than structural differences" indicating that these features are especially suited to providing non-semantic information such as syntactic qualities.

4.2 WeeBit Experiments

The WeeBit corpus was analyzed in two perspectives: the downsampled dataset and the full dataset. Raw results and model rankings were largely comparable between the two dataset sizes.

4.2.1 Downsampled WeeBit Experiments

As with the Newsela corpus, the downsampled WeeBit corpus demonstrates no gains from being analyzed with linguistic features. The best performing model, a transformer, did not utilize linguistic features. The results for some of the best performing models are shown in table 2.

Differing with the Newsela corpus, the word type models performed near the top results on the WeeBit corpus comparably to the transformer models. Word type models have no access to word order, thus semantic and topic analysis form their core analysis. Therefore, this result supports the hypothesis of Martinc et al. (2019) that the pretrained transformer is especially attentive to semantic content. This result also indicates that the word type features can provide a significant portion of the information needed for successful readability assessment.

The differing best performing model types between the two corpora are likely due to differing compositions. Unlike the Newsela corpus, the WeeBit corpus shows strong correlation between topic and difficulty. Extracting this topic and semantic content is thought to be a particular strength of the transformer (Martinc et al., 2019) leading to its improved results on this corpus.

4.2.2 Full WeeBit Experiments

All of the models were also tested on the full imbalanced WeeBit corpus, the top performing results of which are shown in table 3. Most performance figures increased modestly. However, these gains may not be seen if documents do not match the dis-

Features	Weighted F1
Transformer	0.8387
SVM with transformer, Flesch features, and linguistic features	0.8381
SVM with transformer and Flesch features	0.8359
SVM with transformer and linguistic features	0.8344
SVM with transformer	0.8343
Logistic regression classifier with word types, Flesch features, and linguistic features	0.8135
Logistic regression classifier with word types	0.7894
Logistic regression classifier with word types, word count, and Flesch features	0.7934
SVM with CNN classifier and linguistic features	0.7923
Logistic regression classifier with word types and word count	0.7908
CNN	0.7859
HAN	0.7507

Table 2: Top 10 performing model results, CNN, and HAN on the downsampled WeeBit corpus

tribution of this imbalanced dataset. Additionally, the ranking of models between the downsampled and standard WeeBit corpora showed little change. Although the SVM with transformer and linguistic features performed better than the transformer alone, this difference is extremely small (< 0.005) and thus not likely to be statistically significant.

4.3 Effects of Training Set Size

One hypothesis explaining the lack of effect of linguistic features is that models learn to extract

Features	Weighted F1
SVM with transformer and linguistic features	0.8769
SVM with transformer and Flesch features	0.8746
SVM with transformer	0.8729
Transformer	0.8721
SVM with transformer, Flesch features, and linguistic features	0.8721

Table 3: Top 5 performing model results on the WeeBit corpus

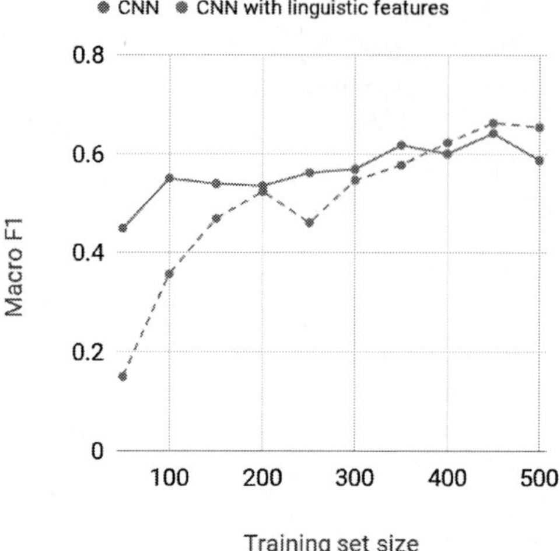

Figure 1: Performance differences across different training set sizes on the downsampled WeeBit corpus

those features given enough data. Thus, perhaps in more data-poor environments the linguistic features would prove more useful. To test this hypothesis, we evaluated two CNN-based models, one with linguistic features and one without, with various sized training subsets of the downsampled WeeBit corpus. The macro F1 at these various dataset sizes is shown in figure 1. Across the trials at different training set sizes, the test set is held constant thereby isolating the impact of training set size.

The hypothesis holds true for extremely small subsets of training data, those with fewer than 200 documents. Above this training set size, the addition of linguistic features results in insubstantial changes in performance. Thus, either the patterns exposed by the linguistic features are learnable with very little data or the patterns extracted by deep learning models differ significantly from the linguistic features. The latter appears more likely given that linguistic features are shown to improve performance for certain corpora (Newsela) and model types (transformers).

This result indicates that the use of linguistic features should be considered for small datasets. However, the dataset size at which those features lose utility is extremely small. Therefore, collecting additional data would often be more efficient than investing the time to incorporate linguistic features.

4.4 Effects of Linguistic Features

Overall, the failure of linguistic features to improve state-of-the-art deep learning models indicates that, given the available corpora, model complexity, and model structures, they do not add information over and beyond what the state-of-the-art models have already learned. However, in certain data-poor contexts, they can improve the performance of deep learning models. Similarly, with more diverse and more accurately and consistently labeled corpora, the linguistic features could prove more useful. It may be the case that the best performing models already achieve near the maximal possible performance on this corpus. The reason the maximal performance may be below a perfect score (an F1 score of 1) is disagreement and inconsistency in dataset labeling. Presumably the dataset was assessed by multiple labelers who may not have always agreed with one another or even with themselves. Thus, if either a new set of human labelers or the original labelers are tasked with labeling readability in this corpus, they may only achieve performance similar to the best performance seen in these experiments. Performing this human experiment would be a useful analysis of corpus validity and consistency. Similarly, a more diverse corpus (differing in length, topic, writing style, etc.) may prove more difficult for the models to label alone without additional training data; in this case, the linguistic features may prove more helpful in providing inductive bias.

Additionally, the lack of improvement from adding linguistic features indicates that deep learning models may already be representing those features. Future work could probe the models for different aspects of the linguistic features, thereby investigating what properties are most relevant for readability.

5 Conclusion

In this paper we explored the role of linguistic features in deep learning methods for readability assessment, and asked: can incorporating linguistic features improve state-of-the-art models? We constructed linguistic features focused on syntactic properties ignored by existing features. We incorporated these features into a variety of model types, both those commonly used in readability research and more modern deep learning methods. We evaluated these models on two distinct corpora that posed different challenges for readability assessment. Additional evaluations were performed with various training set sizes to explore the inductive bias provided by linguistic features. While linguistic features occasionally improved model performance, particularly at small training set sizes, these models did not achieve state-of-the-art performance.

Given that linguistic features did not generally improve deep learning models, these models may be already implicitly capturing the features that are useful for readability assessment. Thus, future work should investigate to what degree the models represent linguistic features, perhaps via probing methods.

Although this work supports disusing linguistic features in readability assessment, this assertion is limited by available corpora. Specifically, ambiguity in the corpora construction methodology limits our ability to measure label consistency and validity. Therefore, the maximal possible performance may already be achieved by state-of-the-art models. Thus, future work should explore constructing and evaluating readability corpora with rigorous consistent methodology; such corpora may be assessed most effectively using linguistic features. For instance, accuracy could be improved by averaging across multiple labelers.

Overall, linguistic features do not appear to be useful for readability assessment. While often used in traditional readability assessment models, these features generally fail to improve the performance of deep learning methods. Thus, this paper provides a starting point to understanding the qualities and abilities of deep learning models in comparison to linguistic features. Through this comparison, we can analyze what types of information these models are well-suited to learning.

References

Martín Abadi, Ashish Agarwal, Paul Barham, Eugene Brevdo, Zhifeng Chen, Craig Citro, Greg S. Corrado, Andy Davis, Jeffrey Dean, Matthieu Devin, Sanjay Ghemawat, Ian Goodfellow, Andrew Harp, Geoffrey Irving, Michael Isard, Yangqing Jia, Rafal Jozefowicz, Lukasz Kaiser, Manjunath Kudlur, Josh Levenberg, Dandelion Mané, Rajat Monga, Sherry Moore, Derek Murray, Chris Olah, Mike Schuster, Jonathon Shlens, Benoit Steiner, Ilya Sutskever, Kunal Talwar, Paul Tucker, Vincent Vanhoucke, Vijay Vasudevan, Fernanda Viégas, Oriol Vinyals, Pete Warden, Martin Wattenberg, Martin Wicke, Yuan Yu, and Xiaoqiang Zheng. 2015. TensorFlow: large-scale machine learning on heterogeneous systems. Technical report.

Rolf Harald Baayen, Richard Piepenbrock, and Leon Gulikers. 1995. The CELEX lexical database.

François Chollet and others. 2015. Keras.

Jacob Devlin, Ming-Wei Chang, Kenton Lee, and Kristina Toutanova. 2019. BERT: Pre-training of Deep Bidirectional Transformers for Language Understanding. In *Proceedings of the 2019 Conference of the North American Chapter of the Association for Computational Linguistics: Human Language Technologies, Volume 1 (Long and Short Papers)*, pages 4171–4186, Minneapolis, Minnesota. Association for Computational Linguistics.

Rudolph Flesch. 1948. A new readability yardstick. *Journal of Applied Psychology*, 32(3):221–233.

Michael Flor, Beata Beigman Klebanov, and Kathleen M. Sheehan. 2013. Lexical tightness and text complexity. In *Proceedings of the Workshop on Natural Language Processing for Improving Textual Accessibility*, pages 29–38, Atlanta, Georgia. Association for Computational Linguistics.

Chih-wei Hsu, Chih-chung Chang, and Chih-Jen Lin. 2003. A practical guide to support vector classification. Technical report.

Yoon Kim. 2014. Convolutional Neural Networks for Sentence Classification. In *Proceedings of the 2014 Conference on Empirical Methods in Natural Language Processing (EMNLP)*, pages 1746–1751, Doha, Qatar. Association for Computational Linguistics.

J. P. Kincaid, Jr. Fishburne, Rogers Robert P., Chissom Richard L., and Brad S. 1975. Derivation of New Readability Formulas (Automated Readability Index, Fog Count and Flesch Reading Ease Formula) for Navy Enlisted Personnel:. Technical report, Defense Technical Information Center, Fort Belvoir, VA.

Diederik P. Kingma and Jimmy Ba. 2015. Adam: A method for stochastic optimization. In *3rd International Conference on Learning Representations, ICLR 2015, San Diego, CA, USA, May 7-9, 2015, Conference Track Proceedings*.

Dan Klein and Christopher D. Manning. 2003. Accurate unlexicalized parsing. In *Proceedings of the 41st Annual Meeting on Association for Computational Linguistics - ACL '03*, volume 1, pages 423–430, Sapporo, Japan. Association for Computational Linguistics.

Solomon Kullback and Richard A. Leibler. 1951. On Information and Sufficiency. *The Annals of Mathematical Statistics*, 22(1):79–86.

Victor Kuperman, Hans Stadthagen-Gonzalez, and Marc Brysbaert. 2012. Age-of-acquisition ratings for 30,000 English words. *Behavior Research Methods*, 44(4):978–990.

Xiaofei Lu. 2010. Automatic analysis of syntactic complexity in second language writing. *International Journal of Corpus Linguistics*, 15(4):474–496.

Matej Martinc, Senja Pollak, and Marko Robnik-Šikonja. 2019. Supervised and unsupervised neural approaches to text readability. *Computing Research Repository*, arXiv:1503.06733. Version 2.

Viet Nguyen. 2020. Hierarchical Attention Networks for Document Classification. Original-date: 2019-01-31T18:56:40Z.

Fabian Pedregosa, Gaël Varoquaux, Alexandre Gramfort, Vincent Michel, Bertrand Thirion, Olivier Grisel, Mathieu Blondel, Peter Prettenhofer, Ron Weiss, Vincent Dubourg, Jake Vanderplas, Alexandre Passos, David Cournapeau, Matthieu Brucher, Matthieu Perrot, and Édouard Duchesnay. 2011. Scikit-learn: Machine Learning in Python. *Journal of Machine Learning Research*, 12:2825-2830.

Sarah E. Schwarm and Mari Ostendorf. 2005. Reading Level Assessment Using Support Vector Machines and Statistical Language Models. In *Proceedings of the 43rd Annual Meeting on Association for Computational Linguistics*, ACL '05, pages 523–530, Stroudsburg, PA, USA. Association for Computational Linguistics. Event-place: Ann Arbor, Michigan.

Sowmya Vajjala and Detmar Meurers. 2012. On Improving the Accuracy of Readability Classification using Insights from Second Language Acquisition. In *Proceedings of the Seventh Workshop on Building Educational Applications Using NLP*, pages 163–173, Montréal, Canada. Association for Computational Linguistics.

Sowmya Vajjala Balakrishna. 2015. *Analyzing Text Complexity and Text Simplification: Connecting Linguistics, Processing and Educational Applications*. Dissertation, Universität Tübingen.

Ashish Vaswani, Noam Shazeer, Niki Parmar, Jakob Uszkoreit, Llion Jones, Aidan N Gomez, Łukasz Kaiser, and Illia Polosukhin. 2017. Attention is all you need. In *Advances in neural information processing systems 30*, pages 5998–6008. Curran Associates, Inc.

Michael Wilson. 1988. MRC psycholinguistic database: Machine-usable dictionary, version 2.00. *Behavior Research Methods, Instruments, & Computers*, 20(1):6–10.

Thomas Wolf, Lysandre Debut, Victor Sanh, Julien Chaumond, Clement Delangue, Anthony Moi, Pierric Cistac, Tim Rault, R'emi Louf, Morgan Funtowicz, and Jamie Brew. 2019. HuggingFace's transformers: state-of-the-art natural language processing. Technical report.

Menglin Xia, Ekaterina Kochmar, and Ted Briscoe. 2016. Text Readability Assessment for Second Language Learners. In *Proceedings of the 11th Workshop on Innovative Use of NLP for Building Educational Applications*, pages 12–22, San Diego, CA. Association for Computational Linguistics.

Zichao Yang, Diyi Yang, Chris Dyer, Xiaodong He, Alex Smola, and Eduard Hovy. 2016. Hierarchical Attention Networks for Document Classification. In *Proceedings of the 2016 Conference of the North American Chapter of the Association for Computational Linguistics: Human Language Technologies*, pages 1480–1489, San Diego, California. Association for Computational Linguistics.

Yukun Zhu, Ryan Kiros, Richard Zemel, Ruslan Salakhutdinov, Raquel Urtasun, Antonio Torralba, and Sanja Fidler. 2015. Aligning Books and Movies: Towards Story-like Visual Explanations by Watching Movies and Reading Books. *Computing Research Repository*, arXiv:1506.06724.

A   Feature Definitions

For the following definitions, if the a ratio is undefined (i.e. the denominator is zero) the result is treated as zero. Vajjala and Meurers (2012) define complex nominals to be: "a) nouns plus adjective, possessive, prepositional phrase, relative clause, participle or appositive, b) nominal clauses, c) gerunds and infinitives in subject positions." Here polysyllabic means more than two syllables and "long words" means a word with seven or more characters. Descriptions of the norms of age of acquisition ratings can be found in Kuperman et al. (2012).

Feature Name	Definition
$PD_x(s)$	The parse deviation, $PD_x(s)$, of sentence s is the standard deviation of the distribution of the x most probable parse log probabilities for s. If s has less than x valid parses, the distribution is taken from all the valid parses.
PDM_x	$PDM_x(s)$ is the difference between the largest parse log probability and the mean of the log probabilities of the x most probable parses for a sentence s. If s has less than x valid parses, the mean is taken over all the valid parses.
$POSD_{dev}$	$POSD_{dev}(d)$ is the standard deviation of the distribution of POS counts for document d.
POS_{div}	Let $P(s)$ be the distribution of POS counts for sentence s in document d. Let Q be the distribution of POS counts for document d. Let $|d|$ be the number of sentences in d. $POS_{div}(d) = \sum_{s \in d} \frac{D_{KL}(P(s) \,\|\, Q)}{|d|}$

Table 4: Novel syntactic feature definitions

Feature Name	Definition
mean t-unit lenght	number of words / number of t-units
mean parse tree height per sentence	mean parse tree height / number of sentences
subtrees per sentence	number of subtrees / number of sentences
SBARs per sentence	number of SBARs / number of sentences
NPs per sentence	number of NPs / number of sentences
VPs per sentence	number of VPs / number of sentences
PPs per sentence	number of PPs / number of sentences
mean NP size	number of children of NPs / number of NPs
mean VP size	number of children of VPs / number of VPs
mean PP size	number of children of PPs / number of PPs
WHPs per sentence	number of wh-phrases / number of sentences
RRCs per sentence	number of reduced relative clauses / number of sentences
ConjPs per sentence	number of conjunction phrases / number of sentences
clauses per sentence	number of clauses / number of sentences
t-units per sentence	number of t-units / number of sentences
clauses per t-unit	number of clauses / number of t-units
complex t-unit ratio	number of t-units that contain a dependent clause / number of t-units
dependent clauses per clause	number of dependent clauses / number of clauses
dependent clauses per t-unit	number of dependent clauses / number of t-units
coordinate clauses per clause	number of coordinate clauses / number of clauses
coordinate clauses per t-unit	number of coordinate clauses / number of t-units
complex nominals per clauses	number of complex nominals / number of clauses
complex nominals per t-unit	number of complex nominals / number of t-units
VPs per t-unit	number of VP / number of t-units

Table 5: Existing syntactic-parse-based feature definitions

Feature Name	Definition
nouns per word	number of nouns / number of words
proper nouns per word	number of proper nouns / number of words
pronouns per word	number of pronouns / number of words
conjuctions per word	number of conjuctions / number of words
adjectives per word	number of adjectives / number of words
verbs per word	number of verbs / number of words
adverbs per word	number of adverbs / number of words
modal verbs per word	number of modal verbs / number of words
prepositions per word	number of prepositions / number of words
interjections per word	number of interjections / number of words
personal pronouns per word	number of personal pronouns / number of words
wh-pronouns per word	number of wh-pronouns / number of words
lexical words per word	number of lexical words / number of words
function words per word	number of function words / number of words
determiners per word	number of determiners / number of words
VBs per word	number of base form verbs / number of words
VBDs per word	number of past tense verbs / number of words
VBGs per word	number of gerund or present participle verbs / number of words
VBNs per word	number of past participle verbs / number of words
VBPs per word	number of non-3rd person singular present verbs / number of words
VBZs per word	number of 3rd person singular present verbs / number of words
adverb variation	number of adverbs / number of lexical words
adjective variation	number of adjectives / number of lexical words
modal verb variation	number of adverbs and adverbs / number of lexical words
noun variation	number of nouns / number of lexical words
verb variation-I	number of verbs / number of unique verbs
verb variation-II	number of verbs / number of lexical words
squared verb variation-I	$(\text{number of verbs})^2$ / number of unique verbs
corrected verb variation-I	number of verbs / $\sqrt{2 * \text{number of unique verbs}}$

Table 6: Existing POS-tag-based feature definitions

Feature Name	Definition
AoA Kuperman	Mean age of acquisition of words (Kuperman database)
AoA Kuperman lemmas	Mean age of acquisition of lemmas
AoA Bird lemmas	Mean age of acquisition of lemmas, Bird norm
AoA Bristol lemmas	Mean age of acquisition of lemmas, Bristol norm
AoA Cortese and Khanna lemmas	Mean age of acquisition of lemmas, Cortese and Khanna norm
MRC familiarity	Mean word familiarity rating
MRC concreteness	Mean word concreteness rating
MRC Imageability	Mean word imageability rating
MRC Colorado Meaningfulness	mean word Colorado norms meaningfulness rating
MRC Pavio Meaningfulness	mean word Pavio norms meaningfulness rating
MRC AoA	Mean age of acquisition of words (MRC database)

Table 7: Existing psycholinguistic feature definitions

Feature Name	Definition
number of sentences	number of sentences
mean sentence length	number of words / number of sentences
number of characters	number of characters
number of syllables	number of syllables
Flesch-Kincaid Formula	$11.8 *$ syllables per word $+ 0.39 *$ words per sentence $- 15.59$
Flesch Fomula	$206.835 - 1.015 *$ words per sentence $- 84.6 *$ syllables per word
Automated Readability Index	$4.71 *$ characters per word $+ 0.5 *$ words per sentence $- 21.43$
Coleman Liau Formula	$-29.5873 *$ sentences per word $+ 5.8799 *$ characters per word $- 15.8007$
SMOG Formula	$1.0430 * \sqrt{30.0 * \text{polysyllabic words per sentence}} + 3.1291$
Fog Fomula	(words per sentence $+$ proportion of words that are polysylabic) $* 0.4$
FORCAST Readability Formula	$20 - 15 *$ monosylabic words per word
LIX Readability Formula	words per sentence $+$ long words per $word * 100.0$

Table 8: Existing traditional feature definitions

Feature Name	Definition
type token ratio	number of word types / number of word tokens
corrected type token ratio	number of word types / $\sqrt{2 * \text{number of word tokens}}$
root type token ratio	number of word types / $\sqrt{\text{number of word tokens}}$
bilogorathmic type token ratio	$log(\text{number of word types}) / log(\text{number of word tokens})$
uber index	$(log(\text{number of word types}))^2 / log(\frac{\text{number of word tokens}}{\text{number of word types}})$
measure of textual lexical diversity (MTLD)	see McCarthy and Jarvis, 2010
number of senses	total number of senses across all words / number of word tokens
hyeprnyms per word	number of hypernyms / number of word tokens
hyponyms per word	total number of senses hyponyms / number of word tokens

Table 9: Existing traditional feature definitions

B Full Model Results

Features	Weighted F1	Macro F1	SD weighted F1	SD macro F1
Linear classifier with Flesch Score	0.2147	0.2156	0.0347	0.0253
Linear classifier with Flesch features	0.3973	0.3976	0.0154	0.0087
SVM with HAN	0.5531	0.5499	0.1944	0.1928
SVM with Flesch features	0.5908	0.5905	0.0157	0.0168
SVM with CNN ordered class regression	0.6703	0.6700	0.0360	0.0334
SVM with CNN age regression	0.6743	0.6742	0.0339	0.0314
Linear classifier with word types	0.7202	0.7189	0.0063	0.0085
SVM with CNN ordered classes regression, and linguistic features	0.7265	0.7262	0.0326	0.0297
Logistic regression classification with word types, Flesch features, and linguistic features	0.7382	0.7376	0.0710	0.0684
SVM with CNN age regression and linguistic features	0.7384	0.7376	0.0361	0.0346
HAN	0.7507	0.7501	0.0306	0.0302
SVM with linguistic features and Flesch features	0.7664	0.7667	0.0109	0.0114
SVM with linguistic features	0.7665	0.7666	0.0146	0.0153
CNN	0.7859	0.7852	0.0171	0.0166
SVM with HAN and linguistic features	0.7862	0.7864	0.0631	0.0633
SVM with CNN classifier	0.7882	0.7879	0.0217	0.0195
Logistic regression with word types	0.7894	0.7887	0.0151	0.0202
Logistic regression classification with word types and word count	0.7908	0.7899	0.0130	0.0182
SVM with CNN classifier and linguistic features	0.7923	0.7919	0.0210	0.0193
Logistic regression classification with word types, word count, and Flesch features	0.7934	0.7926	0.0135	0.0187
Logistic regression with word types, Flesch features, and linguistic features	0.8135	0.8130	0.0131	0.0169
SVM with transformer	0.8343	0.8340	0.0131	0.0135
SVM with transformer and linguistic features	0.8344	0.8347	0.0106	0.0091
SVM with transformer and Flesch features	0.8359	0.8358	0.0151	0.0154
SVM with transformer, Flesch features, and linguistic features	0.8381	0.8377	0.0128	0.0118
Transformer	0.8387	0.8388	0.0097	0.0073

Table 10: WeeBit downsampled model results sorted by weighted F1 score

Features	Weighted F1	Macro F1	SD weighted F1	SD Macro F1
Linear classifier with Flesch Score	0.3357	0.1816	0.0243	0.0079
SVM with HAN	0.3625	0.2134	0.0400	0.0331
Linear classifier with Flesch features	0.3939	0.2639	0.0239	0.0305
SVM with Flesch features	0.4776	0.3609	0.0222	0.0190
SVM with CNN age regression	0.7279	0.6431	0.0198	0.0205
SVM with CNN ordered class regression	0.7316	0.6482	0.0142	0.0141
SVM with CNN age regression and linguistic features	0.7779	0.7088	0.0156	0.0194
SVM with CNN ordered classes regression, and linguistic features	0.7797	0.7114	0.0130	0.0120
Linear classifier with word types	0.7821	0.7109	0.0162	0.0127
SVM with Linguistic features and Flesch features	0.7952	0.7367	0.0121	0.0157
SVM with Linguistic features	0.7952	0.7366	0.0130	0.0164
HAN	0.8065	0.7435	0.0123	0.0220
Logistic regression classification with word types	0.8088	0.7497	0.0127	0.0152
Logistic regression classification with word types and word count	0.8088	0.7497	0.0121	0.0148
Logistic regression classification with word types, word count, and Flesch features	0.8098	0.7505	0.0130	0.0163
Logistic regression classification with word types, Flesch features, and linguistic features	0.8206	0.7664	0.0428	0.0500
CNN	0.8282	0.7748	0.0211	0.0183
SVM with CNN classifier and linguistic features	0.8286	0.7753	0.0222	0.0209
Logistic regression classification with word types, Flesch features, and ling features	0.8293	0.7760	0.0152	0.0172
SVM with CNN classifier	0.8296	0.7754	0.0163	0.0136
SVM with HAN and linguistic features	0.8441	0.7970	0.0643	0.0827
SVM with transformer, Flesch features, and linguistic features	0.8721	0.8273	0.0095	0.0121
Transformer	0.8721	0.8272	0.0071	0.0102
SVM with transformer	0.8729	0.8288	0.0064	0.0090
SVM with transformer and Flesch features	0.8746	0.8305	0.0054	0.0107
SVM with transformer and linguistic features	0.8769	0.8343	0.0077	0.0129

Table 11: WeeBit model results sorted by weighted F1 score

Features	Weighted F1	Macro F1	SD weighted F1	SD Macro F1
Linear classifier with Flesch Score	0.1668	0.0915	0.0055	0.0043
SVM with Flesch score	0.2653	0.1860	0.0053	0.0086
Logistic regression with word types	0.2964	0.2030	0.0144	0.0103
Logistic regression with word types and word count	0.2969	0.2039	0.0145	0.0095
Logistic regression with word types, word count, and Flesch features	0.3006	0.2097	0.0139	0.0088
Linear classifier with Flesch features	0.3080	0.2060	0.0110	0.0077
Logistic regression with word types, Flesch features, and linguistic features	0.3333	0.2489	0.0118	0.0162
Linear classifier with word types	0.3368	0.2485	0.0089	0.0153
CNN	0.3379	0.2574	0.0038	0.0111
SVM with CNN classifier	0.3407	0.2616	0.0079	0.0142
SVM with CNN ordered class regression	0.5207	0.4454	0.0092	0.0193
SVM with CNN age regression	0.5223	0.4469	0.0149	0.0244
SVM with transformer	0.5430	0.4711	0.0095	0.0258
Transformer	0.5435	0.4713	0.0106	0.0264
Linear classifier with linguistic features	0.5573	0.4748	0.0053	0.0140
SVM with CNN classifier, and linguistic features	0.7058	0.5510	0.0079	0.0357
SVM with Flesch features	0.7177	0.6257	0.0079	0.0292
SVM with transformer and Flesch features	0.7186	0.6305	0.0074	0.0282
SVM with CNN ordered classes regression and linguistic features	0.7231	0.6053	0.0062	0.0331
SVM with CNN age regression and linguistic features	0.7281	0.6104	0.0057	0.0337
SVM with linguistic features	0.7582	0.6432	0.0089	0.0379
SVM with transformer, Flesch features, and linguistic features	0.7627	0.6263	0.0075	0.0301
SVM with transformer and linguistic features	0.7678	0.6656	0.0230	0.0385
SVM with linguistic features and Flesch Features	0.7694	0.6446	0.0060	0.0406
SVM with HAN	0.7931	0.6724	0.0448	0.0449
SVM with HAN and linguistic features	0.8014	0.6751	0.0263	0.0379
HAN	0.8024	0.6775	0.1116	0.1825

Table 12: Newsela model results sorted by weighted F1 score

Using PRMSE to evaluate automated scoring
systems in the presence of label noise

Anastassia Loukina, Nitin Madnani, Aoife Cahill
Lili Yao, Matthew S. Johnson, Brian Riordan, Daniel F. McCaffrey
{aloukina,nmadnani,acahill}@ets.org
lili.yao@gmail.com, {msjohnson,briordan,dmccaffrey}@ets.org
Educational Testing Service, NJ, USA

Abstract

The effect of noisy labels on the performance
of NLP systems has been studied extensively
for system *training*. In this paper, we focus
on the effect that noisy labels have on system
evaluation. Using automated scoring as an example, we demonstrate that the quality of human ratings used for system evaluation have a
substantial impact on traditional performance
metrics, making it impossible to compare system evaluations on labels with different quality. We propose that a new metric, proportional
reduction in mean squared error (PRMSE), developed within the educational measurement
community, can help address this issue, and
provide practical guidelines on using PRMSE.

1 Introduction

NLP systems are usually trained and evaluated using human labels. For automated scoring systems,
these would be scores assigned by human raters.
However, human raters do not always agree on the
scores they assign (Eckes, 2008; Ling et al., 2014;
Davis, 2016; Carey et al., 2011) and the inter-rater
agreement can vary substantially across prompts
as well as across applications. For example, in the
ASAP-AES data (Shermis, 2014), the agreement
varies from Pearson's $r=0.63$ to $r=0.85$ across "essay sets" (writing prompts) .

In many automated scoring studies, the data for
training and evaluating the system are randomly
sampled from the same dataset, which means that
the quality of human labels may affect both system
training and evaluation. Notably, the effect of label quality on training and evaluation may not be
the same. Previous studies (Reidsma and Carletta,
2008; Loukina et al., 2018) suggest that when annotation noise is relatively random, a system trained
on noisier annotations may perform as well as a
system trained on clean annotations. On the other
hand, noise in the human labels used for evaluation

can have a substantial effect on the estimates of
system performance even if the noise is random.

In this paper, our focus is the effect of noise in
human labels on system *evaluation*. How do we
compare two systems evaluated on datasets with
different quality of human labels? While there exist
several public data sets that can be used to benchmark and compare automated scoring systems, in
many practical and research applications the scoring systems are customized for a particular task and,
thus, cannot be evaluated appropriately on a public
dataset. As a result, the research community has to
rely on estimates of system performance to judge
the effectiveness of the proposed approach. In an
industry context, the decision to deploy a system is
often contingent on system performance meeting
certain thresholds which may even be codified as
company- or industry-wide standards.

A typical solution to the problem of different human-human agreement across evaluation
datasets is to use human-human agreement itself
as a baseline when evaluating a system (Shermis,
2014). In this case, the system can be evaluated
either via a binary distinction (did its performance
reach human-human agreement?) or by looking
at the differences in agreement metrics as measured between two humans and between a single
human and the machine, known as "degradation"
(Williamson et al., 2012). Yet how do we interpret
these numbers? Is a system that exceeds a human-
human agreement of $r=0.4$ on one dataset better
than another that performs just below a human-
human agreement of $r=0.9$ on a *different* dataset?

In this paper, we use simulated data to demonstrate that the rate of human-human agreement has
a substantial effect on estimates of system performance, making it difficult to compare systems that
are evaluated on different datasets. We also show
that this problem cannot be resolved by simply
looking at the difference between human-human

Proceedings of the 15th Workshop on Innovative Use of NLP for Building Educational Applications, pages 18–29
July 10, 2020. ©2020 Association for Computational Linguistics

and machine-human agreement. We then show that one possible solution is to use proportional reduction in mean squared error (PRMSE) (Haberman, 2008), a metric developed in the educational measurement community, which relies on classical test theory and can adjust for human error when computing estimates of system performance.

2 Related work

The effect of noisy labels on machine learning algorithms has been extensively studied in terms of their effect on system training in both general machine learning literature (see, for example, Frénay and Verleysen (2014) for a comprehensive review), NLP (Reidsma and Carletta, 2008; Beigman Klebanov and Beigman, 2009; Schwartz et al., 2011; Plank et al., 2014; Martínez Alonso et al., 2015; Jamison and Gurevych, 2015) and automated scoring (Horbach et al., 2014; Zesch et al., 2015).

One key insight that emerged from such work is that the nature of the noise is extremely important for the system performance. Machine learning algorithms are greatly affected by systematic noise but are less sensitive to random noise (Reidsma and Carletta, 2008; Reidsma and op den Akker, 2008). A typical case of random noise is when the labeling is done by multiple annotators which minimizes the individual bias introduced by any single annotator. For example, in a study on crowdsourcing NLP tasks, Snow et al. (2008) showed that a system trained on a set of non-expert annotations obtained from multiple annotators outperformed a system trained with labels from one expert, on average.

The studies discussed so far vary the model training set, or training regime, or both while keeping the evaluation set constant. Fewer studies have considered how inter-annotator agreement may affect system *evaluation* when the training set is held constant. These studies have shown that in the case of evaluation, the label quality is likely to have a substantial impact on the estimates of system performance even if the annotation noise is random.

Reidsma and Carletta (2008) used simulated data to explore the effect of noisy labels on classifier performance. They showed that the performance of the model, measured using Cohen's Kappa, when evaluated against the 'real' (or gold-standard) labels was higher than the performance when evaluated against the 'observed' labels with added random noise. This is because for some instances, the classifier's predictions were correct, but the 'observed'

labels contained errors.

Loukina et al. (2018) used two different datasets to train and evaluate an automated system for scoring spoken language proficiency. They showed that training an automated system on perfect labels did not give any advantage over training the system on noisier labels, confirming previous findings that automated scoring systems are likely to be robust to random noise in the data. At the same time, the choice of evaluation set led to very different estimates of system performance *regardless of what data was used to train the system.*

Metrics such as Pearson's correlation or quadratically-weighted kappa, commonly used to evaluate automated scoring systems (Williamson et al., 2012; Yannakoudakis and Cummins, 2015; Haberman, 2019), compare automated scores to observed human scores without correcting for any errors in human scores. In order to account for differences in human-human agreement, these are then compared to the same metrics computed for the human raters using measures such as "degradation": the difference between human-human and human-machine agreement (Williamson et al., 2012).

In this paper, we build on findings from the educational measurement community to explore an alternative approach where estimates of system performance are corrected for measurement error in the human labels. Classical test theory (Lord and Novick, 1968) assumes that the human holistic score is composed of the test's true score and some measurement error. A "true" score is defined as the expected score over an infinite number of independent administrations of the test. While such true scores are latent variables, unobservable in real life, their underlying distribution and measurement error can be estimated if a subset of responses is scored by two independently and randomly chosen raters. Haberman (2008); Haberman et al. (2015); Haberman and Yao (2015); Yao et al. (2019a,b); Zhang et al. (2019) proposed a new metric called proportional reduction in mean squared error (PRMSE) which evaluates how well the machine scores predict the *true* score, after adjusting for the measurement error. The main contribution of this paper is a further demonstration of the utility of this metric in the context of automated scoring. Outside of educational measurement, a similar approach has been been explored in pattern recognition by Lam and Stork (2003), for example, who used estimated error rates in human labels to adjust performance estimates.

We further explore how agreement between human raters affects the *evaluation* of automated scoring systems. We focus on a specific case where the human rating process is organized in such a way that annotator bias is minimized. In other words, the label noise can be considered *random*. We also assume that the scores produced by an automated scoring system are on a continuous scale. This is typical for many automated scoring contexts including essay scoring (Shermis, 2014), speech scoring (Zechner et al., 2009) and, to some extent, content scoring (Madnani et al., 2017a; Riordan et al., 2019) but, of course, not for all possible contexts: for example, some of the SemEval 2013 shared tasks on short answer scoring (Dzikovska et al., 2016) use a different scoring approach.

3 Simulated data

In this paper, we use simulated gold-standard (or "true") scores, human scores and system scores for a set of 10,000 responses. Since "true" scores are not available for real data, using simulated data allows us to compare multiple raters and systems to the known ground-truth.[1] We focus on evaluation only and make no assumptions about the quality of the labels in the training set or any other aspects of system training. The only thing we know is that different human raters and different systems in our data set assign different scores and have different performances when evaluated against true scores.

As our gold-standard, we use a set of *continuous* scores simulated for each response and consider these to be the correct "true" score for the response. Note that the continuous nature of gold-standard scores allows us to capture the intuition that some responses fall between the ordinal score points usually assigned by human raters. To create such gold-standard scores, we randomly sampled 10,000 values from a normal distribution using the mean and standard deviation of human scores observed in a large-scale assessment (mean=3.844, std=0.74). Since the scores in the large-scale assessment we use as reference varied from 1 to 6, the gold-standard scores below 1 and above 6 were also truncated to 1 and 6 respectively.

Next, we simulated scores from 200 human raters for each of these 10,000 "responses". For

each rater, its score for a response was modeled as the gold-standard score for the response plus a random error. We model different groups of raters: with low (inter-rater correlation r=0.4), moderate (r=0.55), average (r=0.65) and high (r=0.8) agreement. The correlations for different categories were informed by correlations we have observed in empirical data from various studies. The errors for each rater were drawn from a normal distribution with a mean of 0. We chose the standard deviation values used to sample the errors in order to create 4 categories of 50 raters, each defined by a specific average inter-rater correlation. Since in most operational scenarios, human raters assign an integer score, all our simulated human scores were rounded to integers and truncated to lie in $[1, 6]$, if necessary. Table 1 shows the correlations between the simulated human rater scores within each category.

Category	# raters	HH-corr	mean	std
Low	50	0.40	3.83	1.14
Moderate	50	0.55	3.83	0.99
Average	50	0.65	3.83	0.91
High	50	0.80	3.83	0.83

Table 1: A description of the 4 categories of simulated human raters used in this study. The table shows the label of each category, the number of raters in the category, the average correlation between pairs of raters within the category, and the mean and standard deviation of the scores assigned by raters in the category.

For each response, we also simulated 25 automated scores. Like human scores, automated scores were simulated as gold-standard scores plus random error. We chose the standard deviation values used to sample the random errors so as to obtain specific levels of performance against the gold-standard scores: the worst system had a Root Mean Squared Error (RMSE) of 0.74 score points while the best system had an error of 0.07 score points. Since the interpretation of RMSE depends on the score scale, we chose these values as the percentage of gold-standard score variance.

Table 2 summarizes different automated systems simulated for this study. We created 5 categories of systems with 5 systems in each category. For the worst systems ("poor"), the mean squared error was equal to the variance of gold-standard scores (R^2=0). In other words, in terms of scoring error, a system from the "poor" category performed no

---

[1]cf. Reidsma and Carletta (2008); Yannakoudakis and Cummins (2015) who also used simulated data to model system evaluation.

better than a constant.[2] For the best system (from the "perfect" category), the mean squared error was only 0.1% of gold-standard score variance with the system achieving an R^2 of 0.99. The systems *within* each category were very close in terms of performance as measured by mean squared error but the actual simulated scores for each system were different. These simulated systems will help evaluate whether performance metrics can both differentiate systems with different performance and correctly determine when two systems have similar performance.

Category	N	R^2 (GS)	r (GS)	r ('Average')
Poor	5	0.01	0.71	0.57
Low	5	0.40	0.79	0.64
Medium	5	0.65	0.86	0.69
High	5	0.80	0.91	0.74
Perfect	5	0.99	1.00	0.80

Table 2: A description of the 5 categories of simulated systems used in this study. The table shows the label of each category, the number of systems in the category, the average R^2 of the systems within the category, and the r when evaluating the systems in the category against the gold-standard scores ("GS"). The last column shows the average correlation of the systems' scores with simulated rater scores from the "Average" category.

To summarize, the final simulated dataset consisted of 10,000 "responses". Each response had 1 "gold-standard" score, 200 "human" scores and 25 "system" scores. [3]

4 Problems with traditional metrics

4.1 Rating quality and performance

We first considered how the quality of human labels affects the estimates of the metrics that are typically used to evaluate automated scoring engines. For the analyses in this section, we used the scores from one of our simulated systems from the "High" system category (R^2 with gold-standard scores =

0.8). We then randomly sampled 50 pairs of simulated raters from each rater category and evaluated the human-machine agreement for each pair. We used both the score from the first rater in the pair as well as the average of the the two rater scores in the pair as our reference score and computed four metrics: Pearson's r[4], quadratically-weighted kappa (QWK)[5], R^2, and degradation (correlation between the scores of the two humans minus the correlation between scores of our chosen system and the reference human score). Figure 1 shows how these metrics *for the same system* vary depending on the human agreement in the evaluation dataset.

As the figure shows, the estimates of performance *for the same set of scores* vary drastically depending on the quality of human ratings whether we use the score from the first human rater or the average of the two scores. For example, estimates of correlation vary from mean $r = 0.69$ when computed against the average scores of two raters with low agreement to $r = 0.86$ when computed against the average score of two raters with high agreement. The difference between $r = 0.69$ and $r = 0.86$ is considerable and, at face value, could influence both deployment decisions in an industry context as well as conclusions in a research context. Yet all it actually reflects is the amount of noise in human labels: both correlations were computed using the *same* set of automated scores. Looking at degradation does not resolve the issue: the degradation in our simulation varied from -0.05 to -0.30. It is obvious that the metrics improve when the human-human agreement goes from low to high, regardless of which metric is used, and do not provide a stable estimate of model performance. This pattern is consistent across different sets of automated scores.

4.2 Rating quality and ranking

Given how much the estimates of system performance vary depending on the quality of human ratings, it is clear that the quality of human ratings will also affect the comparison between different systems if they are evaluated on different datasets.

To demonstrate this, we randomly sampled 25 pairs of simulated raters with different levels of human-human agreement, the same as the number of simulated systems in our data, and "assigned" a different pair to each system. Each pair of raters

---

[2] $R^2 = 1 - \frac{\sum (y_i - \hat{y}_i)^2}{\sum (y_i - \bar{y})^2}$ where y_i are the observed values (human scores), $\hat{y}_i$ are the predicted values and $\bar{y}$ is the mean of observed score. R^2 standardizes the MSE by the total variance of the observed values leading to a more interpretable metric that generally varies from 0 to 1, where 1 corresponds to perfect prediction and 0 indicates that the model is no more accurate than simply using mean value as the prediction.

[3] The data and the code are publicly available at https://github.com/EducationalTestingService/prmse-simulations. We encourage the readers to use this code to run further simulations with varying input parameters.

[4] We use raw correlation coefficients, not z-transforms, as is the norm in automated scoring literature.

[5] QWK for continuous scores was computed cf. Haberman (2019) as implemented in RSMTool (Madnani et al., 2017b)

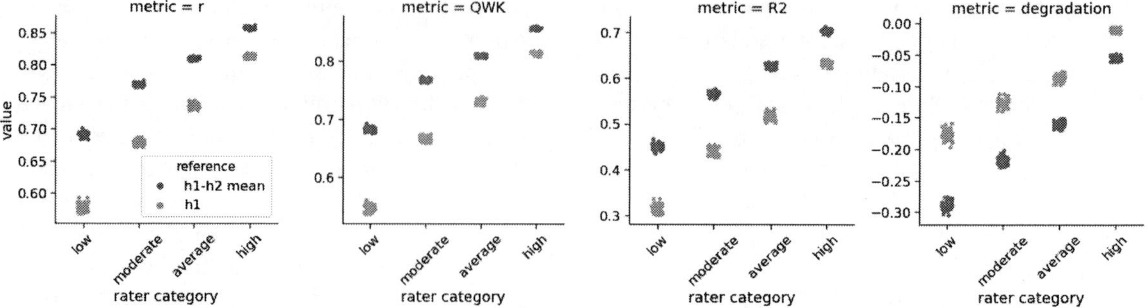

Figure 1: The effect of human-human agreement on the evaluation results for the same set of automated scores against either the first human rater or the average of two human raters. Note that the metrics are on different scales.

is always sampled from the same rater category but different systems are evaluated on pairs from different rater categories. Thus, for example, 3 of 5 systems in the "low" system category were evaluated against rater pairs with "high" agreement, while the remaining two systems in that category were evaluated against rater pairs with "average" agreement. At the same time, for "medium" category systems, 3 out of 5 systems were evaluated on raters with "low" agreement (see also Table 1 in the Appendix). This simulation was designed to mimic, in a simplified fashion, a situation where different research studies might evaluate their systems on datasets with *different* quality of human ratings [6].

We then evaluated each system against their assigned rater pairs using the standard agreement metrics and ranked the systems based on each of the metrics. The results are presented in the first four subplots in Figure 2.[7] For comparison, we also evaluated the systems against a single pair of raters from the "average" rater category, i.e., using the *same* rater pair for each system. The system ranking when systems are evaluated against this same rater pair are shown as red dots. The figure shows that when different systems are evaluated against the same pair of raters, their ranking is consistent with what we know to be the correct ranking in our simulated dataset. However, when different systems are evaluated against *different* pairs of raters, their ranking can vary depending on the quality of the ratings and the chosen metric. All metrics - except degradation - correctly ranked the worst performing systems (in the "poor" system category),

but they could **not** reliably differentiate between the other categories. In our simulated dataset, we see substantial overlaps in R^2 between systems in the "medium", "high", and "perfect" system categories, with even larger overlaps for other metrics.

Notably, when rater quality differs across the datasets used to evaluate a system, the degradation between human-human and system-human agreement, a common way to control for differences in said rater quality, does not always provide accurate system rankings. In our simulated dataset, based on degradation, some of the systems from the "perfect" system category ranked lower than some of the systems from the "medium" system category.

4.3 What if we had more than two raters?

Figure 1 showed that evaluating system scores against the average of two raters leads to higher estimates of agreement than when the system is evaluated against a single rater. This is not surprising: in our simulated dataset, the rater error is modeled as random and averaging across several simulated raters means that errors can cancel out when the number of raters is sufficiently large. In fact, we expect that evaluating the system against the average of *multiple* raters should provide performance estimates close to the known performance against the gold-standard scores. In this section, we simulated a situation where each response is scored by up to 50 raters.

For each category of raters, we randomly ordered the raters within this category and computed the cumulative average score of an increasing number of raters. We then evaluated the same system from the "high" system category used in §4.1 against this cumulative average score. The results are presented in Figure 3. The red lines indicate the values when evaluating the system's performance against the

---

[6]Note that the random assignment between rater categories and systems is a key aspect of this simulation since we are exploring a situation where the system performance is *independent* of the quality of human labels used to evaluate such systems.

[7]The last subplot will be explained in §5.2.

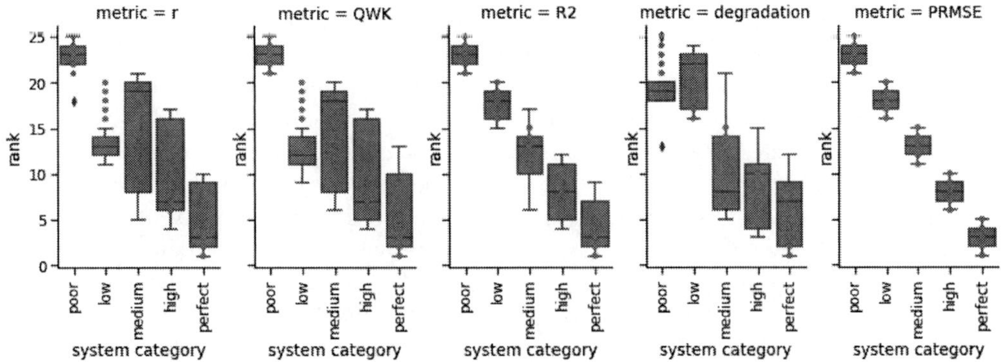

Figure 2: The ranking of systems from different categories when evaluated against randomly selected pairs of raters with different human-human agreement levels. The X axis shows the known ranking of the simulated systems in terms of their performance measured against the gold-standard scores. The red dots show the ranking when the systems are evaluated against the *same* pair of raters.

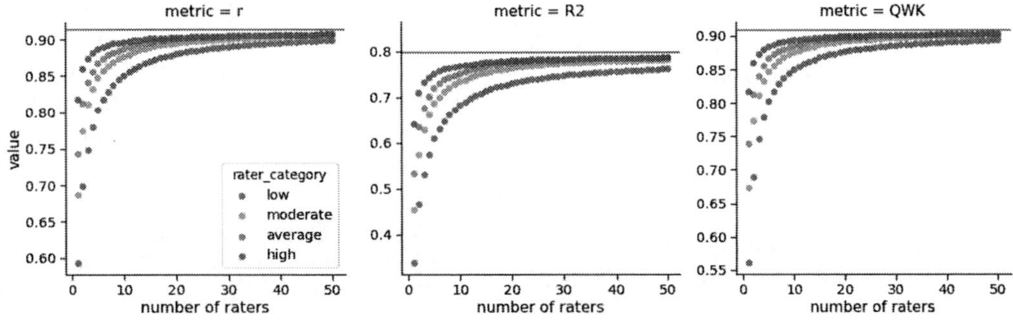

Figure 3: The effect of number of raters on several common metrics. Each plot shows a different metric computed for a randomly chosen system in our dataset against an increasing number of human raters. The red line indicates the metric value computed against the gold-standard scores & different colors indicate different rater categories.

gold-standard scores. As expected, for all rater categories, the performance estimates for the system approach the known gold-standard performance as the number of raters increases.

5   PRMSE **with reference to true scores**

The simulations in the previous sections demonstrate that the values of metrics usually used to evaluate automated scoring systems are directly dependent on the quality of human ratings used to evaluate the system. In fact, the effect of human label quality can be so large such that two identical systems may appear drastically different while the performance of two very different systems may appear very similar. One possible solution is to collect additional ratings for each response from multiple raters as we showed in §4.3. This solution is likely to be too expensive to be feasible: for example, in our simulated dataset, we would need to collect at least 10 additional ratings for each re-

sponse in order to obtain stable estimates of system performance, more if the rater agreement is low.

The solution we propose comes from the educational measurement community and draws on test theory methods to adjust the system performance estimates for measurement error.

5.1   The definition of PRMSE

The main idea behind PRMSE is to evaluate the automated scores against the true scores rather than the observed human scores. Classical test theory assumes that the human label H consists of the true score T and a measurement error E and $\mathrm{Var}(H) = \mathrm{Var}(T) + \mathrm{Var}(E)$. While it is impossible to compare system scores to the latent true scores *for each individual response*, it is possible to use the variability in human ratings to estimate the rater error and to compute an overall measure of agreement between automated scores and true scores after subtracting the rater error from the variance of the human labels.

Just like R^2, PRMSE relies on the concepts of mean squared error (MSE) and proportional reduction in mean squared error (hence PRMSE), but in this case, these measures are computed between the automated score M and *the true score* T instead of the human label H, where $\text{MSE} = E(M - T)^2$ and $\text{PRMSE} = 1 - \frac{\text{MSE}}{\text{Var}(T)}$.

Also similar to R^2, PRMSE is expected to fall between 0 and 1. A value of 0 indicates that system scores explain none of the variance of the true scores, while a value of 1 implies that system scores explains all the variance of true scores. In general, the higher the PRMSE, the better the system scores are at predicting the true scores.

We provide a detailed derivation for PRMSE in the Appendix. A Python implementation of PRMSE is available in RSMTool in the `rsmtool.utils.prmse` module[8].

5.2 PRMSE **and human-human agreement**

In this section, we show how PRMSE can help address the issues discussed in §4. We first considered the case where the same system is evaluated against ratings of different quality. As shown in §4.1, *all* traditional metrics of system performance are affected by human-human agreement and, therefore, estimates for these metrics vary depending on which pair of raters is used to evaluate the system. Therefore, in this section, we only compare PRMSE to R^2.

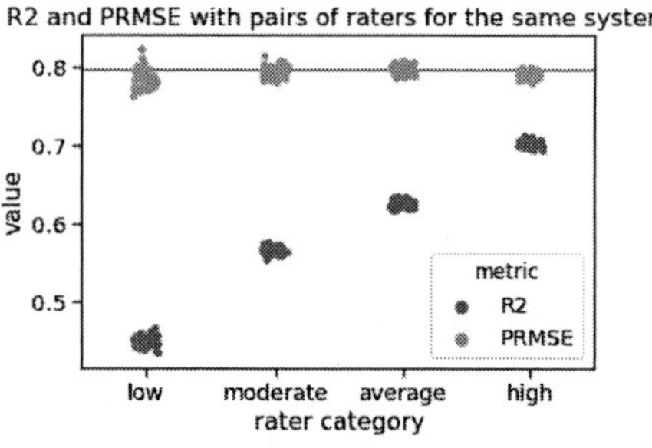

Figure 4: R^2 with average human score and PRMSE for the same system when evaluated against human ratings with different levels of agreement. The red line shows the value of R^2 when evaluating system performance against gold-standard scores.

We used the same pairs of raters and the same systems as in §4.1 to compute PRMSE and then

compared its values to the values of R^2 for the same pair of raters. Both these metrics rely on comparing the mean prediction error to the variance of gold-standard scores. For R^2, the gold-standards scores are the *observed* human-assigned scores that are available and can be used for computation. The gold-standard scores for PRMSE are the *latent* true scores that cannot be used directly: the metric is instead computed using the observed human scores and the estimates of rater variance as explained in the previous section.[9] Figure 4 shows the values of R^2 when evaluating the same system against different categories of human raters and the values of PRMSE for the same evaluations. While R^2, as we have already seen, varies between 0.43 and 0.71 depending on the quality of human ratings, PRMSE remains relatively stable between 0.76 and 0.82. We also note that the values of PRMSE are centered around the R^2 between system scores and gold-standard scores (0.8 in this case), as expected.

Next, we considered whether PRMSE can help obtain stable system rankings when systems are evaluated against human ratings with different qualities. We used the same combinations of simulated rater pairs and systems as in §4.2 and computed PRMSE for each system and rater pair. We then ranked the systems based on their PRMSE values. The results are presented in the last subplot in Figure 2. The figure shows that even though different systems were evaluated against human ratings of different quality, their final ranking based on PRMSE was consistent with the *known* correct ranking based on the gold-standard scores.

In summary, PRMSE is more robust to the quality of human ratings used for system evaluation and can reliably rank systems regardless of the quality of human labels used to evaluate them.

5.3 PRMSE **and double-scoring**

In §5.2, we considered a situation where all responses are double-scored. In reality, often only a subset of responses has several scores available to compute inter-rater agreement. The formula for PRMSE presented in the Appendix also allows us to compute PRMSE in such a situation: in this case, the variance of human errors is computed using *only* the double-scored responses. The prediction error

---

[8] https://rsmtool.readthedocs.io/en/stable/api.html#prmse-api

[9] Although the true scores are known in our simulation, the values of PRMSE in this and the following sections are computed using *observed* human scores only following the formulas in the Appendix, *without* using the simulated true scores.

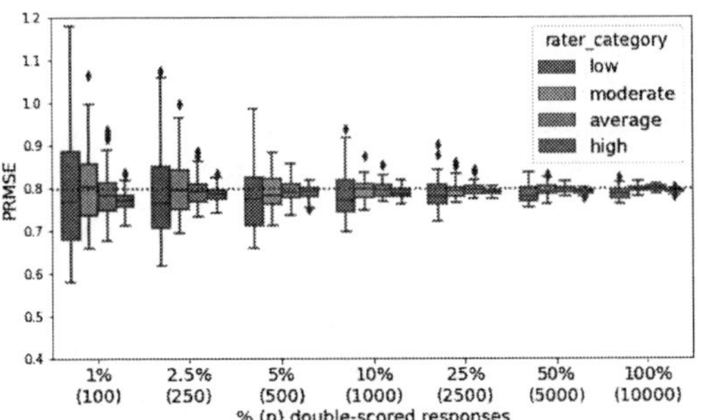 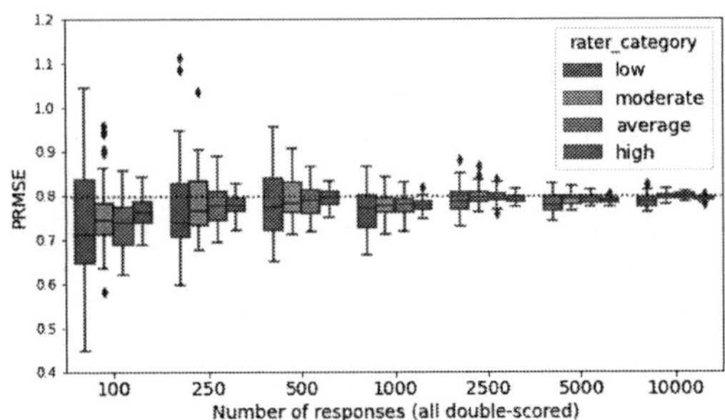

Figure 5: The distribution of PRMSE values depending on the percentage (left) or number (right) of double-scored responses. Different colors indicate levels of inter-rater agreement, i.e, rater category. The dotted line shows the known R^2 against gold-standard scores. Some PRMSE values for N=100 and "low" agreement were around 1.6 and are omitted for clarity. PRMSE values > 1 indicate that sample size is too small to reliably estimate error variance.

and variance are computed using *all* responses in the sample and either the average of two scores when available or the single available score. The numbers are adjusted for the percentage of the total number of ratings available for each response.

To test how PRMSE values depend on the percentage of double scored responses, we randomly sampled 50 pairs of raters from each rater category and created, for each of these 200 pairs, 7 new datasets each with a different percentage of double-scored responses. We then computed PRMSE for a randomly selected system from the "high" category for each of these 1,400 datasets. To check whether it is the *percentage* of double-scored responses that matters or the *number* of double-scored responses, we also computed a second PRMSE value over *only* the double-scored responses available in each case. For example, when simulating the scenario where we only have 10% of the responses double-scored, we compute two PRMSE values: (a) over the full dataset (10,000 responses) with 10% (1,000) double-scored and 90% (9,000) single-scored responses and (b) over a smaller dataset that *only* includes the 1,000 double-scored responses. The results are shown in Figure 5 (see also Table 2 in the Appendix). These results show that PRMSE values are much more stable with a larger number of double-scored responses and what matters is the total *number* of double-scored responses, not their percentage in the sample. There is substantial variability in PRMSE values when the number of double-scored responses is low, especially when computed on human ratings with low inter-rater agreement. In our simulated experiments, consistent values of PRMSE (to the first decimal) were achieved with 1,000 responses if the quality of

human ratings was moderate-to-high. More responses would be necessary to reliably estimate PRMSE with low inter-rater agreement.

6   Discussion

The performance of automated systems is often lower on data with lower human-human agreement. While this may mean that responses harder to score for humans are also harder to score for machines, our analyses show that this is not always true. Furthermore, since subsets of the same dataset are often used for both system training and evaluation, separating the effect of noisy labels on *training* from that on *evaluation* may be impossible.

In this paper, we showed that even for the *same* set of automated scores, estimates of system performance depend directly on the the quality of the human labels used to compute the agreement metrics. We also showed that using standard performance metrics to compare two systems may be misleading if the systems are evaluated against human scores with different inter-rater agreements. Comparing system performance to human-human agreement using degradation does not resolve this issue.

We proposed that a new metric, PRMSE, developed within the educational measurement community for evaluation is an effective way to obtain estimates of system performance that are adjusted for human-human agreement. PRMSE provides system evaluation against 'true' scores, thus making it possible to compare different systems on the same scale and offering a performance metric that is robust to the quality of human labels.

We emphasize that PRMSE does not affect the evaluation results when the systems are evaluated on the *same* set of human labels, for example, in the context of a shared task or a benchmark dataset. However, it can help compare system performance across studies as well as within studies, for example, when the dataset includes multiple items with varying levels of human-human agreement in their respective human scores.

The theory behind PRMSE makes certain assumptions about the nature of the rater error: it is assumed to be random with a mean of 0 and finite variance. Furthermore, the rater error is assumed to be independent of the item and its true score. There are several steps one can take to make sure the data meets these assumptions. For example, a standard way to randomize rater error is to set up the scoring process in a way such that multiple raters each score a different set of responses. Furthermore, one should additionally check whether human ratings have similar mean and variance. We note that other models discussed in the NLP literature (see §2), made other assumptions, for example that noisier labeling is more likely for some items ("hard" cases) than others. The performance of PRMSE under such conditions remains subject for future studies.

Finally, while PRMSE can adjust estimates of system performance for human error, it does not fully address the issue of different datasets. Users of automated scoring still need to use their judgement – or additional extrinsic criteria – to decide whether two systems can be deemed comparable.

7 Practical guidelines for PRMSE

We conclude with guidelines for using PRMSE.
- PRMSE estimates of system performance are robust to human-human agreement and can be used to compare systems across datasets.
- PRMSE computation assumes that the rating process is set up to randomize rater error: e.g. even if most responses only have a single score, the scoring process should involve multiple raters each scoring a different set of responses to minimize individual rater bias.
- Both sets of human ratings used to estimate PRMSE should have similar mean and variance and similar agreement with system scores.
- Responses selected for double-scoring must be a random sample of all responses.
- We recommend a total of at least 1000 double-scored responses to reliably estimate the human error. For human-human correlations > 0.65, a smaller sample (such as 500) might suffice.

PRMSE values above 1 indicate that the double-scored sample is too small.
- PRMSE should be used in combination with other metrics of human-machine agreement.

Acknowledgments

We thank Beata Beigman Klebanov, Oren Livne, Paul Deane and the three anonymous BEA reviewers for their comments and suggestions that greatly improved this paper.

References

Beata Beigman Klebanov and Eyal Beigman. 2009. From Annotator Agreement to Noise Models. *Computational Linguistics*, 35(4):495–503.

Michael D. Carey, Robert H. Mannell, and Peter K. Dunn. 2011. Does a Rater's Familiarity with a Candidate's Pronunciation Affect the Rating in Oral Proficiency Interviews? *Language Testing*, 28(2):201–219.

Larry Davis. 2016. The influence of training and experience on rater performance in scoring spoken language. *Language Testing*, 33(1):117–135.

Myroslava O. Dzikovska, Rodney D. Nielsen, and Claudia Leacock. 2016. The joint student response analysis and recognizing textual entailment challenge: making sense of student responses in educational applications. *Language Resources and Evaluation*, 50(1):67–93.

Thomas Eckes. 2008. Rater types in writing performance assessments: A classification approach to rater variability. *Language Testing*, 25(2):155–185.

Benoît Frénay and Michel Verleysen. 2014. Classification in the presence of label noise: A survey. *IEEE Transactions on Neural Networks and Learning Systems*, 25(5):845–869.

Shelby J. Haberman. 2008. When can subscores have value? *Journal of Educational and Behavioral Statistics*, 33:204–229.

Shelby J. Haberman. 2019. Measures of Agreement Versus Measures of Prediction Accuracy. *ETS Research Report Series*, 2019(1):1–23.

Shelby J. Haberman and L. Yao. 2015. Repeater analysis for combining information from different assessments. *Journal of Educational Measurement*, 52:223–251.

Shelby J. Haberman, L. Yao, and S. Sinharay. 2015. Prediction of true test scores from observed item scores and ancillary data. *British Journal of Mathematical and Statistical Psychology*, 68:363–385.

Andrea Horbach, Alexis Palmer, and Magdalena Wolska. 2014. Finding a Tradeoff between Accuracy and Rater's Workload in Grading Clustered Short Answers. *Proceedings of the Ninth International Conference on Language Resources and Evaluation (LREC'14)*, pages 588–595.

Emily K. Jamison and Iryna Gurevych. 2015. Noise or additional information? Leveraging crowdsource annotation item agreement for natural language tasks. In *Proceedings of EMNLP 2015*, pages 291–297, Lisbon, Portugal. Association for Computational Linguistics.

Chuck P. Lam and David G. Stork. 2003. Evaluating classifiers by means of test data with noisy labels. *IJCAI International Joint Conference on Artificial Intelligence*, pages 513–518.

Guangming Ling, Pamela Mollaun, and Xiaoming Xi. 2014. A Study on the Impact of Fatigue on Human Raters when Scoring Speaking Responses. *Language Testing*, 31:479–499.

Frederic M. Lord and Melvin R. Novick. 1968. *Statistical Theories of Mental Test Scores*. Addison Wesley, Reading, MA.

Anastassia Loukina, Klaus Zechner, James Bruno, and Beata Beigman Klebanov. 2018. Using exemplar responses for training and evaluating automated speech scoring systems. In *Proceedings of the Thirteenth Workshop on Innovative Use of NLP for Building Educational Applications*, pages 1–12, Stroudsburg, PA, USA. Association for Computational Linguistics.

Nitin Madnani, Anastassia Loukina, and Aoife Cahill. 2017a. A Large Scale Quantitative Exploration of Modeling Strategies for Content Scoring. In *Proceedings of the 12th Workshop on Innovative Use of NLP for Building Educational Applications*, pages 457–467, Copenhagen, Denmark. Association for Computational Linguistics.

Nitin Madnani, Anastassia Loukina, Alina Von Davier, Jill Burstein, and Aoife Cahill. 2017b. Building Better Open-Source Tools to Support Fairness in Automated Scoring. In *Proceedings of the First Workshop on ethics in Natural Language Processing, Valencia, Spain, April 4th, 2017*, pages 41–52, Valencia. Association for Computational Linguistics.

Héctor Martínez Alonso, Barbara Plank, Arne Skjærholt, and Anders Søgaard. 2015. Learning to parse with IAA-weighted loss. In *Proceedings of the 2015 Conference of the North American Chapter of the Association for Computational Linguistics: Human Language Technologies*, pages 1357–1361, Denver, Colorado. Association for Computational Linguistics.

Barbara Plank, Dirk Hovy, and Anders Søgaard. 2014. Learning part-of-speech taggers with inter-annotator agreement loss. In *Proceedings of the 14th Conference of the European Chapter of the Association for Computational Linguistics*, pages 742–751, Gothenburg, Sweden. Association for Computational Linguistics.

Dennis Reidsma and Rieks op den Akker. 2008. Exploiting subjective annotations. In *COLING 2008 workshop on Human Judgments in Computational Linguistics*, pages 8–16, Manchester, UK.

Dennis Reidsma and Jean Carletta. 2008. Reliability Measurement without Limits. *Computational Linguistics*, 34(3):319–326.

Brian Riordan, Michael Flor, and Robert Pugh. 2019. How to account for mispellings: Quantifying the benefit of character representations in neural content scoring models. In *Proceedings of the 14th Workshop on Innovative Use of NLP for Building Educational Applications (BEA)*.

Roy Schwartz, Omri Abend, Roi Reichart, and Ari Rappoport. 2011. Neutralizing linguistically problematic annotations in unsupervised dependency parsing evaluation. In *Proceedings of the 49th Annual Meeting of the Association for Computational Linguistics: Human Language Technologies - Volume 1*, HLT '11, pages 663–672, Stroudsburg, PA, USA. Association for Computational Linguistics.

Mark D. Shermis. 2014. State-of-the-art automated essay scoring: Competition, results, and future directions from a United States demonstration. *Assessing Writing*, 20:53–76.

Rion Snow, Brendan O'Connor, Daniel Jurafsky, and Andrew Y. Ng. 2008. Cheap and fast—but is it good?: Evaluating non-expert annotations for natural language tasks. In *Proceedings of the Conference on Empirical Methods in Natural Language Processing*, EMNLP '08, pages 254–263, Stroudsburg, PA, USA. Association for Computational Linguistics.

David M. Williamson, Xiaoming Xi, and F. Jay Breyer. 2012. A Framework for Evaluation and Use of Automated Scoring. *Educational Measurement: Issues and Practice*, 31(1):2–13.

Helen Yannakoudakis and Ronan Cummins. 2015. Evaluating the performance of Automated Text Scoring systems. In *Proceedings of the 10th Workshop on Innovative Use of NLP for Building Educational Applications*, pages 213–223.

Lili Yao, Shelby J. Haberman, and Mo Zhang. 2019a. Penalized best linear prediction of true test scores. *Psychometrika*, 84 (1):186–211.

Lili Yao, Shelby J. Haberman, and Mo Zhang. 2019b. Prediction of writing true scores in automated scoring of essays by best linear predictors and penalized best linear predictors. ETS Research Report RR-19-13, ETS, Princeton, NJ.

Klaus Zechner, Derrick Higgins, Xiaoming Xi, and David M. Williamson. 2009. Automatic scoring of non-native spontaneous speech in tests of spoken English. *Speech Communication*, 51(10):883–895.

Torsten Zesch, Michael Heilman, and Aoife Cahill. 2015. Reducing Annotation Efforts in Supervised Short Answer Scoring. In *Proceedings of the Tenth Workshop on Innovative Use of NLP for Building Educational Applications*, pages 124–132, Denver, Colorado.

Mo Zhang, Lili Yao, Shelby J. Haberman, and Neil J. Dorans. 2019. Assessing scoring accuracy and assessment accuracy for spoken responses. In *Automated Speaking Assessment*, pages 32–58. Routledge.

A The distribution between system and rater categories

The table below shows how systems from different categories were assigned to different pairs of raters.

| System | Human-human agreement | | | |
	Low	Moderate	Average	High
Poor	1	3	0	1
Low	0	0	2	3
Medium	3	0	1	1
High	2	1	1	1
Perfect	2	0	2	1

Table 3: The distribution between different systems and different pairs of raters. The table shows how many systems from each system category were evaluated using pairs of raters from different rater categories.

B Deriving the PRMSE formula

Let
- N denote the total number of responses in the evaluation set
- c_i denote the number of human ratings for response i,
- H_{ij} denote human rating $j = 1, \ldots, c_i$ for response i, and
- $\bar{H}_i = \frac{1}{c_i} \sum_{j=1}^{c_i} H_{ij}$ denote the average human rating for response i.
- $\bar{H} = \frac{\sum_i c_i \bar{H}_i}{\sum_i c_i}$ denote the average of all human ratings.
- Let M_i denote the predicted score for response i.

The true human score model assumes a hypothetical infinite population/sequence of human raters that could score responses and assumes that the raters a response actually receives are an unbiased sample from this population. The raters H_{ij} are assumed to have the same error variance and the errors e_{ij} are uncorrelated. The model defines the true human score by

$$T_i = \lim_{c_i \to \infty} \frac{1}{c_i} \sum_{j=1}^{c_i} Y_{ij} = E[H_{ij}] \qquad (1)$$

and the error ϵ_{ij} as $\epsilon_{ij} = H_{ij} - T_i$, or stated differently $H_{ij} = T_i + \epsilon_{ij}$.

B.1 Estimating the error variance

If we have only two ratings per response then we estimate the error variance by recognizing

$$V_\epsilon = \frac{1}{2} E[(H_{i2} - H_{i1})^2] \qquad (2)$$

which can easily be estimated with the unbiased estimator

$$\hat{V}_\epsilon = \frac{1}{2N} \sum_{i=1}^{N} (H_{i2} - H_{i1})^2 \qquad (3)$$

When we have more than two raters, the variance of rater errors is computed as a pooled variance estimator. We first calculate the within-subject variance of human ratings V_i for each response i using denominator $c_i - 1$:

$$V_i = \frac{\sum_{j=1}^{c} (H_{i,j} - \bar{H}_i)^2}{c_i - 1} \qquad (4)$$

We then take a weighted average of those within-responses variances:

$$\hat{V}_\epsilon = \frac{\sum_{i=1}^{N} V_i * (c_i - 1)}{\sum_{i=1}^{N} (c_i - 1)} \qquad (5)$$

B.2 Estimating true score variance

An unbiased estimator of the true score variance is

$$\hat{V}_T \equiv \widehat{\mathrm{Var}}(T) = \frac{\sum_{i=1}^{N} c_i (\bar{H}_i - \bar{H})^2 - (N-1)\hat{V}_\epsilon}{c. - \frac{\sum_{i=1}^{N} c_i^2}{c.}} \qquad (6)$$

where $c. = \sum_{i=1}^{N} c_i$ is the total number of observed human scores.

B.3 Estimating mean squared error

We estimate the mean squared error of the automated scores M_i with the following unbiased estimator.

$$\widehat{\mathrm{MSE}}(T|M) = \frac{1}{c.} \left(\sum_{i=1}^{N} c_i (\bar{H}_i - M_i)^2 - N\hat{V}_\epsilon \right) \qquad (7)$$

B.4 Estimating PRMSE

With estimators for the MSE and the variance of the true score available, estimation of PRMSE is simple.

$$\widehat{\mathrm{PRMSE}} = 1 - \frac{\widehat{\mathrm{MSE}}(T|M)}{\hat{V}_T} \qquad (8)$$

C Impact of double-scoring

Table 4 shows the range of PRMSE values we observed for different number of double-scored responses and human-human agreement.

	Human-human agreement			
N	Low	Moderate	Average	High
100	1.01	0.41	0.26	0.12
250	0.46	0.30	0.15	0.09
500	0.33	0.17	0.12	0.07
1,000	0.24	0.13	0.08	0.06
2,500	0.18	0.09	0.07	0.03
5,000	0.08	0.07	0.04	0.02
10,000	0.06	0.03	0.02	0.02

Table 4: The range of observed PRMSE values for different number double-scored responses and different levels of human-human agreement.

Multiple Instance Learning for Content Feedback Localization without Annotation

Scott Hellman, William R. Murray, Adam Wiemerslage, Mark Rosenstein, Peter W. Foltz, Lee Becker and Marcia Derr
Pearson
Boulder, CO
{scott.hellman, william.murray, adam.wiemerslage, mark.rosenstein, peter.foltz, lee.becker, marcia.derr} @pearson.com

Abstract

Automated Essay Scoring (AES) can be used to automatically generate holistic scores with reliability comparable to human scoring. In addition, AES systems can provide formative feedback to learners, typically at the essay level. In contrast, we are interested in providing feedback specialized to the content of the essay, and specifically for the content areas required by the rubric. A key objective is that the feedback should be localized alongside the relevant essay text. An important step in this process is determining where in the essay the rubric designated points and topics are discussed. A natural approach to this task is to train a classifier using manually annotated data; however, collecting such data is extremely resource intensive. Instead, we propose a method to predict these annotation spans without requiring any labeled annotation data. Our approach is to consider AES as a Multiple Instance Learning (MIL) task. We show that such models can both predict content scores and localize content by leveraging their sentence-level score predictions. This capability arises despite never having access to annotation training data. Implications are discussed for improving formative feedback and explainable AES models.

1 Introduction

The assessment of writing is an integral component in the pedagogical use of constructed response items. Often, a student's response is scored according to a rubric that specifies the components of writing to be assessed – such as content, grammar, and organization – and establishes an ordinal scale to assign a score for each of those components. Furthermore, there is strong evidence of learning improvements when instructors provide feedback to their students (Graham et al., 2011). Their comments can take the form of holistic, document-level feedback, or more specific, targeted feedback that addresses an error or praises an insight at relevant locations in the paper.

As far back as the 1960s, computers have been employed in essay scoring (Page, 1966). Thus, automated essay scoring (AES) is a well-studied area, and with modern approaches, AES systems are often as reliable as human scorers (Shermis and Burstein, 2003, 2013). However, many of these systems are limited to providing holistic scores – that is, they assign an ordinal value for every component in the rubric.

Furthermore, some AES systems can provide document-level feedback, but this requires students to interpret which parts of their text the feedback refers to. When an automated scoring system additionally provides location information, students can leverage a more specific frame of reference to better understand the feedback. Indeed, students are more likely to understand and implement revisions when given feedback that summarizes and localizes relevant information (Patchan et al., 2016).

We are interested in automatically providing localized feedback on the content of an essay. The specific kinds of feedback provided can vary, ranging from positive feedback reinforcing that a student correctly covered a specific topic, to feedback indicating areas that the student could improve. This latter category includes errors such as domain misconceptions or inadequate citations. We consider wholly omitted topics to be outside the scope of localized feedback, as they represent an overall issue in the essay that is best addressed by essay-level feedback.

From a machine learning perspective, content localization is difficult. Current automated localization is often very fine-grained, e.g., grammar checkers can identify spelling or grammar mistakes at the word level. However, we view the content of a student's essay as primarily a sentence-level aspect of student writing. Critically, to provide this type of content feedback, we need to be able to

Proceedings of the 15th Workshop on Innovative Use of NLP for Building Educational Applications, pages 30–40
July 10, 2020. ©2020 Association for Computational Linguistics

detect where in their essay a student is discussing that particular content. One approach would be to collect a corpus of training data containing essays with annotations indicating text spans where topics of interest were discussed. A supervised machine learning classifier could be trained on this data, and this localization model could then be integrated into a full AES feedback system. For example, a scoring model could identify the degree of coverage of rubric-required topics $t_1, \ldots, t_n$. A formative feedback system could generate suggestions for inadequately covered topics. Finally, the localization system could identify *where* this formative feedback should be presented. In this work, we address the localization part of this process.

While AES systems typically provide scoring of several rubric traits, we are interested primarily in the details of an essay's content, and so our work here focuses on a detailed breakdown of content coverage into individual topics. For example, consider a prompt that asks students to discuss how to construct a scientific study on the benefits of aromatherapy. Each student answer is a short essay, and is scored on its coverage of six content topics. Examples of these topics include discussion of independent and dependent variables, defining a blind study, and discussing the difficulties in designing a blind study for aromatherapy. These kinds of content topics are what our localization efforts are focused on. Figure 1 shows a a screenshot from an annotation tool containing an example essay with human-provided annotations and scores.

The downside of building a localization classifier based on annotation data is that such annotation data is very expensive to collect. Holistic scoring data itself is expensive to collect, and obtaining reliable annotations is even more difficult to orchestrate. Due to these issues, an approach that eliminates annotation training data is desirable. We propose a weakly-supervised multiple instance learning (MIL) approach to content localization, that relies on either document-level scoring information, or on a set of manually curated reference sentences. We show that both approaches can perform well at the topic localization task, without having been trained on localization data.

2 Automated Essay Scoring and Feedback

Automated Essay Scoring systems for providing holistic scoring are well studied (Shermis and Burstein, 2003, 2013). Some systems are specifically designed to provide formative feedback, with or without an accompanying overall score. Roscoe et al. (2012) presents an automated feedback system that measures attributes of the student response and provides specific feedback if certain thresholds are met (e.g., "use larger words" when the mean syllables per word is too low). In Foltz et al. (2000) an AES system is shown that uses Latent Semantic Analysis (LSA) to measure similarities between student sentences and reference sentences. Each required topic has a set of 1–3 reference sentences, and if no sentence in the student essay is similar to any reference sentences for that topic, feedback encouraging the student to more fully describe the topic is presented. Summary Street® provides students with content feedback during the summarization task, and specifically uses a reference document with LSA for semantic comparison (Steinhart, 2001; Franzke et al., 2005).

There has been effort toward providing students with localized feedback as well. Burstein et al. (2003) presents a system that uses an ensemble of supervised machine learning models to locate and provide feedback on discourse components such as thesis statements. Similarly, Chukharev-Hudilainen and Saricaoglu (2016) presents a system that provides feedback on discourse structure in essays written by English language learners.

A major drawback of these more localized feedback systems is the requirement that they be trained on annotation data, which is expensive to gather. Our work, which removes this constraint, is inspired by approaches that determine the contribution of individual sentences to the overall essay score. One such approach is described in Dong et al. (2017), which presents a neural network that generates an attention vector over the sentences in a response. This attention vector directly relates to the importance of each individual sentence in the computation of the final predicted score.

Woods et al. (2017) attempts to localize feedback based purely on the output of a holistic AES model. Specifically, they train an ordinal logistic regression model on a feature space consisting of character, word, and part-of-speech n-grams. They show that this model performs well on the AES task. They then propose a method for determining the contribution of each sentence to the overall score by measuring how much more likely a lower (or higher) score would be if that sentence was re-

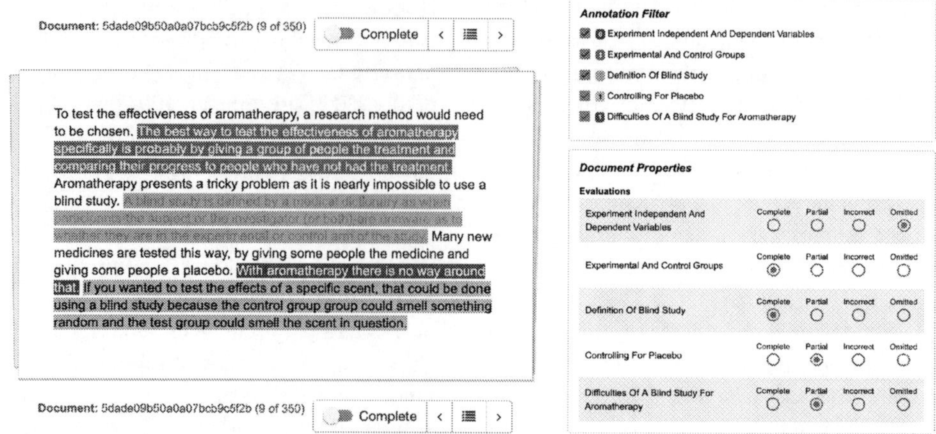

Figure 1: Screenshot from an annotation tool containing an example essay with colored text indicating human-provided annotations (left), the color-coded annotation key (top right) and holistic scores (bottom right).

moved. They then use the Mahalanobis distance to compute how much that sentence's contribution differs from a known distribution of sentence contributions. Finally, they present feedback to the student, localized to sentences that were either noticeably beneficial or detrimental to the overall essay.

We are interested in almost exactly the same task as Woods et al. (2017) – the only difference is that we aim to predict the locations humans would annotate, while their goal was to evaluate the effectiveness of their localized feedback. Specifically, we frame annotation prediction as a task with a set of essays and a set of labels, such that each sentence in each essay has a binary label indicating whether or not the specified topic was covered in that sentence. The goal is to develop a model that can predict these binary labels given the essays.

Latent Dirichlet Allocation (LDA) is an unsupervised method for automatically identifying topics in a document (Blei et al., 2003), and is related to our goal of identifying sentences that received human annotations. This requires an assumption that the human annotators identified sentences that could match a specific topic learned by LDA. While there is some work on using LDA to aid in annotation (Camelin et al., 2011), we are unaware of any attempts to extend it to the educational writing domain. Our approach differs from LDA in that we use supervised techniques whose predictions can be transferred to the annotation domain, rather than approaching the problem as a wholly unsupervised task. Additionally, we are classifying sentences by topics rather than explicitly creating word topic models for the topics.

If one views student essays as summaries (e.g., of the section of the textbook that the writing prompt corresponds to), then summarization evaluation approaches could be applicable. In particular, the PEAK algorithm (Yang et al., 2016) builds a hypergraph of subject-predicate-object triples, and then salient nodes in that graph are identified. These salient nodes are then collected into summary content units (SCUs), which can be used to score summaries. In our case, these SCUs would correspond to recurring topics in the student essays. One possible application of PEAK to our annotation prediction problem would be to run PEAK on a collection of high-scoring student essays. Similarity to the identified SCUs could then be used as a weak signal of the presence of a human annotation for a given sentence. Our approach differs from this application of PEAK in that we not only utilize similarity to sentences from high-scoring essays, but also use sentences from low-scoring essays as negative examples for a given topic.

3 Multiple Instance Learning

To accomplish our goal of predicting annotations without having access to annotation data, we approach AES as a multiple instance learning regression problem. Multiple instance learning is a supervised learning paradigm in which the goal is to label bags of items, where the number of items in a bag can vary. The items in a bag are also referred to as *instances*. MIL is a well-studied area of machine learning, with a broad literature into its applications both in NLP (e.g., Bunescu and Mooney (2007)) and in general settings (e.g., Dietterich et al. (1997)). The description provided here is based on Carbonneau et al. (2016).

The standard description of MIL assumes that the goal is a binary classification. Intuitively, each bag has a known binary label, and we can think of the instances in a bag as having unknown binary labels. We then assume that the bag label is some aggregation of the unknown instance labels. We first describe MIL in these terms, and then extend those ideas to regression.

Formally, let $\mathcal{X}$ denote our collection of training data, and let i denote an index over bags, such that each $X_i \in \mathcal{X}$ is of the form $X_i = \{x_{i,1}, x_{i,2}, \ldots, x_{i,m}\}$. Note that m can differ among the elements of X, that is, the cardinalities of two elements $X_i, X_j \in \mathcal{X}$ need not be equal. Let Y denote our training labels, such that each X_i has a corresponding $Y_i \in \{0, 1\}$. We assume that there is a latent label for each instance $x_{i,j}$, denoted by $y_{i,j}$. Note that, in our specific application, $x_{i,j}$ corresponds to the j-th sentence of the i-th document in our corpus. The *standard assumption* in MIL asserts that

$$Y_i = \begin{cases} 0 & \text{if } \forall x_{i,j} \in X_i, y_{i,j} = 0 \\ 1 & \text{if } \exists x_{i,j} \in X_i, y_{i,j} = 1 \end{cases}$$

That is, the standard assumption holds that a bag is positive if *any* of its constituent instances are positive. Another way of framing this assumption is that a single instance is responsible for an entire bag being positive.

In contrast, the *collective assumption* holds that Y_i is determined by some aggregation function over *all* of the instances in a bag. Thus, under the collective assumption, a bag's label is dependent upon more than one and possibly all of the instances in that bag.

AES is usually approached as a regression task, so these notions must be extended to regression. We adapt the standard assumption, that a single instance determines the bag label, by using a function that selects a single instance value from the bag. In this work, we use the maximum instance label. We adapt the collective assumption, that all instance labels contribute to the bag label, by using a function that aggregates across all instance labels. In this work, we use the mean instance label.

The application of MIL to natural language processing tasks is quite common. Wang et al. (2016) trains a convolutional neural network to aggregate predictions across sentences in order to predict discussion of events in written articles. By framing this task as a MIL problem, not only can they learn to predict the types of events articles pertain to, they can also predict which sentences specifically discuss those events. A variety of similar approaches that assign values to sentences and then use aggregation to create document scores have been used for sentiment analysis (Kotzias et al., 2015; Pappas and Popescu-Belis, 2017; Angelidis and Lapata, 2018; Lutz et al., 2019).

To the best of our knowledge, applications of MIL in educational domains are rare, and we are not aware of any attempts to explicitly approach AES as a MIL task. The educational MIL work that we are aware of uses MIL to determine overall student performance given their trajectory over the duration of a course (Zafra et al., 2011).

4 Automated Essay Scoring with Multiple Instance Learning

By framing AES as a MIL problem, the goal becomes predicting, for each sentence, the score for that sentence, and then aggregating those sentence-level predictions to create a document-level prediction. This goal requires determining both how to predict these sentence-level scores, and how to aggregate them into document-level scores. Note that we perform this task independently for each topic $t_1, \ldots, t_n$, but this discussion is limited to a single topic for clarity.

We define the AES task as follows. Assume we are given a collection of student essays D and corresponding scores y. We assume these scores are numeric and lie in a range defined by the rubric – we use integers, but continuous values could also work. For example, if the rubric for a concept defined the possible scores as *Omitted/Incorrect*, *Partially Correct*, and *Correct*, the corresponding entries in y could be drawn from $\{0, 1, 2\}$. The AES task is to predict y given D.

The intuition for why MIL is appropriate for AES is that, for many kinds of topics, the content of a single sentence is sufficient to determine a score. For example, consider a psychology writing prompt that requires students to include the definition of a specific kind of therapy. If an essay includes a sentence that correctly defines that type of therapy, then the essay as a whole will receive a high score for that topic.

We approach the sentence-level scoring task using k-Nearest Neighbors (kNN) (Cover and Hart, 1967). Denote the class label of a training example

a as y_a. For each document in our training corpus, we project each sentence into a semantic vector space, generating a corresponding vector that we denote as x. We assign to x the score of its parent document. We then train a kNN model on all of the sentences in the training corpus. We use the Euclidean distance as the metric for our nearest neighbor computations.

To predict the score of a new document using this model, we first split the document into sentences, project those sentences into our vector space, and use the kNN model to predict the score of each sentence. We define this sentence-level scoring function ϕ as

$$\phi(x) = \frac{1}{k} \sum_{a \in \text{knn}(x)} y_a$$

where $\text{knn}(x)$ denotes the set of k nearest neighbors of x. We aggregate these sentence-level scores through a document-level scoring function θ:

$$\theta(X_i) = \underset{x_{i,j} \in X_i}{\text{agg}} (\phi(x_{i,j}))$$

where agg corresponds to either the maximum or the mean – that is, agg determines whether we are making the standard or collective assumption.

We consider three semantic vector spaces. We define our vocabulary V as the set of all words appearing in the training sentences. The first vector space is a tf-idf space, in which each sentence is projected into $\mathbb{R}^{|V|}$ and each dimension in that vector corresponds to the term frequency of the corresponding vocabulary term multiplied by the inverse of the number of documents that contained that term.

We also consider a pretrained latent semantic analysis space. This space is constructed by using the singular value decomposition of the tf-idf matrix of a pretraining corpus to create a more compact representation of that tf-idf matrix (Landauer et al., 1998).

Finally, we consider embedding our sentences using SBERT (Reimers and Gurevych, 2019). SBERT is a version of BERT (Devlin et al., 2019) that has been fine-tuned on the SNLI (Bowman et al., 2015) and Multi-Genre NLI (Williams et al., 2018) tasks. These tasks involves predicting how sentences relate to one another. Critically, this means that the SBERT network has been specifically fine-tuned to embed individual sentences into a common space.

5 Weakly Supervised Localization

While this kNN-MIL model is ultimately trained to predict document-level scores for essays, as a side effect, it also generates a score prediction for each sentence. The central idea is that we can directly use these sentence-level scores as weak signals of the presence of annotation spans in the sentences.

Concretely, given our trained kNN-MIL model and an essay X_i, we predict the presence of annotations as follows. Assume that the minimum and maximum scores allowed by the rubric for the given topic are S_{min} and S_{max}, respectively. We leverage the sentence-level scoring function ϕ to compute an annotation prediction function α:

$$\alpha(x_{i,j}) = \frac{\phi(x_{i,j}) - S_{min}}{S_{max} - S_{min}}$$

That is, our annotation prediction function α is a rescaling of ϕ such that it lies in $[0, 1]$, allowing us to interpret it as a normalized prediction of a sentence having an annotation.

As our goal is to predict annotation spans without explicit annotation data, we also consider a modification of this process. Rather than training our kNN-MIL model on a corpus of scored student essays, we could instead use a set of manually curated reference sentences to train the model. We consider two sources of reference sentences.

First, we consider reference sentences pulled from the corresponding rubric, labeled by the topic they belong to. Rubrics often have descriptions of ideal answers and their key points, so generating such a set is low-cost. However, sentences from rubric descriptions may not discuss a topic in the same way that a student would, or they may fail to anticipate specific correct student answers.

For these reasons, we also consider selecting reference sentences by manually picking sentences from the training essays. We consider all training essays that received the highest score on a topic as candidates and choose one to a few sentences that clearly address the topic. We specifically look for exemplars making different points and written in different ways. These identified sentences are manually labeled as belonging to the given topic, and each one is used as a different reference sentence when training our kNN-MIL model. Typically, just a few exemplars per topic is sufficient (Foltz et al., 2000).

Whether we collect examples of formal wording from the rubric or informal wording from student answers, or both, we must then label the reference sentences for use in our kNN-MIL model. For a given topic, the references drawn from other topics provide negative examples of it. To convert these manual binary topic labels into the integer space that we use for the AES task, we assign to each reference sentence the maximum score for the topic(s) it was labeled as belonging to, and the minimum score to it for all other topics.

The key benefit of our approach is that it never requires access to annotation training data. Instead, given a collection of student essays for a new prompt, training a kNN-MIL model for that prompt requires one of a few sources of data. If we have human-provided document-level scores for the topics we are interested in, we can train a kNN-MIL model on those labeled documents. Otherwise, if the rubric contains detailed enough reference sentences and descriptions for the various topics, we can train a kNN-MIL model using reference sentences collected from the rubric. And finally, we can have a human expert collect examples of the topics of interest from the essays, and then train a kNN-MIL model using those examples as reference sentences.

6 Datasets

To evaluate the performance of kNN-MIL, we need student essays that have both document-level scores and annotation spans. To the best of our knowledge, there is no publicly available dataset that contains both.

Thus, we make use of an existing Pearson proprietary corpus developed to explore fine-grained content assessment for formative feedback. This corpus consists of student responses to four university-level psychology writing prompts. While the essays were originally written and scored against holistic writing traits, a subsequent annotation effort factored the content trait into multiple topics that represent core ideas or assertions an instructor would expect a student to address within the essay. For example, the topic *Comparing Egocentrism* from a prompt about Piaget's stages of development has the following reference answer:

> *A child in the pre-operational stage is unable to see things from another person's point of view, whereas a child in the concrete operational stage can.*

Annotators were tasked with assigning an essay-level rating for each topic with a judgment of *Com-*

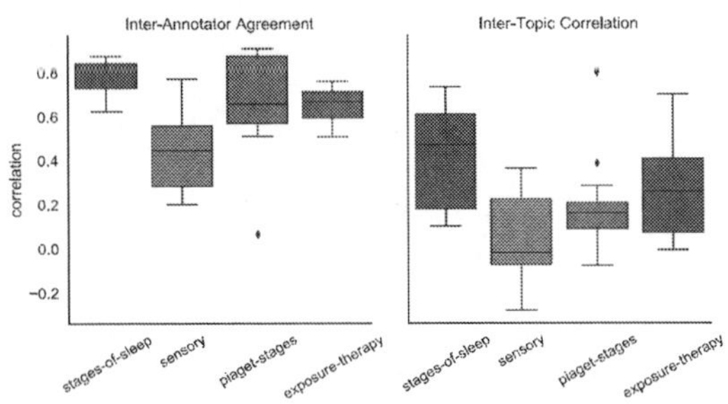

Figure 2: Box plots of inter-annotator correlations of the sentence-level annotation labels for each topic (left) and correlation between scores for all topic pairs (right).

plete, Partial, Incorrect or *Omitted*. Additionally, they were asked to mark spans in the essay pertaining to the topic – these could be as short as a few words or as long as multiple sentences. Two psychology subject matter experts (SMEs) performed the rating and span selection tasks. Ideally, rating and span annotations would have also been adjudicated by a third SME. However, due to time and cost constraints, we lack adjudicated labels for three of the four prompts. For this reason, we ran our experiments on both annotators separately.

As our techniques work at a sentence-level, but the human annotations can be shorter or longer than a single sentence, we frame the annotation prediction task as the task of predicting, for a given sentence, whether an annotation overlapped with that sentence. We show the distribution of inter-annotator agreements for the topics in the four prompts in the left panel of Figure 2, calculated as the correlation between these sentence-level annotation labels. The annotators achieved reasonable reliability except on the Sensory prompt, where the median correlation was below 0.5, and one topic in the Piaget prompt, where the annotators had a correlation near 0.

The features of these four prompts are shown in Table 1. Essays had 5–8 topics and covered areas such as the stages of sleep; the construction of a potential experimental study on aromatherapy; Piaget's stages of cognitive development; and graduated versus flooding approaches to exposure therapy for a hypothetical case of agoraphobia. Table 2 shows how many sentences were available for training the kNN-MIL models for each prompt.

Our approach assumes that the topic scores are numeric. We convert the scores in this dataset by mapping both *Omitted* and *Incorrect* to 0, *Partial*

Prompt	# of Essays	# of Topics	Mean Words	Annotator 1	Annotator 2
Sleep Stages	283	7	361	9%	8%
Sensory Study	348	6	395	7%	14%
Piaget Stages	448	8	367	10%	6%
Exposure Therapy	258	5	450	15%	9%

Table 1: Characteristics and summary statistics of prompts used in the experiments. The Annotator columns indicate, for a specific topic, the average percentage of sentences annotated with that topic.

Prompt	Rubric	Student	Training
Sleep Stages	15	19	4741
Sensory Study	11	13	5362
Piaget Stages	26	22	6342
Exposure Therapy	20	48	5184

Table 2: Number of sentences available for kNN-MIL training. The Rubric column shows the number of reference sentences taken from the rubric, while the Student column shows the number manually chosen from the student essays. The Training column shows the total number of sentences in the full set of essays.

to 1, and *Complete* to 2. As our approach uses these topic scores to generate annotation predictions, its ability to predict different annotations for different topics depends on the topic scores not being highly correlated. The right panel of Figure 2 shows the distribution of inter-topic correlations for each prompt. While there is considerable variation between the prompts, we do see that, except for one topic pair on the Piaget prompt, all inter-topic correlations are less than 0.8, and the median correlations are all below 0.5.

7 Experiments

Our goal is to determine how well the kNN-MIL approaches perform on the annotation prediction task. We also want to verify that our approaches perform reasonably well on the essay scoring task – while we are not directly interested in essay scoring, if our approaches are incapable of predicting essay scores, that would indicate that the underlying assumptions of our kNN-MIL approaches are likely invalid.

For each prompt, we construct 30 randomized train/test splits, holding out 20% of the data as the test set. We then train and evaluate our models on those splits, recording two key values: the correlation of the model's document-level scores to the human scorer, and the area under the ROC curve of the model's sentence-level annotation predictions.

We compare results between three categories of models. The first is the kNN-MIL model, trained on the training set. We refer to this model as the Base kNN-MIL model. The second is the kNN-MIL model trained on a manually curated reference set, which we refer to as the Manual kNN-MIL model. Finally, we compare to the ordinal logistic regression-based approach presented in Woods et al. (2017), which we will refer to as the OLR model. Additionally, as a baseline for comparison on the annotation prediction task, we train a sentence-level kNN model directly on the human annotation data, which we refer to as the Annotation kNN model. We consider the Annotation kNN model to provide a rough upper bound on how well the kNN-MIL approaches can perform. Finally, for our kNN-MIL models, we investigate how varying k and the vector space impacts model performance.

We use the all-threshold ordinal logistic regression model from mord (Pedregosa-Izquierdo, 2015) and the part of speech tagger from spaCy (Honnibal and Montani, 2017) in our implementation of the OLR model. The Mahalanobis distance computation for this approach requires a known distribution of score changes, for this we use the distribution of score changes of the training set.

We use the kNN and tf-idf implementations from scikit-learn (Pedregosa et al., 2011) and the LSA implementation from gensim (Řehůřek and Sojka, 2010). Our pretrained LSA space is 300 dimensional, and is trained on a collection of 45,108 English documents sampled from grade 3-12 readings and augmented with material from psychology textbooks. (Landauer et al., 1998). After filtering very common and uncommon words, this space includes 37,013 terms, covering 85% of the terms appearing in the training data.

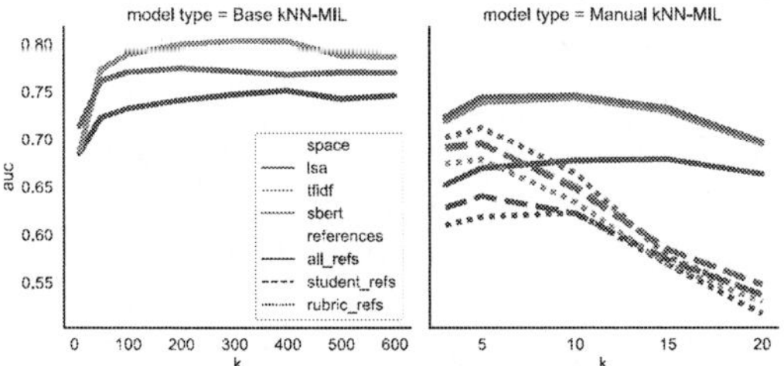

Figure 3: Annotation prediction performance of the kNN-MIL models as k is varied, averaged across all prompts, concepts, and annotators. Error bars omitted for clarity.

8 Discussion

We present the average annotation prediction performance of the kNN-MIL models for different values of k in Figure 3. While all approaches achieve AUCs above 0.5, the LSA-based space performs relatively poorly. The tf-idf space performs well, especially for the Base kNN-MIL model. In the tf-idf space, Base kNN-MIL performance peaks at $k = 400$. For the Manual kNN-MIL models, best performance occurs with the combined reference set using the tf-idf or SBERT spaces, around $k = 10$. Performance for Manual kNN-MIL with only rubric references or student references peaks and declines sooner than for combined due to the set of possible neighbors being smaller.

Note that the substantial difference in k between Base kNN-MIL and Manual kNN-MIL is due to the fact that we have orders of magnitude fewer manual reference sentences than training set sentences.

In light of these results, for clarity in the rest of this discussion, we focus on $k = 400$ for Base kNN-MIL, $k = 10$ and the combined reference set for Manual kNN-MIL, and exclude the LSA space.

To determine how annotation prediction differs across model types, we show the average overall AUC of all models in Table 3. In this table, we see that our best performance is achieved when we train a kNN model on actual annotation data. In contrast, the OLR model performs relatively poorly, suggesting that its success at predicting sentences that require some sort of feedback does not directly translate into an ability to predict locations of annotations.

Between the different kNN-MIL approaches, Base kNN-MIL using a tf-idf vector space performs best on three of the four prompts, and regardless of vector space, Base kNN-MIL performs as well or better than Manual kNN-MIL on those same three prompts. On the remaining prompt, Exposure Therapy, Manual kNN-MIL with SBERT performs best, but the differences between the various kNN-MIL approaches are relatively small on this prompt.

These annotation predictions results show that the kNN-MIL approach performs well despite never being explicitly trained on the annotation prediction task. While the Base kNN-MIL approach is overall better than the Manual kNN-MIL approach, it also requires a large amount of scored data for training. Which kNN-MIL approach is best for a particular situation thus depends on if the additional performance gain of Base kNN-MIL is worth the added cost of obtaining essay scoring data.

Finally, we show performance on the essay scoring task in Table 4. On this task, the OLR model and the Base kNN-MIL model with a tf-idf space perform the best, and the Manual kNN-MIL models perform the worst. We had predicted that the standard MIL assumption would perform well for AES, and our results show that this is true – for both Base and Manual kNN-MIL, using the maximum sentence topic score in an answer outperforms using the mean sentence topic score.

The Base kNN-MIL model can perform relatively well at both the document scoring task and the annotation prediction task. This suggests that it could be used as an explainable AES model, as the annotation predictions are directly tied to the document-level scores it provides. In this quite different application, the localization would be used to explain the sentences contributing to the final score, rather than to provide context for formative feedback.

9 Conclusions and Future Work

We have presented a novel approach of using MIL to train annotation prediction models without access to annotation training data. This technique performs well and can allow for automated localization without expensive data annotation. It also performs relatively well on the document-level scoring task, suggesting that its sentence-level score predictions could be used as part of an explainable model for AES.

Given that our kNN-MIL approach operates at the sentence level, it is unlikely to correctly locate annotations that exist across multiple sentences. Adapting our method to better incorporate information across sentences (e.g., by incorporating co-

Model	Space	Exposure Therapy	Piaget Stages	Sensory Study	Sleep Stages
Annotation kNN	sbert	0.88 (0.04)	0.89 (0.08)	0.85 (0.06)	0.91 (0.03)
	tfidf	0.87 (0.04)	0.92 (0.07)	0.89 (0.06)	0.93 (0.02)
Base kNN-MIL	sbert	0.76 (0.08)	0.78 (0.09)	0.77 (0.09)	0.78 (0.06)
	tfidf	0.74 (0.06)	0.84 (0.10)	0.81 (0.09)	0.80 (0.07)
Manual kNN-MIL	sbert	0.78 (0.07)	0.73 (0.12)	0.70 (0.10)	0.78 (0.06)
	tfidf	0.74 (0.08)	0.77 (0.09)	0.68 (0.10)	0.75 (0.07)
OLR		0.55 (0.04)	0.63 (0.08)	0.63 (0.07)	0.61 (0.05)

Table 3: Area under the ROC curve on the annotation prediction task, averaged over all topics and annotators. Standard deviation shown in parentheses.

Model	agg	Space	Exposure Therapy	Piaget Stages	Sensory Study	Sleep Stages
Base kNN-MIL	max	sbert	0.49 (0.14)	0.51 (0.18)	0.41 (0.15)	0.60 (0.11)
		tfidf	0.47 (0.12)	0.61 (0.19)	0.52 (0.17)	0.67 (0.12)
	mean	sbert	0.39 (0.15)	0.44 (0.16)	0.36 (0.15)	0.61 (0.14)
		tfidf	0.40 (0.14)	0.52 (0.16)	0.46 (0.14)	0.63 (0.13)
Manual kNN-MIL	max	sbert	0.41 (0.15)	0.30 (0.18)	0.25 (0.15)	0.37 (0.14)
		tfidf	0.38 (0.14)	0.40 (0.15)	0.23 (0.16)	0.34 (0.18)
	mean	sbert	0.29 (0.15)	0.23 (0.15)	0.16 (0.15)	0.27 (0.14)
		tfidf	0.29 (0.16)	0.29 (0.13)	0.19 (0.16)	0.22 (0.20)
OLR			0.50 (0.18)	0.63 (0.16)	0.51 (0.18)	0.69 (0.14)

Table 4: Pearson correlation coefficients on the document-level scoring task, averaged over all topics. Standard deviation shown in parentheses.

reference resolution) could help improve its overall performance. Additionally, as the Base kNN-MIL approach uses topics as negative examples for each other, we expect that it would not work well in situations where the inter-topic score correlations were high. We expect the Manual kNN-MIL approach to be less sensitive to this issue. Determining other ways to include negative examples would allow the Base kNN-MIL approach to be applied to prompts whose topics were highly correlated.

In our current domain, psychology, and in the context of low-stakes formative feedback, incorrect answers are uncommon compared to omitted or partial answers. In contrast, for domains that require chained reasoning over more complex mental models, such as accounting, cell biology, or computer science, we expect the ability to correctly detect misconceptions and errors to be far more important. In general, future work is required to determine how well our approach will work in other domains, and which domains it is best suited to.

Determining where topics are discussed is only one step in the full formative feedback process. More work is required to determine the path from holistic scoring and topic localization to the most helpful kinds of feedback for a student. In particular, we need to consider different kinds of pedagogical feedback and how such feedback could be individualized. Additionally, we could provide not just text but also video, peer interaction, worked examples, and other approaches from the full panoply of potential pedagogical interventions. Finally, we need to decide what actions will help the student the most, which relies on our pedagogical theory of how to help a student achieve their current instructional objectives.

Acknowledgements

We would like to thank Alok Baikadi, Julio Bradford, Jill Budden, Amy Burkhardt, Dave Farnham, Andrew Gorman and Jorge Roccatagliata for their efforts in collecting the annotated dataset used in this work.

References

Stefanos Angelidis and Mirella Lapata. 2018. Multiple instance learning networks for Fine-Grained sentiment analysis. *Transactions of the Association for Computational Linguistics*, 6:17–31.

David M Blei, Andrew Y Ng, and Michael I Jordan. 2003. Latent dirichlet allocation. *Journal of Machine Learning Research.*, 3(Jan):993–1022.

Samuel R. Bowman, Gabor Angeli, Christopher Potts, and Christopher D. Manning. 2015. A large annotated corpus for learning natural language inference. In *Proceedings of the 2015 Conference on Empirical Methods in Natural Language Processing (EMNLP)*. Association for Computational Linguistics.

Razvan Bunescu and Raymond Mooney. 2007. Learning to extract relations from the web using minimal supervision. In *Proceedings of the 45th Annual Meeting of the Association of Computational Linguistics*, pages 576–583.

Jill Burstein, Daniel Marcu, and Kevin Knight. 2003. Finding the write stuff: Automatic identification of discourse structure in student essays. *Intelligent Systems, IEEE*, 18:32 – 39.

Nathalie Camelin, Boris Detienne, Stéphane Huet, Dominique Quadri, and Fabrice Lefèvre. 2011. Unsupervised concept annotation using latent dirichlet allocation and segmental methods. In *Proceedings of the First workshop on Unsupervised Learning in NLP*, pages 72–81.

Marc-André Carbonneau, Veronika Cheplygina, Eric Granger, and Ghyslain Gagnon. 2016. Multiple instance learning: A survey of problem characteristics and applications. *Pattern Recognition*.

Evgeny Chukharev-Hudilainen and Aysel Saricaoglu. 2016. Causal discourse analyzer: improving automated feedback on academic ESL writing. *Computer Assisted Language Learning*, 29(3):494–516.

T. Cover and P. Hart. 1967. Nearest neighbor pattern classification. *IEEE Transactions on Information Theory*, 13(1):21–27.

Jacob Devlin, Ming-Wei Chang, Kenton Lee, and Kristina Toutanova. 2019. BERT: pre-training of deep bidirectional transformers for language understanding. In *Proceedings of the 2019 Conference of the North American Chapter of the Association for Computational Linguistics: Human Language Technologies, NAACL-HLT 2019, Minneapolis, MN, USA, June 2-7, 2019, Volume 1 (Long and Short Papers)*, pages 4171–4186. Association for Computational Linguistics.

Thomas G. Dietterich, Richard H. Lathrop, and Tomás Lozano-Pérez. 1997. Solving the multiple instance problem with axis-parallel rectangles. *Artificial Intelligence*, 89(1–2):31–71.

Fei Dong, Yue Zhang, and Jie Yang. 2017. Attention-based recurrent convolutional neural network for automatic essay scoring. In *Proceedings of the 21st Conference on Computational Natural Language Learning (CoNLL 2017)*, pages 153–162.

Peter W Foltz, Sara Gilliam, and Scott A Kendall. 2000. Supporting Content-Based feedback in On-Line writing evaluation with LSA. *Interactive Learning Environments*, 8(2):111–127.

Marita Franzke, Eileen Kintsch, Donna Caccamise, Nina Johnson, and Scott Dooley. 2005. Summary street®: Computer support for comprehension and writing. *Journal of Educational Computing Research*, 33:53–80.

Steve Graham, Karen Harris, and Michael Hebert. 2011. Informing Writing: The Benefits of Formative Assessment. A Report from Carnegie Corporation of New York. *Carnegie Corporation of New York*.

Matthew Honnibal and Ines Montani. 2017. spaCy 2: Natural language understanding with Bloom embeddings, convolutional neural networks and incremental parsing. To appear.

Dimitrios Kotzias, Misha Denil, Nando de Freitas, and Padhraic Smyth. 2015. From group to individual labels using deep features. In *Proceedings of the 21th ACM SIGKDD International Conference on Knowledge Discovery and Data Mining*, pages 597–606. ACM.

Thomas K Landauer, Peter W. Foltz, and Darrell Laham. 1998. An introduction to latent semantic analysis. *Discourse processes*, 25(2-3):259–284.

Bernhard Lutz, Nicolas Pröllochs, and Dirk Neumann. 2019. Sentence-level sentiment analysis of financial news using distributed text representations and multi-instance learning. In *Proceedings of the 52nd Hawaii International Conference on System Sciences*.

Ellis B Page. 1966. The imminence of grading essays by computer. *The Phi Delta Kappan*, 47(5):238–243.

Nikolaos Pappas and Andrei Popescu-Belis. 2017. Explicit document modeling through weighted multiple-instance learning. *Journal of Artificial Intelligenece Research.*, 58(1):591–626.

Melissa Patchan, Christian Schunn, and Richard Correnti. 2016. The nature of feedback: How peer feedback features affect students' implementation rate and quality of revisions. *Journal of Educational Psychology*, 108.

Fabian Pedregosa, Gaël Varoquaux, Alexandre Gramfort, Vincent Michel, Bertrand Thirion, Olivier Grisel, Mathieu Blondel, Peter Prettenhofer, Ron Weiss, Vincent Dubourg, Jake Vanderplas, Alexandre Passos, David Cournapeau, Matthieu Brucher,

Matthieu Perrot, and Édouard Duchesnay. 2011. Scikit-learn: Machine Learning in Python. *Journal of Machine Learning Research*, 12(Oct):2825–2830.

Fabian Pedregosa-Izquierdo. 2015. *Feature extraction and supervised learning on fMRI : from practice to theory*. Theses, Université Pierre et Marie Curie - Paris VI.

Radim Řehůřek and Petr Sojka. 2010. Software Framework for Topic Modelling with Large Corpora. In *Proceedings of the LREC 2010 Workshop on New Challenges for NLP Frameworks*, pages 45–50, Valletta, Malta. ELRA.

Nils Reimers and Iryna Gurevych. 2019. Sentence-bert: Sentence embeddings using siamese bert-networks. In *Proceedings of the 2019 Conference on Empirical Methods in Natural Language Processing*. Association for Computational Linguistics.

Rod Roscoe, Danica Kugler, Scott A Crossley, Jennifer L Weston, and Danielle McNamara. 2012. Developing pedagogically-guided threshold algorithms for intelligent automated essay feedback. In *Proceedings of the 25th International Florida Artificial Intelligence Research Society Conference, FLAIRS-25*, pages 466–471.

Mark D. Shermis and Jill C. Burstein, editors. 2003. *Automated essay scoring: A cross-disciplinary perspective*. Lawrence Erlbaum Associates, Inc., Mahway, NJ.

Mark D. Shermis and Jill C. Burstein, editors. 2013. *Handbook of automated essay evaluation: Current applications and new directions*. Routledge, New York.

David J. Steinhart. 2001. *Summary street: An intelligent tutoring system for improving student writing through the use of latent semantic analysis*. Doctor of philosophy (thesis), University of Colorado at Boulder.

Wei Wang, Yue Ning, Huzefa Rangwala, and Naren Ramakrishnan. 2016. A multiple instance learning framework for identifying key sentences and detecting events. In *Proceedings of the 25th ACM International on Conference on Information and Knowledge Management*, pages 509–518. ACM.

Adina Williams, Nikita Nangia, and Samuel Bowman. 2018. A broad-coverage challenge corpus for sentence understanding through inference. In *Proceedings of the 2018 Conference of the North American Chapter of the Association for Computational Linguistics: Human Language Technologies, Volume 1 (Long Papers)*, pages 1112–1122, New Orleans, Louisiana. Association for Computational Linguistics.

Bronwyn Woods, David Adamson, Shayne Miel, and Elijah Mayfield. 2017. Formative essay feedback using predictive scoring models. In *Proceedings of the 23rd ACM SIGKDD International Conference on Knowledge Discovery and Data Mining*, KDD '17, page 2071–2080, New York, NY, USA. Association for Computing Machinery.

Qian Yang, Rebecca J Passonneau, and Gerard De Melo. 2016. Peak: Pyramid evaluation via automated knowledge extraction. In *Thirtieth AAAI Conference on Artificial Intelligence*.

Amelia Zafra, Cristóbal Romero, and Sebastián Ventura. 2011. Multiple instance learning for classifying students in learning management systems. *Expert Systems with Applications*, 38(12):15020–15031.

Complementary Systems for Off-Topic Spoken Response Detection

Vatsal Raina, Mark J.F. Gales, Kate Knill
Dept. of Engineering, Cambridge University
Cambridge, UK
`{vr311, mjfg, kate.knill}@eng.cam.ac.uk`

Abstract

Increased demand to learn English for business and education has led to growing interest in automatic spoken language assessment and teaching systems. With this shift to automated approaches it is important that systems reliably assess all aspects of a candidate's responses. This paper examines one form of spoken language assessment; whether the response from the candidate is relevant to the prompt provided. This will be referred to as off-topic spoken response detection. Two forms of previously proposed approaches are examined in this work: the hierarchical attention-based topic model (HATM); and the similarity grid model (SGM). The work focuses on the scenario when the prompt, and associated responses, have not been seen in the training data, enabling the system to be applied to new test scripts without the need to collect data or retrain the model. To improve the performance of the systems for unseen prompts, data augmentation based on easy data augmentation (EDA) and translation based approaches are applied. Additionally for the HATM, a form of prompt dropout is described. The systems were evaluated on both seen and unseen prompts from Linguaskill Business and General English tests. For unseen data the performance of the HATM was improved using data augmentation, in contrast to the SGM where no gains were obtained. The two approaches were found to be complementary to one another, yielding a combined $F_{0.5}$ score of 0.814 for off-topic response detection where the prompts have not been seen in training.

1 Introduction

Spoken language assessment of English is on the rise as English is the chosen language of discourse for many situations. Businesses and academic institutes demand rigorous assessment methods to ensure prospective employees and students exceed a baseline standard for English proficiency so they can succeed and contribute in their new environment. Standardised assessments such as IELTS (Cullen et al., 2014), Pearson Test of English Academic (Longman, 2010) and TOEFL (ETS, 2012) include *"free speaking"* tasks where the candidate speaks spontaneously in response to a prompted question to ensure their speaking skills are fully assessed. A candidate might attempt to achieve a higher grade by speaking a pre-prepared response, irrelevant to the prompt. For scoring validity it is important that measures are taken to detect any off-topic responses so they do not influence the final grade. This is particularly true for automatic assessment systems which are increasingly being deployed to cope with the growing demand for examinations and may see increased cheating if candidates are aware that a computerised system is responsible for grading them (e.g. (Mellar et al., 2018)). These systems are more susceptible to inaccurate scoring due to emphasis given to criteria such as fluency, pronunciation and language use, over topic relevance (Lochbaum et al., 2013; Higgins and Heilman, 2014).

Automatic off-topic spoken response detection systems based on attention (Malinin et al., 2017b,a) and similarity grid (Wang et al., 2019) models have shown good performance for prompts seen in training. For operational reasons it would be cost and time effective to be able to use the same systems on responses to new prompts, unseen in training i.e. removing the need to collect new data and retrain models prior to deployment. Yoon et al. (2017) has had some success with handling unseen prompts. This is still a challenging research problem, however, with significant degradation observed on even the best performing hierarchical attention-based topic model (HATM) (Malinin et al., 2017a), and with no assessment to date of Wang et al. (2019)'s similarity grid model (SGM) approach. This paper

Proceedings of the 15th Workshop on Innovative Use of NLP for Building Educational Applications, pages 41–51
July 10, 2020. ©2020 Association for Computational Linguistics

therefore focuses on investigating how to improve performance on unseen prompts for these models. It presents extensions to the HATM and SGM with the goal of learning robust representations of seen prompts for effective generalisation to unseen prompts. The resulting systems are shown to have complementary detection characteristics, yielding improved off-topic response detection when combined.

The remainder of the paper is structured as follows: Section 2 presents related work; Section 3 details the components of the HATM and SGM, proposing modifications to each (universal regularisation and multi-channel cosine-similarity, respectively) to make them more robust; data augmentation is proposed in Section 4 to overcome limited training data; the experimental set-up and structure of the data is described in Section 5; Section 6 presents the experimental results and analysis; conclusions are given in Section 7.

2   Related Work

Initial off-topic spoken response detection systems were based on vector space models, measuring the relevance between the spoken response and test prompts inspired by systems for written essays (Higgins et al., 2006; Louis and Higgins, 2010). Cheng and Shen (2011)'s approach using speech confidence derived features is unsuited to general free speaking tasks, whereas Yoon and Xie (2014) required hundreds of example responses for each prompt from highly proficient speakers.

Using word embeddings and deep neural networks to measure sentence similarity has since become dominant. Rei and Cummins (2016) generated sentence-level relevance scores for written essays by using various similarity metrics based on word embeddings. For spoken responses, Malinin et al. (2016) proposed a topic-adapted recurrent neural network language model (RNNLM) to rank prompt-response pairs. This handles sequential information but cannot handle prompts unseen in training so Malinin et al. (2017b) introduced an attention-based topic model (ATM) which can. The deep learning ATM architecture uses an attention mechanism to attend over response word embeddings with the prompt sentence embedding as the key. A hierarchical variant of the ATM (HATM) is proposed in Malinin et al. (2017a) where an additional (prompt) attention mechanism is incorporated to attend over sentence embeddings of a set

of seen prompts with the test prompt embedding acting as the key. Hence, an unseen prompt is able to lock onto the vector representation of a combination of the seen prompts. The HATM assumes the set of seen prompts are sufficiently diverse to capture aspects of all possible unseen prompts. Malinin et al. (2017a) observed lower performance on unseen prompts due to a lack of diversity.

A radically different approach was proposed by Wang et al. (2019) based on initial work in Lee et al. (2017) and Yoon et al. (2017). Very deep CNNs are employed for automatic detection of off-topic spoken responses in which a prompt-response pair is represented as a similarity grid that can be interpreted as an image (this model will be referred to here as *SGM*). Similarity measurements are made based on word embeddings (or other distance metrics) of the prompt/response content words. The training data used in Wang et al. (2019) was from exams with generally short prompts which resulted in a limited number of content words to use. It was not assessed on unseen prompts.

3   Off-Topic Spoken Response Detection

This paper builds upon the hierarchical attention-based topic model (HATM) (Malinin et al., 2017a) (section 3.1) and the similarity grid in CNNs model (SGM) (Wang et al., 2019) (section 3.2) for detection of off-topic spoken responses to prompted questions. The candidate can answer freely so automatic speech recognition (ASR) is needed to determine the words in their response in each case. Both systems assign a probability that the ASR obtained response, $\hat{z}$, is relevant to the prompt, $\hat{x}$.

The performance of the HATM and SGM models on responses to prompts *seen* in training is high, with $F_{0.5}$ scores above 0.9. A key issue, however, in the practical deployment of off-topic response detection systems is handling responses to prompts that were *unseen* in training so that new examination questions can be asked without requiring example responses to be collected and the detection system retrained. Although Malinin et al. (2017a) improved off-topic detection on *unseen* prompts compared to earlier work, the performance is still quite far below that of *seen*, and the SGM has not been evaluated in the unseen prompt scenario. This section presents two approaches to potentially improve performance on unseen prompts: universal regularisation in an attention mechanism as a structural modification to the HATM in order to encourage generalisation; multi-channel SGM based on cosine distance (MSGM). Data augmentation strategies to increase the number of prompts available for training are presented in Section 4.

3.1 Attention-Based Model

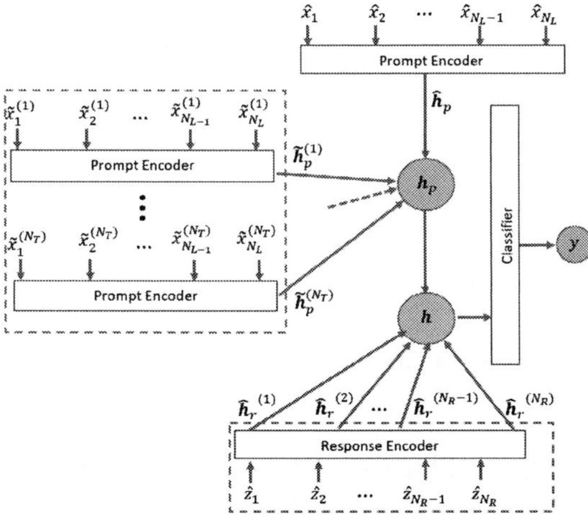

Figure 1: Hierarchical Attention-based Topic Model (HATM).

The Hierarchical Attention-based Topic Model (HATM) (Malinin et al., 2017a) is depicted in Figure 1. The system uses an encoding of the prompt word sequence, $\mathbf{h}_p$, as the key for an attention mechanism over an embedding of the response to yield a fixed length vector, $\mathbf{h}$, that is used to predict the probability, y, that the response was relevant to the prompt. To improve the robustness of the estimate of the prompt embedding an additional attention mechanism is run over all N_T embeddings of the prompts seen in training, $\tilde{\mathbf{h}}_p^{(1)}, \ldots, \tilde{\mathbf{h}}_p^{(N_T)}$. This attention mechanism uses an embedding of the test prompt, $\hat{\mathbf{h}}_p$, as the key to yield $\mathbf{h}_p$. This additional attention mechanism over the prompts was found to improve the performance of the system when the prompt had not been seen in the training data (Malinin et al., 2017a). The same network configuration as that used in Malinin et al. (2017a) was implemented in this work:

- bi-directional (Schuster and Paliwal, 1997) LSTMs (Hochreiter and Schmidhuber, 1997) were used as the encoders for both the prompts and the responses. Separate models were used for the prompt and response encoders[1];

---

[1] More complex sentence and word embeddings, such as BERT (Devlin et al., 2019) were examined in initial experiments but were not found to yield performance gains.

- additive attention mechanisms were used for both the attention mechanism over the training prompts and that over the responses;

- the classifier used ReLU activation functions.

The parameters of the network were optimised using cross-entropy training. For the training of the prompt attention mechanism, the actual prompt was excluded from the attention mechanism, otherwise the attention mechanism simply focuses on the matched prompt embedding.

One of the issues observed with the HATM is that the performance of the system on unseen prompts is significantly poorer than the performance on seen prompts that have been seen, along with relevant responses, in the training data. This motivates the need for the model to improve the generalisation of the system to unseen prompts. Here, the prompt attention mechanism (see Figure 1) is targeted. A specific form of dropout, where training prompt embeddings are excluded from the prompt attention mechanism, referred to as *prompt-dropout*, is proposed. Denoting $\alpha_k = \texttt{Softmax}\left[\hat{\mathbf{h}}_p, \tilde{\mathbf{h}}_p^{(k)}, \theta_{pa}\right]$ as the attention weight for the kth training prompt embedding, $\tilde{\mathbf{h}}_p^{(k)}$, with the test prompt embedding, $\hat{\mathbf{h}}_p$, as the key, random attention weights are set to zero during training in prompt-dropout such that

$$\alpha_k = \begin{cases} 0 & \text{w.p. } 1 - \kappa \\ \texttt{Softmax}\left[\hat{\mathbf{h}}_p, \tilde{\mathbf{h}}_p^{(k)}, \theta_{pa}\right] & \text{w.p. } \kappa \end{cases} \tag{1}$$

where κ represents the keep-probability. The attention weights must be re-normalised after prompt-dropout. Sampling κ from a probabilistic distribution for each attention weight is motivated by Garnelo et al. (2018). In initial experiments this distribution of dropout rate was found to outperform selecting a fixed dropout rate.

3.2 Similarity Grid Model

The Similarity Grid Model (SGM) (Wang et al., 2019) represents a prompt-response pair as a "similarity image". This image is transformed by an Inception network into a measure of the degree of relevance between the test prompt and test response.

Initially all stop words are removed such that a given prompt and response pair only consists of

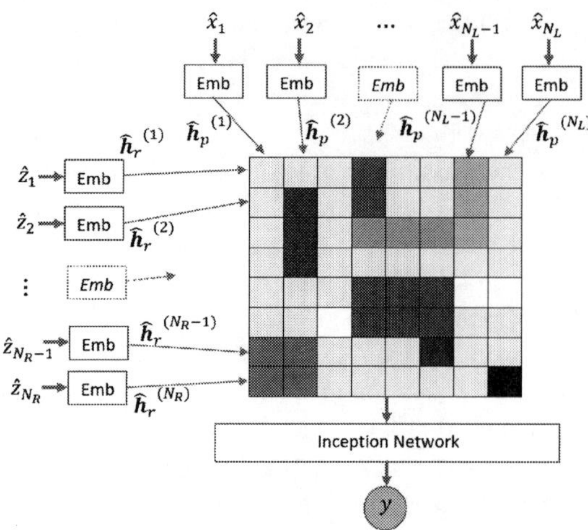

Figure 2: Similarity Grid Model (SGM) where the grid "pixel" colours indicate the level of similarity.

content words[2]. After this pre-processing the similarity grid model for a prompt-response pair is as shown in Figure 2. For all content words in the test prompt, $\{\hat{x}_i\}_{i=1}^{N_L}$, and test response, $\{\hat{z}_i\}_{i=1}^{N_R}$, word embeddings, $\left\{\hat{\mathbf{h}}_p^{(i)}\right\}_{i=1}^{N_L}$ and $\left\{\hat{\mathbf{h}}_r^{(i)}\right\}_{i=1}^{N_R}$, are computed. These word embeddings are used to construct a similarity grid, $\mathbf{S}$. This two-dimensional grid has N_L columns and N_R rows and the cell position (i, j) holds an inverse similarity metric between the ith prompt word embedding, $\hat{\mathbf{h}}_p^{(i)}$, and the jth response word embedding, $\hat{\mathbf{h}}_r^{(j)}$. $\mathbf{S}$ is then resized to 180×180 in order to make the similarity grid of standard size regardless of the number of content words in the test prompt and response. Perceiving the similarity grid as an image, an Inception network transforms the resized image to a value $0 \leq y \leq 1$, indicating the degree of relevance between the test prompt and test response.

The network configuration used in this work is closely related to that used in Wang et al. (2019):

- context independent word embeddings are computed for each word in the prompt and the response. The embeddings for both the prompt and response are tied;

- a cosine distance to compute the distance between each prompt response word embedding pair, followed by a bilinear transform was used to resize the similarity grid;

---

[2]A comprehensive list of stop words is provided by `nltk.corpus` https://www.nltk.org/api/ nltk.corpus.html.

- the Resnet-152 (He et al., 2016b) Inception network was used.

The similarity grid has one channel i.e. one single measurement value per cell. This can be extended to multiple channels (MSGM), with different forms of embeddings or distance functions used to compute the grid in each channel. Wang et al. (2019) used cosine distances in the first channel and inverse document frequency (IDF) values of the prompt and response words for the second and third channel, respectively. For this paper a MSGM with three channels where each channel represents the cosine distance between prompt and response word embeddings with a different set of word embeddings learnt for each channel is used[3]. The variety in the embeddings, and resulting channel, is achieved by using different initialisation seeds with the same network configuration. As the Inception network filters over the channels are simultaneously trained the resulting filters will be complementary.

4 Data Augmentation

In general, the performance of off-topic response systems is limited by insufficient unique prompts being available for training. Data augmentation, where the training data is modified in some way to create new examples, is regularly applied on low resource tasks in areas such as speech recognition (e.g. (Cui et al., 2015)) and computer vision (e.g. (Shorten and Khoshgoftaar, 2019)) and has had some success in NLP (e.g. (Zhang et al., 2015; Kafle et al., 2017; Wei and Zou, 2019)). This motivates investigating if augmentation of the training prompts such that multiple versions of each prompt are generated can help improve robustness[4]. Prompt augmentation will permit the model to explore the region around each unique prompt rather than being restricted to a discrete point in the high-dimensional prompt-space.

Both structured and unstructured data augmentation techniques are considered here. Augmentation of prompts is performed *on-the-fly* during training. Note, the hierarchy of seen prompts of the HATM

---

[3]In this work, the use of IDF values in the second and third MSGM channels did not improve performance over the SGM so was not used.

[4]Data augmentation of training responses is also possible. This was found to degrade performance in initial experiments, possibly due to there being a large number of diverse responses available for training without augmentation and issues with generating sensible back-translations on ASR output.

in the prompt attention mechanism (Figure 1) does not include the additional augmented prompts because the expectation is that augmented prompts will not dramatically differ from the original unique prompts.

Easy Data Augmentation (EDA) techniques were trialled by Wei and Zou (2019). They proposed that different variants of any textual data can be generated using a combination of synonym replacement, random insertion, random swap and random deletion of words. A single hyper-parameter, α, controls the fraction of words that are modified in the original text. Using the default value of $\alpha = 0.1$, prompts are augmented using the above techniques to replace, insert, swap or delete 10% of the words randomly in the original prompt. This structured augmentation approach should enable the model to learn a more robust representation of each unique prompt.

Back-translation is employed as an unstructured method to augment the amount of available training data. A machine translation model is employed to translate a given training prompt into a foreign language by taking the maximum likelihood output. Then a reverse machine translation model takes the prompt in the foreign language and translates it back into English. The expectation is that the original and final pair of English prompts will be very similar in meaning but will have a different ordering and choice of specific words. Therefore, the back-translated prompt can be treated as a new prompt which can be paired with the original prompt's response to generate a new prompt-response pair. The use of several different languages permits the creation of several variants of the same prompt. Translation can be achieved using standard machine translation packages.

5 Data and Experimental Set-Up

The HATM and SGM models and the proposed extensions were assessed on their ability to detect off-topic responses to prompts in free speaking tests where the candidates can talk for up to one minute in answering the question.

5.1 Training and evaluation data

Data from the Cambridge Assessment English Linguaskill Business and Linguaskill General English tests[5] are used in the training and evaluation of the

---

systems. The two tests are similar in format but with different foci and therefore vary in the topics discussed by candidates and their associated vocabularies. They are multi-level, global, tests - i.e. taken by candidates from across the CEFR levels, A1-C2, with a wide range of first languages (L1s) and variation in response proficiency.

Both Linguaskill speaking tests are comprised of five parts. For this paper only prompts and corresponding responses from the three long free speaking parts are used. The candidate has 60 seconds in parts 3 and 4 to talk on a topic such as *advice for a colleague/friend* and discuss a picture or graph, respectively. Part 5 consists of 20 second responses to a set of five contextualised prompts, such as *starting a retail business*, or *talk about a hobby*. The diversity of these prompts is discussed by Malinin et al. (2017a).

Data		TRN	SEEN	UNS
#Prompts		379	219	56
#Responses		257.2K	40.8K	85.0K
Avg. prompt length		51	51	55
content words		28	28	29
Avg. resp. length		48	43	42
content words		22	20	19

Table 1: Prompt/response statistics for training (TRN) and *seen* (SEEN) and *unseen* (UNS) evaluation data sets.

Table 1 outlines the statistics for the training (TRN) and two evaluation data sets (SEEN and UNS). TRN and SEEN are taken from the Linguaskill Business test and UNS from the Linguaskill General English test. There is no overlap in speakers between any of the data sets. The response texts are generated automatically from the 1-best hypotheses from an ASR system with a word error rate (WER) of 25.7% on Business English data. TRN consists of a total of 257.2K responses to 379 unique prompts, an average of 679 responses per prompt compared with 186 for SEEN and 1518 for UNS. The average number of words are similar across the 3 data sets, with prompts (51-55) being slightly longer than responses (42-48) on average. This reduces by about half when content words only are included. The HATM is trained and evaluated using all the words in every textual prompt-response pair while the SGM is trained and evaluated using only the content words in every prompt-response pair.

5.1.1 Training data construction

All responses are taken from tests assessed by human examiners, which permits the assumption that all responses in the data are on-topic. Therefore synthetic off-topic responses have to be created to train the systems. The off-topic data is generated using a dynamic sampling mechanism; this matches responses from one prompt with a different prompt. Balance is maintained such that the empirical distribution of topics in the on-topic examples is mimicked in the generation of synthetic off-topic examples. Off-topic examples for training data are generated *on-the-fly* (Malinin et al., 2017a) instead of producing a fixed set of negative examples prior to training as in Malinin et al. (2016) because dynamic sampling allows the diversity of negative examples to be efficiently increased. For each on-topic example, one off-topic example is generated.

For the data augmentation experiments the number of prompts was increased by a factor of 10 using EDA (Wei and Zou, 2019) or machine translation, and 20 when both were applied. The default value of $\alpha = 0.1$ was used in EDA to change 10% of words in the original prompt by replacing, inserting, swapping and/or deleting. Machine translation was performed offline using the Babylon MT system [6]. Back-translations were generated using 9 different languages[7].

5.1.2 Evaluation data construction

Due to the scarcity of real off-topic examples, negative off-topic examples are generated by permuting on-topic examples for SEEN and UNS. Each on-topic example has ten off-topic examples generated and duplicated ten times to maintain balance. Data set SEEN is formed from prompts that have been seen during training and negative responses that correspond to a different set of prompts seen during training. Data set UNS consists of prompts that are unseen during training and negative responses that correspond to prompts that are unseen during training too. Forming negative examples by permuting on-topic examples is reasonable because real off-topic examples by candidates are anticipated to consist of responses to a different prompt to that being answered.

5.2 Hyper-parameters and models

The HATM consists of two 400 dimensional BiL-STM encoders with 200 forward and backward states each and TanH non-linearities. 200 dimensional parameters are used for the prompt attention mechanism. The binary classifier is a DNN with 2 hidden layers of 200 rectified linear (ReLU) units and a 1-dimensional logistic output. Dropout regularisation (Srivastava et al., 2014) with a keep probability of 0.8 is applied to all layers except for the LSTM recurrent connections and word embeddings. The universal regularisation samples its keep probability using $\kappa \sim \mathcal{U}(0.05, 0.95)$. The HATM is initialised from an attention-topic model (ATM) as described in Malinin et al. (2017a). It is trained for 3 epochs using an Adam optimizer, with an exponentially decaying learning rate initialised at 1e-3 and decay factor of 0.85 per epoch. The first two epochs train only the prompt attention mechanism and the final epoch is used to train the whole network apart from the DNN binary classifier. This configuration was optimised using seen development data, similarly for the SGM. The ATM takes approximately 3 hours to train and an additional 1 hour for the HATM on an nVidia GTX 980M graphics card.

The SGM learns 200 dimensional word embeddings for each word in the prompt and response. ResNet-152 (He et al., 2016a)[8] with 152 residual layers is used as the Inception network with a 1-dimensional logistic output. The SGM is trained for 1 epoch using an Adam optimizer with a learning rate of 1e-3. It takes about 2 hours to train on an nVidia GTX 980M graphics card. The extended HATM and the SGM were built in Tensorflow[9].

The HATM and SGM results reported are computed on an ensemble of 15 models unless noted otherwise. Each model has an identical architecture and training parameters but each has a different initial seed value, creating modeling diversity. For this work a large ensemble is reported to minimise variance on the ensemble performance results. No analysis of efficiency is given. Approaches such as ensemble distillation (Hinton et al., 2015) can be directly applied to reduce computational cost.

---

[6]`https://translation.babylon-software.com/english/Offline/`

[7]Machine translation languages: Arabic, French, German, Greek, Hebrew, Hindi, Japanese, Korean, Russian.

[8]Code available at `https://github.com/KaimingHe/resnet-1k-layers`.

[9]Code available at `https://github.com/VatsalRaina/HATM`.

5.3 Performance criteria

Following Wang et al. (2019), precision and recall are used to assess performance except $F_{0.5}$ is preferred over F_1 as there is a greater interest in achieving a higher precision compared to recall: a candidate's response should not be mistakenly classified as off-topic as such responses are to be assigned a score of 0. This is a more standard metric than the area under the curve (AUC) used in Malinin et al. (2017a) and more intuitive in terms of test evaluation. Note, the results are given for a particular instance of permuting the off-topic examples for evaluation.

6 Experimental Results

This section presents the results of experiments performed on SGM, MSGM and extended HATM systems. Section 6.1 compares the performance of the baseline HATM with the MSGM on the *unseen* (UNS) and *seen* (SEEN) evaluation data sets. Section 6.2 explores the improvement in performance due to extending the baseline HATM using universal regularisation and prompt augmentation strategies. Finally, 6.3 investigates the complementary nature of the MSGM and the extended HATM. The prompt-specific performance of the combined system is considered in Section 6.4.

6.1 Baseline systems

	Model	P	R	$F_{0.5}$
SEEN	HATM	—	—	0.918 ±0.010
	-ensemble	0.963	0.841	0.936
	MSGM	—	—	0.905 ±0.009
	-ensemble	0.943	0.838	0.920
UNS	HATM	—	—	0.612 ±0.032
	-ensemble	0.815	0.370	0.657
	MSGM	—	—	0.767 ±0.019
	-ensemble	0.833	0.691	0.800

Table 2: Comparison of baseline HATM $[\mathcal{B}]$ and MSGM, for *seen* (SEEN) and *unseen* (UNS).

Table 2 shows the baseline performance for the HATM and MSGM models. There is a relatively low variance between individual system results but combining the outputs in an ensemble improves the $F_{0.5}$ score in each case, with a larger gain (0.045/0.033 vs 0.018/0.015) observed on the unseen data. The

HATM performs slightly better on the seen data than the MSGM, with a higher $F_{0.5}$ and a similar but always slightly higher precision-recall curve (Figure 3). For unseen data, however, the reverse is true with MSGM having a higher $F_{0.5}$ score of 0.800 compared to 0.657 for the baseline HATM. From Figure 3 it can be seen that the precision-recall curves for the HATM and SGM/MSGM systems on unseen data are quite different in shape. The HATM has a higher precision at the lowest recall but this drops quickly as the threshold increases. The degradation in the MSGM precision is much more gradual.

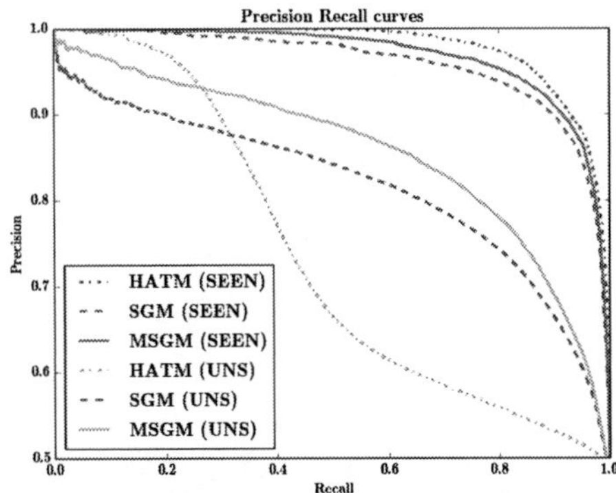

Figure 3: Comparison of precision-recall curves for baseline ensemble systems for HATM, SGM and MSGM for *seen* (SEEN) and *unseen* (UNS).

Figure 3 confirms that the focus should be on improving the performance on the unseen evaluation data set. The use of multi-channels benefits the similarity grid model as can be seen in Figure 3, with a SGM $F_{0.5}$ score of 0.908 on the seen and 0.768 on the unseen data sets, respectively. These gains are similar to those observed in Wang et al. (2019). Therefore, the results in the following sections will only be presented for the unseen evaluation data set and MSGM systems.

6.2 Regularisation and data augmentation

Universal regularisation and data augmentation were applied to the HATM to see if they improved detection performance. From Table 3 and Figure 4, it is evident that the universal regularisation on the prompt attention mechanism yields an increase in the $F_{0.5}$ score. Both the structured techniques and the machine translation (MT) prompt data augmentation strategies produce a boost in performance on the baseline HATM with universal regularisation. MT yields a much larger gain but the structured technique is shown to be complementary by

Model	P	R	$F_{0.5}$
$\mathcal{B}$	0.815	0.370	0.657
$\mathcal{B} \oplus \mathcal{P_D}$	0.846	0.386	0.683
$\mathcal{B} \oplus \mathcal{P_D} \oplus \mathcal{A_E}$	0.790	0.464	0.693
$\mathcal{B} \oplus \mathcal{P_D} \oplus \mathcal{A_M}$	0.877	0.529	0.775
$\mathcal{B} \oplus \mathcal{P_D} \oplus \mathcal{A_E} \oplus \mathcal{A_M}$	0.891	0.524	0.782

Table 3: Impact of universal regularisation, $\mathcal{P_D}$, and data augmentation ($\mathcal{A_E}$ = structured techniques and $\mathcal{A_M}$ = machine translation) on baseline HATM, $\mathcal{B}$, for *unseen* (UNS).

	Model	P	R	$F_{0.5}$
	HATM	0.956	0.802	0.921
SEEN	MSGM	0.943	0.838	0.920
	Comb	0.962	0.839	0.935
	HATM	0.891	0.524	0.782
UNS	MSGM	0.833	0.691	0.800
	Comb	0.875	0.635	0.814

Table 4: Impact of combining models SGM and extended HATM $[\mathcal{B} \oplus \mathcal{P_D} \oplus \mathcal{A_E} \oplus \mathcal{A_M}]$ on *seen* (SEEN) and *unseen* (UNS). Comb = HATM & MSGM.

a further improvement when prompts are generated by both methods which was larger than observed when simply doubling the MT augmented prompts. Hence, the extended HATM is defined as $\mathcal{B} \oplus \mathcal{P_D} \oplus \mathcal{A_E} \oplus \mathcal{A_M}$.

for the HATM and MSGM systems, respectively (Table 4). For comparison with Wang et al. (2019), the combined system here has an F_1 score of 0.922 and 0.807 on the seen and unseen data sets respectively.

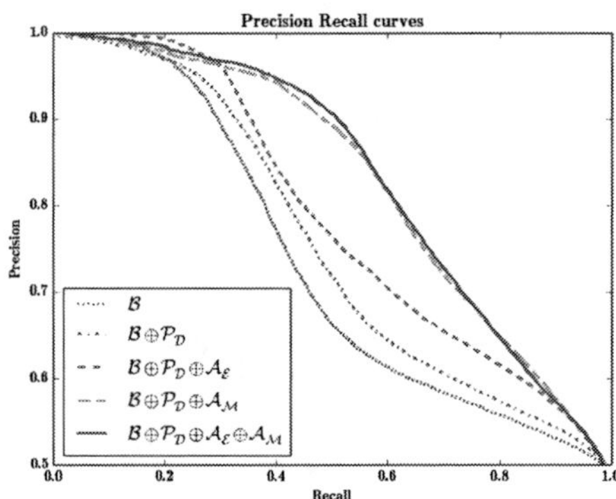

Figure 4: Impact of universal regularisation, $\mathcal{P_D}$, and data augmentation ($\mathcal{A_E}$ = structured techniques and $\mathcal{A_M}$ = machine translation) on baseline HATM, $\mathcal{B}$, on precision-recall curves for *unseen* (UNS).

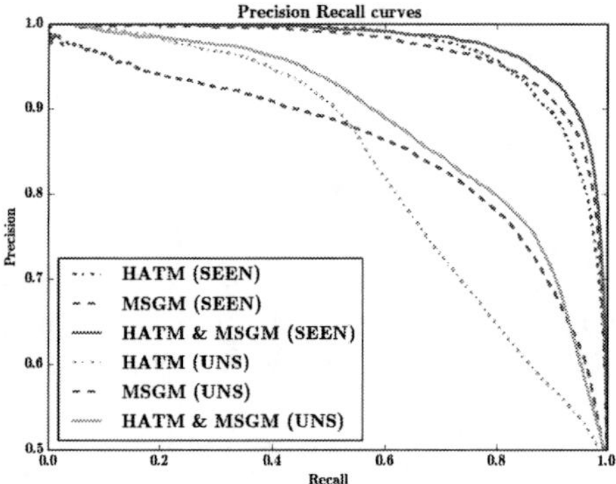

Figure 5: Impact of combining models MSGM and extended HATM $[\mathcal{B} \oplus \mathcal{P_D} \oplus \mathcal{A_E} \oplus \mathcal{A_M}]$ on *seen* (SEEN) and *unseen* (UNS).

Experiments were also run on applying data augmentation to SGM. This led to significant drops in $F_{0.5}$, probably as a result of the SGM over-fitting to the training data.

6.3 Combining MSGM and extended HATM

As for the baseline HATM, the precision-recall curve for the extended HATM displays different characteristics to MSGM on the unseen data set as shown in Figure 5. These systems are complementary; combining the systems by averaging their outputs yields precision-recall curves which boost the precision at each recall level, giving a small gain over the best individual system at each threshold. The individual $F_{0.5}$ scores are boosted on the unseen data set from 0.782 and 0.800 to 0.814 and from 0.921 and 0.920 to 0.935 on the seen data set

6.4 Prompt-specific performance analysis

The performance of any off-topic response detection system is expected to depend on both the nature of the prompts, and how "close" a test prompt is to one seen in the training data. Yoon et al. (2017) found that performance varied substantially across different prompts. In this work the 10 most common, in the sense of having a large number of responses, unseen prompts in UNS were used to analyse the prompt specific performance. These common prompts should give robust per-prompt $F_{0.5}$ scores. The average performance of the combined MSGM and extended HATM system on this subset of prompts was 0.832, with a standard deviation of 0.048. This standard deviation across prompts is approximately half of the value presented in Yoon et al. (2017). As the prompts for that data are not available, however, it is unclear whether this reduction is due to the nature of the prompts or improved generalisation of the combined model.

From Table 4 there is a large $F_{0.5}$ performance difference between prompts seen during training, 0.935, and those not seen, 0.814. Given this variation in performance, it is interesting to see whether the performance of an individual test prompt can be predicted given the set of training prompts. For prompts that are expected to perform poorly it would then be possible to collect training data.

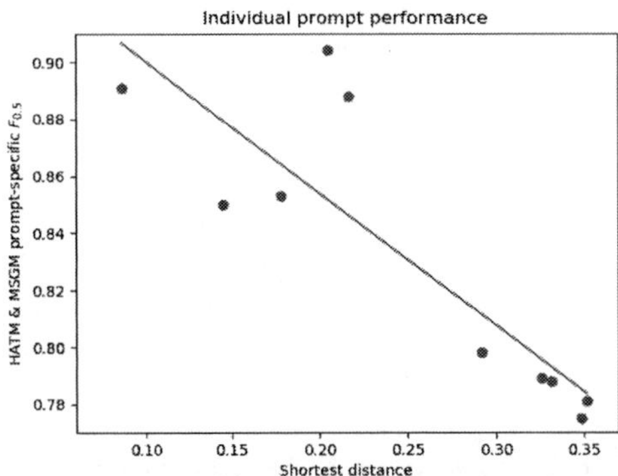

Figure 6: Relationship between unseen prompt distance to closest seen prompt and $F_{0.5}$ performance of MSGM & extended HATM $[\mathcal{B} \oplus \mathcal{P}_\mathcal{D} \oplus \mathcal{A}_\mathcal{E} \oplus \mathcal{A}_\mathcal{M}]$ on the unseen prompts subsets.

In Malinin et al. (2017a) the entropy of the prompt attention mechanism was used to rank performance of the prompts based on area under the curve metrics. From initial experiments this was not found to be a good predictor of $F_{0.5}$ score on these unseen test prompts. In this work, the cosine distance from the test prompt embedding, $\hat{\mathbf{h}}_p$, and each of the training prompt embeddings, $\tilde{\mathbf{h}}_p^{(i)}$, was computed. The closest distance was then used as the measure of similarity of the individual test prompt to the training data prompts. Figure 6 shows the individual $F_{0.5}$ score against this distance again using the 10 most common unseen prompts. There is a strong negative correlation, an R^2 statistic of 0.739, between the individual prompt performance and its distance to the closest seen prompt, showing the cosine distance between the prompt embeddings is a good indicator of unseen prompt performance.

From Figure 6 the cosine distance allows the unseen prompts to be partitioned into two distinct groups, *close* and *far* prompts with respect to the training prompts. The performance of all the unseen prompts was then evaluated using a distance threshold of 0.24 at the same operating point as Table 4. This yielded $F_{0.5}$ of 0.833 for *close*, and 0.777 for *far* prompts. Note for all distance thresholds examined, that resulted in a split of the unseen prompts, *close* always outperformed *far*.

7 Conclusion

This paper addresses the issue of off-topic detection in the context of unconstrained spoken responses to prompts. In particular, the problem of robustness to prompts unseen in training is considered. The Hierarchical Attention-based Topic Model (HATM) (Malinin et al., 2017a) and Similarity Grid Model (Wang et al., 2019) are compared and extended. Universal regularisation and data augmentation, from structured techniques and machine translation, increased the HATM $F_{0.5}$ by 19% relative to 0.782 on the unseen evaluation set. This contrasts with a three channel SGM (MSGM) based on cosine distances between prompt and response embeddings which yielded $F_{0.5}$ of 0.800.

The extended HATM and MSGM are shown to have very different precision-recall characteristics on unseen prompts, with the HATM having a very high precision at low recall but with a fairly sharp drop-off whilst the SGM's precision does not reach quite the same level but degrades at a much more gradual rate. The best individual systems are found to be complementary, with system combination boosting off-topic response detection on both unseen and seen prompts, achieving the best performance of $F_{0.5}$ of 0.814 on unseen and 0.935 on seen prompts. This combined system closely follows, and slightly enhances, the envelope of the best precision-recall path across the two individual systems. Finally the distance between a test prompt and the closest training is shown to predict the system performance, indicating which prompts may require additional training data to be collected.

8 Acknowledgements

This paper reports on research supported by Cambridge Assessment, University of Cambridge. Thanks to Cambridge English Language Assessment for support and access to the Linguaskill data. The authors would like to thank members of the ALTA Speech Team for generating the ASR transcriptions for the responses, and the initial implementation of the code from Malinin et al. (2017a).

References

J. Cheng and J. Shen. 2011. Off-topic detection in automated speech assessment applications. In *Proc. INTERSPEECH 2011*, pages 1597–1600.

X. Cui, V. Goel, and B. Kingsbury. 2015. Data augmentation for deep neural network acoustic modeling. *IEEE/ACM Transactions on Audio, Speech, and Language Processing*, 23(9):1469–1477.

P. Cullen, A. French, and V. Jakeman. 2014. *The Official Cambridge Guide to IELTS*. Cambridge University Press.

J. Devlin, M.-W. Chang, K. Lee, and K. Toutanova. 2019. BERT: Pre-training of deep bidirectional transformers for language understanding. In *Proc. 2019 Conf. North American Chapter of the Association for Computational Linguistics: Human Language Technologies, Volume 1 (Long and Short Papers)*, pages 4171–4186.

ETS. 2012. *The Official Guide to the TOEFL® Test*, fourth edition edition. McGraw-Hill.

M. Garnelo, D. Rosenbaum, C. Maddison, T. Ramalho, D. Saxton, M. Shanahan, Y. W. Teh, D. Jimenez Rezende, and S. M. Ali Eslami. 2018. Conditional Neural Processes. In *Proc. 35th International Conference on Machine Learning, ICML*, pages 1690–1699.

K. He, X. Zhang, S. Ren, and J. Sun. 2016a. Deep residual learning for image recognition. In *Proc. IEEE Conference on Computer Vision and Pattern Recognition, CVPR 2016*, pages 770–778.

K. He, X. Zhang, S. Ren, and J. Sun. 2016b. Identity mappings in deep residual networks. In *Proc. European Conference Computer Vision (ECCV)*, pages 630–645.

D. Higgins, J. Burstein, and Y. Attali. 2006. Identifying off-topic student essays without topic-specific training data. *Natural Language Engineering*, 12:145 – 159.

D. Higgins and M. Heilman. 2014. Managing what we can measure: Quantifying the susceptibility of automated scoring systems to gaming behavior. *Educational Measurement: Issues and Practice*, 33(3):36–46.

G. E. Hinton, O. Vinyals, and J. Dean. 2015. Distilling the knowledge in a neural network. *CoRR*, abs/1503.02531.

S. Hochreiter and J. Schmidhuber. 1997. Long short-term memory. *Neural computation*, 9:1735–80.

K. Kafle, M. Yousefhussien, and C. Kanan. 2017. Data augmentation for visual question answering. In *Proc. 10th International Conference on Natural Language Generation*, pages 198–202.

C. H. Lee, S.-Y. Yoon, X. Wang, M. Mulholland, I. Choi, and K. Evanini. 2017. Off-topic spoken response detection using Siamese convolutional neural networks. In *Proc. INTERSPEECH 2017*, pages 1427–1431.

K. E. Lochbaum, M. Rosenstein, P. Foltz, and M. A. Derr. 2013. Detection of gaming in automated scoring of essays with the IEA. In *Proc. 75th Annual meeting of NCME*.

P. Longman. 2010. *The Official Guide to Pearson Test of English Academic*. Pearson Education ESL.

A. Louis and D. Higgins. 2010. Off-topic essay detection using short prompt texts. In *Proc. NAACL HLT 2010 Fifth Workshop on Innovative Use of NLP for Building Educational Applications*, pages 92–95.

A. Malinin, R. C. van Dalen, K. Knill, Y. Wang, and M. J. F. Gales. 2016. Off-topic response detection for spontaneous spoken english assessment. In *Proc. 54th Annual Meeting of the Association for Computational Linguistics, ACL 2016*.

A. Malinin, K. Knill, and M. J. F. Gales. 2017a. A hierarchical attention based model for off-topic spontaneous spoken response detection. In *Proc. 2017 IEEE Automatic Speech Recognition and Understanding Workshop, ASRU*, pages 397–403.

A. Malinin, K. Knill, A. Ragni, Y. Wang, and M. J. F. Gales. 2017b. An attention based model for off-topic spontaneous spoken response detection: An initial study. In *Proc. 7th ISCA International Workshop on Speech and Language Technology in Education, SLaTE 2017*, pages 144–149.

H. Mellar, R. Peytcheva-Forsyth, S. Kocdar, A. Karadeniz, and B. Yovkova. 2018. Addressing cheating in e-assessment using student authentication and authorship checking systems: teachers' perspectives. *Int. J. Educ. Integr.*, 14(2).

Marek Rei and Ronan Cummins. 2016. Sentence similarity measures for fine-grained estimation of topical relevance in learner essays. In *Proc. 11th Workshop on Innovative Use of NLP for Building Educational Applications, BEA@NAACL-HLT 2016*, pages 283–288.

M. Schuster and K. Paliwal. 1997. Bidirectional recurrent neural networks. *Signal Processing, IEEE Transactions on*, 45:2673 – 2681.

C. Shorten and T. M. Khoshgoftaar. 2019. A survey on image data augmentation for deep learning. *J. Big Data*, 6:60.

N. Srivastava, G. Hinton, A. Krizhevsky, I. Sutskever, and R. Salakhutdinov. 2014. Dropout: A simple way to prevent neural networks from overfitting. *J. Mach. Learn. Res.*, 15(1):1929–1958.

X. Wang, S.-Y. Yoon, K. Evanini, K. Zechner, and Y. Qian. 2019. Automatic detection of off-topic spoken responses using very deep convolutional neural networks. In *Proc. INTERSPEECH 2019*, pages 4200–4204.

J. Wei and K. Zou. 2019. EDA: Easy data augmentation techniques for boosting performance on text classification tasks. In *Proc. 2019 Conference on Empirical Methods in Natural Language Processing and the 9th International Joint Conference on Natural Language Processing (EMNLP-IJCNLP)*, pages 6382–6388.

Su-Youn Yoon, Chong Min Lee, Ikkyu Choi, Xinhao Wang, Matthew Mulholland, and Keelan Evanini. 2017. Off-topic spoken response detection with word embeddings. In *Proc. INTERSPEECH 2017*, pages 2754–2758.

Su-Youn Yoon and Shasha Xie. 2014. Similarity-based non-scorable response detection for automated speech scoring. In *Proc. Ninth Workshop on Innovative Use of NLP for Building Educational Applications*, pages 116–123.

X. Zhang, J. Zhao, and Y. LeCun. 2015. Character-level convolutional networks for text classification. In *Advances in Neural Information Processing Systems 28*, page 649–657.

CIMA: A Large Open Access Dialogue Dataset for Tutoring

Katherine Stasaski
UC Berkeley
katie_stasaski@berkeley.edu

Kimberly Kao
Facebook*
kimkao957@gmail.com

Marti A. Hearst
UC Berkeley
hearst@berkeley.edu

Abstract

One-to-one tutoring is often an effective means to help students learn, and recent experiments with neural conversation systems are promising. However, large open datasets of tutoring conversations are lacking. To remedy this, we propose a novel asynchronous method for collecting tutoring dialogue via crowdworkers that is both amenable to the needs of deep learning algorithms and reflective of pedagogical concerns. In this approach, extended conversations are obtained between crowdworkers role-playing as both students and tutors. The CIMA collection, which we make publicly available, is novel in that students are exposed to overlapping grounded concepts between exercises and multiple relevant tutoring responses are collected for the same input.

CIMA contains several compelling properties from an educational perspective: student role-players complete exercises in fewer turns during the course of the conversation and tutor players adopt strategies that conform with some educational conversational norms, such as providing hints versus asking questions in appropriate contexts. The dataset enables a model to be trained to generate the next tutoring utterance in a conversation, conditioned on a provided action strategy.

1   Introduction

There is a pressing societal need to help students of all ages learn new subjects. One-on-one tutoring is one of the most effective techniques for producing learning gains, and many studies support the efficacy of conversational tutors as educational aids (VanLehn et al., 2007; Nye et al., 2014; Graesser, 2015; Ruan et al., 2019).

Tutoring dialogues should exhibit a number of important properties that are not present in existing open datasets. The conversation should be grounded around common concepts that both the student and the tutor recognize are the topics to be learned (Graesser et al., 2009). The conversation should be *extended*, that is, long enough for the student to be exposed to new concepts, givin students the opportunity to recall them in future interactions. The collection should contain varied responses, to reflect the fact that there is more than one valid way for a tutor to respond to a student at any given point in the conversation. And lastly, the dialogue should not contain personally identifiable information so it can be available as open access data.

We propose a novel method for creating a tutoring dialogue collection that exhibits many of the properties needed for training a conversational tutor. In this approach, extended conversations are obtained between crowdworkers role-playing as both students and tutors. Students work through an exercise, which involves translating a phrase from English to Italian. The workers do not converse directly, but rather are served utterances from prior rounds of interaction asynchronously in order to obtain multiple tutoring responses for the same conversational input. Special aspects of the approach are:

- Each exercise is grounded with both an image and a concept representation.
- The exercises are linked by subsets of shared concepts, thus allowing the student to potentially transfer what they learn from one exercise to the next.
- Each student conversational turn is assigned three responses from distinct tutors.
- The exercises are organized into two datasets, one more complex (Prepositional Phrase) than the other (Shape).
- Each line of dialogue is manually labeled with a set of action types.

We report on an analysis of the Conversa-

---

*Research performed while at UC Berkeley.

Proceedings of the 15ᵗʰ Workshop on Innovative Use of NLP for Building Educational Applications, pages 52–64
July 10, 2020. ©2020 Association for Computational Linguistics

tional Instruction with Multi-responses and Actions (CIMA) dataset,[1] including the difference in language observed among the two datasets, how many turns a student requires to complete an exercise, actions tutors choose to take in response to students, and agreement among the three tutors on which actions to take. We also report results of a neural dialogue model trained on the resulting data, measuring both quality of the model responses and whether the model can reliably generate text conditioned on a desired set of tutoring actions.

2 Prior Work

2.1 Tutoring Dialogue Corpus Creation

Past work in creation of large publicly-available datasets of human-to-human tutoring interactions has been limited. Relevant past work which utilizes tutoring dialogue datasets draws from proprietary data collections (Chen et al., 2019; Rus et al., 2015a) or dialogues gathered from a student's interactions with an automated tutor (Niraula et al., 2014; Forbes-Riley and Litman, 2013).

Open-access human-to-human tutoring data has been released in limited contexts. In particular, we draw inspiration from the BURCHAK work (Yu et al., 2017b), which is a corpus of humans tutoring each other with the names of colored shapes in a made-up foreign language. In each session, an image is given to help scaffold the dialogue. The corpus contains 177 conversations with 2454 turns in total. This corpus has been utilized to ground deep learning model representations of visual attributes (colors and shapes) in dialogue via interacting with a simulated tutor (Ling and Fidler, 2017; Yu et al., 2017b). Follow-up work has used this data to model a student learning names and colors of shapes using a reinforcement learning framework (Yu et al., 2016, 2017a).

Our approach differs from that of Yu et al. (2017b) in several ways, including that we tie the colored shape tutoring interactions to the more complex domain of prepositional phrases. Additionally, by using a real foreign language (Italian) we are able to leverage words with similar morphological properties in addition to well-defined grammar rules.

2.2 Learning Tutoring Dialogue Systems

Modern work in dialogue falls into two categories: chit-chat models and goal-oriented models. Chit-chat models aim to creating interesting, diversely-worded utterances which further a conversation and keep users engaged. These models have the advantage of leveraging large indirectly-collected datasets, such as the Cornell Movie Script Dataset which includes 300,000 utterances (Danescu-Niculescu-Mizil and Lee, 2011).

By contrast, goal oriented dialogue systems have a specific task to complete, such as restaurant (Wen et al., 2017) and movie (Yu et al., 2017c) recommendations as well as restaurant reservations (Bordes et al., 2017).

Neural goal-oriented dialogue systems require large amounts of data to train. Bordes et al. (2017) include 6 restaurant reservation tasks, with 1,000 training dialogues in each dataset. Multi-domain datasets such as MultiWOZ include 10k dialogues spanning multiple tasks (Budzianowski et al., 2018). For longer-term interactions, a dataset involving medical diagnosis has approximately 200 conversations per disease (Wei et al., 2018).

By contrast, prior work in the field of intelligent tutoring dialogues has widely relied on large rule-based systems injected with human-crafted domain knowledge (Anderson et al., 1995; Aleven et al., 2001; Graesser et al., 2001; VanLehn et al., 2002; Rus et al., 2015b). Many of these systems involve students answering multiple choice or fill-in-the-blank questions and being presented with a hint or explanation when they answer incorrectly. However, curating this domain knowledge is time-expensive, rule-based systems can be rigid, and the typical system does not include multiple rephrasings of the same concept or response.

Some recent work has brought modern techniques into dialogue-based intelligent tutoring, but has relied on hand-crafted rules to both map a student's dialogue utterance onto a template and generate the dialogue utterance to reply to the student (Dzikovska et al., 2014). A limitation of this is the assumption that there is a single "correct" response to show a student in a situation.

2.3 Crowdwork Dialogue Role-Playing

Prior work has shown that crowdworkers are effective at role-playing. Self-dialogue, where a single crowdworker role-plays both sides of a conversation, has been used to collect chit-chat data (Krause

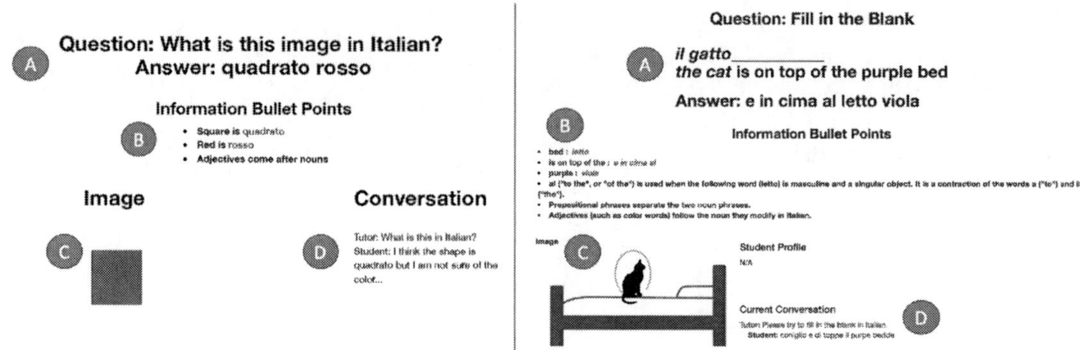

Figure 1: Example exercises as seen by a tutor (Left: Shape task, Right: Prepositional Phrase task). Shown are (A) the exercise with the correct answer that the student must produce, (B) knowledge in the form of information bullet points, (C) the image stimulus, and (D) the conversation so far. The student view is similar but does not include the information bullet points or the correct answer.

et al., 2017). Crowdworkers have been effective participants in peer learning studies (Coetzee et al., 2015); multiple crowdworkers can confirm lexical information within a dialogue (Ono et al., 2017).

3 Tutoring Dataset Creation

We create two dialogue datasets within CIMA: Shapes and Prepositional Phrases with colored objects.

3.1 Stimuli

We constructed stimuli for the two tasks at different levels of complexity. The Shape task follows the BURCHAK (Yu et al., 2017b) format of learning the words for adjective-noun modifiers when viewing shapes of different colors (see Figure 1, left). The Prepositional Phrase stimuli involves pairs of objects in relation to one another, with the task of learning the words for the prepositional phrase and its object, where the object is a noun with a color modifier and a determiner (see Figure 1, right).

Each stimulus consists of an image, a set of information points, and a question and answer pair. Importantly, the stimuli across the two tasks are linked by shared color terms. Intentionally including a set of common vocabulary words across datasets can potentially aid with transfer learning experiments (both human and machine). Initial tests were all done with English speakers learning the words in Italian. However, other language pairs can easily be associated with the image stimuli.

Vocabulary for the Shape task includes six colors (red, blue, green, purple, pink, and yellow) and five shapes (square, triangle, circle, star, and heart). There is only one grammar rule associated with the questions: that adjectives follow nouns in Italian.

The Prepositional Phrase task includes 6 prepositional phrases (on top of, under, inside of, next to, behind, and in front of) with 10 objects (cat, dog, bunny, plant, tree, ball, table, box, bag, and bed). Additionally, the same six colors as the Shape dataset modify the objects. Students are not asked to produce the subjects or the verbs, only the prepositional phrases. The full list of grammar rules (e.g. "l'" ("the") is prepended to the following word when it begins with a vowel) appears in Appendix A, and the full distribution of prepositional phrases, objects, and colors is in Appendix B.

3.2 Dialogue Collection with Crowdworkers

We hired crowdworkers on Amazon Mechanical Turk to role-play both the the student and the tutor. (Throughout this paper we will refer to them as students and tutors; this should be read as people taking on these roles.) In order to collect multiple tutoring responses at each point in a student conversation in a controllable way, student and tutor responses are gathered asynchronously. A diagram of this process can be seen in Figure 2. We collect several student conversations from crowdworkers with a fixed collection of hand-crafted and crowdworker-generated tutor responses. Afterwards, we show those student conversations to tutors to collect multiple appropriate crowdworker-generated responses. We then feed the newly-collected responses into the fixed collection of tutor responses for the next

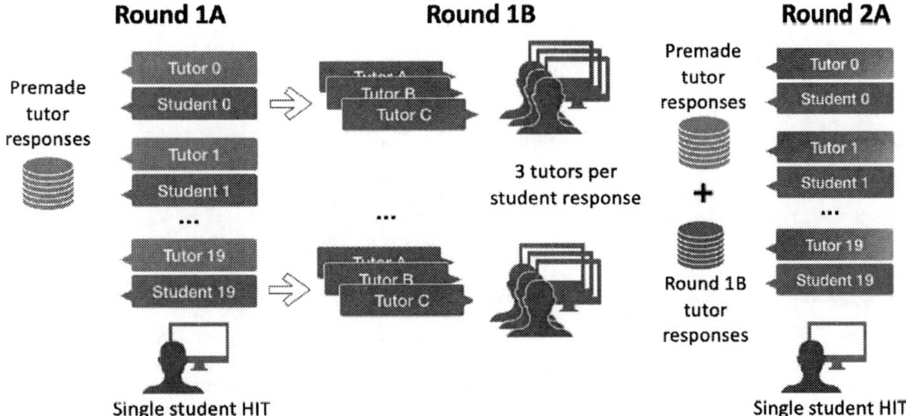

Figure 2: Progression of data collection process. In the first round of data gathering (1A), the student is exposed to 20 conversational responses from a hand-curated set of templates (shown in blue). After gathering data from 20-40 students, each student conversation is subsequently sent to three tutors to gather responses (1B). These responses (shown in pink) are placed into the pool of tutor responses for subsequent rounds (ex: 2A).

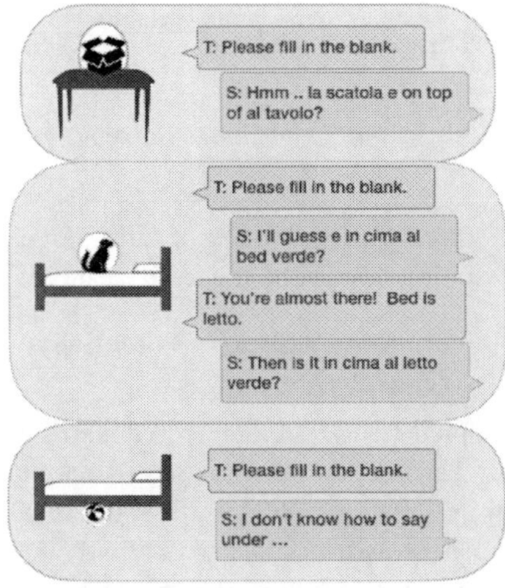

Figure 3: Example student exercise progression, showing shared features across stimuli. In this case, the student sees images for the words for bed and on top of twice within one session.

round of student data collection.

Tutors are asked to construct a *response* to the prior conversation with two outputs: the text of an *utterance* continuing the conversation and a discrete classification of the *action(s)* associated with the utterance. A summary of these actions for both the student and tutor can be seen in Table 1.

Similarly, students produce utterances which they label with actions as they work through *exercises* (defined as a question and corresponding answer, see (A) in Figure 1). Students complete as many exercises as possible in a *HIT*, defined as the crowdworking task consisting of a fixed number of turns. Each *turn* is defined as a pair consisting of the student's utterance and the most recent tutor response it is replying to. A *conversation* is defined as the set of utterances that comprise completion of an exercise.

Each participant can complete a maximum of 100 combined responses as a tutor or student for each task, to ensure diversity of responses. For the Shape task, students generate 5 responses per HIT. For the Prepositional Phrase task, however, we increase this to 20 responses per HIT due to the more complex domain.

To ensure response quality, crowdworkers were required to have 95% approval over at least 1,000 HITs. A subset of responses from each crowdworker were manually checked. We prohibited workers from copying from the prior conversation or writing a blank response. Crowdworkers were paid the equivalent of $8/hour and were required not to know Italian to participate as a student.

3.3 The Student Role

Figure 3 shows an example student interaction progression, in which students converse with the system to complete multiple exercises. Because the data collection process is asynchronous, when a student converses with the system, we serve a tutor response from a static collection to respond to them instantly. There are four rounds of data collection; in each phase, the pool of tutor responses

Student Actions

Action Label	Description	Example
Guess	The student attempts to answer the question	"Is it 'il gatto e vicino alla scatola rosa'?"
Clarification Question	The student asks a question to the tutor, ranging from directly asking for a translated word to asking why their prior guess was incorrect.	"How would I say 'pink' in Italian?"
Affirmation	When the student affirms something previously said by the tutor.	"Oh, I understand now!"
Other	We allow students to define a category if they do not believe their utterance fits into the predefined categories.	"Which I just said."

Tutor Actions

Action Label	Description	Example
Hint	The tutor provides knowledge to the student via a hint.	"Here's a hint - "tree" is "l'albero" because l' ("the") is prepended to the following word when it begins with a vowel."
Open-Ended Question	The tutor asks a question of the student, which can attempt to determine a student's understanding or continue the conversation.	"Are you sure you have all the words in the right order?"
Correction	The tutor corrects a mistake or addresses a misconception a student has.	"Very close. Everything is correct, expect you flipped 'viola' and 'coniglio'."
Confirmation	The tutor confirms a student's answer or understanding is correct.	"Great! Now say the whole sentence, starting with the dog..."
Other	We allow tutors to define a category if they do not believe their response fits into the predefined categories.	"Correct! Although try to think of the complete word as 'la scatola.' I find that the easiest way to remember what gender everything is - I just think of the 'the' as part of the noun."

Table 1: Descriptions of Student and Tutor Actions that workers self-assign to their utterances.

is augmented with the student and tutor responses from the prior round. For the Shape task, we gather responses from 20 students at each round; we increase this to 40 for Prepositional Phrase collection.

The conversation is always started by the tutor, with a pre-defined statement. For subsequent turns, we choose a tutor response conditioned on the student's most recent action, a keyword match of a student's most recent text response, and a log of what the student has been exposed to in the current conversation (details are in Appendix C). As tutor responses are gathered from crowdworkers in subsequent rounds, we add them to the collection.

3.3.1 Strategy for Student Exercise Selection

A student session is constrained to have 5 or 20 turns, depending on the task. At the start of the session, the system selects a list of stimuli for the student to work through that contains overlapping concepts (prepositions, colors, objects, shapes). From this list, one is chosen at random to show first to the student. After the student completes the exercise, if another exercise exists in the list which overlaps with at least one concept shown in the prior exercise, it is chosen next. If there is not a question with overlap, an exercise is selected at random. This process continues until the student

reaches the required number of turns. An example of a resulting image chain can be seen in Figure 3.

3.3.2 Mitigating Effects of Potentially Erroneous Responses

We adopted two strategies to reduce the cost of potential errors that may arise from automatically selecting tutoring responses to show to students: (i) Student crowdworkers can explicitly indicate if the tutor response they were served does not make sense. (ii) Because there is more downside to a nonsensical answer to some kinds of student responses than others (e.g., in response to a student's question vs. to an affirmation), each student action type is assigned a probability of being served a templated vs crowdworker-collected response (details in Appendix D).

3.4 The Tutor Role

Tutors for both the Shape and Prepositional Phrase tasks complete five responses per HIT. Because the data collection is asynchronous, the tutor is responding not to five consecutive utterances from the same student, but rather to five different students' conversations.

To ensure good coverage, we inject three different tutors at each utterance within a student's

Action	Shape	Prepositional Phrase
Student Actions		
Guess	448	1318
Question	313	840
Affirmation	289	406
Other	12	12
Tutor Actions		
Question	882	824
Hint	1002	1733
Correction	534	828
Confirmation	854	436
Other	37	59

Table 2: Distribution of student and tutor actions across the two datasets; multiple actions can be associated with each utterance.

conversation. This allows redundant generation of tutor responses to the same student input. We show the tutor the entire conversation up to that point.[2]

To role-play a tutor, crowdworkers were not expected to have any proficiency in Italian. To simulate the knowledge a tutor would have, we show relevant domain information so the tutor could adequately respond to the student (see Figure 1(B)). This includes vocabulary and grammar information which are necessary to answer the question. This domain-specific information can also be used as input knowledge to inform a learning system. In the Prepositional Phrase task, we also showed summaries of prior student conversations, but do not describe this in detail due to space constraints.

4 Dataset Statistics

An analysis of the conversations found that the data contains several interesting properties from an educational perspective. This section summarizes overall statistics of the data collected; the subsequent two sections summarize phenomena associated with the student and tutor data.

4.1 Shape Dataset

A total of 182 crowdworkers participated in the Shape data collection process: 111 as tutors and 90 as students. 2,970 tutor responses were collected, responding to 350 student exercises. A student required an average of 3.09 (standard deviation: 0.85) turns to complete an exercise. The average student turn was 5.38 (3.12) words while the average tutor response length was 7.15 (4.53) words. 4.0% of tutor responses shown to students were explicitly

flagged by the student as not making sense. Table 2 shows the distribution of action types.

4.2 Prepositional Phrase Dataset

A total of 255 crowdworkers participated in the creation of Prepositional Phrase data: 77 as students who completed a total of 391 exercises, and 209 as tutors who completed 2880 responses. The average number of turns a student requires before answering a question correctly is 3.65 (2.12). Of the tutor responses served to students, 4.2% were manually flagged as not making sense. The average student utterance is 6.82 words (2.90) while the average length of a tutor utterance is 9.99 words (6.99).

We analyze the proportion of tutoring responses which include the direct mention of an Italian color word, English translation of a color word, or "color," as this is the domain component which overlaps with the Shapes task. Of the set of tutor responses, 1,292 (40.0%) include a direct mention, indicating substantial overlap with the Shapes task.

5 Student Interactions

By examining a student's interactions over the course of a 20-turn HIT, we find that students take fewer turns on average to complete an exercise at the end than at the beginning of a HIT. We examine the number of turns students take before reaching the correct answer, as we hypothesize this will decrease as students have more exposure to domain concepts. We note this could be due to many factors, such as the students becoming more comfortable with the task or system or learning Italian phrases they were exposed to in prior questions.

We measure this with the prepositional phrase domain, because the students interacted with the system for 20 turns, compared to the 5-turn interactions with the Shape task. For a given HIT, we compare the number of student turns needed to produce their first correct answer with how many turns were needed for their final correct answer.[3]

For each student, we calculate the difference between the number of turns required between their first and final correct answers. The average difference is -0.723, indicating students required fewer turns to achieve their last correct answer than their first. Thus the data set might contain evidence of learning, although it could be as simple as student

---

[2]If a student conversation is longer than 10 turns, or if any point of the conversation has been marked as not making sense, the conversation is not shown to tutors.

[3]Note the final correct question might not be the final question the student attempted to answer, as the HIT is finished at 20-turns regardless of the state of a student's conversation.

workers learning how to more efficiently ask questions of the system.

6 Tutor Phenomena

We examine several characteristics about the tutor interactions: (i) properties about the language tutors use in their responses, (ii) how tutors respond to different student action types, and (iii) characterizing if and how tutors agree when presented with identical student input.

6.1 Tutoring Language

One feature of our dataset construction is the progression from the relatively simple Shape task to the linguistically richer Prepositional Phrase task. We analyze the resulting tutoring responses to see if more complex tutoring language emerges from the syntactically richer domain. We measure complexity in terms of number of non-vocabulary terms (where vocabulary refers to the words that are needed in the task, such as "rosa" for "pink").

We examine the set of tutoring responses from each domain. For each utterance, we remove Italian vocabulary, English translations, and stop words. We further restrict the utterance to words included in the English language[4] to remove typos and misspellings.

We find an average of 2.34 non-domain words per utterance (of average length 9.99 words) in the Prepositional Phrase dataset, compared to 0.40 per utterance (of average length 7.15 words) in the Shape dataset. While accounting for the average difference in length between the two datasets, the Prepositional Phrase dataset results in more non-domain English words than the Shape dataset.

This supports our hypothesis that the added domain complexity makes the Prepositional Phrase collection richer in terms of tutoring language than related work such as Yu et al. (2017b).

6.2 Tutor Response to Student Actions

We additionally examine the tutor action distributions conditioned on the student action taken immediately prior for the Prepositional Phrase dataset. We hypothesize if a student utterance is classified as a question, the tutor will be more likely to respond with the answer to the question (classified as a hint), conforming to conversational expectations. This is supported by the distributions, seen

Tutor Action(s)	Agreement	Individual
Hint	81.1%	39.0%
Question	5.7%	12.5%
Correction	5.2%	12.1%
Hint/Correction	2.8%	8.1%
Confirmation	2.8%	6.2%
Question/Hint	1.4%	7.5%
Correction/Confirmation	0.9%	2.1%
Total	**212**	**2880**

Table 3: Distribution of action sets agreed on by 3-tutor groups. Included are the proportion of individual tutor utterances labeled with each set of actions over the entire dataset for comparison.

in Figure 4. For other student action type responses (e.g., guess, affirmation), we observe that the tutor actions are more evenly distributed.

6.3 Tutor Action Agreement

As there are three tutors responding to each student utterance, we analyze the conditions in which the tutors agree on a unified set of actions to take in response to a student (in the Prepositional Phrase task). In particular, when all three tutors take the same set of action types we measure (i) which action(s) are they agreeing on and (ii) which action(s) the student took in the prior turn.

In 212 out of 1174 tutor tasks, all 3 tutors agreed on the same set of actions to take. We show the distribution of these 212 cases over unified tutor action sets in Table 3. There is a particularly high proportion of agreement on giving hints compared to other action sets. While hint was the most common action taken by tutors compared to the next-highest action by 26.5%, tutor agreement on hint was the most common by 75.4% compared to the next-highest category, a 2.8 times larger difference.

Additionally, we examine how a student's most recent action might influence a group of tutor's potential for action agreement. We measure the proportion of tutor agreement on a unified action set per student action set (the analysis is restricted to student action sets with at least 10 examples). Results can be seen in Table 4.

We note the highest agreement occurs after a student has made a Question or Question/Affirmation. This is consistent with (i) the high likelihood of a tutor to give a hint in response to a question (Figure 4) and (ii) the high proportion of tutor agreement on hints (Table 3). On the contrary, there is relatively low agreement when a student makes a Guess, consistent with the more evenly-distributed tutor action distribution (Figure 4).

---

[4]Stopwords and English vocabulary as defined by NLTK's stop words and English corpus, https://www.nltk.org/

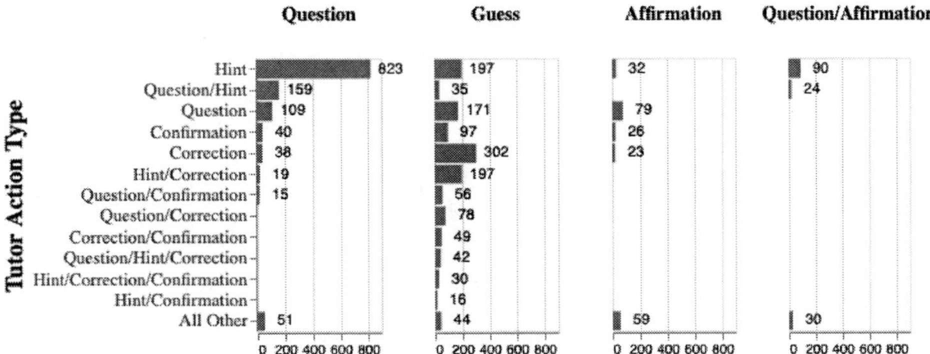

Figure 4: Distribution of tutor action classifications, grouped by the most recent set of student actions. The "All Other" category represents the combination of tutor action sets with fewer than 15 items.

Student Action(s)	Tutor Agreement
Question	36.8%
Question/Affirmation	37.5%
Affirmation	12.3%
Guess	6.4%
Guess/Affirmation	5.6%

Table 4: For each student action(s), percentage of tutor groups who agree on a unified action set in response.

Model	BLEU	BERT F1
Rule-Based Baseline	**0.34**	0.45
Generation Model	0.31	**0.53**

Table 5: Generation quality results comparing a rule-based baseline to the neural Generation model.

7 Tutoring Model

We claim CIMA is useful to train neural models for tutoring tasks. To explore this, we train a Generation model (GM) aimed at producing a tutoring response conditioned on two past conversation utterances.[5] An example input would be:

> Hint, Correction, e di fronte al, giallo, coniglio, is in front of the, yellow, bunny, <EOC> Tutor: Well, "bunny" is "coniglio" Student: il gatto e di fronte al coniglio.

In this representation, domain information and an intended set of actions to take is separated with a special token <EOC> from two sentences of conversation. Model training details are in Appendix E. We split the data along conversations into 2296 train, 217 development, and 107 test utterances.

7.1 Generation Quality Results

One benefit of CIMA is the ability to compare generated text to multiple distinct reference sentences in order to measure quality. We apply two standard generation quality measures: BLEU (Papineni et al., 2002) and BERT F1 Score (Zhang* et al.,

2020), using the maximum score of the model's response compared to each of the three human-generated tutor responses for a turn in the conversation. We compare the quality of the GM's responses to Round 1A of the same rule-based system used to collect CIMA (see Appendix C).

Results can be seen in Table 5. We note the rule-based baseline (which is guaranteed to be grammatical) performs slightly better than GM on BLEU score (which incentivizes exact word overlap) but that GM performs higher on BERT F1 Score (which incentivizes semantic word overlap). Given the comparable BLEU score and the gain on BERT F1 Score, we conclude that using CIMA to train a neural model can produce tutoring utterances of reasonable quality.

7.2 Action Evaluation Results

In addition to quality, we examine whether the Generation model is able to generate utterances consistent with the set of actions it is conditioned on. We train a separate Action Classifier (AC) to predict a set of actions from a tutoring utterance. For example, for the input *Tutor: Well, "bunny" is "coniglio." Do you know the word for yellow?* the classifier would output `Hint Question`. Training details appear in Appendix E.

To examine the classifier's reliability, we mea-

---

[5] As we did not see a gain in quality when including the full conversation, we simplify the task to responding to the most recent tutor and student utterance.

Overall	Question	Hint	Corr.	Conf.
0.72	0.85	0.93	0.67	0.61

Table 6: Action Classification model F1 scores for the test set, where the Overall metric is weighted by class.

sure the F1 for the test set, both overall and for each of the four top action categories (excluding Other due to the low number of utterances). Results can be seen in Table 6. While the Overall, Hint, and Question F1 are relatively high, we note the lower Correction and Confirmation scores.

Using the classifier, we measure the GM's ability to generate utterances consistent with the set of actions it is conditioned on. For each item in the test set, we sample one of the three tutor's responses, identify the action(s) that tutor chose to make, and use GM to generate an utterance conditioned on that action type. To determine if the generated utterance is of the correct action type, we apply the classifier model. The average accuracy over the test set is 89.8%, indicating GM's ability to generate utterances consistent with an action strategy.

8 Discussion

Our analysis finds that tutors are more unified in an action strategy when a student asks a question than other actions. This is consistent with the findings that (i) when tutors agree, they are more likely to agree on a hint and (ii) the most likely action in response to a student question is a hint. Overall tutor agreement was low among the dataset (18.1%), indicating the potential capture of divergent tutoring strategies. Future work can leverage this disagreement to explore the multiple potential actions to take when responding to a student.

Our preliminary experiments show CIMA can be used to train a model that can generate text conditioned on a desired actions. Future work should explore more complex models utilizing CIMA, as well as exploring the other unique qualities of the collection, such as the shared image representation, multiple tutoring utterances for each conversation, and link between the two domains.

Tutoring responses marked as not making sense should be explored, to both improve the process of serving student responses as well as correcting a model when a generated response veers the conversation off track. A benefit to having this explicitly logged is that the collection contains labeled negative examples of tutoring responses, which can be leveraged in training models.

9 Limitations

While past work utilized crowdworkers to collect tutoring utterances (Yu et al., 2017b) and for peer learning studies (Coetzee et al., 2015), future work should examine the similarities and differences between the language and actions taken by crowdworkers and actual tutors and students engaged in the learning process.

Because we were working with untrained crowdworkers, we were constrained in the complexity of language learning concepts we could include in CIMA. It is possible that the resulting dataset only transfers to novice language learners. Future work should examine how well this generalizes to a real language learning setting and how general tutoring language and strategies that emerge from our domain transfer to more complex ones.

The dataset currently does not distinguish the type of hint or correction tutors make. Examples include providing direct corrections versus indirect feedback which states the error and allows the student to self-correct (Chandler, 2003). Future work on CIMA can examine the prevalence of these different types of feedback and potential benefits or shortcomings.

10 Conclusion

We present CIMA: a data collection method and resulting collection of tutoring dialogues which captures student interactions and multiple accompanying tutoring responses. Two datasets of differing complexity have direct applicability to building an automatic tutor to assist foreign language learning, as we examine with a preliminary model. CIMA has the potential to train personalized dialogue agents which incorporate longer-term information, have a well-defined goal to have a student learn and recall concepts, and can explore different correct utterances and actions at given times.

Acknowledgements

This work was supported by an AWS Machine Learning Research Award, an NVIDIA Corporation GPU grant, a UC Berkeley Chancellor's Fellowship, and a National Science Foundation (NSF) Graduate Research Fellowship (DGE 1752814).We thank Kevin Lu, Kiran Girish, and Avni Prasad for their engineering efforts and the three anonymous reviewers for their helpful comments.

References

Vincent Aleven, Octav Popescu, and Kenneth R Koedinger. 2001. A tutorial dialogue system with knowledge-based understanding and classification of student explanations. In *Working Notes of 2nd IJCAI Workshop on Knowledge and Reasoning in Practical Dialogue Systems*.

John R Anderson, Albert T Corbett, Kenneth R Koedinger, and Ray Pelletier. 1995. Cognitive tutors: Lessons learned. *The journal of the learning sciences*, 4(2):167–207.

Antoine Bordes, Y-Lan Boureau, and Jason Weston. 2017. Learning end-to-end goal-oriented dialog. In *5th International Conference on Learning Representations, ICLR 2017, Toulon, France, April 24-26, 2017, Conference Track Proceedings*. OpenReview.net.

Paweł Budzianowski, Tsung-Hsien Wen, Bo-Hsiang Tseng, Iñigo Casanueva, Stefan Ultes, Osman Ramadan, and Milica Gasic. 2018. Multiwoz - a large-scale multi-domain wizard-of-oz dataset for task-oriented dialogue modelling. In *Proceedings of the 2018 Conference on Empirical Methods in Natural Language Processing*, pages 5016–5026. Association for Computational Linguistics.

Jean Chandler. 2003. The efficacy of various kinds of error feedback for improvement in the accuracy and fluency of l2 student writing. *Journal of Second Language Writing*, 12:267–296.

Guanliang Chen, David Lang, Rafael Ferreira, and Dragan Gasevic. 2019. Predictors of student satisfaction: A large-scale study of human-human online tutorial dialogues. In *Proceedings of the 12th International Conference on Educational Data Mining, EDM 2019, Montréal, Canada, July 2-5, 2019*. International Educational Data Mining Society (IEDMS).

D. Coetzee, Seongtaek Lim, Armando Fox, Bjorn Hartmann, and Marti A. Hearst. 2015. Structuring interactions for large-scale synchronous peer learning. In *Proceedings of the 18th ACM Conference on Computer Supported Cooperative Work and Social Computing*, CSCW '15, page 1139–1152, New York, NY, USA. Association for Computing Machinery.

Cristian Danescu-Niculescu-Mizil and Lillian Lee. 2011. Chameleons in imagined conversations: A new approach to understanding coordination of linguistic style in dialogs. In *Proceedings of the 2nd Workshop on Cognitive Modeling and Computational Linguistics*, pages 76–87, Portland, Oregon, USA. Association for Computational Linguistics.

Myroslava O. Dzikovska, Natalie B. Steinhauser, Elaine Farrow, Johanna D. Moore, and Gwendolyn E. Campbell. 2014. Beetle ii: Deep natural language understanding and automatic feedback generation for intelligent tutoring in basic electricity and electronics. *International Journal of Artificial Intelligence in Education*, 24:284–332.

Kate Forbes-Riley and Diane Litman. 2013. When does disengagement correlate with performance in spoken dialog computer tutoring? *Int. J. Artif. Intell. Ed.*, 22(1–2):39–58.

Arthur C. Graesser. 2015. Conversations with autotutor help students learn. *International Journal of Artificial Intelligence in Education*, 26:124–132.

Arthur C Graesser, Sidney D'Mello, and Natalie Person. 2009. Meta-knowledge in tutoring. *The educational psychology series. Handbook of metacognition in education*, pages 361–382.

Arthur C. Graesser, Kurt VanLehn, Carolyn Penstein Rosé, Pamela W. Jordan, and Derek Harter. 2001. Intelligent tutoring systems with conversational dialogue. *AI Magazine*, 22:39–52.

Jiatao Gu, Zhengdong Lu, Hang Li, and Victor O.K. Li. 2016. Incorporating copying mechanism in sequence-to-sequence learning. In *Proceedings of the 54th Annual Meeting of the Association for Computational Linguistics (Volume 1: Long Papers)*, pages 1631–1640, Berlin, Germany. Association for Computational Linguistics.

Diederik P. Kingma and Jimmy Ba. 2015. Adam: A method for stochastic optimization. In *3rd International Conference on Learning Representations, ICLR 2015, San Diego, CA, USA, May 7-9, 2015, Conference Track Proceedings*.

Guillaume Klein, Yoon Kim, Yuntian Deng, Jean Senellart, and Alexander M. Rush. 2017. Opennmt: Open-source toolkit for neural machine translation. In *Proc. ACL*.

Ben Krause, Marco Damonte, Mihai Dobre, Daniel Duma, Joachim Fainberg, Federico Fancellu, Emmanuel Kahembwe, Jianpeng Cheng, and Bonnie Webber. 2017. Edina: Building an open domain socialbot with self-dialogues. *Alexa Prize Proceedings*.

Huan Ling and Sanja Fidler. 2017. Teaching machines to describe images via natural language feedback. In *Proceedings of the 31st International Conference on Neural Information Processing Systems*, NIPS'17, page 5075–5085, Red Hook, NY, USA. Curran Associates Inc.

Nobal Niraula, Vasile Rus, Rajendra Banjade, Dan Stefanescu, William Baggett, and Brent Morgan. 2014. The DARE corpus: A resource for anaphora resolution in dialogue based intelligent tutoring systems. In *Proceedings of the Ninth International Conference on Language Resources and Evaluation (LREC'14)*, pages 3199–3203, Reykjavik, Iceland. European Language Resources Association (ELRA).

Benjamin D Nye, Arthur C Graesser, and Xiangen Hu. 2014. Autotutor and family: A review of 17 years of natural language tutoring. *International Journal of Artificial Intelligence in Education*, 24(4):427–469.

Kohei Ono, Ryu Takeda, Eric Nichols, Mikio Nakano, and Kazunori Komatani. 2017. Lexical acquisition through implicit confirmations over multiple dialogues. In *Proceedings of the 18th Annual SIGdial Meeting on Discourse and Dialogue*, pages 50–59, Saarbrücken, Germany. Association for Computational Linguistics.

Kishore Papineni, Salim Roukos, Todd Ward, and Wei-Jing Zhu. 2002. Bleu: a method for automatic evaluation of machine translation. In *Proceedings of the 40th Annual Meeting of the Association for Computational Linguistics*, pages 311–318, Philadelphia, Pennsylvania, USA. Association for Computational Linguistics.

Jeffrey Pennington, Richard Socher, and Christopher Manning. 2014. Glove: Global vectors for word representation. In *Proceedings of the 2014 Conference on Empirical Methods in Natural Language Processing (EMNLP)*, pages 1532–1543, Doha, Qatar. Association for Computational Linguistics.

Sherry Ruan, Liwei Jiang, Justin Xu, Bryce Joe-Kun Tham, Zhengneng Qiu, Yeshuang Zhu, Elizabeth L. Murnane, Emma Brunskill, and James A. Landay. 2019. Quizbot: A dialogue-based adaptive learning system for factual knowledge. In *Proceedings of the 2019 CHI Conference on Human Factors in Computing Systems*, CHI '19, New York, NY, USA. Association for Computing Machinery.

Vasile Rus, Nabin Maharjan, and Rajendra Banjade. 2015a. Unsupervised discovery of tutorial dialogue modes in human-to-human tutorial data. In *Proceedings of the Third Annual GIFT Users Symposium*, pages 63–80.

Vasile Rus, Nobal B. Niraula, and Rajendra Banjade. 2015b. Deeptutor: An effective, online intelligent tutoring system that promotes deep learning. In *Proceedings of the Twenty-Ninth AAAI Conference on Artificial Intelligence*, AAAI'15, page 4294–4295. AAAI Press.

Kurt VanLehn, Arthur C Graesser, G Tanner Jackson, Pamela Jordan, Andrew Olney, and Carolyn P Rosé. 2007. When are tutorial dialogues more effective than reading? *Cognitive science*, 31(1):3–62.

Kurt VanLehn, Pamela W. Jordan, Carolyn Penstein Rosé, Dumisizwe Bhembe, Michael Böttner, Andy Gaydos, Maxim Makatchev, Umarani Pappuswamy, Michael A. Ringenberg, Antonio Roque, Stephanie Siler, and Ramesh Srivastava. 2002. The architecture of why2-atlas: A coach for qualitative physics essay writing. In *Proceedings of the 6th International Conference on Intelligent Tutoring Systems*, ITS '02, page 158–167, Berlin, Heidelberg. Springer-Verlag.

Zhongyu Wei, Qianlong Liu, Baolin Peng, Huaixiao Tou, Ting Chen, Xuanjing Huang, Kam-Fai Wong, and Xiangying Dai. 2018. Task-oriented dialogue system for automatic diagnosis. In *Proceedings of the 56th Annual Meeting of the Association for Computational Linguistics (Volume 2: Short Papers)*, pages 201–207. Association for Computational Linguistics.

Tsung-Hsien Wen, David Vandyke, Nikola Mrkšić, Milica Gašić, Lina M. Rojas-Barahona, Pei-Hao Su, Stefan Ultes, and Steve Young. 2017. A network-based end-to-end trainable task-oriented dialogue system. In *Proceedings of the 15th Conference of the European Chapter of the Association for Computational Linguistics: Volume 1, Long Papers*, pages 438–449, Valencia, Spain. Association for Computational Linguistics.

Yanchao Yu, Arash Eshghi, and Oliver Lemon. 2016. Training an adaptive dialogue policy for interactive learning of visually grounded word meanings. In *Proceedings of the 17th Annual Meeting of the Special Interest Group on Discourse and Dialogue*, pages 339–349, Los Angeles. Association for Computational Linguistics.

Yanchao Yu, Arash Eshghi, and Oliver Lemon. 2017a. Learning how to learn: An adaptive dialogue agent for incrementally learning visually grounded word meanings. In *Proceedings of the First Workshop on Language Grounding for Robotics*, pages 10–19, Vancouver, Canada. Association for Computational Linguistics.

Yanchao Yu, Arash Eshghi, Gregory Mills, and Oliver Lemon. 2017b. The BURCHAK corpus: a challenge data set for interactive learning of visually grounded word meanings. In *Proceedings of the Sixth Workshop on Vision and Language*, pages 1–10, Valencia, Spain. Association for Computational Linguistics.

Zhou Yu, Alan W. Black, and Alexander I. Rudnicky. 2017c. Learning conversational systems that interleave task and non-task content. In *Proceedings of the 26th International Joint Conference on Artificial Intelligence*, IJCAI'17, page 4214–4220. AAAI Press.

Tianyi Zhang*, Varsha Kishore*, Felix Wu*, Kilian Q. Weinberger, and Yoav Artzi. 2020. Bertscore: Evaluating text generation with bert. In *International Conference on Learning Representations*.

A Prepositional Phrase Collection Grammar Rules

Listed below is the complete collection of Prepositional Phrase grammar rules:

- "il" ("the") is used for when the following word is masculine.
- "alla" ("to the") is used when the following word is feminine and a singular object. It is a contraction of a ("to") and la ("the").
- "al" ("to the") is used when the following word is masculine and a singular object. It is a contraction of the words a ("to") and il ("the").
- "l'" ("the") is prepended to the following word when it begins with a vowel.
- "all'" ("to the" is prepended to the following word when it begins with a vowel. This is a contraction of al ("to") and l' ("the").
- "rossa" is the feminine form of red because the noun it modifies is feminine
- Adjectives (such as color words) follow the noun they modify in Italian.
- Prepositional phrases separate the two noun phrases.

B Phrase Breakdown

Table 7 shows the coverage of Prepositional Phrase exercises over the potential objects, prepositional phrase, and colors.

C Algorithm

Algorithmic specifications for data collection can be viewed in Figure 5. In order to serve a tutor-crafted response to a student, we match the current student utterance to a prior-collected student utterance which has been responded to by a tutor. The most similar student utterance is determined by maximizing word overlap of the student's most recent utterance to the prior-collected student utterances, excluding domain vocabulary words. The English and Italian words are replaced with the information relevant to the current exercise in the associated tutor utterance before showing this to the student.

D Hand-Crafted Response Probabilities

Throughout different rounds of data collection, we balance the probability of a student receiving a pre-made tutor response with a crowdworker-generated response from a prior round of data collection. As we collect more tutoring responses in subsequent rounds, the probabilities shift from pre-made, safe choices to the crowd-worker generated responses, because with more data, the choices should be more likely to more closely match a student utterance. The probabilities were manually set and can be seen in Table 8.

Category	Number of Questions
First Object (students don't translate these)	
'the dog'	134
'the cat'	161
'the plant'	49
'the bunny'	129
'the ball'	47
'the bag'	28
'the box'	17
Prepositional phrases	
'is in front of the'	126
'is next to the'	106
'is inside of the'	74
'is under the'	73
'is behind the'	127
'is on top of the'	59
Colors	
'green'	88
'pink'	77
'blue'	100
'yellow'	91
'red'	101
'purple'	108
Second Object	
'tree'	128
'box'	160
'plant'	14
'cat'	13
'bunny'	49
'dog'	23
'bed'	69
'table'	89
'bag'	20

Table 7: Phrase Breakdown of Student conversations

	G	Q	A	O
Shape	1.0	1.0	0.0	0.5
PP R1	1.0	1.0	1.0	1.0
PP R2	0.75	0.75	0.5	0.5
PP R3	0.75	0.75	0.5	0.5
PP R4	0.65	0.65	0.4	0.4

Table 8: Probabilities for serving hand crafted responses instead of tutor-provided responses for the shape and the prepositional phrase task, rounds 1 - 4. for Guess, Question, Action, and Other student question types.

E   Model Training Details

For the Generation Model, we use OpenNMT (Klein et al., 2017) to train a 4-layer LSTM of size 1000 with global attention. We use the Adam optimizer (Kingma and Ba, 2015) with a learning rate of 0.001. We allow the model to have a copy mechanism to copy relevant words (such as translation information) from the input (Gu et al., 2016). We use 300-dimensional pre-trained GloVe embeddings (Pennington et al., 2014), which are allowed to be updated throughout training. At decode time, we replace unknown words with the input word with the highest attention.

We train the Action Classification model using OpenNMT (Klein et al., 2017). The model is a 4-layer bidirectional LSTM with 1024 hidden state size, general attention, a learning rate of 0.001, and batch size of 16. It utilizes pre-trained 300-dimensional GloVe embeddings (Pennington et al., 2014) which can be updated. This model is trained on the same training set as the generation model, taking in the human-created utterances and predicting the corresponding classifications.

```
if Guess and Correct then
    Move on to next question
else if Guess and Incorrect then
    Flip a coin with probability = G
    if Heads then
        Compile a list of pre-defined responses containing
        vocabulary missing from the student response
        Randomly select from this list
    else
        Return the most similar past-tutor response from the
        set of responses of type G.
    end if
end if


if Question then
    Flip a coin with probability = Q
    if Heads then
        Attempt to find words from a set list of pre-defined
        hints associated with each vocabulary word in the
        question.
        if Match is Found then
            Serve that hint
        else
            Choose a random hint that the student has not
            seen and serve that.
        end if
    else
        Return the most similar past-tutor response from the
        set of responses of type Q.
    end if
end if


if Affirmation or Other then
    Flip a coin with probability = A / O
    if Heads then
        Flip a coin with probability = 0.5
        if Heads then
            Ask the student for an attempt at a guess.
        else
            Give a pre-defined hint for a vocabulary or gram-
            mar concept that the student has not yet seen.
        end if
    else
        Return the most similar past-tutor response from the
        set of responses of type A/O.
    end if
end if
```

Figure 5: Algorithm for serving tutoring responses.

Becoming Linguistically Mature: Modeling English and German Children's Writing Development Across School Grades

Elma Kerz[1], Yu Qiao[1], Daniel Wiechmann [2], and Marcus Ströbel[1]
[1]RWTH Aachen University, Germany
[2]University of Amsterdam, Netherlands
{elma.kerz|marcus.stroebel}@ifaar.rwth.aachen.de
yu.qiao@rwth-aachen.de d.wiechmann@uva.nl

Abstract

In this paper we employ a novel approach to advancing our understanding of the development of writing in English and German children across school grades using classification tasks. The data used come from two recently compiled corpora: The English data come from the the GiC corpus (983 school children in second-, sixth-, ninth- and eleventh-grade) and the German data are from the FD-LEX corpus (930 school children in fifth- and ninth-grade). The key to this paper is the combined use of what we refer to as 'complexity contours', i.e. series of measurements that capture the progression of linguistic complexity within a text, and Recurrent Neural Network (RNN) classifiers that adequately capture the sequential information in those contours. Our experiments demonstrate that RNN classifiers trained on complexity contours achieve higher classification accuracy than one trained on text-average complexity scores. In a second step, we determine the relative importance of the features from four distinct categories through a Sensitivity-Based Pruning approach.

1 Introduction

There is growing recognition among researchers, educators and policymakers that literacy and the language of schooling (other terms include academic language, language of education, scientific language) are key to children's overall educational success and academic achievement (see, e.g., Commission, 2019; Lorenzo and Meyer, 2017). Children are expected to acquire the ability to comprehend and produce complex clause and sentence structures, sophisticated vocabulary and informationally dense texts characteristic of language of schooling as they progress through their school career (see, e.g., Berman, 2007; Snow, 2010, for overviews). However, this ability is acquired gradually and for many school children only with diffi-

culty (Snow and Uccelli, 2009; Snow, 2010). Given the key role of academic language, it is somewhat surprising that relatively little empirical research has been conducted on the development of academic language skills across school grades in children's first language, in particular in the area of writing (for exceptions, see, Crossley et al., 2011; Weiss and Meurers, 2019). This paper contributes to and expands the scant literature by investigating the development of linguistic complexity in children's writing from second-, sixth-, ninth- and eleventh-grade in English schools and fifth- and ninth-grade in German schools. We employ a novel approach to the automatic assessment of text complexity. In this approach, a series of scores for a given complexity measure is obtained through a sliding window technique, tracking the progression of complexity within a text, captured in what we refer to as 'complexity contours' (Ströbel, 2014; Ströbel et al., 2020). These contours are then fed into recurrent neural network (RNN) classifiers – adequate to take into account the sequential information in the contours – to perform grade-level classification tasks. We demonstrate the utility of the approach by comparing the performance of 'contour-based' RNN models against those of 'means-based' RNN models trained on text-average performance scores. In a second step, we determine which features drive classification accuracy through a Sensitivity-Based Pruning (SBP) approach. The remainder of the paper is organized as follows: Section 2 provides a concise overview of related work on automated assessment of text complexity in combination with machine learning techniques in the language learning context. Section 3 presents the two data sets representing English and German children's school writing. Section 4 introduces our approach to assessment of text complexity based on a sliding-window technique, whereas Section 5 introduces the features

Proceedings of the 15th Workshop on Innovative Use of NLP for Building Educational Applications, pages 65–74
July 10, 2020. ©2020 Association for Computational Linguistics

investigated in the paper. Sections 6 describes the model architecture and the training procedure (Section 6.1) and the SBP method used to determine the relative feature importance (Section 6.2). Sections 7 presents the results and concluding remarks follow in Section 8.

2 Related work

In recent years, there has been an increased interest in automated assessment of text complexity in authentic contextualized language samples in combination with machine learning techniques (Meurers, 2020, for a recent overview). As a valuable complement to experimental research, this research has the potential to advance our current understanding of (both first and second) language learning and development (Rebuschat et al., 2017; Ellis, 2019). Important steps have been made in this direction through both language input and language output perspectives: Regarding the former, a number of studies have examined whether and to what extent learning materials show an adequate level of linguistic complexity considered to be of crucial importance for successful learning outcomes (see, e.g., François and Fairon, 2012; Pilán et al., 2016; Xia et al., 2019; Chen and Meurers, 2018; Berendes et al., 2018). For example, Berendes et al. (2018) employ a text classification approach to examine to whether and to what extent reading complexity of school textbooks differ systematically across grade levels in line with the so-called 'systematic complexification assumption'. They build text classification models using a Sequential Minimal Optimization (SMO) algorithm trained on a wide range of lexical, syntactic, morphological, and cohesion-related features to predict the grade level (fifth to tenth grade) and school track (high vs. low). The best performing model reached a grade-level classification accuracy of 53.7%, corresponding to a 20.7% over the random baseline, providing only partial support for thee systematic complexification assumption. In addition, they report significant differences across grade levels and tracks for some of the ten linguistic features. Regarding the latter, a rapidly growing body of research has focused on language output aiming to determine to what extent L2 writing and speaking differs from that of their L1 peers and expert writers/speakers, to differentiate levels of language proficiency, to predict human ratings of the quality of learner productions, and to examine to the relationship between L1 and

L2 writing complexity and speaking fluency (see, e.g., Crossley et al., 2014; Lu, 2017; Duran-Karaoz and Tavakoli, 2020; Ströbel et al., 2020). Much research in this area has focused on English and on populations of upper intermediate to advanced L2 learners (but see Crossley et al., 2011; Durrant and Brenchley, 2019; Weiss and Meurers, 2019, for L1 English and German, respectively). Two recent studies are particularly relevant for the purposes of the present study. Durrant and Brenchley (2019) zoom-in on the development of vocabulary sophistication in English children's writing across second-, sixth-, ninth- and eleventh grade. Their corpus (also used in the present paper) consists of 2,898 texts of children's writing produced by 983 children. Through a mixed-effects regression modeling approach, they assess the effects of grade level and genre on lexical sophistication - measured through children's use of low-frequency words and register appropriate words. Their analysis reveals no significant differences with regard to the average frequency of the lexical words used by younger and older children. However, with increasing age children's writing display a shift from a more fiction-like vocabulary to a more academic-like vocabulary, reflecting a development towards more register appropriate word use. Weiss and Meurers (2019) focus on German children's writing development through a text classification approach based on a broad range of complexity and accuracy measures. Their dataset includes 1,633 texts of writing from 727 German elementary school children from first to fourth grade and 906 secondary school students from fifth to eighth grade, who attended either a basic or an intermediate school track. Using SMO classifiers with a linear kernel, their best performing classification model employed a combination of linguistic complexity features, error rate and meta information on topic and school track to reach an accuracy of 72.68% in classifying four grade level categories. Their analysis further revealed a shift in the primary locus of development from accuracy to complexity within elementary school and an increasing linguistic complexity in secondary school, in particular in the lexical complexity domain.

3 Data

The data used in this study come from two recently compiled corpora representing school writing: The English data come from the the Growth in Grammar corpus (GIG, `https://gigcorpus.com/`) that comprises 2,898 texts produced by 983 children in 24 different schools from 14 cities in Great Britain. The texts in the GiG corpus were sampled at four points that mark 'key stages' of the English school system: the ends of Key Stage (KS) 1 (Year 2, when children are 6-7 years old) and KS2 (Year 9, when children are 10-11 years old), encompassing the primary phase of the school system, and the ends of KS3 (Year 9, when children are 13-14 years old) and KS4 (Year 11, when children are 15-16 years old), encompassing the secondary stage. The texts were classified into two text types (literary and non-literary texts) on the basis of their overall purpose. Approximately 13% of the texts were written by children categorized as speaking English as an additional language. The German data come from the Forschungsdatenbank Lernertexte (FD-LEX; https://fd-lex.Uni-koeln.de/), a research database of learner texts compiled in joint project of the Mercator Institute for Language Promotion and German as a Second Language. It contains a total of 5,628 texts from two text types (report and argumentation) collected from a total of 930 school children in grades five (when children are 10-11 years old) and nine (when children are 14-15 years old) at comprehensive and grammar schools in two German cities. These texts were elicited using a narrative and an argumentative writing prompt. The database contains information on a number of learner background variables, including the learners language background distinguishing monolingual German students from students who have German as a their first language (L1) and know at least one additional language and students for whom German is not their first language. Table 1 shows the distribution of texts along with descriptive statistics of text sizes across grade levels and registers for each language.

4 Automatic Assessment of Text Complexity through a Sliding Window Technique

Text complexity of the writing samples in the two corpora is automatically assessed using the Complexity Contour Generator (CoCoGen), a computational tool that implements a sliding-window technique to generate a series of measurements for a given complexity measure (CM) (Ströbel, 2014; Ströbel et al., 2018; Ströbel et al., 2020). This approach enables a 'local assessment' of complexity within a text, in contrast to the standard approach

English data: GIG				
Grade	Register	N Texts	M	SD
2	lit	263	83.56	58.36
2	non-lit	376	71.18	43.09
4	lit	23	169.7	111.6
4	non-lit	26	151.58	96.65
6	lit	293	371.58	200.61
6	non-lit	575	208.68	104.53
9	lit	220	422.22	186.69
9	non-lit	584	277.25	187.95
11	lit	63	422.22	186.69
11	non-lit	475	415.3	264.46
German data: FD-LEX				
5	arg	1462	49.26	27.94
5	nar	1460	67.65	32.68
9	arg	1282	70.67	32.24
9	nar	1305	80.69	32.54

Table 1: Composition of two corpora of children's school writing. 'lit' = literary, 'non-lit' = non-literary, 'arg' = argumentative, 'nar' = narrative; M = mean number of words, SD = standard deviation

that represents text complexity as a single score, providing a 'global assessment' of the complexity of a text. A sliding window can be conceived of as a window with a certain size (ws) defined by the number of sentences it contains. The window is moved across a text sentence-by-sentence, computing one complexity score per window for a given CM. The series of measurements generated by CoCoGen track the progression of linguistic complexity within a text captured in what we refer to as 'complexity contours'. These contours faithfully represent that complexity is typically not uniformly distributed within a text but rather by characterized peaks and troughs and that complexity contours of individual measures may exhibit different trajectories (see Figure 1. For a text comprising n sentences, there are $w = n - ws + 1$ windows.[1] To compute the complexity score of a given window, a measurement function is called for each sentence in the window and returns a fraction wn_S/wd_S, where wn_S is the numerator of the complexity score for a sentence and wd_S is the denominator of the complexity score for that sentence. If the window size is specified to be greater than one sentences, the denominators and numerators of the fractions from the first to the last sentence

---

[1]Given the constraint that there has to be at least one window, a text has to comprise at least as many sentences at the ws is wide $n \geq w$.

in the window are added up to form the denominator and numerator of the resulting complexity score of a given window (see Figure 3 in the Appendix). The size of the window is user-defined parameter whose value depends on the goals of the analysis: When windows is set to the minimum, i.e. complexity is measured at each sentence of a text, the resulting complexity contour will typically exhibit many sharp turns. By increasing the window size, i.e. the number of sentences in a window, the complexity contour can be smoothened akin to a moving average technique (see Figure 4 in the Appendix). To compute the complexity scores, CoCoGen uses the Stanford CoreNLP suite (Manning et al., 2014) for performing tokenization, sentence splitting, part-of-speech tagging, lemmatization and syntactic parsing using the probabilistic context free grammar parsers for English (Klein and Manning, 2003) and German (Rafferty and Manning, 2008).

5 Features

In its current version CoCoGen features 57 complexity measures (CMs) for English of which 13 are also available for German.[2] These features cover (1) surface measures, (2) measures of syntactic complexity, (3) measures of lexical richness, (4) information theoretic measures, and (5) register-based n-gram frequency measures. The operationalizations of the syntactic and lexical CMs follow those given in Lu (2011) and Lu (2012). For details on the operationalization of the information theoretic CMs, see Ströbel (2014). The operationalization of the register-based n-gram frequency measures is provided below. Surface measures concern the length of production units and include Mean Length of Words in characters (MLWc), Mean Length of Words in syllable (MLWs), Mean length of clause (MLC), Mean length of sentence (MLS), and Mean length of T-Unit (MLT). Syntactic complexity is typically quantified in terms of measures of the type and incidence of embeddings (Sentence complexity ratio (C/S), T-Unit complexity ratio (C/T), Complex T-Unit ratio (CT/T), Dependent clause ratio (DC/C), Dependent clauses per T-Unit (DC/T), T-Units per Sentence (T/S), and Verb Phrases per

T-Unit (VP/T)), the types and number of coordinations between clauses and phrasal units (Coordinate phrases per clause (CP/C), Coordinate phrases per T-Unit (CP/T)), and the type of particular structures (Complex nominals per T-Unit(CN/T), Complex nominals per Clause (CN/C), Noun Phrase Premodification in words (NPpreW), Noun Phrase Postmodification in words (NPpostW)) (see Lu, 2017, for a recent overview). The lexical richness measures fall into three distinct sub-types: (1) Lexical density, i.e. the ratio of the number of lexical (as opposed to grammatical) words to the total number of words in a text (Lexical Density (LD)), (2) Lexical variation, i.e. the range of a learner's vocabulary as displayed in his or her language use (Number of Different Words (NDW), Type-Token Ratio (TTR), Log Type-Token Ratio (logTTR), Root Type-Token Ratio (rTTR), Corrected Type-Token Ratio (cTTR)) and (3) Lexical sophistication, i.e. the proportion of relatively unusual or advanced words in the learner's text (words from the New Academic Word List (NAWL), words from the New Academic Formula List (NAFL), words that are not part of the New General Service List (NGSL), Lexical Sophistication BNC (LS.BNC), Lexical Sophistication ANC (LS.ANC)). The three information-theoretic measures are Kolmogorov Deflate (KolDef), Kolmogorov Deflate Syntactic (KolDefSyn), Kolmogorov Deflate Morphological (KolDefMor) (see Ehret and Szmrecsanyi, 2019, for the benefits of using these measures in the assessment of text complexity in the context of language learning). These measures, use the Deflate algorithm (Deutsch and Gailly, 1996) to compress a given text and obtain performance scores by relating the size of the compressed file to the size of the original file (Ströbel, 2014). The fifth group of register-based n-gram frequency measures was based on list of the top 100,000 most frequent ngrams (for $n \in [1, 5]$) from the five register sub-components of the COCA corpus[3] (spoken, magazine, fiction, news, academic language). The general definition of these CMs is given in (1) and

---

[2]CoCoGen was designed with extensibility in mind, so that additional CMs can easily be added. It uses an abstract measure class for the implementation of CMs. Currently, additional CMs from the cognitive science (psycholinguistic) literature are being implemented for both English and German.

[3]The Contemporary Corpus of American English (Davies, 2008) is the largest genre-balanced corpus of American English, which at the time the measures were derived comprised 560 million words.

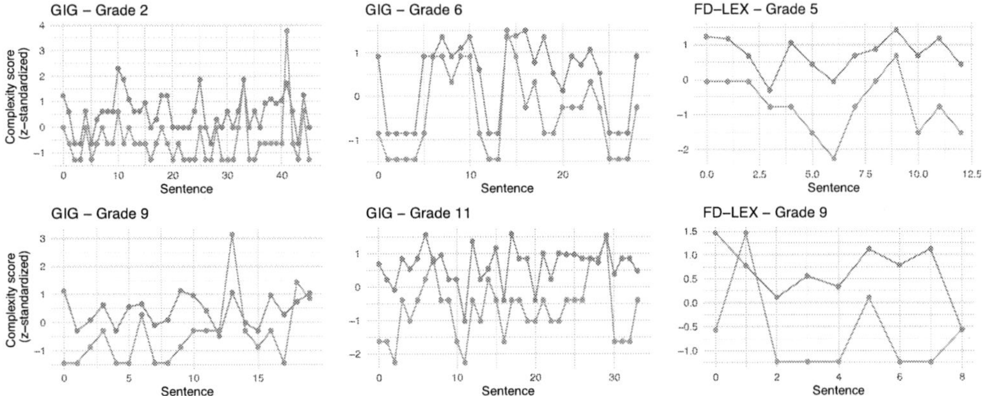

Figure 1: Complexity contours for two different measures (red: Type Token Ratio, blue: Clauses per Sentence) for six randomly selected texts from different grade levels for each language

(2):

$$\text{Score}_{n,s,r} = \frac{|C_{n,s,r}| \cdot \log\left[\prod_{c\in|C_{n,s,r}|} freq_{n,r}(c)\right]}{|U_{n,s}|} \tag{1}$$

where

$$C_{n,s,r} = A_{n,s} \cap B_{n,r} \tag{2}$$

Let $A_{n,s}$ be the list of n-grams ($n \in [0,5]$) contained within a sentence s, $B_{n,r}$ the list of n-grams on the n-gram frequency list of a register r ($r \in \{\text{acad, acad, fic, mag, news, spok}\}$) and $C_{n,s,r} = A_{n,s} \cap B_{n,r}$ the intersection list. Furthermore, $U_{n,s}$ denotes the list of unique n-grams in s, and $freq_{n,r}(a)$ the frequency of n-gram a in the n-gram frequency list of register r. The score of a given n-gram-based CMs is thus obtained by multiplying the number of n-grams in a sentence that are on the n-gram list with the log of the product of the corresponding frequencies of those n-grams divided by the number of distinct n-grams in the sentence.

6   Classification Models

6.1   Model Architecture

We used a Recurrent Neural Network (RNN) classifier, specifically a dynamic RNN model with Gated Recurrent Unit (GRU) cells (Cho et al., 2014). A dynamic RNN was chosen as it can handle sequences of variable length[4]. As shown in Figure 2, the input of the contour-based model is a sequence $X = (x_1, x_2, \ldots, x_l, x_{l+1}, \ldots, x_n)$, where x_i, the

output of CoCoGen for the ith window of a document, is a 13 dimensional vector (for German) or a 57 dimensional vector (for English), l is the length of the sequence, $n \in \mathbb{Z}$ is a number, which is greater or equal to the length of the longest sequence in the dataset and $x_{l+1}, \cdots, x_n$ are padded 0-vectors. The input of the contour-based model is be fed into a RNN which consists of two layers of GRU cells with 20 hidden units each. To predict the class of a sequence, the last output of the RNN, i.e. the output of RNN right after the feeding of x_l, concatenated with the variables (text type and learner background), which are encoded into one-hot vectors, is transformed through a feed-forward neural network. The feed-forward neural-network consists of three fully connected layers, whose output dimensions are 512, 256, 1 (German) and 3 (English). The Rectifier Linear Unit (ReLU) was used as activation function. Two dropout layers were added between fully connected layers 1 and 2 and between layers 2 and 3, both with a dropout rate of 0.3. Before the final output, a sigmoid layer was applied. For the mean-based model, we used the same neural network as in the contour-based model, except that the network was trained on vectors of text-average complexity scores. For the purpose of comparison, we also built two baseline models based on the control variables and the prior probability distribution. The first one is a statistics-based baseline model. We trained this model by grouping the instances in the dataset by the control variables and computed the empirical distribution over grades for each group. For prediction, we classified instances of the test set into grades by

---

[4]The lengths of the feature vector sequences depends on the number of sentences of the texts in our corpus.

$$p(y|x, c) = p(y|c) = \frac{N_{c,y}}{N_c}$$

where y is the class label, i.e. grade, x the features of an instance from the test set, and c is a control variable. $N_{c,y}$ denotes the number of instances in the training set, for a control variable c and class label y, while $N_c = \sum_y N_{c,y}$ is the total number of instances in the training set, which has c as their control variable. The second baseline model is a neural network model that has the same structure of the upper part of the RNN model which is a feedforward neural network. The input of this model is one-hot encoded control variables and the output stay the same as the RNN model.

Since the task is to classify instances of the dataset into a set of ordered categories, i.e. grade $2 < 6 < 9 < 11$ for English and grade $5 < 9$ for German, our task can be treated as an ordinal classification problem. To adapt the neural network classifier to the ordinal classification task, we followed the NNRank approach described in (Cheng et al., 2008), which is a gerneralization of ordinal perceptron learning in neural networks(Crammer and Singer, 2002) and outperforms a neural network classifier on serveral benchmark datasets. Instead of one-hot encoding of class labels and using softmax as the output layer of a neural network, in NNRank, a class label for class k is encoded as $(y_1, y_2, \ldots, y_i, \ldots, y_{C-1})$, in which $y_i = 1$ for $i \leq k$ and $y_i = 0$ otherwise, where C is the number of classes. For the output layer, a sigmoid function was used. For prediction, the output of the neural network $(o_1, y_2, \ldots, o_{C-1})$ is scanned from left to right. It stops after encountering o_i, which is the first element of the output vector that is smaller than a threshold T (e.g. 0.5), or when there is no element left to be scanned. The predicted class of the output vector is the index k of the last element, whose value is greater than or equal to T.

We use ten-fold cross-validation, using a 90%–10% split into training and testing sets. As the loss function for training, binary cross entropy was used:

$$\mathcal{L}(\hat{Y}, c) = -\frac{1}{N} \sum_{i=1}^{N} (y_i \log(\hat{y}) + (1-y_i) \log(1-\hat{y}))$$

in which $c = (y_1, y_2, \ldots, y_N)$, $N = C - 1$ is the true class label of the current observation encoded in accordance with the NNRank method, where C is the number of classes and $\hat{Y} = (\hat{y}_1, \hat{y}_2, \ldots, \hat{y}_N)$

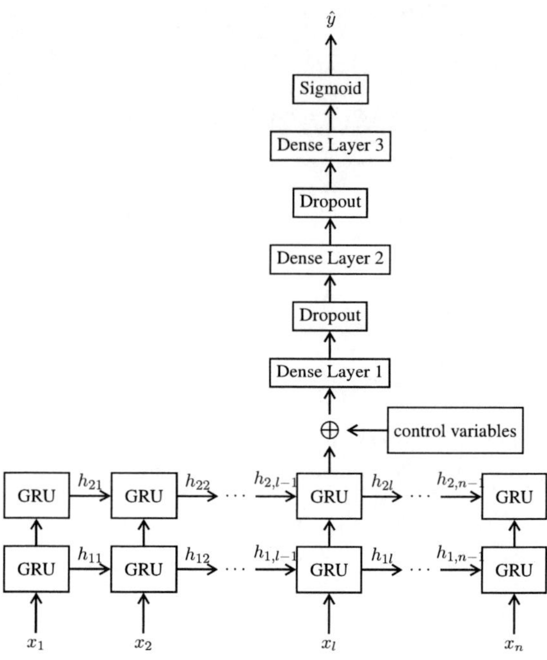

Figure 2: Roll-out of the RNN model based on complexity contours

is the output vector of the sigmoid layer. For optimization, we used Adamax with a learning rate $\eta = 0.001$ and weight decay $= 1 \times 10^{-6}$. The minibatch size is 32, which was shown as a reasonable value for modern GPUs (Masters and Luschi, 2018). All models were implemented using PyTorch (Pytorch, 2019).

6.2 Feature Importance

To determine the relative importance of the complexity features, we conducted feature ablation experiments for the contour-based RNN. Classical forward or backward sequential selection algorithms that proceed by sequentially adding or discarding features require a quadratic number of model training and evaluation in order to obtain a feature ranking (Langley, 1994). In the context of neural network model training a quadratic number of models can become prohibitive. To alleviate this problem, we used an adapted version of the iterative sensitivity-based pruning algorithm proposed by Díaz-Villanueva et al. (2010). This algorithm ranks the features based on a 'sensitivity measure' (see, (Moody, 1994; Utans and Moody, 1991)) and removes the least relevant variables one at a time. The classifier is then retrained on the resulting subset and a new ranking is calculated over the remaining features. This process is repeated until all features are removed (see Algorithm 1). In this fashion, rather than training $\frac{n(n+1)}{2}$ models required for sequential algorithms, the number of models trained is reduced to $\frac{n}{m}$, where m is the number of features that can be removed at each step. We report the results obtained with m = 1, i.e. the results after the removal of a single feature at each step. At step t, neural network models $M_{t,n}, n \in \{1, \dots, k\}$ are trained on the training sets of a 10-fold cross-validation, where n is the fold ID. The training sets at step t consist of instances with feature set $F_t = \{f_1, f_2, \dots, f_{D_t}\}$ where $f_1, \dots f_{D_t}$ are the remaining features at the current step, whose importance rank is to be determined. We define $X_{t,n}$ as the test set of the nth fold with feature set F_t and $X_{t,n}^i$ as the same dataset as $X_{t,n}$ except we set the ith feature f_i of each instance within the dataset to its average. Furthermore, we define $g(X)$ as the classification accuracy of $M_{t,n}$ for a dataset X. The sensitivity of feature f_i on the nth fold at step t is obtained from:

$$S_{i,t,n} = g(X_{t,n}) - g(X_{t,n}^i)$$

The final sensitivity for a feature f_i at step t is:

$$S_{i,t} = \frac{1}{k} \sum_{n=1}^{k} S_{i,t,n}$$

The most important feature at step t can be found by:

$$f_{\hat{i}} : \hat{i} = \arg\max_{i:f_i \in F_t} (S_{i,t})$$

Then we set the rank for feature $f_{\hat{i}}$:

$$Rank_{\hat{i}} = t$$

In the end, feature $f_{\hat{i}}$ is dropped from F_t and the corresponding columns in training and test dataset are also dropped simultaneously:

$$F_{t+1} = F_t - \{f_{\hat{i}}\}$$

This procedure is repeated, until $|F_{t'}| = 1$. To increase the robustness of the feature importance rank order, 10-fold cross-validation was applied.

7   Results

We report the results of classification with 10-fold cross-validation (see Figures 5 and 6 in the Appendix for a visualization of model accuracy for the means-based and contour-based models over 200 epochs across the 10 cross-validation folds). We first present the results of the experiments on the English data, before moving to results for the German data. The performance metrics of the classification models for English (global accuracy, precision, recall and macro F1 scores per grade level) are presented in Table 2. Both the means-based and the contour-based models achieved grade-level-based classification accuracy of $> 75\%$, a substantial improvement over the baseline model (28%, see Table 4 in the Appendix for details). These findings indicate that text complexity increases with children's age/competence level and provide further empirical evidence in support of grade-level-based complexification assumption (see the study by Berendes et al, 2018 described above). The contour-based model outperforms the means-based model in terms of both precision and recall across all classes, resulting in an increase in global classification accuracy of 6%, from 76% (means-based model) to 82% (contour-based model). Precision and recall rates are found to be highest for grade 2, followed by grades 6 and 11, and lowest for grade 11. Inspection of the confusion matrix for the contour-based model (see Table 7 in the Appendix) indicates that misclassified samples are close to the actual class, indicating that the model was sensitive to the grade ordering.[5] These results suggest that the change in complexity was most pronounced in the earlier grades and decreased with increasing grade levels. The results of the feature importance analysis reveal that classification is mainly driven by features related to vocabulary (the feature importance statistics for the top 30 measures can be found in Table 6 in the Appendix). The top 14 of the 57 measures are related to lexical sophistication, word length and the use of register-based n-grams. These findings are consistent with the available body of research suggesting that the development of children's writing during adolescent years is primarily characterized by higher proportions of unusual/advanced words and words of greater surface length (compare *same* vs. *equal* vs. *identical* vs. *tantamount*) (see, Berman 2007) and replicate and extend the findings reported in Durrant and Brenchley (2019) that the shift towards more academic vocabulary can also be observed in the use of multi-word sequences. The information theoretic measures are

---

[5]We also examined all pairwise classification errors among the four grades (see Table 8).

	Means-based		Contour-based	
	M	SD	M	SD
Accuracy	0.76	0.03	**0.82**	0.02
Precision 2	0.87	0.06	**0.90**	0.07
Recall 2	0.85	0.04	**0.90**	0.04
F1 score 2	0.86	0.03	**0.90**	0.03
Precision 6	0.78	0.02	**0.82**	0.04
Recall 6	0.78	0.03	**0.81**	0.04
F1 score 6	0.78	0.01	**0.81**	0.03
Precision 9	0.72	0.04	**0.76**	0.06
Recall 9	0.71	0.05	**0.76**	0.04
F1 score 9	0.71	0.03	**0.76**	0.03
Precision 11	0.71	0.09	**0.82**	0.06
Recall 11	0.75	0.06	**0.82**	0.05
F1 score 11	0.73	0.07	**0.82**	0.04

Table 2: Performance statistics of the means-based (left) and contour-based (right) RNN classifiers aggregated over 10 crossvalidation runs (English data). Baseline classification accuracy was 28%.

	Means-based		Contour-based	
	M	SD	M	SD
Accuracy	0.70	0.02	**0.74**	0.02
Precision 5	0.71	0.02	**0.75**	0.02
Recall 5	0.74	0.02	**0.79**	0.02
F1 score 5	0.72	0.02	**0.77**	0.01
Precision 9	0.69	0.03	**0.74**	0.03
Recall 9	0.66	0.03	**0.7**	0.03
F1 score 9	0.67	0.02	**0.72**	0.03

Table 3: Performance statistics of the means-based (left) and contour-based (right) RNN classifiers aggregated over 10 crossvalidation runs (German data). Baseline classification accuracy was 51%.

situated at ranks 15, 18 and 22. The group of lexical diversity measures (NDW and variants of TTR) is located in the mid-field (ranks 34, 36, 37, 38, 39). Syntactic complexity is found to play only a subsidiary role: with the exception of one measure (VP/T, rank 19) features from this class appeared only after rank 30.

Even with a more restricted features set compared to English, grade-level-based classification accuracy on the German dataset displays considerable - albeit less pronounced - improvement of $\geq 19\%$ over the baseline model (51% classification accuracy) (see Table 5 in the appendix). These findings thus provide additional, though somewhat weaker, empirical evidence in support of grade-level-based complexification assumption. As is the case in the English data, the performance of the model based on complexity contours exceeds that of the means-based model on the German data both in terms of precision and recall across the two school grades, leading to an 4% increase in overall classification accuracy from 70% to 74%. Table 3 presents the performance statistics. The feature ablation analysis reveals that the most important features are more evenly distributed across the four groups of CMs (see Table 9 in the Appendix): The top eight features include surface CMs pertaining to the length of production unit (MLWc, MLC, MLS), lexical diversity (NDW, RTTR, CTTR), syntactic complexity (Cl/S), and information density

(KolDef). Within this set of eight CMs, the removal of individual CMs is associated with a relatively minor drop in classification accuracy of less than 1.5%, suggesting that the network is able to compensate for the loss of information from a given feature by relying on the other features. However, when the last feature of the top-8 group is removed, classification accuracy drops by almost 5%, indicating that the remaining features played subsidiary roles in the grade-level classification. These findings nicely complement those reported in the paper by Weiss and Meurers (2019) described above focusing on basic (Hauptschule) and intermediate school tracks (Realschule) by assessing writing skills in the other two tracks of the German educational system: comprehensive school (Gesamtschule) and grammar school (Gymnasium).

8 Conclusion and Outlook

In this paper, we demonstrated how the automatic assessment of text complexity through a sliding window approach in combination with machine learning techniques can provide valuable and unique insights into the development of children's writing as they progress through their school education. Such an approach has the added advantage of capturing the progression of complexity within a text. In classification tasks on two data sets representing children's school writing in L1 English and German, we showed that the inclusion of this sequential information can substantially increase classification performance across grade-levels. We also show that Sensitivity-Based Pruning is a viable complementary approach to other approaches aimed at assessing feature importance to identify 'criterial features' that are characteristic and indicative of language competencies at a given level (Hawkins and Filipović, 2012). More generally, the type of research presented in this paper has the potential to advance our understanding of the development of literacy skills in children during adolescent years, a key stage that is still not well understood. In future work, we intend to extend the approach presented here to larger cross-sectional data sets covering additional school grades in search of valid and reliable benchmarks and norms that can be used to inform school curricula and educational standards.

References

Karin Berendes, Sowmya Vajjala, Detmar Meurers, Doreen Bryant, Wolfgang Wagner, Maria Chinkina, and Ulrich Trautwein. 2018. Reading demands in secondary school: Does the linguistic complexity of textbooks increase with grade level and the academic orientation of the school track? *Journal of Educational Psychology*, 110(4):518.

Ruth A Berman. 2007. Developing linguistic knowledge and language use across adolescence.

Xiaobin Chen and Detmar Meurers. 2018. Word frequency and readability: Predicting the text-level readability with a lexical-level attribute. *Journal of Research in Reading*, 41(3):486–510.

Jianlin Cheng, Zheng Wang, and Gianluca Pollastri. 2008. A neural network approach to ordinal regression. In *2008 IEEE International Joint Conference on Neural Networks (IEEE World Congress on Computational Intelligence)*, pages 1279–1284. IEEE.

KyungHyun Cho, Bart van Merrienboer, Dzmitry Bahdanau, and Yoshua Bengio. 2014. On the properties of neural machine translation: Encoder-decoder approaches. *CoRR*, abs/1409.1259.

European Commission. 2019. Proposal for a council recommendation on a comprehensive approach to the teaching and learning of languages.

Koby Crammer and Yoram Singer. 2002. Pranking with ranking. In *Advances in neural information processing systems*, pages 641–647.

Scott A Crossley, Rod Roscoe, and Danielle S McNamara. 2014. What is successful writing? an investigation into the multiple ways writers can write successful essays. *Written Communication*, 31(2):184–214.

Scott A Crossley, Jennifer L Weston, Susan T McLain Sullivan, and Danielle S McNamara. 2011. The development of writing proficiency as a function of grade level: A linguistic analysis. *Written Communication*, 28(3):282–311.

Peter Deutsch and Jean-Loup Gailly. 1996. Zlib compressed data format specification version 3.3. Technical report, RFC 1950, May.

Wladimiro Díaz-Villanueva, Francesc J Ferri, and Vicente Cerverón. 2010. Learning improved feature rankings through decremental input pruning for support vector based drug activity prediction. In *International Conference on Industrial, Engineering and Other Applications of Applied Intelligent Systems*, pages 653–661. Springer.

Zeynep Duran-Karaoz and Parvaneh Tavakoli. 2020. Predicting L2 fluency from L1 fluency behavior: The case of L1 Turkish and L2 English speakers. *Studies in Second Language Acquisition*, pages 1–25.

Philip Durrant and Mark Brenchley. 2019. Development of vocabulary sophistication across genres in english children's writing. *Reading and Writing*, 32(8):1927–1953.

Katharina Ehret and Benedikt Szmrecsanyi. 2019. Compressing learner language: An information-theoretic measure of complexity in sla production data. *Second Language Research*, 35(1):23–45.

Nick C Ellis. 2019. Essentials of a theory of language cognition. *The Modern Language Journal*, 103:39–60.

Thomas François and Cédrick Fairon. 2012. An ai readability formula for french as a foreign language. In *Proceedings of the 2012 Joint Conference on Empirical Methods in Natural Language Processing and Computational Natural Language Learning*, pages 466–477. Association for Computational Linguistics.

John A Hawkins and Luna Filipović. 2012. *Criterial features in L2 English: Specifying the reference levels of the Common European Framework*, volume 1. Cambridge University Press.

Dan Klein and Christopher D Manning. 2003. Accurate unlexicalized parsing. In *Proceedings of the 41st Annual Meeting on Association for Computational Linguistics-Volume 1*, pages 423–430. Association for Computational Linguistics.

Pat Langley. 1994. Selection of relevant features in machine learning. In *Proceedings of the AAAI Fall symposium on relevance*, pages 1–5.

Francisco Lorenzo and Oliver Meyer. 2017. Special issue: Languages of schooling: explorations into disciplinary literacies.

Xiaofei Lu. 2011. A corpus-based evaluation of syntactic complexity measures as indices of college-level esl writers' language development. *Tesol Quarterly*, 45(1):36–62.

Xiaofei Lu. 2012. The relationship of lexical richness to the quality of esl learners' oral narratives. *The Modern Language Journal*, 96(2):190–208.

Xiaofei Lu. 2017. Automated measurement of syntactic complexity in corpus-based l2 writing research and implications for writing assessment. *Language Testing*, 34(4):493–511.

Christopher Manning, Mihai Surdeanu, John Bauer, Jenny Finkel, Steven Bethard, and David McClosky. 2014. The stanford corenlp natural language processing toolkit. In *Proceedings of 52nd annual meeting of the association for computational linguistics: system demonstrations*, pages 55–60.

Dominic Masters and Carlo Luschi. 2018. Revisiting small batch training for deep neural networks. *arXiv preprint arXiv:1804.07612*.

Detmar Meurers. 2020. Natural language processing and language learning. In Carol A. Chapelle, editor, *The Concise Encyclopedia of Applied Linguistics*. Wiley.

John Moody. 1994. Prediction risk and architecture selection for neural networks. In *From statistics to neural networks*, pages 147–165. Springer.

Ildikó Pilán, David Alfter, and Elena Volodina. 2016. Coursebook texts as a helping hand for classifying linguistic complexity in language learners' writings. In *Proceedings of the Workshop on Computational Linguistics for Linguistic Complexity (CL4LC)*, pages 120–126.

Pytorch. 2019. Pytorch: Tensors and dynamic neural networks in python with strong gpu acceleration. https://github.com/pytorch/pytorch.

Anna N Rafferty and Christopher D Manning. 2008. Parsing three german treebanks: Lexicalized and unlexicalized baselines. In *Proceedings of the Workshop on Parsing German*, pages 40–46.

Patrick Emanuel Rebuschat, Meurers Detmar, and Tony McEnery. 2017. Language learning research at the intersection of experimental, computational and corpus-based approaches. *Language Learning*, 67(S1):6–13.

Catherine E Snow. 2010. Academic language and the challenge of reading for learning about science. *science*, 328(5977):450–452.

Catherine E Snow and Paola Uccelli. 2009. The challenge of academic language. *The Cambridge handbook of literacy*, pages 112–133.

Marcus Ströbel. 2014. *Tracking complexity of l2 academic texts: A sliding-window approach*. Master thesis. RWTH Aachen University.

Marcus Ströbel, Elma Kerz, Daniel Wiechmann, and Yu Qiao. 2018. Text genre classification based on linguistic complexity contours using a recurrent neural network. In *MRC@ IJCAI*, pages 56–63.

Marcus Ströbel, Elma Kerz, and Daniel Wiechmann. 2020. The relationship between first and second language writing: Investigating the effects of first language complexity on second language complexity in advanced stages of learning. *Language Learning*, n/a(n/a).

Joachim Utans and John Moody. 1991. Selecting neural network architectures via the prediction risk: Application to corporate bond rating prediction. In *Proceedings First International Conference on Artificial Intelligence Applications on Wall Street*, pages 35–41. IEEE.

Zarah Weiss and Detmar Meurers. 2019. Analyzing linguistic complexity and accuracy in academic language development of german across elementary and secondary school. In *Proceedings of the Fourteenth Workshop on Innovative Use of NLP for Building Educational Applications*, pages 380–393.

Menglin Xia, Ekaterina Kochmar, and Ted Briscoe. 2019. Text readability assessment for second language learners. *arXiv preprint arXiv:1906.07580*.

Annotation and Classification of Evidence and Reasoning Revisions in Argumentative Writing

Tazin Afrin, Elaine Wang, Diane Litman, Lindsay C. Matsumura, Richard Correnti
Learning Research and Development Center
University of Pittsburgh
Pittsburgh, Pennsylvania 15260
`tazinafrin@cs.pitt.edu, ewang@rand.org`
`{dlitman,lclare,rcorrent}@pitt.edu`

Abstract

Automated writing evaluation systems can improve students' writing insofar as students attend to the feedback provided and revise their essay drafts in ways aligned with such feedback. Existing research on revision of argumentative writing in such systems, however, has focused on the types of revisions students make (e.g., surface vs. content) rather than the extent to which revisions actually respond to the feedback provided and improve the essay. We introduce an annotation scheme to capture the nature of sentence-level revisions of evidence use and reasoning (the 'RER' scheme) and apply it to 5th- and 6th-grade students' argumentative essays. We show that reliable manual annotation can be achieved and that revision annotations correlate with a holistic assessment of essay improvement in line with the feedback provided. Furthermore, we explore the feasibility of automatically classifying revisions according to our scheme.

1 Introduction

Automated writing evaluation (AWE) systems are intended to help improve students' writing by providing formative feedback to guide students' essay revision. Such systems are only effective if students attend to the feedback provided and revise their essays in ways aligned with such feedback.

To date, few AWE systems assess (and are assessed on) the extent to which students' revisions respond to the feedback provided and thus improve the essay in suggested ways. Moreover, we know little about what students do when they do not revise in expected ways. For example, most natural language processing (NLP) work on writing revision focuses only on annotating and classifying revision purposes (Daxenberger and Gurevych, 2013; Zhang et al., 2017), rather than on assessing the quality of a revision in achieving its purpose. A few

studies do focus on revision quality, but without relating revisions to feedback (Tan and Lee, 2014; Afrin and Litman, 2018).

In this study, we take a step towards advancing automated revision analysis capabilities. First, we develop a sentence-level revision scheme to annotate the nature of students' revision of evidence use and reasoning (hereafter, we refer to this as the 'RER scheme') in a text-based argumentative essay writing task. By evidence use, we refer to the selection of relevant and specific details from a source text to support an argument. By reasoning, we mean an explanation connecting the text evidence to the claim and overall argument. Table 4 shows examples of evidence and reasoning revisions from first draft to second draft. Next, we demonstrate inter-rater reliability among humans in the use of the RER scheme. In addition, we show that only desirable revision categories in the scheme relate to a holistic assessment of essay improvement in line with the feedback provided. Finally, we adapt word to vector representation features to automatically classify desirable versus undesirable evidence revisions, and examine how automatically predicted evidence revisions relate to the holistic assessment of essay improvement.

2 Related Work

Automated revision detection work has centered on classifying edits on largely non-content level features of writing, such as spelling and morphosyntactic revisions (Max and Wisniewski, 2010), error correction, paraphrase or vandalism detection (Daxenberger and Gurevych, 2013), factual versus fluency edits (Bronner and Monz, 2012), and document- versus word-level revisions (Roscoe et al., 2015). Other research has focused on patterns of revision behavior, for example, the addition, deletion, substitution, and reorganization of

Proceedings of the 15th Workshop on Innovative Use of NLP for Building Educational Applications, pages 75–84
July 10, 2020. ©2020 Association for Computational Linguistics

information (Zhang, 2020). However, these categories center on general writing features and behaviors. In the context of AWE systems, this could be seen as a limitation because feedback is most useful to students and teachers alike when it is keyed to critical features of a genre – such as claims, reasons, and evidence use in argumentative writing – that are most challenging to teach and learn.

Some research has begun to take up the challenge of investigating student revision for argumentative writing (Zhang and Litman, 2015; Zhang et al., 2017). Results show a high level of agreement for human annotation and some relationship to essay improvement, though not at the level of individual argument elements (Zhang and Litman, 2015). Existing schemes also lack in specificity, e.g., they do not distinguish between desirable and undesirable revisions for each argument element in terms of improving essay quality.

Prior work on assessing revision quality has evaluated revision in general terms (e.g., strength (Tan and Lee, 2014) or overall improvement (Afrin and Litman, 2018)), but without consideration of the feedback students were provided. We instead focus on analyzing revisions in response to feedback from an AWE system. Although prior studies have focused on all revision categories (e.g., claim, evidence, and word-usage (Zhang and Litman, 2015)), we focus on only evidence and reasoning revisions that correspond to the scope of the AWE system's feedback. Also, we focus not only on why the student made a revision (e.g., add evidence) but also analyze if the revision was desirable or not (e.g., relevant versus irrelevant evidence).

3   Corpus

Our corpus consists of the first draft (Draft1) and second draft (Draft2) of 143 argumentative essays. The corpus draws from our effort to develop an automated writing evaluation system - eRevise, to provide 5th- and 6th-grade students feedback on a response-to-text essay (Zhang et al., 2019; Wang et al., 2020). The writing task administration involved teachers reading aloud a text while students followed along with their copy. Then, students were given a writing prompt[1] to write an argumentative essay.

No	Feedback Message
1	Use more evidence from the article
2	Provide more details for each piece of evidence you use
3	Explain the evidence
4	Explain how the evidence connects to the main idea & elaborate

Table 1: Top-level feedback from the AWE system.

Each student wrote Draft1 and submitted their essay to the AWE system. Students then received feedback focused specifically on the use of text evidence and reasoning. Table 1 shows the top-level feedback messages[2] that the system provided. Finally, students were directed to revise their essay in response to the feedback, yielding Draft2.

As part of a prior exploration of students' implementation of the system's feedback, this corpus of 143 essays was coded holistically on a scale from 0 to 3 for the extent to which use of evidence and reasoning improved from Draft1 to Draft 2 in line with the feedback provided (Wang et al., 2020)[3]. A code, or score, of 0 indicated no attempt to implement the feedback given; 1= no perceived improvement in evidence use or reasoning, 2= slight improvement; and 3= substantive improvement. Note again that this score represents a subjective, holistic (i.e., not sentence-level) assessment of whether Draft2 improved in evidence use and/or reasoning specifically in alignment with the feedback that a particular student received. We refer to this as **'improvement score'** in the rest of the paper.

3.1   Preparing the corpus for annotation

On average, Draft1 essays contain 14 sentences and 253 words, and Draft2 essays contain 18 sentences and 334 words. To prepare the corpus for annotation, we first segmented each Draft1 and Draft2 essay into sentences, then manually aligned them at sentence-level. For example, if a sentence is added to Draft2, it is aligned with a null sentence in Draft1. If a sentence is deleted from Draft1, it is aligned with a null sentence in Draft2. A modified sentence, or a sentence with no change in Draft2, is aligned with the corresponding sen-

---

[1]"Based on the article, did the author provide a convincing argument that winning the fight against poverty is achievable in our lifetime? Explain why or why not with 3-4 examples from the text to support your answer."

[2]See (Zhang et al., 2019) for detailed feedback messages.

[3]In the prior study, two researchers double-coded 35 of the 143 essays (24 percent). Cohen's kappa was 0.77, indicating 'substantial' agreement (McHugh, 2012).

#Sentence	Draft2	#No Change	#Revision
Total	2652	1362	1475
Avg.	18.545	9.524	10.315

Table 2: Essay statistics (N=143).

#Revision	Evidence (N=93)	Reasoning (N=111)	Other (N=129)
Total	386	389	700
Min	0	0	0
Max	36	17	21
Avg.	4.151	3.505	5.426

Table 3: Revision statistics.

tence in Draft1[4]. Based on this alignment, we then extracted the 1475 sentence pairs where students made either additions, deletions, or modifications as *revisions*. The remaining 1362 aligned sentences had no changes between drafts and were thus not extracted as revisions.

Each revision was next manually annotated[5] for its revision purpose according to the scheme proposed in (Zhang and Litman, 2015), which categorizes revisions into surface versus content changes. Surface revisions are changes to fluency or word choice, convention or grammar, and organization. Content revisions are meaningful textual changes such as claim or thesis, evidence, reasoning, counter-arguments etc. From among these revisions, only evidence and reasoning revisions are used for the current study, due to their alignment with the AWE feedback messages in Table 1.

Table 2 shows the descriptive statistics of the essay corpus at the sentence-level. The second column shows the total and average number of sentences for Draft2. The third column shows that, on average, about 9 sentences per essay were unchanged. The final column shows that, on average, 10 sentences per essay were revised[6]. Out of those 10 sentences, only two to three sentences were revised with respect to evidence, and another two to three sentences with respect to reasoning, on average over all 143 students. This indicates that students engaged in very limited revisions of evidence and reasoning, even when provided feedback targeted to these argument elements.

Table 3 shows the statistics for the students who did revise their essay. Note that out of 143 students, 50 students (35%) did not make any evidence-use revisions; 32 students (22%) did not make any reasoning revisions. Only 10 students (7%) did not make any evidence or reasoning revisions. 4 students (3%) did not make any revision at all. From these students we extracted 386 evidence revisions and 389 reasoning revisions, a total of 775 sentence-

level revisions. We do not consider the other 700 revisions (claim, word-usage, grammar mistakes, etc.) in this study.

To better understand how students did revise, whether their revisions were desirable, and whether desirable revisions relate to a measure of essay improvement that includes alignment with feedback, we developed a revision categorization scheme and conducted the analysis described below.

4 Revision Categorization (RER Scheme)

We propose a new scheme for annotating revisions of evidence use and reasoning (RER scheme) that will be useful for assessing the improvement of the essay in line with the feedback provided. The initial set of codes drew from the qualitative exploration of students' implementation of feedback from our AWE system (Wang et al., 2020), in which the authors inductively and holistically coded how students successfully and unsuccessfully revised their essays with respect to evidence use and reasoning. For example, students sometimes added evidence that repeated evidence they had already provided in Draft1. Or they successfully modified sentences to better link the evidence to the claim.

Both the initial set of codes and our AWE system's feedback messages were informed by writing experts and research suggesting that strong argument writing generally features multiple pieces of specific evidence that are relevant to the argument and clear explication (or reasoning) of how the evidence connects to the claim and helps to support the argument (see, for example, (De La Paz et al., 2012; O'Hallaron, 2014; Wang et al., 2018)).

For the present study, two annotators read through each extracted evidence or reasoning-related revision in the context of the entire essay. They labeled each instance of revision with a code. The annotators iteratively expanded or refined the initial codes until they finalized a set of codes for evidence use revisions and another for reasoning revisions (see sections 4.1 and 4.2). Together these

---

[4]Sentence order substitution is evaluated as deleted then inserted.

[5]Annotator Cohen's kappa of 0.753.

[6]#Revision also includes deleted sentences, hence #Revision + #No Change does not equal #Sentence in Draft2.

Draft1	Draft2	Operation	Purpose	RER code
In the story, "A Brighter Future," the author convinced me that "winning the fight against poverty is achievable in our life time."	In the story, "A Brighter Future," the author of the story convinced me that winning the fight against poverty is achievable in our lifetime.	Modify	Fluency	
	I think that in Sauri, Kenya [where poverty is all around], people were in poverty.	Add	Claim	
	In the story it states "The Yala sub-District Hospital has medicine."	Add	Evidence	Relevant
For example, we have good food and clean water		Delete	Evidence	Irrelevant
	This shows that there was a change at the hospital because they had medicine which is good for the peoples health when they get sick.	Add	Reasoning	Linked to Claim and Evidence

Table 4: Example revisions from aligned drafts of an essay and application of RER codes.

two sets comprise the RER scheme. Subsequently, the two annotators applied the RER scheme to all instances of evidence use or reasoning-related revisions in all 143 students' essays.[7] Annotators selected the best code; no sentence received more than one code.

Table 4 presents an example of corpus preparation (Operation and Purpose, section 3.1) and RER coding (see below) as applied to an excerpted essay and its revision. Table 5 presents an example of each code, though for parsimony, we only present additive revisions – not deletions or modification, as these are less common. Table 6 shows the distribution for each RER code.

4.1 Revision of evidence use

Revisions related to evidence are characterized by one of the following five codes. All codes apply to added, deleted, or modified revisions, except 'Minimal', which only applies to modified evidence. **Relevant** applies to examples or details that support (i.e., are appropriate and related to) the particular claim. **Irrelevant** applies to examples or details that are unnecessary, impertinent to, or disconnected from the claim. They do not help with the argument. **Repeat evidence** applies to examples or

details that were already present in Draft1; students are merely repeating the information. **Non-text based** applies to examples or details outside of the provided text. **Minimal** applies to minor modifications to existing evidence that may add some specificity, but do not affect the argument much.

4.2 Revision of reasoning

Reasoning revisions are characterized by one of the following six codes. All codes apply to added, deleted, or modified revisions, except 'Minimal', which only applies to modified reasoning. **Linked claim-evidence (LCE)** applies to an explanation that connects the evidence provided with the claim. **Not LCE** applies to an explanation that does not connect the evidence provided with the claim. **Paraphrase evidence** applies to an attempt at explanation that merely paraphrases the evidence rather than explain or elaborate upon it. **Generic** applies to a non-specific explanation that is reused multiple times, after each piece of evidence (e.g., "This is why I am convinced that we can end poverty.") **Commentary** applies to an explanation that is unrelated to the main claim or source text; most of the time, it comes from the writer's personal experience. **Minimal** applies to minor modifications that do not affect the argument much.

---

[7]33 of the essays, or 23 percent, were double-coded for reliability, see Section 5 for kappa score.

	Example of "Add" Revision ("Modify" for Minimal Revision)
Evidence	
*Relevant	To support the point that conditions in Sauri were bleak, a student added this new example: "The hospitals don't have the medicine for their sick patients so therefore they can get even more ill and eventually die [if] the [immune] system is not strong enough."
Irrelevant	To support the claim that winning the fight against poverty is possible, the student wrote, "Students could not attend school because they did not have enough money to pay the school fee." This does not support the claim.
Repeat Evidence	"Malaria causes adults to get sick and cause children to die" was added as sentence #27 in a student's Draft2, but sentence #5 already said, "Around 20,000 kids die a day from malaria and the adults get very ill from it."
Non-Text-Based	Student provided example of an uncle living in poverty, rather than draw from examples in the source text about poverty in Kenya.
Minimal	In Draft1, the student wrote, "Now during the project there are no school fees, the schools serve the students lunch, and the attendance rate is way up." In Draft 2, the student specified "Millennium Villages" project.
Reasoning	
*LCE	The student argued that we can end poverty because Sauri has already made significant progress. After presenting the evidence about villagers receiving bednets to protect against malaria, the student added, "This shows that the people of Sauri have made progress and have taken steps to protect everyone using the bed nets and other things."
Not LCE	The student claims that Sauri is overcoming poverty. After presenting the evidence that "Each net costs $5," the student wrote, "This explain how low prices are but we may not get people to lower them more."
Paraphrase	After presenting the evidence that "People's crops were dying because they could not afford the necessary fertilizer," the student added, "This evidence shows that the crops were dying and the people could not get the food that they needed because the farmers could not afford any fertilizer..."
Generic	After the first piece of evidence, the student added, "This evidence helps the statement that there was a lot of poverty." Then after the second piece of evidence, the student added almost the same generic sentence, "This statement also supports that there were a lot of problems caused by poverty."
Commentary	After a piece of evidence, a student wrote, "We think that we are poor because we can not get toys that we want, but we go to school and its not free."
Minimal	In Draft1, the student wrote, "I believe that because it states that we have enough hands and feet to get down and dirty and help these kids that are suffering.". In Draft2, the student only added "and are in poverty" to the end of the sentence.

* indicates desirable revision, as the revision has hypothesized utility in improving the assigned essay in alignment with provided feedback given in Table 1. Other codes may also be desirable given a different writing task with different feedback (e.g., students may be asked to provide non-text-based evidence from their own experience).

Table 5: Example of each RER code.

RER Code	Add	Delete	Modify	Total
Evidence	265	63	58	386
Relevant	159	50	30	239
Irrelevant	26	9	8	43
Repeat Evidence	70	4	0	74
Non-Text-Based	10	0	0	10
Minimal	0	0	20	20
Reasoning	270	59	60	389
LCE	90	18	13	121
Generic	20	0	1	21
Paraphrase	50	10	5	65
Not LCE	62	11	12	85
Commentary	48	20	7	75
Minimal	0	0	22	22
Total	535	122	118	775

Table 6: RER code distribution (N=143).

5 Evaluation of the RER Scheme

We evaluated our annotated corpus to answer the following research questions (RQ):

RQ1: What is the inter-rater reliability for annotating revisions of evidence use and reasoning?

RQ2: Is the number of each type of revision related to essay 'improvement score'?

RQ3: Is there any difference in the 'improvement score' based on the kinds of revisions?

RQ4: Is there a cumulative benefit to predicting essay 'improvement score' when students made multiple types of revisions?

To answer RQ1, we calculated Cohen's kappa for inter-rater agreement on the 33 essays (23 percent) that were double-coded. Our results show that we were able to achieve substantial inter-rater agreement on reasoning (k = .719) and excellent inter-rater agreement for evidence use (k = .833) (see, e.g., (McHugh, 2012)).

To answer RQ2, we calculated the Pearson correlation between the raw number of revisions per code to the 'improvement score' described in Section 3. Table 7 shows that the total number of evidence-related revisions was not significantly correlated with 'improvement score' (r = .15), while the total number of reasoning revisions was (r = .30). Table 7 also shows that positive correlations were found for added evidence or reasoning (r = .17 and .40, respectively), whereas deletions and modification were not significantly correlated.

Looking at the correlations for our proposed RER codes (which sub-categorize the Evidence and Reasoning codes (Zhang and Litman, 2015)), we see that the RER codes yield more and generally stronger results. We found that, as hypothesized, adding relevant pieces of evidence was significantly positively correlated with the 'improvement score', while the addition of irrelevant evidence, non-text based evidence or repeating prior evidence were all unrelated to this score. Similarly, we found that adding reasoning that linked evidence to the claim (LCE) was significantly correlated with the 'improvement score' and so was paraphrasing evidence. Other reasoning codes, as expected, were not significantly related to the 'improvement score'. We did not initially consider paraphrases as a desirable type of revision; yet, this code showed a significant positive correlation. While unexpected, we were not altogether surprised as two of the feedback messages (shown in Table 1) did explicitly ask for students to put ideas into their own words (see (Zhang et al., 2019) for details). Although addition of evidence and reasoning revisions demonstrated correlation to the 'improvement score', deletions and modifications did not show any intuitive correlation. We suspect that this is due to the comparatively small number of delete and modify revisions.

To answer RQ3, we performed one-way ANOVAs for different levels of the 'improvement score' (0=no attempt, 1=no improvement, 2=slight improvement, 3=substantive improvement, aligned with feedback provided) comparing means of the number of revisions added, modified, or deleted. ANOVAs showed overall significance for the cate-

RER Code	Add	Delete	Modify	Total
Evidence	0.17*	0.00	0.13	0.15
Relevant	0.25**	0.02	0.09	0.20*
Irrelevant	0.05	-0.00	0.07	0.06
Repeat Evidence	0.01	-0.06	–	0.00
Non-Text-Based	0.07	–	–	0.07
Minimal	–	–	0.06	0.06
Reasoning	0.40**	0.09	-0.10	0.30**
LCE	0.45**	0.05	0.09	0.41**
Generic	-0.03	–	-0.04	-0.04
Paraphrase	0.22**	0.09	0.02	0.22**
Not LCE	0.09	0.00	-0.07	0.04
Commentary	-0.02	0.08	-0.08	0.01
Minimal	–	–	-0.14	-0.14

Table 7: Revision correlation to 'Improvement Score'. (N=143, * $p <$ .05, ** $p <$ .01)

RER Code	Add	Modify	Total
Evidence:			
Relevant	3*>1	3*>2	
Reasoning:			
LCE	3*>0,1,2	3*>1	3*>0,1,2
Not LCE	2*>0,3		2*>0,3

Table 8: ANOVA results showing differences among 'Improvement Scores' (coded as 0, 1, 2, 3). Only categories with significant results are shown. All categories were tested. (N=143, * $p <$ .05, ** $p <$ .01)

Model	Variables	Coef.	R^2
Model_E	add Relevant	0.25**	0.06
Model_R	add LCE	0.05**	0.25
	add Paraphrase	0.08**	
Model_ER	add LCE	0.45**	0.32
	add Paraphrase	0.20**	
	add Relevant	0.29**	
	del Relevant	-0.21*	

Table 9: Stepwise linear regression results predicting 'Improvement Score'. (N=143, * $p <$ .05, ** $p <$ .01)

gories shown in Table 8. Tukey post-hoc analyses showed that students whose essays substantively improved made more revisions in which they added or modified relevant pieces of evidence. Students who substantively improved also added or modified their reasoning linking evidence to their claims (LCE) more than students in all other groups. Finally, students with slightly improved essays added more explanations not linking evidence to claim (Not-LCE) than did students who made no attempt at revision or whose essays substantively improved.

To answer RQ4, we examined three stepwise linear regression models to understand whether adding more revision codes had a cumulative influence explaining more variance in 'improvement score'. *Model_E* included only revisions related to evidence use. *Model_R* included only revisions related to reasoning. *Model_ER* included all evidence use and reasoning revisions. As shown in Table 9, *Model_ER* shows significant positive coefficients for the addition of relevant evidence, rea-

soning that links evidence to the claim (LCE), and reasoning that paraphrases evidence. The positive relationship shows that more of these kinds of revisions are more likely to lead to a higher 'improvement score'. Note that the order of the coefficients is related to the magnitude of the r-squared they explain - thus linked claim and evidence (LCE) has the strongest relationship with the score. Meanwhile, deleting relevant pieces of evidence has a negative relationship when adjusting for the other covariates in the model, which means that, all else being equal, this is an undesirable revision.

6 Automatic RER Classification

The ultimate goal for developing the RER scheme is to implement it in an AWE system to provide feedback to students about revision outcome not only at the essay-level but also at a more actionable, sentence-level. While the previous section demonstrated the utility of the RER scheme, this section explores its automatic classification. Since

	Precision	Recall	F1-score
Majority	0.309	0.500	0.377
LogR	**0.615****	**0.622****	**0.594****

Table 10: 10-fold cross-validation result for classifying Evidence as 'Relevant' or not. (N=386, ** $p<$ .01)

	Add	Delete	Modify	Total
Gold	0.25**	0.02	0.09	0.20*
Majority	0.17*	0.00	0.13	0.15
LogR	0.17*	-0.01	0.03	0.15

Table 11: Correlation of predicted 'Relevant' evidence to 'Improvement Score'. (N=143, * $p<$ .05, ** $p<$ .01)

our overall revision dataset is small, we focus on the simplified task of developing a binary classifier to predict whether an Evidence revision is 'Relevant' or not. 'Relevant' is both the most frequent RER code and relates positively to the improvement score.

The input is a revision sentence pair – the sentence from Draft1 (S1) and its aligned sentence from Draft2 (S2). The pair can have 3 variations: (null, S2) for added sentences, (S1, null) for deleted sentences, and (S1, S2) for modified sentences. Since we are focusing on 'Relevant' evidence prediction, and by our definition in Section 4.1 'Relevant' evidence supports the claim, we also consider the given source text (A) in extracting features.

Features. We explore Word2vec as features for our classification task[8]. We extract representations of S1, S2, and A using the pre-trained GloVe word embedding (Pennington et al., 2014). For each word representation (w) we use the vector of dimension 100, $w = [v_1, \ldots, v_{100}]$. Then the sentence or document vector (d) is calculated as the average of all word vectors $d = [d_1, \ldots, d_{100}]$, where $d_i = mean(v_{1i}, \ldots, v_{ni})$, for n words in the document. Following this method we extract vectors d_{s1}, d_{s2}, and d_a for S1, S2, and A respectively. Finally, we take the average of those 3 vectors to represent the feature vector, $f = [f_1, \ldots, f_{100}]$, where $f_j = mean(d_{s1j}, d_{s2j}, d_{aj})$.

For machine learning, we use off-the-shelf Logistic Regression (LogR) from the scikit-learn toolkit.[9] We did not perform any parameter tuning or feature selection. In an intrinsic evaluation, we compare whether there are significant differences between the classifier's performance and a majority baseline in terms of average un-weighted precision, recall and F1, using paired sample t-tests over 10-folds of cross-validation. In an extrinsic evaluation, we repeat the Pearson correlation study in Section 5 for the predicted code, 'Relevant' evidence.

---

[8]We also explored n-gram features from a previous revision classification task (Zhang and Litman, 2015). Our classification algorithm performed better with word2vec features.

[9]We also explored Support Vector Machines (SVM) but Logistic Regression outperformed SVM in our experiment.

Intrinsic evaluation. Table 10 presents the results of the binary classifier predicting 'Relevant' evidence. The results show that the logistic regression classifier significantly outperforms the baseline using our features for all metrics.

Extrinsic evaluation. Table 11 shows the Pearson correlation of 'Relevant' evidence to 'Improvement Score' using 'Gold' human labels (repeated from Table 7) versus predicted labels from the majority and logistic regression classifiers. First, the number of 'Add Relevant' revisions, whether gold or predicted, significantly correlates to improvement. While it is not surprising that the correlation is lower for LogR than for Gold (upper bound), it is unexpected that LogR and Majority (baseline) are the same. This likely reflects the Table 7 result that adding any type of Evidence, relevant or not, correlates with improvement. In contrast, the predicted models are not yet accurate enough to replicate the statistical significance of the 'Gold' correlation between improvement and 'Total Relevant' revisions.

7   Discussion

In our corpus, students revised only about half of the sentences from Draft1 to Draft2. Among the revisions, only a small proportion focused on evidence or reasoning, despite feedback targeting these argument elements exclusively. This resonates with writing research (though not in the context of AWE) showing that students often struggle to revise (Faigley and Witte, 1981; MacArthur, 2018), and that novice writers – like our 5th- and 6th-graders – tend to focus on local word- and sentence level problems rather than content or structure (MacArthur et al., 2004; MacArthur, 2018). When novices do revise, their efforts frequently result in no improvement or improvement only in surface features (Patthey-Chavez et al., 2004).

We knew of no revision schemes that assessed the extent to which evidence use and reasoning-related revisions aligned with desirable features of argumentative writing (i.e., showed responsiveness to system feedback to use more relevant evidence, give more specific details, or provide explanations connecting evidence to the claim); hence, we developed the RER scheme. The scheme – along with the reliability we established and the positive correlations we demonstrated between its sentence-level application and a holistic assessment of essay improvement in line with provided feedback – is an important contribution because the codes are keyed to critical features of the argument writing genre. Therefore, it is more useful than existing schemes that focus on general revision purposes (surface vs. content) or operations (addition, deletion, modification) for assessing the quality of students' revisions.

This assessment capability is important for at least two related reasons. First, an AWE system is arguably only effective if it helps to improve writing in line with any feedback provided. It is easier to attribute other types of revisions or improvements to the general opportunity to revisit the essay than to any inputs the system provides to students. For argument writing (and our AWE system), then, it is necessary, to be able to identify specific revision behaviors related to evidence use and reasoning. With the RER scheme, we were able to distinguish among revision behaviors. On the whole, predictably undesirable revisions (e.g., deleting relevant evidence) were not correlated with the 'improvement score'.

Second, gaining insight into how students specifically revise evidence use and reasoning can help hone the content of AWE feedback so that it better supports students to make desirable revisions that impact the overall argument quality. From our coding, we learned that students make deletion or modification revisions less frequently; rather they tend to make additions, even if they do not improve the essay. We also learned that repeating existing evidence accounted for about 19 percent of the evidence-use revisions. We could refine our feedback to preempt students from making these undesirable revisions. Or, once automated revision detection is implemented, we could develop a finer-grained set of feedback messages to provide students to guide their second revision (i.e., production of Draft 3).

Finally, our study takes a step towards advancing automated revision detection for AWE by developing a simple machine learning algorithm for classifying relevant evidence. However, it is important to note that the classifier's input is currently based on the gold (i.e., human) alignments of the essay drafts and the gold revision purpose labels (e.g., Evidence). An actual end-to-end system would have lower performance due to the propagation of errors from both alignment and revision purpose classification. In addition, due to the small size of our current corpus, our classification study was simplified to focus on evidence rather than both evidence and reasoning, and to focus on binary rather than 5-way classification. Although our algorithm is thus limited to predicting only relevant evidence, the classifier nonetheless outperforms the baseline given little training data.

8 Conclusion and Future Work

We developed the RER scheme as a step towards advancing automated revision detection capabilities of students' argument writing, which is critical to supporting students' writing development in AWE systems. We demonstrated that reliable manual annotation can be achieved and that the RER scheme correlates in largely expected ways with a holistic assessment of the extent to which revisions address the feedback provided. We conclude that this scheme has promise in guiding the development of an automated revision classification tool.

Although the RER scheme was developed with a specific corpus and writing assignment, we believe some of the categories (e.g., reasoning linked to claim and evidence) can easily be adapted to data we have from other revision tasks. With more data, we also plan to improve the current classification method with state-of-the-art machine learning models, and extend the classification for all categories.

Acknowledgments

The research reported here was supported, in whole or in part, by the Institute of Education Sciences, U.S. Department of Education, through Grant R305A160245 to the University of Pittsburgh. The opinions expressed are those of the authors and do not represent the views of the Institute or the U.S. Department of Education.

References

Tazin Afrin and Diane Litman. 2018. Annotation and classification of sentence-level revision improvement. In *Proceedings of the Thirteenth Workshop on Innovative Use of NLP for Building Educational Applications*, pages 240–246, New Orleans, Louisiana.

Amit Bronner and Christof Monz. 2012. User edits classification using document revision histories.

In *Proceedings of the 13th Conference of the European Chapter of the Association for Computational Linguistics*, EACL '12, pages 356–366, Avignon, France. Association for Computational Linguistics.

Johannes Daxenberger and Iryna Gurevych. 2013. Automatically classifying edit categories in wikipedia revisions. In *Proceedings of the 2013 Conference on Empirical Methods in Natural Language Processing*, EMNLP '13, pages 578–589, Seattle, Washington, USA. Association for Computational Linguistics.

Susan De La Paz, Ralph Ferretti, Daniel Wissinger, Laura Yee, and Charles MacArthur. 2012. Adolescents' disciplinary use of evidence, argumentative strategies, and organizational structure in writing about historical controversies. *Written Communication*, 29(4):412–454.

Lester Faigley and Stephen Witte. 1981. Analyzing revision. *College Composition and Communication*, 32(4):400–414.

Charles MacArthur, Steve Graham, and Karen Harris. 2004. *Insights from Instructional Research on Revision with Struggling Writers*, pages 125–137. Springer.

Charles A MacArthur. 2018. Evaluation and revision. *Best practices in writing instruction*, 287.

Aurélien Max and Guillaume Wisniewski. 2010. Mining naturally-occurring corrections and paraphrases from Wikipedia's revision history. In *Proceedings of the Seventh International Conference on Language Resources and Evaluation (LREC'10)*, Valletta, Malta. European Language Resources Association (ELRA).

Mary McHugh. 2012. Interrater reliability: The kappa statistic. *Biochem Med (Zagreb)*, 22:276–82.

Catherine L O'Hallaron. 2014. Supporting fifth-grade ells' argumentative writing development. *Written Communication*, 31(3):304–331.

Genevieve Patthey-Chavez, Lindsay Clare Matsumura, and Rosa Valdés. 2004. Investigating the process approach to writing instruction in urban middle schools. *Journal of Adolescent and Adult Literacy*, 47:462–477.

Jeffrey Pennington, Richard Socher, and Christopher D. Manning. 2014. Glove: Global vectors for word representation. In *Empirical Methods in Natural Language Processing (EMNLP)*, pages 1532–1543.

Rod D Roscoe, Erica L Snow, Laura K Allen, and Danielle S McNamara. 2015. Automated detection of essay revising patterns: Applications for intelligent feedback in a writing tutor. *Technology, Instruction, Cognition and Learning*, 10(1):59–79.

Chenhao Tan and Lillian Lee. 2014. A corpus of sentence-level revisions in academic writing: A step towards understanding statement strength in communication. In *Proceedings of the 52nd Annual Meeting of the Association for Computational Linguistics*, volume 2: Short Papers, pages 403–408, Baltimore, MD, USA.

Elaine Lin Wang, Lindsay Clare Matsumura, and Richard Correnti. 2018. Student writing accepted as high-quality responses to analytic text-based writing tasks. *The Elementary School Journal*, 118:357–383.

Elaine Lin Wang, Lindsay Clare Matsumura, Richard Correnti, Diane Litman, Haoran Zhang, Emily Howe, Ahmed Magooda, and Rafael Quintana. 2020. erevis(ing): Students' revision of text evidence use in an automated writing evaluation system. *Assessing Writing*, 44:100449.

Fan Zhang, Homa Hashemi, Rebecca Hwa, and Diane Litman. 2017. A corpus of annotated revisions for studying argumentative writing. In *Proceedings of the 55th Annual Meeting of the Association for Computational Linguistics (Volume 1: Long Papers)*, pages 1568–1578. Association for Computational Linguistics.

Fan Zhang and Diane Litman. 2015. Annotation and classification of argumentative writing revisions. In *Proceedings of the 10th Workshop on Innovative Use of NLP for Building Educational Applications*, pages 133–143, Denver, Colorado. Association for Computational Linguistics.

Haoran Zhang, Ahmed Magooda, Diane Litman, Richard Correnti, Elaine Lin Wang, Lindsay Clare Matsumura, Emily Howe, and Rafael Quintana. 2019. erevise: Using natural language processing to provide formative feedback on text evidence usage in student writing. In *Proceedings of the AAAI Conference on Artificial Intelligence*, volume 33, pages 9619–9625.

Zhe Victor Zhang. 2020. Engaging with automated writing evaluation (AWE) feedback on l2 writing: Student perceptions and revisions. *Assessing Writing*, 43:100439.

Can Neural Networks Automatically Score Essay Traits?

Sandeep Mathias and **Pushpak Bhattacharyya**
Center for Indian Language Technology
Department of Computer Science and Engineering
Indian Institute of Technology, Bombay
{sam,pb}@cse.iitb.ac.in

Abstract

Essay traits are attributes of an essay that can help explain how well written (or badly written) the essay is. Examples of traits include Content, Organization, Language, Sentence Fluency, Word Choice, *etc.* A lot of research in the last decade has dealt with automatic holistic essay scoring - where a machine rates an essay and gives a score for the essay. However, writers need feedback, especially if they want to improve their writing - which is why trait-scoring is important. In this paper, we show how a deep-learning based system can outperform feature-based machine learning systems, as well as a string kernel system in scoring essay traits.

1 Introduction

An **essay** is a piece of text that is written in response to a topic, called a prompt. Writing a good essay is a very useful skill. However, evaluating the essay consumes a lot of time and resources. Hence, in 1966, Ellis Page proposed a method of evaluation of essays by computers (Page, 1966). The aim of automatic essay grading (AEG) is to have machines, rather than humans, score the text.

An AEG system is a software that takes an essay as input and returns a score as output. That score could either be an overall score for the essay, or a trait-specific score, based on essay traits like content, organization, style, etc. To the best of our knowledge, most of the systems today use feature engineering and ordinal classification / regression to score essay traits.

From the late 1990s / early 2000s onwards, there were many commercial systems that used automatic essay grading. Shermis and Burstein (2013) cover a number of systems that are used commercially, such as E-Rater (Attali and Burstein, 2006), Intelligent Essay Assessor (Landauer, 2003), Lightside (Mayfield and Rosé, 2013), etc.

In 2012, Kaggle conducted a competition called the Automatic Student Assessment Prize (ASAP), which had 2 parts - the first was essay scoring, and the second was short-answer scoring. The release of the ASAP AEG dataset[1] led to a large number of papers on automatic essay grading using a number of different techniques, from machine learning to deep learning. Section 3 lists the different work in automatic essay grading.

In addition to the Kaggle dataset, another dataset - the International Corpus of Learner's English (ICLE) - is also used in some trait-specific essay grading papers (Granger et al., 2009). Our work, though, makes use of only the ASAP dataset, and the trait specific scores provided by Mathias and Bhattacharyya (2018a) for that dataset.

The rest of the paper is organized as follows. In Section 2, we give the motivation for our work. In Section 3, we describe related work done for trait-specific automatic essay grading. In Section 4, we describe the Dataset. In Section 5, we describe the experiments, such as the baseline machine learning systems, the string kernel and super word embeddings, the Neural Network system, *etc.* We report the results and analyze them in Section 6, and conclude our paper and describe future work in Section 7.

2 Motivation

Most of the work dealing with automatic essay grading either deals with providing an overall score to the essay, but often doesn't provide any more feedback to the **essay's writer** (Carlile et al., 2018).

One way to resolve this is by using trait-specific scoring, where we either do feature engineering or construct a neural network, for individual traits.

[1]The dataset can be downloaded from https://www.kaggle.com/c/asap-aes/data

Proceedings of the 15th Workshop on Innovative Use of NLP for Building Educational Applications, pages 85–91
July 10, 2020. ©2020 Association for Computational Linguistics

Prompt ID	Trait Scores Range	Word Count	No. of Traits	No. of Essays	Essay Type
Prompt 1	1-6	350	5	1783	Argumentative / Persuasive
Prompt 2	1-6	350	5	1800	Argumentative / Persuasive
Prompt 3	0-3	100	4	1726	Source-Dependent Response
Prompt 4	0-3	100	4	1772	Source-Dependent Response
Prompt 5	0-4	125	4	1805	Source-Dependent Response
Prompt 6	0-4	150	4	1800	Source-Dependent Response
Prompt 7	0-6	300	4	1569	Narrative / Descriptive
Prompt 8	0-12	600	6	723	Narrative / Descriptive

Table 1: Properties of the dataset we used in our experiments.

However, coming up with different systems for measuring different traits is often going to be a challenge, especially if someone decides to come up with a new trait to score. Our work involves showing how we can take existing general-purpose systems, and use them to score traits in essays.

In our paper, we demonstrate that a neural network, built for scoring essays holistically, performs reasonably well for scoring essay traits too. We compare it with a task-independent machine learning system using task independent features (Mathias and Bhattacharyya, 2018a), as well as a state-of-the-art string kernel system (Cozma et al., 2018) and report statistically significant results when we use the attention based neural network (Dong et al., 2017).

3 Related Work

In this section, we describe related work in the area of automatic essay grading.

3.1 Holistic Essay Grading

Holistic essay grading is assigning an overall score for an essay. Ever since the release of Kaggle's Automatic Student Assessment Prize's (ASAP) Automatic Essay Grading (AEG) dataset in 2012, there has been a lot of work on holistic essay grading. Initial approaches, such as those of Phandi et al. (2015) and Zesch et al. (2015) made use of machine learning techniques in scoring the essays. A number of other works used various deep learning approaches, such as Long Short Term Memory (LSTM) Networks (Taghipour and Ng, 2016; Tay et al., 2018) and Convolutional Neural Networks (CNN) (Dong and Zhang, 2016; Dong et al., 2017). The current State-of-the-Art in holistic essay grading makes use of word embedding clusters, called super word embeddings, and string kernels (Cozma et al., 2018).

3.2 Trait-specific Essay Grading

Over the years, there has been a fair amount of work done in trait-specific essay grading, in essay traits such as organization (Persing et al., 2010; Taghipour, 2017), coherence (Somasundaran et al., 2014), thesis clarity (Persing and Ng, 2013; Ke et al., 2019), prompt adherence (Persing and Ng, 2014), argument strength (Persing and Ng, 2015; Taghipour, 2017; Carlile et al., 2018), stance (Persing and Ng, 2016), style (Mathias and Bhattacharyya, 2018b), and narrative quality (Somasundaran et al., 2018). Most of these works use feature engineering with classifiers to score the essay traits.

All the above mentioned works describe systems for scoring different traits *individually*. In our paper, we compare three approaches to score essay traits, which are trait agnostic. The first uses a set of task-independent features as described by Zesch et al. (2015) and Mathias and Bhattacharyya (2018a). The second uses a string kernel-base approach as well as super word embeddings as described by Cozma et al. (2018). The third is a deep learning attention based neural network described by Dong et al. (2017). Our work is also, to the best of our knowledge, the first work that uses *the same* neural network architecture to automatically score essay traits.

4 Dataset

The dataset we use is the ASAP AEG dataset. The original ASAP AEG dataset only has trait scores for prompts 7 & 8. Mathias and Bhattacharyya (2018a) provide the trait scores for the remaining prompts [2]. Tables 1 and 2 describe the different essay sets and the traits for each essay set respectively.

---

[2] The dataset and scores can be downloaded from `http://www.cfilt.iitb.ac.in/~egdata/`.

Essay Set	List of Essay Traits
Prompt 1	Content, Organization, Word Choice, Sentence Fluency, & Conventions
Prompt 2	Content, Organization, Word Choice, Sentence Fluency, & Conventions
Prompt 3	Content, Prompt Adherence, Language, & Narrativity
Prompt 4	Content, Prompt Adherence, Language, & Narrativity
Prompt 5	Content, Prompt Adherence, Language, & Narrativity
Prompt 6	Content, Prompt Adherence, Language, & Narrativity
Prompt 7	Content, Organization, Style, & Conventions
Prompt 8	Content, Organization, Voice, Word Choice, Sentence Fluency & Conventions

Table 2: Traits that are present in each prompt in our dataset. The trait scores are taken from the original ASAP dataset, as well as from ASAP++ (Mathias and Bhattacharyya, 2018a).

5   Experiments

We use the following systems for our experiments:

1. **Feature-Engineering System.** This is a machine-learning system described by Mathias and Bhattacharyya (2018a).

2. **String Kernels and Superword Embeddings.** This is a state-of-the-art system on holistic essay grading developed by Cozma et al. (2018) using string kernels and superword embeddings.

3. **Attention-based Neural Network.** This is a system for holistic automatic essay grading described by Dong et al. (2017), that we adapt for trait-specific essay grading.

5.1   Baseline Feature-Engineering System

The baseline system we use is the one described by Mathias and Bhattacharyya (2018a). Their system used a Random Forest classifier to score the essay traits. The features that they used are length based features (word count, sentence count, sentence length, word length), punctuation features (counts of commas, apostrophes, quotations, etc.), syntax features (parse tree depth, number of clauses (denoted by $SBAR$ in the parse tree), *etc.*), sytlistic features (formality, type-token ratio, etc.), cohesion features (discourse connectives, entity grid (Barzilay and Lapata, 2008)), etc.

5.2   String Kernels and Superword Embeddings

Cozma et al. (2018) showed that using string kernels and a bag of super word embeddings drastically improved on the state-of-the-art for essay grading.

5.2.1   String Kernels

A string kernel is a similarity function that operates on a pair of strings a and b. The string kernel used is the histogram intersection string kernel ($HISK(a, b)$) that is given by the formula:

$$HISK(a, b) = \sum min(\#_x(a), \#_x(b)),$$

where $HISK(a, b)$ is the histogram intersection string kernel between two strings a and b, and $\#_x(a)$ and $\#_x(b)$ is the number of occurrences of the substring x in the strings a and b.

The string kernel is then normalized as follows:

$$\hat{k}(i, j) = \frac{k(i,j)}{\sqrt{k(i,i) \times k(j,j)}},$$

where $\hat{k}(i, j)$ is the normalized value of the string kernel $k(i, j)$ between the strings i and j.

5.2.2   Super Word Embeddings

A super word embedding is a word embedding created by making a cluster of word embeddings (Cozma et al., 2018). The clusters are created using the k means algorithm, with $k = 500$. For each essay, we use the count of words in each cluster as features.

5.3   Attention-based Neural Network

Figure 1 describes the architecture of Dong et al. (2017)'s neural network system. An essay is taken as input and the network outputs the grade for a particular trait. The essay is first split into sentences. For each sentence, we get the embeddings from the **word embedding** layer. The **4000 most frequent words** are used as the vocabulary, with all the other words mapped to a special unknown token.

This sequence of words is given as input to a 1-d CNN layer. The output from the CNN layer is pooled using an attention layer, which gets a word-level representation for every sentence in the essay. This is then sent through a sentence-level LSTM

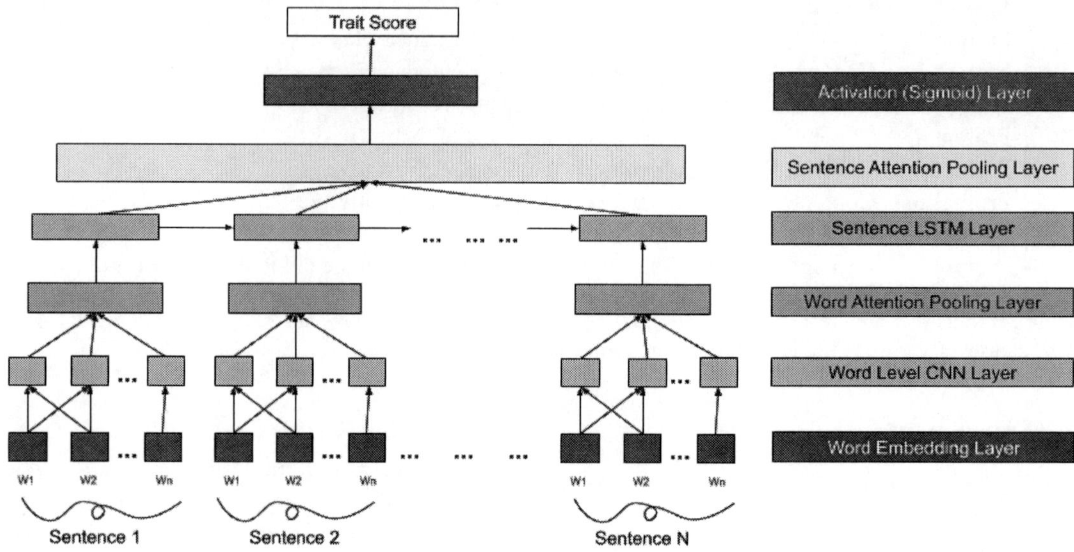

Figure 1: Architecture of Dong et al. (2017) neural network system

layer for getting a sentence-level representation of the essay.

We send the sentence-level representation of the essay through a sentence-level attention pooling layer, to get the representation for the essay. The essay representation is then sent through a Dense layer to score the essay trait. As the scores were converted to the range of $[0, 1]$, we use the **sigmoid activation function** in the activation layer, minimizing the **mean squared error loss** To evaluate the system, we convert the trait scores back to the original score range.

We use the **50 dimension** GloVe pre-trained word embeddings (Pennington et al., 2014). We run the experiments over a **batch size of 100**, for **100 epochs**, and set the learning rate as **0.001**, and a dropout rate of **0.5**. The Word-level CNN layer has a **kernel size of 5**, with **100 filters**. The Sentence-level LSTM layer and modeling layer both have **100 hidden units**. We use the **RMSProp Optimizer** (Dauphin et al., 2015) with a **momentum of 0.9**.

5.4 Experimental Setup

In this section, we describe different experiments.

5.4.1 Evaluation Metric

We choose to use Cohen's Kappa with quadratic weights (Cohen, 1968) - i.e. Quadratic Weighted Kappa (QWK) - as the evaluation metric. We use this as the evaluation metric because of the follow-

ing reasons. Unlike accuracy and F-Score, Kappa takes into account if the classification happened by chance. Secondly, the accuracy and F-score metrics do not consider the fact that classes here are ordered. Thirdly, using weights allows Kappa to consider ordering among the classes. Lastly, by using quadratic weights, we reward matches and punish mismatches more than linear weights. Hence, we use QWK as the evaluation metric, rather than accuracy and F-score.

5.4.2 Evaluation Method

We evaluate the systems using **five-fold cross-validation**, with **60% training data**, **20% development data** and **20% testing data** for each fold. The folds that we use are the same as those used by Taghipour and Ng (2016).

6 Results and Analysis

Table 3 gives the results of the experiments using the different classification systems. In each cell, we compare the results of each of the 3 systems for a given trait and prompt. The bold value in each cell corresponds to the system giving the best value out of all the 3 systems. Traits which are not applicable to different prompts are marked with a "—".

We see that the attention-based neural network system is able to outperform both, the baseline system of Mathias and Bhattacharyya (2018a) and the histogram intersection string kernel system of

Prompt ID	System	Cont.	Org.	WC	SF	Conv.	PA	Lang.	Narr.	Style	Voice
Prompt 1	LREC 2018	0.628	0.606	0.618	0.594	0.588	—	—	—	—	—
	ACL 2018	0.686	0.637	0.659	0.639	0.620	—	—	—	—	—
	CoNLL 2017	**0.703**	**0.664**	**0.675**	**0.648**	**0.638**	—	—	—	—	—
Prompt 2	LREC 2018	0.563	0.551	0.531	0.495	0.486	—	—	—	—	—
	ACL 2018	0.600	0.570	0.583	0.544	0.530	—	—	—	—	—
	CoNLL 2017	**0.617**	**0.623**	**0.630**	**0.603**	**0.601**	—	—	—	—	—
Prompt 3	LREC 2018	0.586	—	—	—	—	0.575	0.534	0.594	—	—
	ACL 2018	0.659	—	—	—	—	0.658	0.590	0.645	—	—
	CoNLL 2017	**0.673**	—	—	—	—	**0.683**	**0.612**	**0.684**	—	—
Prompt 4	LREC 2018	0.646	—	—	—	—	0.636	0.577	0.641	—	—
	ACL 2018	0.702	—	—	—	—	0.702	0.571	0.687	—	—
	CoNLL 2017	**0.751**	—	—	—	—	**0.738**	**0.645**	**0.722**	—	—
Prompt 5	LREC 2018	0.667	—	—	—	—	0.639	0.618	0.647	—	—
	ACL 2018	0.713	—	—	—	—	0.700	0.620	0.635	—	—
	CoNLL 2017	**0.738**	—	—	—	—	**0.719**	**0.638**	**0.700**	—	—
Prompt 6	LREC 2018	0.579	—	—	—	—	0.581	0.555	0.592	—	—
	ACL 2018	0.759	—	—	—	—	0.711	0.624	0.635	—	—
	CoNLL 2017	**0.820**	—	—	—	—	**0.783**	**0.664**	**0.690**	—	—
Prompt 7	LREC 2018	0.495	0.528	—	—	0.533	—	—	—	0.577	—
	ACL 2018	0.737	0.659	—	—	0.504	—	—	—	0.609	—
	CoNLL 2017	**0.771**	**0.676**	—	—	**0.621**	—	—	—	**0.659**	—
Prompt 8	LREC 2018	0.510	0.571	0.518	0.507	0.431	—	—	—	—	0.507
	ACL 2018	0.573	0.572	0.494	0.477	0.455	—	—	—	—	0.489
	CoNLL 2017	**0.586**	**0.632**	**0.559**	**0.586**	**0.558**	—	—	—	—	**0.544**
Mean QWK	LREC 2018	0.584	0.564	0.556	0.532	0.510	0.608	0.571	0.619	0.577	0.507
	ACL 2018	0.679	0.610	0.579	0.553	0.527	0.693	0.601	0.651	0.609	0.489
	CoNLL 2017	**0.707**	**0.649**	**0.621**	**0.612**	**0.605**	**0.731**	**0.640**	**0.699**	**0.659**	**0.544**

Table 3: Results of each of the systems for scoring essay traits, namely Mathias and Bhattacharyya (2018a) (LREC 2018), Cozma et al. (2018) (ACL 2018) and Dong et al. (2017) (CoNLL 2017). — denote that the particular trait is not there for that particular prompt. The different traits are Content (Cont.), Organization (Org.), Word Choice (WC), Sentence Fluency (SF), Conventions (Conv.), Prompt Adherence (PA), Language (Lang.), Narrativity (Narr.), Style and Voice. **Mean QWK** is the mean QWK predicted for the trait across all essay sets.

Cozma et al. (2018) for all the traits, and across all 8 prompts. We also check if the improvements are statistically significant. We find that the improvements of the neural network system over the baseline system Mathias and Bhattacharyya (2018a) and histogram intersection string kernel system Cozma et al. (2018) to be statistically significant for $p < 0.05$ using the Paired T-Test.

Between the other 2 systems, the String Kernels system performed better than the baseline system in most of the cases. The only prompt in which it did not do so was in Prompt 8 - mainly because of the number of essays being very low and the size of the essay being very high compared to the other prompts.

Among the traits, the easiest to score are the traits of content and prompt adherence (where ever they are applicable) as they yielded the best agreement with the human raters. The hardest of the traits to score was Voice, which yielded the lowest QWK in the only prompt in which it was scored.

7 Conclusion and Future Work

In this paper, we describe a comparison between a feature-engineering system, a string kernel-based system, and an attention-based neural network to score different traits of an essay. We found that the neural network system provided the best results. To the best of our knowledge, this is the first work that describes how neural networks are used, in particular, to score essay traits.

As part of future work, we plan to investigate how to incorporate trait scoring as a means of helping to score essays holistically.

Acknowledgements

We would like to acknowledge the work done by the anonymous reviewers in evaluating our submission.

References

Yigal Attali and Jill Burstein. 2006. Automated essay scoring with e-rater® v. 2. *The Journal of Technology, Learning and Assessment*, 4(3).

Regina Barzilay and Mirella Lapata. 2008. Modeling local coherence: An entity-based approach. *Computational Linguistics*, 34(1):1–34.

Winston Carlile, Nishant Gurrapadi, Zixuan Ke, and Vincent Ng. 2018. Give me more Feedback: Annotating Argument Persuasiveness and Related Attributes in Student Essays. In *Proceedings of the 56th Annual Meeting of the Association for Computational Linguistics (Volume 1: Long Papers)*, pages 621–631. Association for Computational Linguistics.

Jacob Cohen. 1968. Weighted kappa: Nominal scale agreement provision for scaled disagreement or partial credit. *Psychological bulletin*, 70(4):213.

Mădălina Cozma, Andrei Butnaru, and Radu Tudor Ionescu. 2018. Automated essay scoring with string kernels and word embeddings. In *Proceedings of the 56th Annual Meeting of the Association for Computational Linguistics (Volume 2: Short Papers)*, pages 503–509, Melbourne, Australia. Association for Computational Linguistics.

Yann Dauphin, Harm De Vries, and Yoshua Bengio. 2015. Equilibrated adaptive learning rates for non-convex optimization. In *Advances in neural information processing systems*, pages 1504–1512.

Fei Dong and Yue Zhang. 2016. Automatic Features for Essay Scoring – An Empirical Study. In *Proceedings of the 2016 Conference on Empirical Methods in Natural Language Processing*, pages 1072–1077, Austin, Texas. Association for Computational Linguistics.

Fei Dong, Yue Zhang, and Jie Yang. 2017. Attention-based Recurrent Convolutional Neural Network for Automatic Essay Scoring. In *Proceedings of the 21st Conference on Computational Natural Language Learning (CoNLL 2017)*, pages 153–162, Vancouver, Canada. Association for Computational Linguistics.

Sylviane Granger, Estelle Dagneaux, Fanny Meunier, and Magali Paquot. 2009. International Corpus of Learner English.

Zixuan Ke, Hrishikesh Inamdar, Hui Lin, and Vincent Ng. 2019. Give me more feedback II: Annotating thesis strength and related attributes in student essays. In *Proceedings of the 57th Annual Meeting of the Association for Computational Linguistics*, pages 3994–4004, Florence, Italy. Association for Computational Linguistics.

Thomas K Landauer. 2003. Automated scoring and annotation of essays with the intelligent essay assessor. *Automated Essay Scoring: A Cross-disciplinary Perspective*.

Sandeep Mathias and Pushpak Bhattacharyya. 2018a. ASAP++: Enriching the ASAP automated essay grading dataset with essay attribute scores. In *Proceedings of the Eleventh International Conference on Language Resources and Evaluation (LREC-2018)*, Miyazaki, Japan. European Languages Resources Association (ELRA).

Sandeep Mathias and Pushpak Bhattacharyya. 2018b. Thank "Goodness"! A Way to Measure Style in Student Essays. In *Proceedings of the 5th Workshop on Natural Language Processing Techniques for Educational Applications*, pages 35–41. Association for Computational Linguistics.

Elijah Mayfield and Carolyn Penstein Rosé. 2013. LightSIDE: Open source machine learning for text. In *Handbook of Automated Essay Evaluation*, pages 146–157. Routledge.

Ellis B Page. 1966. The imminence of... grading essays by computer. *The Phi Delta Kappan*, 47(5):238–243.

Jeffrey Pennington, Richard Socher, and Christopher Manning. 2014. Glove: Global vectors for word representation. In *Proceedings of the 2014 Conference on Empirical Methods in Natural Language Processing (EMNLP)*, pages 1532–1543, Doha, Qatar. Association for Computational Linguistics.

Isaac Persing, Alan Davis, and Vincent Ng. 2010. Modeling Organization in Student Essays. In *Proceedings of the 2010 Conference on Empirical Methods in Natural Language Processing*, pages 229–239. Association for Computational Linguistics.

Isaac Persing and Vincent Ng. 2013. Modeling Thesis Clarity in Student Essays. In *Proceedings of the 51st Annual Meeting of the Association for Computational Linguistics (Volume 1: Long Papers)*, pages 260–269, Sofia, Bulgaria. Association for Computational Linguistics.

Isaac Persing and Vincent Ng. 2014. Modeling Prompt Adherence in Student Essays. In *Proceedings of the 52nd Annual Meeting of the Association for Computational Linguistics (Volume 1: Long Papers)*, pages 1534–1543, Baltimore, Maryland. Association for Computational Linguistics.

Isaac Persing and Vincent Ng. 2015. Modeling Argument Strength in Student Essays. In *Proceedings of the 53rd Annual Meeting of the Association for Computational Linguistics and the 7th International Joint Conference on Natural Language Processing (Volume 1: Long Papers)*, pages 543–552, Beijing, China. Association for Computational Linguistics.

Isaac Persing and Vincent Ng. 2016. Modeling Stance in Student Essays. In *Proceedings of the 54th Annual Meeting of the Association for Computational Linguistics (Volume 1: Long Papers)*, pages 2174–2184, Berlin, Germany. Association for Computational Linguistics.

Peter Phandi, Kian Ming A. Chai, and Hwee Tou Ng. 2015. Flexible domain adaptation for automated essay scoring using correlated linear regression. In *Proceedings of the 2015 Conference on Empirical Methods in Natural Language Processing*, pages 431–439, Lisbon, Portugal. Association for Computational Linguistics.

Mark D Shermis and Jill Burstein. 2013. *Handbook of Automated Essay Evaluation: Current Applications and New Directions*. Routledge.

Swapna Somasundaran, Jill Burstein, and Martin Chodorow. 2014. Lexical Chaining for Measuring Discourse Coherence Quality in Test-taker Essays. In *Proceedings of COLING 2014, the 25th International Conference on Computational Linguistics: Technical Papers*, pages 950–961. Dublin City University and Association for Computational Linguistics.

Swapna Somasundaran, Michael Flor, Martin Chodorow, Hillary Molloy, Binod Gyawali, and Laura McCulla. 2018. Towards evaluating narrative quality in student writing. *Transactions of the Association for Computational Linguistics*, 6:91–106.

Kaveh Taghipour. 2017. *Robust Trait-Specific Essay Scoring Using Neural Networks and Density Estimators*. Ph.D. thesis, National University of Singapore.

Kaveh Taghipour and Hwee Tou Ng. 2016. A Neural Approach to Automated Essay Scoring. In *Proceedings of the 2016 Conference on Empirical Methods in Natural Language Processing*, pages 1882–1891, Austin, Texas. Association for Computational Linguistics.

Yi Tay, Minh Phan, Luu Anh Tuan, and Siu Cheung Hui. 2018. SkipFlow: Incorporating Neural Coherence Features for End-to-End Automatic Text Scoring. In *Proceedings of the 32nd Annual AAAI Conference on Artificial Intelligence*.

Torsten Zesch, Michael Wojatzki, and Dirk Scholten-Akoun. 2015. Task-independent features for automated essay grading. In *Proceedings of the Tenth Workshop on Innovative Use of NLP for Building Educational Applications*, pages 224–232, Denver, Colorado. Association for Computational Linguistics.

Tracking the Evolution of Written Language Competence in L2 Spanish Learners

Alessio Miaschi[⋆][◇]**, Sam Davidson**[•]**, Dominique Brunato**[◇]**,**
Felice Dell'Orletta[◇]**, Kenji Sagae**[•]**, Claudia H. Sánchez-Gutiérrez**[•]**, Giulia Venturi**[◇]
[⋆]Department of Computer Science, University of Pisa
[◇]ItaliaNLP Lab, Istituto di Linguistica Computazionale "Antonio Zampolli", Pisa
[•]University of California Davis
`alessio.miaschi@phd.unipi.it, {ssdavidson,sagae,chsanchez}@ucdavis.edu,`
`{dominique.brunato,felice.dellorletta,giulia.venturi}@ilc.cnr.it`

Abstract

In this paper we present an NLP-based approach for tracking the evolution of written language competence in L2 Spanish learners using a wide range of linguistic features automatically extracted from students' written productions. Beyond reporting classification results for different scenarios, we explore the connection between the most predictive features and the teaching curriculum, finding that our set of linguistic features often reflects the explicit instruction that students receive during each course.

1   Introduction

In the last few years, research on language acquisition has benefited from the use of Natural Language Processing (NLP) technologies applied to large–scale corpora of authentic texts produced by learners, in both the first and second language context. The empirical evidence acquired from learner corpora, complemented with the increased reliability of linguistic features extracted by computational tools and machine learning approaches, has promoted a better understanding of learners' language properties and how they change across time and increasing proficiency level (Crossley, 2020). A first line of research has focused on providing automatic ways of operationalizing sophisticated metrics of language development to alleviate the laborious manual computation of these metrics by experts (Sagae et al., 2005; Lu, 2009). A second line of research has taken the more challenging step of implementing completely data-driven approaches, which use a variety of linguistic features extracted from texts to automatically assign a learner's language production to a given developmental level (Lubetich and Sagae, 2014).

A great amount of work has been carried out in the field of second language acquisition where the study of L2 writings is seen as a proxy of language ability development (Crossley, 2020). In this respect, much related work is devoted to predicting the degree of second language proficiency according to expert–based evaluation (Crossley and McNamara, 2012) or to modelling the evolution of grammatical structures' competence with respect to predefined grades, such as the Common European Framework of Reference for Languages (CEFRL) (Zilio et al., 2018). Given the difficulty of defining a unique indicator of linguistic complexity in the context of L2 language development, a great variety of features from all linguistic levels have been used as input for supervised classification systems trained on authentic learner data for different L2s. Such is the case e.g. of Hancke and Meurers (2013) and Vajjala and Léo (2014), dealing with L2 German and L2 Estonian, respectively, and of Pilán and Volodina (2018), who also provided a features analysis focused on predictive features extracted from both receptive and productive texts in Swedish L2.

This paper adopts this framework and presents an innovative NLP-based stylometric approach to model writing development in learners of Spanish as a second and Heritage language. Our approach relies on a wide set of linguistically motivated features extracted from students' essays, which have already been shown relevant for a number of tasks related to modelling the 'form' of a text rather than the content. While the majority of previous studies on the evolution of language proficiency in L2 uses cross–sectional data, this study is the first, to our knowledge, using a longitudinal corpus of Spanish L2 essays to model writing development. Interestingly, a similar approach resulted in the successful prediction of the development of writing competence in a L1 acquisition scenario for the Italian language (Richter et al., 2015).

Contributions In this paper: (i) we present, to

Proceedings of the 15th Workshop on Innovative Use of NLP for Building Educational Applications, pages 92–101
July 10, 2020. ©2020 Association for Computational Linguistics

the best of our knowledge, the first data–driven study which uses linguistic features from student data to model the evolution of written language competence in Spanish as a Second Language (SSL); (ii) we show that it is possible to automatically predict the relative order of two essays written by the same student at different course levels using a wide spectrum of linguistic features; (iii) we investigate the importance of linguistic features in predicting language growth at different course levels and whether they reflect the explicit instruction that students receive during each course.

2 Motivation and Approach

Studies of L2 writing have focused on linguistic complexity as an indicator of writing development (Lu, 2011; Ortega, 2003). This construct, however, is still ill-defined, as evidenced by the divergent measures of complexity utilized in different studies. Typical measures of complexity have been the length of the T-unit (Hunt, 1965), the number of subordinate clauses in a text, or type to token ratios, among others. Instead of considering the construct as being multidimensional (Norris and Ortega, 2009; Bulté and Housen, 2012) and, thus, encompassing an array of different features, most studies have selected one or two of these measures and used them as single indicators of complexity (Bulté and Housen, 2014). This has prevented the development of much needed research that associates different steps of linguistic and written development with specific sets of characteristics. This situation has also prevented the formation of an in-depth picture of how those specific aspects develop in relation to the grammatical, lexical or stylistic content taught in classes at different language course levels. This second objective of characterizing writing at different proficiency levels may provide useful insights into how writing samples could be used for placement tests or other assessments to determine which language course is best suited to further develop a student's linguistic skills.

In the concrete case of SSL, the literature indicates that one of the most difficult aspects to master for learners is the language's complex verbal morphology (Blake and Zyzik, 2016; Salaberry, 1999), given that verbal inflections express a complex cluster of person, number, tense, aspect and mood. Therefore, SSL courses tend to propose a step-by-step introduction to these different aspects of verbal morphology, generally following this order: (1) person and number in the present indicative, (2) past tenses (i.e., imperfect vs. preterite vs. pluperfect), and (3) mood (subjunctive vs. indicative). If this typical instructional sequence had to influence students' writing, it would be expected that learners show an increase in the variety of inflections that they are able to use over time. Nonetheless, several studies also indicate that a linguistic feature that has been learned in class may be mastered in exercises that focus on explicit knowledge but take additional time to unfold in tasks that require more implicit knowledge, such as free writing (Ellis and Shintani, 2013). This means that a simple classification of students' proficiency based on the presence or absence of features studied in a particular course may not be accurate, as some students may explicitly know the rules for a specific inflectional distinction but still be unable to use them accurately in writing. Taking lack of use in writing as evidence for lack of explicit knowledge could entail that students be mistakenly invited to enroll in courses where those features that do not show in their writing are unnecessarily explained to them again. A better approach would thus be to know what students are able to do when they are enrolled in different courses and, only then, compare those abilities to see which match, or mismatch, the contents seen in that particular class. By using a large set of linguistic features, it is possible to understand which phenomena change across proficiency levels and whether they are explicitly related to the teaching guidelines.

This study aims at tackling some of the still open methodological issues in the literature on Spanish acquisition by decomposing the problem into two main research questions: *(i)* verify if it is possible to predict the relative order of two essays written by the same student at different course levels using a wide set of linguistic predictors automatically extracted from Spanish L2 written productions; *(ii)* understand which typologies of language phenomena contribute more to the identification of writing skills' evolution and whether such properties reflect the teaching guidelines of the courses.

Following the approach devised in Richter et al. (2015) we addressed the first research question as a classification task: given a pair of essays written by the same student and ordered according to the course level (d_1, d_2), we classify whether $C(d_2) > C(d_1)$, where $C(d_1)$ and $C(d_2)$ correspond respectively to the course levels during

Course Level	Essays	Tokens	Students
Beginner (SPA 1-3)	2,058	485,435	1,130
Intermediate (SPA 21-22)	445	120,102	244
Composition (SPA 23-24)	536	151,197	287
Heritage (SPA 31-33)	459	130,684	244
Total	3,498	887,418	1,905[1]

Table 1: Summary of corpus composition.

Terms Enrolled	Students	Essays	Tokens
2	267	984	290,399
3	111	612	179,306
4	32	242	74,956
5	5	48	13,977

Table 2: Longitudinal data summary.

which the student wrote d_1 and d_2. Specifically, we model the problem as a binary classification task, training a Linear Support Vector Machine (LinearSVM) to predict the relative order of two essays written by the same student using a wide range of linguistic predictors automatically extracted from the POS tagged and dependency parsed essays. We rely on LinearSVM rather than more powerful learning algorithms, such as Neural Language Models, in order to obtain meaningful explanations when the classifier outputs its predictions to anchor the observed patterns of language development to explicit linguistic evidence.

We further extracted and ranked the feature weights assigned by the linear model in order to understand which typology of linguistic features contributes more to the classification task at different course levels. The assumption is that the higher the weight associated with a specific feature, the greater its importance in solving the classification task and, consequently, in modeling the student's written language evolution.

3　Corpus and Features

3.1　The COWS-L2H Corpus

We analyzed development of student writing from the *Corpus of Written Spanish of L2 and Heritage Speakers*, or COWS-L2H (Davidson et al., 2020). This corpus consists of 3,498 short essays written by students enrolled in one of ten lower-division Spanish courses at a single American university. Concretely, these courses are organized as follows: Spanish (SPA) 1, 2, and 3 are the introductory

courses, which exposes students to the basic morphosyntax of Spanish; SPA 21 and 22 are the intermediate courses, focused on the development of reading and listening skills with a strong emphasis on lexical development; SPA 23 and 24 are two courses that specifically aim at improving writing skills with an emphasis on academic writing in Spanish; SPA 31, 32, and 33 are the Heritage speakers courses. These courses are grouped into four categories based on student proficiency and experience, as shown in Table 1.

Student compositions in the corpus are written in response to one of four writing prompts, which are changed periodically. During each period (an academic quarter, which consists of ten weeks of instruction) of data collection, students are asked to submit two compositions, approximately one month apart, in response to targeted writing prompts. These composition themes are designed to be relatively broad, to allow for a wide degree of creative liberty and open-ended interpretation by the writer. Prompts are intended to be accessible to writers at all levels of proficiency. Additionally, the use of broad themes invites the use of a variety of verb tenses and vocabulary. The use of specific writing prompts allows us to control for known topic effects on syntactic complexity among L2 learners (Yang et al., 2015).

The essays in the corpus were submitted by 1,370 unique student participants, with 415 student participants having submitted compositions in two or more academic terms (for a maximum of eight writing samples from each student). Thus, the corpus contains both cross-sectional and longitudinal data on the development of student writing in the context of a university language program. The distribution of the essays across the levels is uneven due to the distribution of student enrollment in Spanish courses. Because more students enroll in beginning Spanish courses than in advanced levels, a larger number of essays submitted to the corpus come from these beginner-level courses. The L2 Spanish learners are primarily L1 speakers of English, but due to the diverse student population of the source university, a large number are L1 speakers of other languages such as Mandarin. However, as English is the university's language of instruction, all students are either L1 or fluent L2 speakers of English. Those students enrolled in the Heritage courses (SPA 31 - 33) are, for the most part, L1 speakers of Spanish, having learned Spanish from

---

[1]This number differs from the 1,370 unique participants, as students who participated in more than one category are represented twice.

a young age in the home, and L2 speakers of English; these Heritage learners have had little-to-no academic instruction in Spanish.

We focused our study on the longitudinal data in the COWS-L2H corpus. We were thus able to model the chronological development of L2 Spanish writing by monitoring how the writing quality of an individual student's compositions increase with time. Student participation is summarized in Table 2.

3.2 Linguistic Features

The set of linguistic features considered as predictors of L2 written competence evolution is based on those described in Brunato et al. (2020). It includes a wide range of text properties, from raw text features, to lexical, morpho-syntactic and syntactic properties, which were extracted from different levels of linguistic annotation. For this purpose, the COWS-L2H Corpus was automatically parsed using UDPipe (Straka et al., 2016) trained on the Spanish Universal Dependency Treebank (GSD section), version 2.5. We rely on these features since it has been shown that they have a high predictive power for several tasks all aimed at modelling the linguistic *form* of documents. This is the case for example of the automatic readability assessment task (Dell'Orletta et al., 2011a), of the automatic classification of the textual genre of documents (Cimino et al., 2017), or also of the automatic identification of the L1 of a writer based on his/her language production in a L2 (Cimino et al., 2018). Interestingly, for all mentioned tasks the set of linguistic features plays a very important role in the classification not only of a whole document but also of each single sentence. This is the reason why, as reported in the following sections, we modelled the prediction of the development of writing skills both as document and sentence classification tasks.

Although we used a state–of–the art pipeline, it is well-acknowledged that the accuracy of statistical parsers decreases when tested against texts of a different typology from that used in training (Gildea, 2001). In this respect, learners' data are particularly challenging for general–purpose text analysis tools since they can exhibit deviation from correct and standard language; for instance, missing or anomalous use of punctuation (especially in 1st grade prompts) already impacts on the coarsest levels of text processing, i.e. sentence splitting, and thus may affect all subsequent levels of annotation.

Nevertheless, if we can expect that the predicted value of a given feature might be different from the real one (especially for features extracted from more complex levels of annotation such as syntax), we can also assume that the distributions of errors will be almost similar, at least when parsing texts of the same domain. Note also that the reliability of features checked against automatically annotated data was also empirically shown by Dell'Orletta et al. (2011b), who compared morpho-syntactic and syntactic features extracted from a gold (i.e. manually annotated) and an automatically annotated corpus of the same domain (i.e. biomedical language), showing that results are highly comparable.

As shown in Table 3, the considered features capture linguistic phenomena ranging from the average length of document, sentences and words, to morpho-syntactic information such as parts of speech (POS) distribution and fine–grained features about the inflectional properties of verbs. More complex phenomena are derived from syntactic annotation and model global and local properties of parsed tree structure, with a focus on subtrees of verbal heads, the order of subjects and objects with respect to the verb, the distribution of Universal Dependencies (UD) syntactic relations and features referring to the use of subordination.

Since it is acknowledged that lexical proficiency plays an important role in predicting L2 writing development (Crossley and McNamara, 2012), we also decided to add a small subset of features that model this property in terms of word frequency. Specifically, we considered the average class frequency of all word forms and lemmas in the essays (*Words Frequency Class*), where the class frequency for each word form/lemma was computed exploiting the Spanish Wikipedia (dump of March 2020) using the following measures: $C_{cw} = \lfloor \log_2 \frac{freq(MFW)}{freq(CW)} \rfloor$, $C_{cl} = \lfloor \log_2 \frac{freq(MFL)}{freq(CL)} \rfloor$, where *MFW* and *MFL* are the most frequent word form/lemma in the corpus and *CW* and *CL* are the considered ones.

A first overview of how and to what extent all these features vary across the documents of the COWS-L2H Corpus is provided in Table 4. Essays written by students in the first course levels are longer in terms of number of sentences but they contain shorter sentences compared with those written in the more advanced courses. As concerns the distribution of POS, essays written in the

Level of Annotation	Linguistic Feature	Label
Raw Text	Sentence Length	tokens_per_sent
	Word Length	char_per_tok
	Document Length	n_sentences
	Type/Token Ratio for words and lemmas	ttr_form, ttr_lemma
POS tagging	Distribution of UD and language–specific POS	upos_*, xpos_*
	Lexical density	lexical_density
	Inflectional morphology of lexical verbs and auxiliaries	verbs_*, aux_*
Dependency Parsing	Depth of the whole syntactic tree	parse_depth
	Average length of dependency links and of the longest link	links_len, max_links_len
	Average length of prepositional chains and distribution by depth	prepositional_chain_len, prep_dist_*
	Clause length (n. tokens/verbal heads)	token_per_clause
	Order of subject and object	subj_pre, subj_post, obj_pre, obj_post
	Verb arity and distribution of verbs by arity	verb_edges, verb_edges_*
	Distribution of verbal heads per sentence	verbal_head_sent
	Distribution of verbal roots	verbal_root_perc
	Distribution of dependency relations	dep_dist_*
	Distribution of subordinate and principal clauses	principal_proposition_dist, subord_dist
	Average length of subordination chains and distribution by depth	subord_chain_len, subord_*
	Relative order of subordinate clauses	subord_post, subord_prep

Table 3: Linguistic features according to different levels of annotation.

first years show a lower percentage of e.g. adpositions (*upos_ADP*) and subordinate conjunctions (*upos_SCONJ*) typically contained in longer and well-articulated sentences, while the use of main content words (e.g. *upos_NOUN*, *upos_VERB*) is almost comparable across years. The variation affecting morphosyntactic categories is reflected by the lexical density value, i.e. the ratio between content words over the total number of words, which is slightly higher in beginner essays. If we focus on differences concerning verbal morphology, a linguistic property particularly relevant in the development of Spanish curriculum, we can see how the use of more complex verb forms increases across course levels. Essays of the introductory courses contain a lower percentage of verbs in the past (*verbs_tense_Past*) and imperfect tenses (*verbs_tense_Imp*) (out of the total number of verb tenses) as well as a lower percentage of auxiliary verbs (*aux_**) typically used in more complex verb forms, such as copulative verbs or periphrastic moods and tenses. Interestingly, features related to verb inflectional morphology have the highest standard deviation, suggesting a quite wide variability among learners. A similar trend towards the acquisition of more complex verb structures can also be inferred by considering features extracted from the syntactic level of annotation: essays of the intermediate courses contain for example sentences with a higher average number of dependents of verbs (*verb_edges*) and in particular of verbs with a complex argument structures of 4 dependents (*verb_edges_4*).

As long as Spanish learners start mastering the second language, linguistic properties related to the construction of more complex sentences increase.

This is for example the case of the depth of sentence tree (*parse_depth*) and of the length of syntactic relations (*max_links_len*) as well as of features concerning the use of subordination.

4 Experiments

We train a LinearSVM that takes as input pairs of essays written by the same students according to all the possible pairs of course levels (e.g. SPA 1 - SPA 2, SPA 2 - SPA 3, etc.). Specifically, we extract for each pair the linguistic features corresponding to the first and second essays and the difference between them. We standardize the input features by scaling each component in the range $[0, 1]$. To test the actual efficiency of the model, we perform the experiments with a 5-cross validation using different students during the training and testing phases. In order to provide our system with negative samples, we expand our datasets by adding reversed samples.

Since the students were asked to write essays responding to different prompts, we devise two set of experiments, pairing all the essays written by the same students that have: (i) the same prompt; (ii) both same and different prompts. Also, because of the small number of training samples for certain pairs of course levels we also decide to perform the experiments on a sentence-level, extracting the linguistic features for each sentence in the longitudinal subset of the COWS-L2H corpus and pairing them on the basis of the previously defined criteria. In order to obtain reliable results both on the document and sentence configurations, we consider only datasets at different pairs of course levels that contain at least 50 and 20 samples (including negative pairs) respectively. All the classification

Features	SPA 1	SPA 2	SPA 3	SPA 21	SPA 22	SPA 23	SPA 24	SPA 31	SPA 32	SPA 33
Raw Text Properties										
char_per_tok	4.3 ±.27	4.4 ±.27	4.42 ±.26	4.42 ±.26	4.43 ±.25	4.46 ±.23	4.41 ±.22	4.42 ±.23	4.42 ±.28	4.38 ±.3
n_sentences	20.0 ±7.0	24.01 ±7.15	23.57 ±6.87	20.8 ±5.99	20.17 ±5.15	19.54 ±6.33	17.92 ±5.44	16.06 ±4.05	16.31 ±3.78	15.46 ±3.63
tokens_per_sent	10.7 ±3.43	13.16 ±3.52	13.74 ±3.7	15.71 ±3.95	16.43 ±3.59	17.11 ±3.49	19.01 ±4.27	19.95 ±4.16	20.07 ±3.48	20.94 ±4.04
Morphosyntactic information										
lexical_density	.51 ±.05	.5 ±.04	.5 ±.04	.49 ±.03	.48 ±.04	.48 ±.03	.47 ±.03	.48 ±.04	.47 ±.04	.47 ±.04
upos_ADJ	.07 ±.03	.06 ±.02	.06 ±.02	.06 ±.02	.05 ±.02	.05 ±.02	.05 ±.02	.05 ±.02	.05 ±.02	.05 ±.02
upos_ADP	.09 ±.04	.1 ±.03	.11 ±.03	.11 ±.02	.11 ±.02	.12 ±.02	.12 ±.02	.13 ±.03	.12 ±.02	.13 ±.02
upos_NOUN	.16 ±.04	.16 ±.03	.16 ±.03	.16 ±.03	.16 ±.03	.17 ±.02	.17 ±.03	.17 ±.02	.16 ±.03	.16 ±.03
upos_PRON	.07 ±.04	.07 ±.03	.07 ±.03	.07 ±.03	.07 ±.03	.07 ±.03	.07 ±.03	.07 ±.03	.08 ±.04	.08 ±.04
upos_PUNCT	.14 ±.03	.13 ±.03	.12 ±.03	.12 ±.03	.11 ±.03	.11 ±.03	.11 ±.03	.09 ±.02	.09 ±.02	.09 ±.02
upos_SCONJ	.01 ±.01	.02 ±.01	.03 ±.01	.03 ±.02	.04 ±.02	.04 ±.01	.04 ±.02	.04 ±.02	.05 ±.02	.05 ±.02
upos_VERB	.12 ±.04	.12 ±.03	.12 ±.03	.12 ±.02	.12 ±.02	.12 ±.02	.12 ±.02	.13 ±.02	.13 ±.02	.13 ±.03
Inflectional morphology										
aux_mood_Cnd	.02 ±.09	.03 ±.09	.04 ±.12	.03 ±.07	.06 ±.11	.05 ±.11	.04 ±.08	.05 ±.09	.06 ±.12	.04 ±.11
aux_mood_Ind	.97 ±.14	.96 ±.12	.92 ±.15	.94 ±.14	.91 ±.13	.92 ±.14	.94 ±.1	.91 ±.16	.91 ±.12	.93 ±.12
aux_mood_Sub	.01 ±.04	.01 ±.04	.03 ±.07	.02 ±.05	.03 ±.05	.02 ±.08	.03 ±.06	.03 ±.06	.03 ±.06	.03 ±.05
aux_tense_Imp	.05 ±.16	.16 ±.25	.21 ±.26	.21 ±.25	.24 ±.25	.24 ±.26	.22 ±.24	.23 ±.28	.2 ±.27	.24 ±.29
aux_tense_Past	.02 ±.09	.1 ±.15	.09 ±.15	.12 ±.16	.12 ±.14	.11 ±.15	.12 ±.16	.11 ±.16	.12 ±.17	.11 ±.13
aux_tense_Pres	.92 ±.21	.73 ±.32	.69 ±.33	.65 ±.32	.63 ±.3	.65 ±.32	.66 ±.32	.63 ±.34	.66 ±.34	.63 ±.33
verbs_tense_Imp	.02 ±.06	.08 ±.12	.11 ±.13	.13 ±.13	.16 ±.14	.14 ±.15	.13 ±.13	.17 ±.15	.15 ±.15	.14 ±.14
verbs_tense_Past	.11 ±.19	.28 ±.23	.28 ±.22	.3 ±.2	.35 ±.22	.3 ±.22	.31 ±.19	.31 ±.21	.28 ±.18	.33 ±.19
Verbal Predicate Structure										
verb_edges	2.3 ±.36	2.5 ±.32	2.52 ±.3	2.62 ±.35	2.67 ±.28	2.63 ±.28	2.7 ±.32	2.71 ±.29	2.68 ±.26	2.76 ±.27
verb_edges_4	.09 ±.08	.13 ±.07	.13 ±.07	.16 ±.07	.16 ±.07	.15 ±.08	.16 ±.07	.16 ±.06	.16 ±.06	.16 ±.07
verbal_head_sent	1.52 ±.46	1.8 ±.53	1.92 ±.52	2.13 ±.54	2.26 ±.54	2.3 ±.51	2.54 ±.61	2.73 ±.58	2.86 ±.65	2.95 ±.66
Global and Local Parsed Tree Structures										
parse_depth	2.88 ±.65	3.27 ±.62	3.37 ±.61	3.6 ±.63	3.78 ±.55	3.94 ±.64	4.21 ±.69	4.49 ±.65	4.59 ±.67	4.56 ±.62
max_links_len	.65 ±.44	.7 ±.45	.72 ±.42	.96 ±.74	.92 ±.43	.99 ±.42	1.2 ±.68	1.24 ±.53	1.21 ±.42	1.39 ±.72
5rtoken_per_clause	7.17 ±1.56	7.49 ±1.58	7.28 ±1.39	7.52 ±1.51	7.41 ±1.26	7.55 ±1.26	7.62 ±1.24	7.42 ±1.3	7.16 ±1.09	7.26 ±1.32
Order of elements										
obj_post	.67 ±.18	.68 ±.15	.67 ±.15	.64 ±.16	.65 ±.15	.69 ±.13	.69 ±.14	.6 ±.17	.64 ±.17	.6 ±.16
obj_pre	.33 ±.18	.32 ±.15	.33 ±.15	.35 ±.15	.35 ±.15	.31 ±.13	.31 ±.14	.39 ±.16	.36 ±.17	.4 ±.16
subj_pre	.8 ±.19	.84 ±.15	.82 ±.15	.84 ±.15	.84 ±.13	.84 ±.13	.83 ±.13	.81 ±.12	.78 ±.13	.79 ±.14
Use of Subordination										
subord_chain_len	1.06 ±.25	1.15 ±.16	1.18 ±.14	1.21 ±.18	1.24 ±.15	1.24 ±.14	1.26 ±.16	1.29 ±.23	1.33 ±.16	1.32 ±.2
subord_2	.08 ±.14	.11 ±.11	.13 ±.1	.15 ±.11	.17 ±.1	.17 ±.11	.18 ±.11	.19 ±.11	.2 ±.1	.2 ±.1
subord_dist	.24 ±.14	.33 ±.13	.38 ±.12	.4 ±.12	.44 ±.12	.47 ±.12	.5 ±.12	.56 ±.12	.58 ±.08	.57 ±.1

Table 4: A subset of linguistic features extracted for each course level. For each feature it is reported the average value and the standard deviation.

experiments are performed using the majority class classifier as baseline and accuracy as the evaluation metric.

4.1 Tracking Writing Skills' Evolution

Table 5 reports the results obtained at both the document and sentence levels, pairing essays that have the same prompt (*Same* columns) and both the same and different prompts (*All* columns). As a general remark, we observe that best results are those obtained with the document-level experiments. This is quite expected, since sentence-level classification is a more complex task that often requires a higher number of features to gain comparable accuracy (Dell'Orletta et al., 2014). If we focus instead on the distinction between *Same* and *All* results, we notice that higher scores are mainly achieved considering pairs of essays that also have different prompts. Again, this result is not surprising because adding pairs of essays with different prompts within each datasets increases the number of training samples, thus leading to better scores. Despite this, the results obtained according to the *Same* and *All* configurations are quite similar and this allows us to confirm that classification accuracy is not significantly harmed if the two essay's prompts are the same, thus showing

that our system is actually focusing on written language competence evolution properties rather than prompt-dependent characteristics.

More interestingly, we notice that considering all the possible course level pairs at the same time our system is able to achieve quite good results, especially at document level classification (0.68 and 0.70 of accuracy for *Same* and *All* configurations respectively), thus showing that it is possible to automatically predict the chronological order of two essays written by the same student by using a wide spectrum of linguistic properties.

In general, our best scores are obtained by considering all the experiments that include essays written by students in the Beginner category (SPA 1, 2 and 3). This is particularly evident for the experiments that compare essays written during SPA 1 as one of the two considered course levels, most likely because the evolution from knowing nothing at all of a specific L2 to knowing enough to start writing is actually bigger that the difference between knowing a little and then learning a little more. Additionally, students at this beginning stage of L2 acquisition tend to use markedly fewer words per sentence, and the words they user are shorter; these features are particularly salient for the classifier. Observing instead the results ob-

Course Levels	Documents				Sentences			
	Same		All		Same		All	
	Score	Samples	Score	Samples	Score	Samples	Score	Samples
All Levels	0.68	2,208	0.7	5,536	0.59	1,047,156	0.61	2,570,366
SPA 1 - SPA 2	0.88	280	0.9	624	0.7	143,660	0.71	316,264
SPA 1 - SPA 3	0.97	178	0.95	440	0.75	85,032	0.75	209,048
SPA 1 - SPA 21	#	#	0.91	116	0.61	14,298	0.7	46,738
SPA 2 - SPA 3	0.62	528	0.62	1,192	0.56	323,332	0.56	724,400
SPA 2 - SPA 21	0.61	62	0.61	188	0.57	35,754	0.58	104,442
SPA 2 - SPA 22	#	#	0.59	68	0.55	8,048	0.63	29,670
SPA 2 - SPA 23	#	#	0.77	52	#	#	0.58	27,420
SPA 3 - SPA 21	0.59	158	0.55	364	0.53	82,104	0.54	190,596
SPA 3 - SPA 22	0.61	64	0.58	186	0.54	31,886	0.6	93,486
SPA 3 - SPA 23	#	#	0.89	106	0.59	13,404	0.59	45,804
SPA 3 - SPA 24	#	#	#	#	#	#	0.68	11,276
SPA 21 - SPA 22	0.59	132	0.62	302	0.52	57,326	0.54	132,454
SPA 21 - SPA 23	0.52	58	0.74	154	0.54	27,038	0.57	67,634
SPA 21 - SPA 24	#	#	0.7	92	0.47	9,268	0.56	35,384
SPA 22 - SPA 23	0.71	76	0.69	186	0.55	35,272	0.56	79,168
SPA 22 - SPA 24	0.69	158	0.73	164	0.5	23,446	0.56	66,184
SPA 23 - SPA 24	0.45	168	0.49	386	0.48	61,654	0.49	137,786
SPA 31 - SPA 32	0.8	100	0.63	212	0.55	27,608	0.55	57,790
SPA 31 - SPA 33	0.52	100	0.53	198	0.51	24,830	0.48	48,990
SPA 32 - SPA 33	0.54	96	0.59	256	0.5	24,154	0.55	66,466

Table 5: Classification results in terms of accuracy obtained both at document and sentence levels along with number of samples for each dataset. **Same** and **All** columns report the results obtained by pairing essays that have same prompt and both same and different prompts respectively. Since the labels within each dataset has been balanced, baseline accuracy is 0.50.

tained pairing student essays belonging to the other three course level categories (Intermediate, Composition and Heritage), we notice a considerable drop in classifier performance. For instance, if we compare essays written by students in the Composition category (SPA 23 - SPA 24) we can see that all the classification results are below the majority class baseline classifier. A possible reason might be that these two courses are specifically aimed at improving learners' writing skills, with an emphasis on academic writing in Spanish, thus involving specific properties, such as discourse-level characteristics, which are possibly not covered by our set of features.

4.2 Understanding Linguistic Predictors

Beyond classification results, we were interested in understanding which typologies of linguistic phenomena are more important for solving the classification task and whether such properties correlate to the teaching curriculum. To better explore this second research question, we perform a feature ranking analysis along with the classification experiments, which allows us to establish a ranking of the most important features according to the different classification scenarios. That is, we evaluate the importance of each linguistic property by extracting and ranking the feature weights assigned by the

LinearSVM. Table 6 reports the feature rankings obtained with sentence-level classification results, including pairs of essays that have the same prompt (*Same* configuration). We considered in particular six different course level pairs which are mostly representative of different stages of writing development. The focus on sentence-level results rather than document-level allows capturing more fine-grained linguistic phenomena.

Because the COWS-L2H corpus was collected from a single university with set curriculum, we are able to compare the features utilized by the LinearSVM with the course curriculum. We find that the feature rankings as obtained from the LinearSVM can in many cases be explained by differences in curriculum at each level. For example, from SPA 1 to SPA 2 the most important features used by the model are all related to verbal morphology, particularly morphology of auxiliary verbs. This can be explained by the fact that SPA 1 and 2 are the courses where students are introduced for the first time to the notions of verb tense and person. SPA 1 is focused on managing the idea of person and number in a tense that is not particularly difficult to understand for a speaker of English: the present tense. SPA 2, however, introduces the difficult difference between the three tenses in the past: imperfect, preterite and plus-perfect. This

SPA 1 - SPA 2	SPA 1 - SPA 3	SPA 2 - SPA 3	SPA 3 - SPA 21	SPA 22 - SPA 23	SPA 31 - SPA 32
aux_mood_Ind	lexical_density *	aux_tense_dist_Pres *	lexical_density	upos_PUNCT	upos_ADP *
aux_tense_Pres *	upos_ADP *	aux_mood_Ind	upos_DET	dep_punct	dep_case *
aux_tense_Imp *	upos_VERB *	aux_tense_Imp *	dep_punct	upos_ADV	verbal_head_sent
aux_tense_Past *	upos_NOUN *	aux_tense_Past	upos_VERB	dep_advmod	upos_PUNCT
upos_ADP *	upos_ADJ	dep_punct *	aux_tense_Pres	upos_CCONJ	upos_PRON
verbs_tense_Past *	upos_PRON	upos_PUNCT *	upos_ADJ	dep_cc *	dep_mark
upos_VERB *	dep_det	dep_nsubj *	upos_NOUN	upos_VERB	dep_punct
upos_INTJ *	upos_PUNCT *	dep_iobj	dep_nsubj *	dep_case	aux_tense_Imp
verbal_head_sent *	upos_PROPN	upos_PRON	upos_PRON	aux_form_Part	verbs_tense_Pres
verbs_tense_Imp *	dep_case *	verbal_head_sent *	upos_SCONJ	upos_ADP	subord_dist
upos_ADJ *	upos_SCONJ *	dep_cop	upos_ADV *	dep_mark	dep_cop
ttr_form	upos_AUX	subj_post *	upos_PUNCT	dep_compound	dep_cc
upos_PRON *	dep_punct *	aux_form_Fin	aux_form_Fin	upos_INTJ *	lexical_density
upos_PROPN *	subord_dist *	verbs_tense_Imp *	dep_cc *	dep_nsubj *	upos_AUX
upos_PUNCT *	upos_CCONJ *	upos_AUX	aux_tense_Imp	upos_AUX	upos_ADV

Table 6: Feature rankings obtained with sentence-level (*Same*) classification results for six different course level pairs. Features that vary in a statistically significant way with Wilcoxon Rank-Sum test are marked with *.

fact explains why distribution of past tense main verbs (*verbs_tense_Past*) differs between essays written during SPA 1 and SPA 2. Additionally, SPA 2 introduces composed verb tenses that require an auxiliary. Specifically, the auxiliary verbs "haber", "estar", and "ser" are introduced in SPA 2 as part of the past tense forms. Thus, it is not surprising that the top four features used by our classifier for distinguishing between essays written in SPA 1 and SPA 2 are related to the use of auxiliary verbs.

Classification of essays written by students while enrolled in SPA 2 and SPA 3 also relies largely on differences in verbal morphology. While the distribution of present tense auxiliary verbs is the most important distinguishing feature, other compound verb tenses play a role at these levels. For example, differences in the distribution of imperfect auxiliary verbs (*aux_tense_Imp*) may be explained by the use of the pluperfect tense.

Between SPA 1 and SPA 3, the most important discriminating feature is lexical density. While there is no specific focus on lexical density in the course curriculum, this feature is a natural extension of increasing sentence complexity. Davidson et al. (2019) shows that as students progress through the Spanish course sequence, lexical density tends to decrease due to the increased use of function words in more complex sentences. Additionally, one of the final items covered in the SPA 1 curriculum is the use of the prepositions "por" and "para". Also, at all three beginning levels students are taught to use prepositions in constructing more complex sentence structures. This may explain why preposition usage (*upos_ADP*) is a key discriminating feature between essays written in SPA 1 and SPA2, as well as between SPA 1 and SPA 3. The prominence of this feature indicates that students are learning to more confidently use prepositions as their writing skills develop. The fact that (*upos_ADP*) is not a key discriminating feature between SPA 2 and SPA3 indicates that these changes are occurring primarily at the SPA 2 level, which accords with the course curriculum.

In spite of the still reasonable accuracy in discriminating more advanced levels, making a direct connection between the features used by the SVM and the course curriculum becomes more difficult. At these more advanced levels students have developed an individual writing style which results in a more complex relationship between the curriculum and the syntax used by students. At the SPA 3 - SPA 21 interval, the only three features which vary in a statistically significant way are the distributions of nominal subjects (*dep_nsubj*), adverbs (*upos_ADV*), and coordinating conjunctions (*dep_cc*). While the increased use of adverbs may be seen as a general sign of increased writing complexity, coordinating conjunctions are taught explicitly during SPA 3. Conjunctions are also practiced intensively during both SPA 21 and SPA 22 explaining their importance as a discriminating feature between these levels.

One of the clearest connections between curriculum and the features used by the LinearSVM occurs at the Heritage levels SPA 31 and SPA 32. Heritage learners of Spanish raised in an English-dominant country are known to use "English-like" prepositions in Spanish. For example, Pascual y Cabo and Soler (2015) report on preposition stranding (which is grammatical in English by ungrammatical in Spanish) among Heritage speakers of Spanish in the United States. We find that distributional differences in the use of prepositions, represented by the features *upos_ADP* and *dep_case*, is the key distinguishing feature between essays written by the same student during SPA 31 and SPA 32. This difference indicates that students are learning to use prepositions in a more "Spanish-like" manner, which is one of the major areas of feedback which instructors provide to Heritage students.

5 Conclusion

We present a first study aimed at modeling the evolution of written language competence in Spanish as a Second and Heritage Language, using data from the COWS-L2H Corpus. We have described a rich set of linguistic features automatically extracted from student writing, and have demonstrated that it is possible to automatically predict the relative order of two essays written by the same student at different course levels using these features, especially when considering students enrolled in beginner-level Spanish courses. Finally, we have shown that the linguistic features most important in predicting essay order often reflect the explicit instruction that students receive during each course.

This work can help instructors and language researchers better understand the specific linguistic factors which contribute to improved writing proficiency. Additionally, the appearance of features in the LinearSVM ranking helps clarify the effect of instruction on writing performance, specifically on effects such as the known delay between students being taught a concept and that concept appearing in the students' writing. We also believe that this work may contribute to the development of better language assessment and placement tools.

In future work we intend to explore the influence of student L1 on feature rankings, as L1 (and L2) transfer and interference effects may influence the rate at which students acquire specific linguistic features. Additionally we plan to conduct a cross-lingual analysis, investigating how the feature rankings we see in Spanish writing development relate to those seen in the acquisition of other languages.

Acknowledgments

Reported research started in the framework of a Short Term Mobility program of international exchanges funded by CNR. This work was also funded in part by the UC Davis Grant for Collaborative Interdisciplinary Research and by a gift from Microsoft Azure.

References

Robert J Blake and Eve C Zyzik. 2016. *El espanol y la linguistica aplicada*. Georgetown University Press.

Dominique Brunato, Andrea Cimino, Felice Dell'Orletta, Giulia Venturi, and Simonetta Montemagni. 2020. Profiling-ud: a tool for linguistic profiling of texts. In *Proceedings of The 12th Language Resources and Evaluation Conference*, pages 7147–7153, Marseille, France. European Language Resources Association.

Bram Bulté and Alex Housen. 2012. Defining and operationalising L2 complexity. *Dimensions of L2 performance and proficiency: Complexity, accuracy and fluency in SLA*, pages 23–46.

Bram Bulté and Alex Housen. 2014. Conceptualizing and measuring short-term changes in L2 writing complexity. *Journal of second language writing*, 26:42–65.

Diego Pascual y Cabo and Inmaculada Soler. 2015. Preposition Stranding in Spanish as a Heritage Language. *Heritage Language Journal*, 12:186–209.

A. Cimino, F. Dell'Orletta, D. Brunato, and G. Venturi. 2018. Sentences and Documents in Native Language Identification. In *Proceedings of 5th Italian Conference on Computational Linguistics (CLiC-it)*, pages 1–6, Turin.

A. Cimino, M. Wieling, F. Dell'Orletta, S. Montemagni, and G. Venturi. 2017. Identifying Predictive Features for Textual Genre Classification: the Key Role of Syntax. In *Proceedings of 4th Italian Conference on Computational Linguistics (CLiC-it)*, pages 1–6, Rome.

Scott Crossley. 2020. Linguistic features in writing quality and development: An overview. *Journal of Writing Research*.

Scott A Crossley and Danielle S McNamara. 2012. Predicting second language writing proficiency: The roles of cohesion and linguistic sophistication. *Journal of Research in Reading*, 35(2):115–135.

Sam Davidson, Aaron Yamada, Agustina Carando, Kenji Sagae, and Claudia Sánchez Gutiérrez. 2019. Word use and lexical diversity in second language learners and heritage speakers of spanish: A corpus study. In *American Association for Applied Linguistics*.

Sam Davidson, Aaron Yamada, Paloma Fernandez Mira, Agustina Carando, Claudia H. Sanchez Gutierrez, and Kenji Sagae. 2020. Developing nlp tools with a new corpus of learner spanish.

In *Proceedings of The 12th Language Resources and Evaluation Conference*, pages 7240–7245, Marseille, France. European Language Resources Association.

F. Dell'Orletta, S. Montemagni, and G. Venturi. 2011a. READ-IT: assessing readability of Italian texts with a view to text simplification. In *Proceedings of Second Workshop on Speech and Language Processing for Assistive Technologies*, pages 73–83, Edinburgh, UK.

Felice Dell'Orletta, Giulia Venturi, and Simonetta Montemagni. 2011b. Ulisse: an unsupervised algorithm for detecting reliable dependency parses. In *CoNLL*.

Felice Dell'Orletta, Martijn Wieling, Giulia Venturi, Andrea Cimino, and Simonetta Montemagni. 2014. Assessing the readability of sentences: which corpora and features? In *Proceedings of the Ninth Workshop on Innovative Use of NLP for Building Educational Applications*, pages 163–173.

Rod Ellis and Natsuko Shintani. 2013. *Exploring language pedagogy through second language acquisition research*. Routledge.

Daniel Gildea. 2001. Corpus variation and parser performance. In *Proceedings of the 2001 Conference on Empirical Methods in Natural Language Processing*.

Julia Hancke and Detmar Meurers. 2013. Exploring CEFR classification for German based on rich linguistic modeling. In *Proceedings of the Learner Corpus Research (LCR) conference*.

K. W. Hunt. 1965. Grammatical structures written at three grade levels. *(NCTE Research Report Number 3). Urbana, IL: National Council of Teachers of English.*

Xiaofei Lu. 2009. Automatic measurement of syntactic complexity in child language acquisition. In *International Journal of Corpus Linguistics, 14(1):3–28.*

Xiaofei Lu. 2011. A corpus-based evaluation of syntactic complexity measures as indices of college-level ESL writers' language development. *TESOL quarterly*, 45(1):36–62.

Shannon Lubetich and Kenji Sagae. 2014. Data-driven measurement of child language development with simple syntactic templates. In *Proceedings of COLING 2014, the 25th International Conference on Computational Linguistics: Technical Papers*, pages 2151–2160.

John Norris and Lourdes Ortega. 2009. Measurement for understanding: An organic approach to investigating complexity, accuracy, and fluency in SLA. *Applied Linguistics*, 30(4):555–578.

Lourdes Ortega. 2003. Syntactic complexity measures and their relationship to l2 proficiency: A research synthesis of college-level l2 writing. *Applied linguistics*, 24(4):492–518.

Ildikó Pilán and Elena Volodina. 2018. Investigating the importance of linguistic complexity features across different datasets related to language learning. In *Proceedings of the Workshop on Linguistic Complexity and Natural Language Processing*, pages 49–58, Santa Fe, New-Mexico. Association for Computational Linguistics.

Stefan Richter, Andrea Cimino, Felice Dell'Orletta, and Giulia Venturi. 2015. Tracking the Evolution of Written Language Competence: an NLP–based Approach. *CLiC it*, page 236.

Kenji Sagae, Alon Lavie, and Brian MacWhinney. 2005. Automatic measurement of syntactic development in child language. In *Proceedings of the 43rd Annual Meeting of the Association for Computational Linguistics*, pages 197–204. Association for Computational Linguistics.

M Rafael Salaberry. 1999. The development of past tense verbal morphology in classroom L2 spanish. *Applied Linguistics*, 20(2):151–178.

M. Straka, J. Hajic, and J. Strakova. 2016. UDPipe: Trainable pipeline for processing CoNLL-U files performing tokenization, morphological analysis, POS tagging and parsing. In *Proceedings of the Tenth International Conference on Language Resources and Evaluation (LREC)*.

Sowmya Vajjala and Kaidi Lēo. 2014. Automatic CEFR Level Prediction for Estonian Learner Text. In *NEALT Proceedings Series Vol. 22, pages 113–127.*

Weiwei Yang, Xiaofei Lu, and Sara Cushing Weigle. 2015. Different topics, different discourse: Relationships among writing topic, measures of syntactic complexity, and judgments of writing quality. *Journal of Second Language Writing*, 28:53–67.

Leonardo Zilio, Rodrigo Wilkens, and Cédrick Fairon. 2018. An SLA corpus annotated with pedagogically relevant grammatical structures. In *Proceedings of the Eleventh International Conference on Language Resources and Evaluation (LREC-2018)*, Miyazaki, Japan. European Languages Resources Association (ELRA).

Distractor Analysis and Selection for Multiple-Choice Cloze Questions for Second-Language Learners

Lingyu Gao[1], Kevin Gimpel[1], Arnar Jensson[2]
[1]Toyota Technological Institute at Chicago, [2]Cooori Japan
`{lygao, kgimpel}@ttic.edu`

Abstract

We consider the problem of automatically suggesting distractors for multiple-choice cloze questions designed for second-language learners. We describe the creation of a dataset including collecting manual annotations for distractor selection. We assess the relationship between the choices of the annotators and features based on distractors and the correct answers, both with and without the surrounding passage context in the cloze questions. Simple features of the distractor and correct answer correlate with the annotations, though we find substantial benefit to additionally using large-scale pretrained models to measure the fit of the distractor in the context. Based on these analyses, we propose and train models to automatically select distractors, and measure the importance of model components quantitatively.

1 Introduction

Multiple-choice cloze questions (MCQs) are widely used in examinations and exercises for language learners (Liang et al., 2018). The quality of MCQs depends not only on the question and choice of blank, but also on the choice of **distractors**, i.e., incorrect answers. Distractors, which could be phrases or single words, are incorrect answers that distract students from the correct ones.

According to Pho et al. (2014), distractors tend to be syntactically and semantically homogeneous with respect to the correct answers. Distractor selection may be done manually through expert curation or automatically using simple methods based on similarity and dissimilarity to the correct answer (Pino et al., 2008; Alsubait et al., 2014). Intuitively, optimal distractors should be sufficiently similar to the correct answers in order to challenge students, but not so similar as to make the question unanswerable (Yeung et al., 2019). However, past

work usually lacks direct supervision for training, making it difficult to develop and evaluate automatic methods. To overcome this challenge, Liang et al. (2018) sample distractors as negative samples for the candidate pool in the training process, and Chen et al. (2015) sample questions and use manual annotation for evaluation.

In this paper, we build two datasets of MCQs for second-language learners with distractor selections annotated manually by human experts. Both datasets consist of instances with a sentence, a blank, the correct answer that fills the blank, and a set of candidate distractors. Each candidate distractor has a label indicating whether a human annotator selected it as a distractor for the instance. The first dataset, which we call MCDSENT, contains solely the sentence without any additional context, and the sentences are written such that they are understandable as standalone sentences. The second dataset, MCDPARA, contains sentences drawn from an existing passage and therefore also supplies the passage context.

To analyze the datasets, we design context-free features of the distractor and the correct answer, including length difference, embedding similarities, frequencies, and frequency rank differences. We also explore context-sensitive features, such as probabilities from large-scale pretrained models like BERT (Devlin et al., 2018). In looking at the annotations, we found that distractors are unchosen when they are either too easy or too hard (i.e., too good of a fit in the context). Consider the examples in Table 1. For the sentence "The large automobile **manufacturer** has a factory near here.", "beer" is too easy and "corporation" is too good of a fit, so both are rejected by annotators. We find that the BERT probabilities capture this tendency; that is, there is a nonlinear relationship between the distractor probability under BERT and the likelihood of annotator selection.

Proceedings of the 15th Workshop on Innovative Use of NLP for Building Educational Applications, pages 102–114
July 10, 2020. ©2020 Association for Computational Linguistics

dataset	context with **correct answer**	distractor	label
MCDSENT	How many people are planning to **attend** the party?	contribute	T
	The large automobile **manufacturer** has a factory near here.	beer	F
	The large automobile **manufacturer** has a factory near here.	corporation	F
	The large automobile **manufacturer** has a factory near here.	apartment	T
MCDPARA	Stem cells are special cells that can divide to produce many different kinds of cells. When they divide, the new cells may be the same type of **cell** as the original cell....	plastic	F
	...These circumstances made it virtually impossible for salmon to mate. Therefore, the number of **salmon** declined dramatically.	thousands	T

Table 1: Example instances from MCDSENT and MCDPARA. Contexts are shown and correct answers are bold and underlined. Part of the paragraph contexts are replaced by ellipses.

We develop and train models for automatic distractor selection that combine simple features with representations from pretrained models like BERT and ELMo (Peters et al., 2018). Our results show that the pretrained models improve performance drastically over the feature-based models, leading to performance rivaling that of humans asked to perform the same task. By analyzing the models, we find that the pretrained models tend to give higher score to grammatically-correct distractors that are similar in terms of morphology and length to the correct answer, while differing sufficiently in semantics so as to avoid unanswerability.

2 Datasets

We define an **instance** as a tuple $\langle x, c, d, y \rangle$ where x is the **context**, a sentence or paragraph containing a blank; c is the **correct answer**, the word/phrase that correctly fills the blank; d is the **distractor candidate**, the distractor word/phrase being considered to fill the blank; and y is the **label**, a true/false value indicating whether a human annotator selected the distractor candidate.[1] We use the term **question** to refer to a set of instances with the same values for x and c.

2.1 Data Collection

We build two datasets with different lengths of context. The first, which we call MCDSENT ("Multiple Choice Distractors with SENTence context"), uses only a single sentence of context. The second, MCDPARA ("Multiple Choice Distractors with PARAgraph context"), has longer contexts (roughly one paragraph).

Our target audience is Japanese business people with TOEIC level 300-800, which translates to pre-intermediate to upper-intermediate level. Therefore, words from two frequency-based word lists, the New General Service List (NGSL; Browne et al., 2013) and the TOEIC Service List (TSL; Browne and Culligan, 2016), were used as a base for selecting words to serve as correct answers in instances. A proprietary procedure was used to create the sentences for both MCDSENT and MCDPARA tasks, and the paragraphs in MCDPARA are excerpted from stories written to highlight the target words chosen as correct answers. The sentences are created following the rules below:

- A sentence must have a particular minimum and maximum number of characters.

- The other words in the sentence should be at an equal or easier NGSL frequency level compared with the correct answer.

- The sentence theme should be business-like.

All the MCDSENT and MCDPARA materials were created in-house by native speakers of English, most of whom hold a degree in Teaching English to Speakers of Other Languages (TESOL).

2.2 Distractor Annotation

We now describe the procedure used to propose distractors for each instance and collect annotations regarding their selection.

A software tool with a user interface was created to allow annotators to accept or reject distractor candidates. Distractor candidates are sorted automatically for presentation to annotators in order to favor those most likely to be selected. The distractor candidates are drawn from a proprietary dictionary, and those with the same part-of-speech (POS) as the correct answers (if POS data is available) are preferred. Moreover, the candidates that

---

[1] Each instance contains only a single distractor candidate because this matches our annotation collection scenario. Annotators were shown one distractor candidate at a time. The collection of simultaneous annotations of multiple distractor candidates is left to future work.

have greater similarity to the correct answers are preferred, such as being part of the same word learning section in the language learning course and the same NGSL word frequency bucket. There is also preference for candidates that have not yet been selected as distractors for other questions in the same task type and the same course unit.[2] After the headwords are decided through this procedure, a morphological analyzer is used to generate multiple inflected forms for each headword, which are provided to the annotators for annotation. Both the headwords and inflected forms are available when computing features and for use by our models.

Six annotators were involved in the annotation, all of whom are native speakers of English. Out of the six, four hold a degree in TESOL. Selecting distractors involved two-step human selection. An annotator would approve or reject distractor candidates suggested by the tool, and a different annotator, usually more senior, would review their selections. The annotation guidelines for MCD-SENT and MCDPARA follow the same criteria. The annotators are asked to select distractors that are grammatically plausible, semantically implausible, and not obviously wrong based on the context. Annotators also must accept a minimum number of distractors depending on the number of times the correct answer appears in the course. Table 1 shows examples from MCDSENT and MCDPARA along with annotations.

2.3 Annotator Agreement

Some instances in the datasets have multiple annotations, allowing us to assess annotator agreement. We use the term "sample" to refer to a set of instances with the same x, c, and d. Table 2 shows the number of samples with agreement and disagreement for both datasets.[3] Samples with only one annotation dominate the data. Of the samples with multiple annotations, nearly all show agreement.

2.4 Distractor Phrases

While most distractors are words, some are phrases, including 16% in MCDSENT and 13% in MCD-PARA. In most cases, the phrases are constructed by a determiner or adverb ("more", "most", etc.) and another word, such as "most pleasant" or

---

[2]More specific details about this process are included in the supplementary material.

[3]We are unable to compute traditional inter-annotator agreement metrics like Cohen's kappa since we lack information about annotator identity for each annotation.

# anno.	MCDSENT			MCDPARA		
	agree	disagree	total	agree	disagree	total
1	-	-	232256	-	-	734063
2	2553	122	2675	9680	152	9841
3	121	2	123	493	3	496
4	17	0	17	62	0	62
5	10	0	10	12	0	12
6	0	0	0	2	0	2

Table 2: Numbers of samples for which annotators agree or disagree.

dataset	type	y	train	dev	test
MCDSENT	questions	-	2,713	200	200
	instances	T	30,737	1,169	1,046
		F	191,908	6,420	6,813
MCDPARA	questions	-	14,999	1,000	1,000
	instances	T	49,575	597	593
		F	688,804	7,620	8,364

Table 3: Dataset sizes in numbers of questions (a "question" is a set of instances with the same x and c) and instances, broken down by label (y) and data split.

"more recently". However, some candidates show other patterns, such as noun phrases "South Pole", erroneously-inflected forms "come ed" and other phrases (e.g. "Promises Of", "No one").

2.5 Dataset Preparation

We randomly divided each dataset into train, development, and test sets. We remind the reader that we define a "question" as a set of instances with the same values for the context x and correct answer c, and in splitting the data we ensure that for a given question, all of its instances are placed into the same set. The dataset statistics are shown in Table 3. False labels are much more frequent than true labels, especially for MCDPARA.

3 Features and Analysis

We now analyse the data by designing features and studying their relationships with the annotations.

3.1 Features

We now describe our features. The dataset contains both the headwords and inflected forms of both the correct answer c and each distractor candidate d. In defining the features below based on c and d for an instance, we consider separate features for the headword pair and the inflected form pair. For features that require embedding words, we use the 300-dimensional GloVe word embeddings (Pennington et al., 2014) pretrained on the 42 billion token Common Crawl corpus. The GloVe embeddings are provided in decreasing order by frequency, and some features below use the line numbers of words in the GloVe embeddings, which correspond to frequency ranks. For words that are not in the GloVe vocabulary, their frequency ranks are $|N| + 1$, where N is the size of the GloVe vocabulary. We use the four features listed below:

- **length difference**: absolute value of length difference (in characters, including whitespace) between c and d.

- **embedding similarity**: cosine similarity of the embeddings of c and d. For phrases, we average the embeddings of the words in the phrase.

- **distractor frequency**: negative log frequency rank of d. For phrases, we take the max rank of the words (i.e., the rarest word is chosen).

- **freq. rank difference**: feature capturing frequency difference between c and d, i.e., $\log(1 + |r_c - r_d|)$ where r_w is the frequency rank of w.

3.2 Label-Specific Feature Histograms

Figure 1 shows histograms of feature values for each label.[4] Since the data is unbalanced, the histograms are "label-normalized", i.e., normalized so that the sum of heights for each label is 1. So, we can view each bar as the fraction of that label's instances with feature values in the given range.

The annotators favor candidates that have approximately the same length as the correct answers (Fig. 1, plot 1), as the true bars are much higher in the first bin (length difference 0 or 1). Selected distractors have moderate embedding similarity to the correct answers (Fig. 1, plot 2). If cosine similarity is very high or very low, then those distractors are much less likely to be selected. Such distractors are presumably too difficult or too easy, respectively.

Selected distractors are moderately frequent (Fig. 1, plot 3). Very frequent and very infrequent distractors are less likely to be selected. Distractors with small frequency rank differences (those on the left of plot 4) are more likely to be chosen (Fig. 1, plot 4). Large frequency differences tend to be found with very rare distractors, some of which may be erroneously-inflected forms.

We also computed Spearman correlations between feature values and labels, mapping the T/F

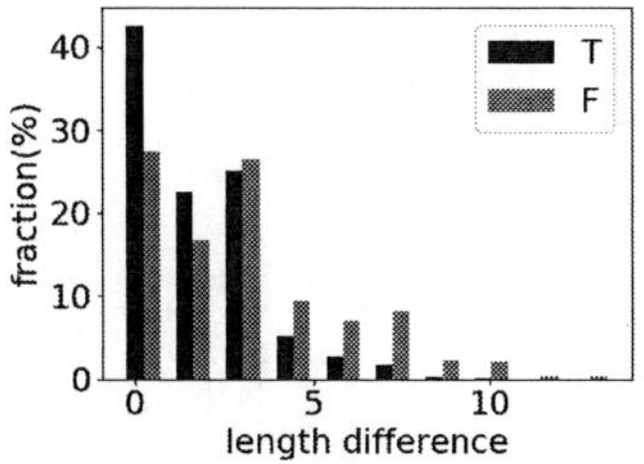

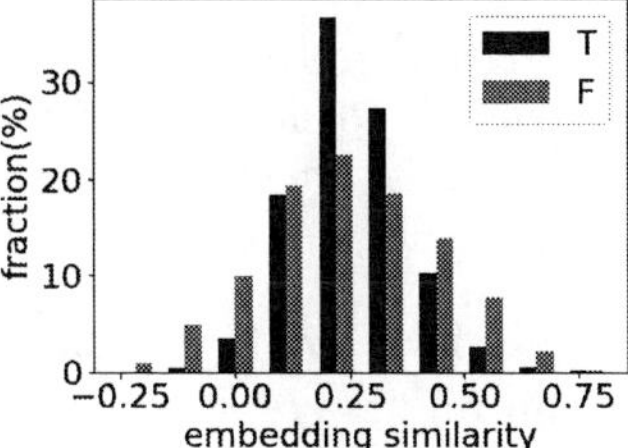

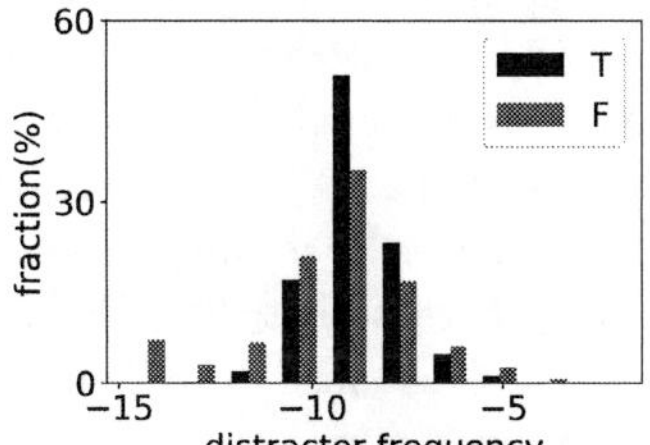

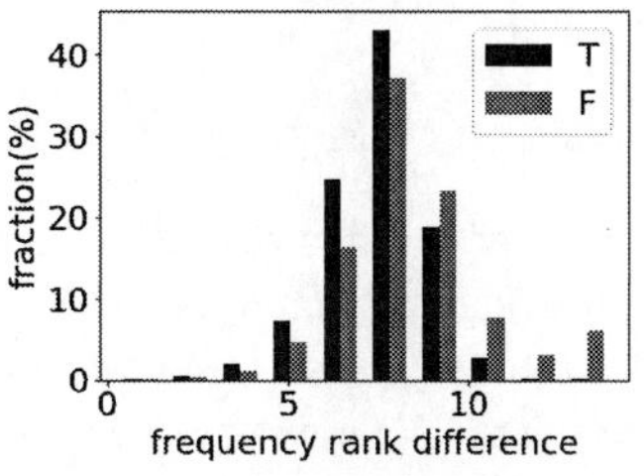

Figure 1: Label-specific feature histograms for MCD-SENT.

labels to 1/0. Aside from what are shown in the feature histograms, we find that a distractor with a rare headword but more common inflected form is more likely to be selected, at least for MCDSENT. The supplementary material contains more detail on these correlations.

3.3 Probabilities of Distractors in Context

We use BERT (Devlin et al., 2018) to compute probabilities of distractors and correct answers in the given contexts in MCDSENT. We insert a mask symbol in the blank position and compute the probability of the distractor or correct answer at that position.[5] Figure 2 shows histograms for correct answers and distractors (normalized by label). The

---

[4]We show plots here for the inflected form pairs; those for headword pairs are included in the supplementary material.

[5]For distractors with multiple tokens, we mask each position in turn and use the average of the probabilities.

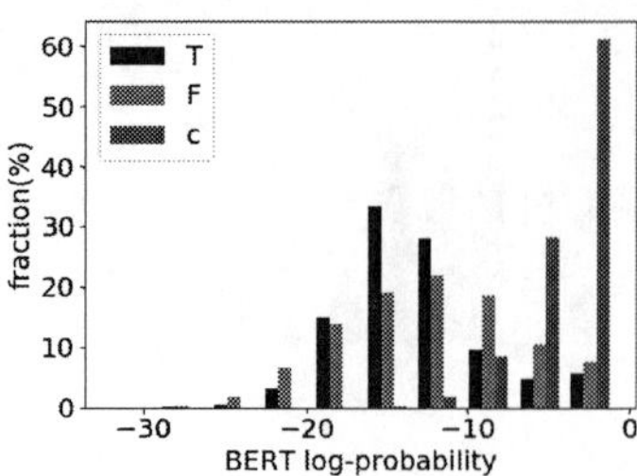

Figure 2: Histograms of BERT log-probabilities of selected distractors ("T"), unselected distractors ("F"), and correct answers ("c") in MCDSENT.

correct answers have very high probabilities. The distractor probabilities are more variable and the shapes of the histograms are roughly similar for the true and false labels. Interestingly, however, when the probability is very high or very low, the distractors tend to not be selected. The selected distractors tend to be located at the middle of the probability range. This pattern shows that BERT's distributions capture (at least partially) the nonlinear relationship between goodness of fit and suitability as distractors.

4   Models

Since the number of distractors selected for each instance is uncertain, our datasets could be naturally treated as a binary classification task for each distractor candidate. We now present models for the task of automatically predicting whether a distractor will be selected by an annotator. We approach the task as defining a predictor that produces a scalar score for a given distractor candidate. This score can be used for ranking distractors for a given question, and can also be turned into a binary classification using a threshold. We define three types of models, described in the subsections below.

4.1   Feature-Based Models

Using the features described in Section 3, we build a simple feed-forward neural network classifier that outputs a scalar score for classification. Only inflected forms of words are used for features without contexts, and all features are concatenated and used as the input of the classifier. For features that use BERT, we compute the log-probability of the distractor and the log of its rank in the distribution. For distractors that consist of multiple subword units, we mask each individually to compute the above features for each subword unit, then use the

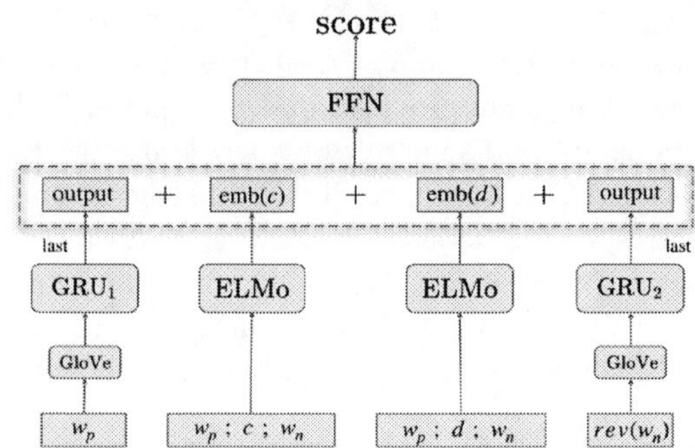

Figure 3: Illustration of the ELMo-based model M_{ELMo}, where semicolon refers to vector concatenation.

concatenation of mean, min, and max pooling of the features over the subword units. We refer to this model as M_{feat}.

4.2   ELMo-Based Models

We now describe models that are based on ELMo (Peters et al., 2018) which we denote M_{ELMo}. Since MCDPARA instances contain paragraph context, which usually includes more than one sentence, we denote the model that uses the full context by $M_{ELMo}(\ell)$. By contrast, M_{ELMo} uses only a single sentence context for both MCDSENT and MCDPARA. We denote the correct answer by c, distractor candidate by d, the word sequence before the blank by w_p, and the word sequence after the blank by w_n, using the notation $rev(w_n)$ to indicate the reverse of the sequence w_n.

We use GloVe (Pennington et al., 2014) to obtain pretrained word embeddings for context words, then use two separate RNNs with gated recurrent units (GRUs; Cho et al., 2014) to output hidden vectors to represent w_p and w_n. We reverse w_n before passing it to its GRU, and we use the last hidden states of the GRUs as part of the classifier input. We also use ELMo to obtain contextualized word embeddings for correct answers and distractors in the given context, and concatenate them to the input. An illustration of this model is presented in Figure 3.

A feed-forward network (FFN) with 1 ReLU hidden layer is set on top of these features to get the score for classification:

$$FFN(z) = \max(0, zW_1 + b_1)W_2 + b_2$$

where z is a row vector representing the inputs shown in Figure 3. We train the model as a binary classifier by using a logistic sigmoid function on

dataset	precision		recall		F1	
	A	B	A	B	A	B
MCDSENT	62.9	48.5	59.5	43.2	61.1	45.7
MCDPARA	32.1	25.0	36.0	24.0	34.0	24.5

Table 4: Results of human performance on distractor selection for two human judges labeled A and B.

the output of $FFN(z)$ to compute the probability of the true label. We also experiment with the following variations:

- Concatenate the features from Section 3 with z.

- Concatenate the correct answer to the input of the GRUs on both sides (denoted $gru+c$).

- Concatenate the GloVe embeddings of the correct answers and distractors with z. We combine this with $gru+c$, denoting the combination *all*.

4.3 BERT-Based Models

Our final model type uses a structure similar to M_{ELMo} but using BERT in place of ELMo when producing contextualized embeddings, which we denote by M_{BERT} and $M_{BERT}(\ell)$ given different types of context. We also consider the variation of concatenating the features to the input to the classifier, i.e., the first variation described in Section 4.2. We omit the $gru+c$ and *all* variations here because the BERT-based models are more computationally expensive than those that use ELMo.

5 Experiments

We now report the results of experiments with training models to select distractor candidates.

5.1 Evaluation Metrics

We use precision, recall, and F1 score as evaluation metrics. These require choosing a threshold for the score produced by our predictors. We also report the area under the precision-recall curve (AUPR), which is a single-number summary that does not require choosing a threshold.

5.2 Baselines

As the datasets are unbalanced (most distractor candidates are not selected), we report the results of baselines that always return "True" in the "baseline" rows of Tables 5 and 6. MCDSENT has a higher percentage of true labels than MCDPARA.

5.3 Estimates of Human Performance

We estimated human performance on the distractor selection task by obtaining annotations from NLP researchers who were not involved in the original data collection effort. We performed three rounds among two annotators, training them with some number of questions per round, showing the annotators the results after each round to let them calibrate their assessments, and then testing them using a final set of 30 questions, each of which has at most 10 distractors.

Human performance improved across rounds of training, leading to F1 scores in the range of 45-61% for MCDSENT and 25-34% for MCDPARA (Table 4). Some instances were very easy to reject, typically those that were erroneous word forms resulting from incorrect morphological inflection or those that were extremely similar in meaning to the correct answer. But distractors that were at neither extreme were very difficult to predict, as there is a certain amount of variability in the annotation of such cases. Nonetheless, we believe that the data has sufficient signal to train models to provide a score indicating suitability of candidates to serve as distractors.

5.4 Modeling and Training Settings

All models have one hidden layer for the feed-forward classifier. The M_{feat} classifier has 50 hidden units, and we train it for at most 30 epochs using Adam (Kingma and Ba, 2014) with learning rate 1e−3. We stop training if AUPR keeps decreasing for 5 epochs.[6] Although our primary metric of interest is AUPR, we also report optimal-threshold F1 scores on dev and test, tuning the threshold on the given set (so, on the test sets, the F1 scores we report are oracle F1 scores). The threshold is tuned within the range of 0.1 to 0.9 by step size 0.1.

For M_{ELMo} and $M_{ELMo}(\ell)$, we use ELMo (Original[7]) for the model, and BERT-large-cased to compute the BERT features from Section 3 (only applies to rows with "features = yes" in the tables). We increase the number of classifier hidden units to 1000 and run 20 epochs at most, also using Adam with learning rate 1e−3. We stop training if AUPR does not improve for 3 epochs.

For M_{BERT} and $M_{BERT}(\ell)$, we applied the same training settings as M_{ELMo} and $M_{ELMo}(\ell)$. We com-

---

[6]We also tune by F1 score as another set of settings with similar trends, which are included in the supplementary material.

[7]https://allennlp.org/elmo

model	variant	development set				test set				BERT	features	best epoch	threshold
		precision	recall	F1	AUPR	precision	recall	F1	AUPR				
baseline		15.4	100	26.7	-	13.3	100	23.5	-	-	-	-	-
M_{feat}		33.6	62.9	43.8	36.5	23.7	55.4	33.2	24.6	none	yes	28	0.2
		44.5	57.1	**50.0**	46.1	28.2	70.9	40.3	32.4	base	yes	25	0.2 (0.3)
		36.4	77.8	49.6	**47.0**	30.0	71.3	**42.2**	**34.5**	large	yes	22	0.2
M_{ELMo}	none	43.2	87.5	57.8	59.0	41.4	88.0	56.3	54.6	-	no	2	0.3
	gru+c	44.8	84.4	58.5	57.4	47.6	68.4	56.1	54.1	-	no	2	0.3 (0.4)
	all	47.2	88.9	61.7	61.2	48.3	75.0	58.7	55.8	-	no	2	0.3 (0.4)
	none	51.7	77.8	62.1	64.6	50.4	76.5	60.8	57.2	large	yes	3	0.3
	gru+c	55.7	73.3	63.3	65.3	49.1	82.3	61.5	**63.1**	large	yes	5	0.4 (0.3)
	all	56.2	74.4	**64.0**	**66.5**	49.8	80.8	**61.6**	58.8	large	yes	5	0.4 (0.3)
M_{BERT}		47.9	78.1	59.4	60.8	44.8	81.0	57.7	55.7	base	no	1	0.3
		49.6	79.3	61.0	64.1	45.3	80.2	57.9	53.4	large	no	1	0.3
		50.6	83.9	**63.2**	65.3	44.8	78.5	57.0	53.8	base	yes	12	0.1
		53.8	73.1	62.0	**66.5**	49.7	73.9	**59.4**	**56.3**	large	yes	2	0.4

Table 5: Results for MCDSENT. Boldface indicates the best F1/AUPR on dev/test for each model type. We include the threshold tuned on the test set in parentheses when it differs from the threshold tuned on dev.

model	development set				test set				BERT	features	best epoch	threshold
	precision	recall	F1	AUPR	precision	recall	F1	AUPR				
baseline	7.3	100	13.5	-	6.6	100	12.4	-	-	-	-	-
M_{feat}	15.3	63.1	24.6	17.3	14.5	63.6	23.6	15.5	-	yes	23	0.1
	18.2	69.2	28.9	21.6	16.3	65.6	26.1	**19.1**	base	yes	27	0.1
	19.8	64.0	**30.2**	**22.3**	16.9	64.2	**26.8**	18.8	large	yes	22	0.1
M_{ELMo}	35.4	47.7	40.7	38.4	26.1	75.6	38.8	30.4	-	no	5	0.3 (0.2)
	37.9	61.3	**46.9**	**46.8**	34.6	63.9	44.9	37.6	large	yes	7	0.3
$M_{ELMo}(\ell)$	30.5	61.1	40.7	36.6	29.1	61.6	39.5	33.2	-	no	5	0.3
	37.1	62.7	46.6	43.7	34.4	65.1	**45.0**	**40.1**	large	yes	6	0.3
M_{BERT}	35.4	61.6	45.0	40.9	29.2	58.7	39.0	30.1	base	no	2	0.2
	33.0	63.7	43.5	40.9	29.1	65.1	40.2	32.4	large	no	2	0.2
	44.3	55.4	**49.3**	**47.3**	31.5	73.2	**44.0**	36.7	base	yes	2	0.3 (0.2)
	35.6	66.0	46.2	45.0	35.5	54.5	43.0	36.6	large	yes	2	0.2 (0.3)
$M_{BERT}(\ell)$	33.1	65.3	43.9	39.7	28.8	66.4	40.2	29.8	base	no	2	0.2
	37.4	67.3	48.1	46.0	31.3	69.1	43.1	**37.0**	base	yes	2	0.2

Table 6: Results for MCDPARA.

pare the BERT-base-cased and BERT-large-cased variants of BERT. When doing so, the BERT features from Section 3 use the same BERT variant as that used for contextualized word embeddings.

For all models based on pretrained models, we keep the parameters of the pretrained models fixed. However, we do a weighted summation of the 3 layers of ELMo, and all layers of BERT except for the first layer, where the weights are trained during the training process.

5.5 Results

We present our main results for MCDSENT in Table 5 and for MCDPARA in Table 6.

Feature-based models. The feature-based model, shown as M_{feat} in the upper parts of the tables, is much better than the trivial baseline. Including the BERT features in M_{feat} improves performance greatly (10 points in AUPR for MCDSENT), showing the value of using the context effectively with a powerful pretrained model. There is not a large difference between using BERT-base and BERT-large when computing these features.

ELMo-based models. Even without features, M_{ELMo} outperforms M_{feat} by a wide margin. Adding features to M_{ELMo} further improves F1 by 2-5% for MCDSENT and 5-6% for MCDPARA. The F1 score for M_{ELMo} on MCDSENT is close to human performance, and on MCDPARA the F1 score outperforms humans (see Table 4). For

MCDSENT, we also experiment with using the correct answer as input to the context GRUs (*gru+c*), and additionally concatenating the GloVe embeddings of the correct answers and distractors to the input of the classifier (*all*). Both changes improve F1 on dev, but on test the results are more mixed.

BERT-based models. For M_{BERT}, using BERT-base is sufficient to obtain strong results on this task and is also cheaper computationally than BERT-large. Although M_{BERT} with BERT-base has higher AUPR on dev, its test performance is close to M_{ELMo}. Adding features improves performance for MCDPARA (3-5% F1), but less than the improvement found for M_{ELMo}. While M_{feat} is aided greatly when including BERT features, the features have limited impact on M_{BERT}, presumably because it already incorporates BERT in its model.

Long-context models. We now discuss results for the models that use the full context in MCD-PARA, i.e., $M_{ELMo}(\ell)$ and $M_{BERT}(\ell)$. On dev, M_{ELMo} and M_{BERT} outperform $M_{ELMo}(\ell)$ and $M_{BERT}(\ell)$ respectively, which suggests that the extra context for MCDPARA is not helpful. However, the test AUPR results are better when using the longer context, suggesting that the extra context may be helpful for generalization. Nonetheless, the overall differences are small, suggesting that either the longer context is not important for this task or that our way of encoding the context is not helpful. The judges in our manual study (Sec. 5.3) rarely found the longer context helpful for the task, pointing toward the former possibility.

5.6 Statistical Significance Tests

For better comparison of these models' performances, a paired bootstrap resampling method is applied (Koehn, 2004). We repeatedly sample with replacement 1000 times from the original test set with sample size equal to the corresponding test set size, and compare the F1 scores of two models. We use the thresholds tuned by the development set for F1 score computations, and assume significance at a p value of 0.05.

- For M_{ELMo}, $M_{ELMo}(\ell)$, M_{BERT} and $M_{BERT}(\ell)$, the models with features are significantly better than their feature-less counterparts ($p < 0.01$).[8]
- When both models use features, $M_{ELMo}(\ell)$ is almost the same as M_{ELMo} ($p = 0.477$). How-

ever, when both do not use features, $M_{ELMo}(\ell)$ is significantly better ($p < 0.01$).

- When using BERT-base-cased, $M_{BERT}(\ell)$ is better than M_{BERT}, but not significantly so ($p = 0.4$ with features and 0.173 without features).
- On MCDPARA, switching from BERT-base to BERT-large does not lead to a significant difference for M_{BERT} without features (BERT-large is better with $p = 0.194$) or M_{BERT} with features (BERT-base is better with $p = 0.504$). For MCDSENT, M_{BERT} with BERT-large is better both with and without features ($p < 0.2$).
- On MCDPARA, $M_{BERT}(\ell)$ outperforms $M_{ELMo}(\ell)$ without features but not significantly. With features, $M_{ELMo}(\ell)$ is better with $p = 0.052$.
- On MCDSENT, M_{BERT} without features (BERT-large-cased) is better than M_{ELMo} without features, but not significantly so ($p = 0.386$). However, if we add features or use M_{BERT} with BERT-base-cased, M_{ELMo} is significantly better ($p < 0.01$).
- On MCDPARA, M_{ELMo} is nearly significantly better than M_{BERT} when both use features ($p = 0.062$). However, dropping the features for both models makes M_{BERT} significantly outperform M_{ELMo} ($p = 0.044$).

5.7 Examples

Figure 4 shows an example question from MCD-SENT, i.e., "The bank will **notify** its customers of the new policy", and two subsets of its distractors. The first subset consists of the top seven distractors using scores from M_{ELMo} with features, and the second contains distractors further down in the ranked list. For each model, we normalize its distractor scores with min-max normalization.[9]

Overall, model rankings are similar across models, with all distractors in the first set ranked higher than those in the second set. The high-ranking but unselected distractors ("spell", "consult", and "quit") are likely to be reasonable distractors for second-language learners, even though they were not selected by annotators.

We could observe the clustering of distractor ranks with similar morphological inflected form in some cases, which may indicate that the model makes use of the grammatical knowledge of pre-trained models.

---

[8] We only use BERT-base-cased for $M_{BERT}(\ell)$ due to computational considerations.

[9] Given original data x, we use $(x - \min(x))/(\max(x) - \min(x))$ to normalize it.

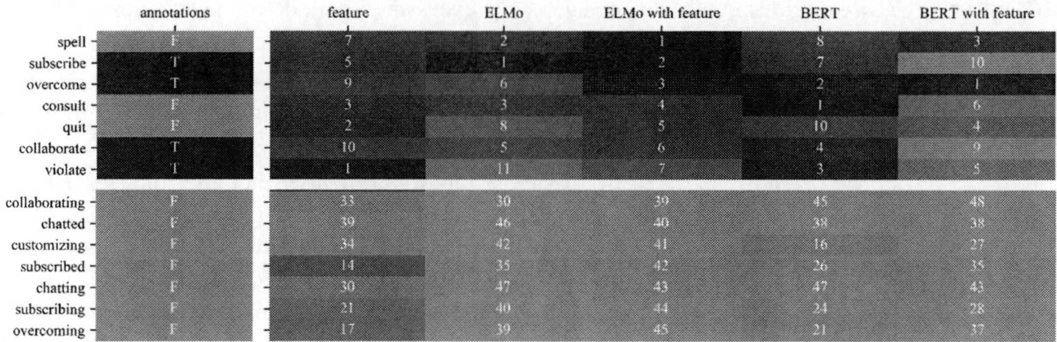

Figure 4: Ranks of distractors for question "The bank will **notify** its customers of the new policy." The colors represent the normalized scores of the models and the numbers in the cells are the ranks of the candidates.

6 Related Work

Existing approaches to distractor selection use WordNet (Fellbaum, 1998) metrics (Mitkov and Ha, 2003; Chen et al., 2015), word embedding similarities (Jiang and Lee, 2017), thesauruses (Sumita et al., 2005; Smith et al., 2010), and phonetic and morphological similarities (Pino and Eskenazi, 2009). Other approaches consider grammatical correctness, and introduce structural similarities in an ontology (Stasaski and Hearst, 2017), and syntactic similarities (Chen et al., 2006). When using broader context, bigram or n-gram co-occurrence (Susanti et al., 2018; Hill and Simha, 2016), context similarity (Pino et al., 2008), and context sensitive inference (Zesch and Melamud, 2014) have also been applied to distractor selection.

Based on these heuristic features, Liang et al. (2018) assemble these features and apply neural networks, training the model to predict the answers within a lot of candidates. Yeung et al. (2019) further applies BERT for ranking distractors by masking the target word. As we have two manually annotated datasets that have different lengths of contexts, we adopt both word pair features and the context-specific distractor probabilities to build our feature-based models. Moreover, we build both ELMo-based and BERT-based models, combining them with our features and measuring the impact of these choices on performance.

7 Conclusion

We described two datasets with annotations of distractor selection for multiple-choice cloze questions for second-language learners. We designed features and developed models based on pretrained language models. Our results show that the task is challenging for humans and that the strongest models are able to approach or exceed human performance. The rankings of distractors provided by our models appear reasonable and can reduce a great deal of human burden in distractor selection. Future work will use our models to collect additional training data which can then be refined in a second pass by limited human annotation. Other future work can explore the utility of features derived from pretrained question answering models in scoring distractors.

References

Tahani Alsubait, Bijan Parsia, and Uli Sattler. 2014. Generating multiple choice questions from ontologies: Lessons learnt. In *OWLED*, pages 73–84. Citeseer.

C. Browne and B. Culligan. 2016. The TOEIC Service List. http://www.newgeneralservicelist.org.

C. Browne, B. Culligan, and J. Phillips. 2013. The New General Service List. http://www.newgeneralservicelist.org.

Chia-Yin Chen, Hsien-Chin Liou, and Jason S Chang. 2006. Fast–an automatic generation system for grammar tests. In *Proceedings of the COLING/ACL 2006 Interactive Presentation Sessions*, pages 1–4.

Tao Chen, Naijia Zheng, Yue Zhao, Muthu Kumar Chandrasekaran, and Min-Yen Kan. 2015. Interactive second language learning from news websites. In *Proceedings of the 2nd Workshop on Natural Language Processing Techniques for Educational Applications*, pages 34–42.

Kyunghyun Cho, Bart van Merriënboer, Caglar Gulcehre, Dzmitry Bahdanau, Fethi Bougares, Holger Schwenk, and Yoshua Bengio. 2014. Learning phrase representations using RNN encoder–decoder for statistical machine translation. In *Proceedings of the 2014 Conference on Empirical Methods in Natural Language Processing (EMNLP)*, pages 1724–1734, Doha, Qatar. Association for Computational Linguistics.

Jacob Devlin, Ming-Wei Chang, Kenton Lee, and Kristina Toutanova. 2018. Bert: Pre-training of deep bidirectional transformers for language understanding. *arXiv preprint arXiv:1810.04805*.

Christiane Fellbaum, editor. 1998. *WordNet: An Electronic Lexical Database*. Language, Speech, and Communication. MIT Press, Cambridge, MA.

Jennifer Hill and Rahul Simha. 2016. Automatic generation of context-based fill-in-the-blank exercises using co-occurrence likelihoods and google n-grams. In *Proceedings of the 11th Workshop on Innovative Use of NLP for Building Educational Applications*, pages 23–30.

Shu Jiang and John Lee. 2017. Distractor generation for chinese fill-in-the-blank items. In *Proceedings of the 12th Workshop on Innovative Use of NLP for Building Educational Applications*, pages 143–148.

Diederik P Kingma and Jimmy Ba. 2014. Adam: A method for stochastic optimization. *arXiv preprint arXiv:1412.6980*.

Philipp Koehn. 2004. Statistical significance tests for machine translation evaluation. In *Proceedings of the 2004 Conference on Empirical Methods in Natural Language Processing*, pages 388–395, Barcelona, Spain. Association for Computational Linguistics.

Chen Liang, Xiao Yang, Neisarg Dave, Drew Wham, Bart Pursel, and C Lee Giles. 2018. Distractor generation for multiple choice questions using learning to rank. In *Proceedings of the thirteenth workshop on innovative use of NLP for building educational applications*, pages 284–290.

Ruslan Mitkov and Le An Ha. 2003. Computer-aided generation of multiple-choice tests. In *Proceedings of the HLT-NAACL 03 workshop on Building educational applications using natural language processing-Volume 2*, pages 17–22. Association for Computational Linguistics.

Jeffrey Pennington, Richard Socher, and Christopher D. Manning. 2014. Glove: Global vectors for word representation. In *Empirical Methods in Natural Language Processing (EMNLP)*, pages 1532–1543.

Matthew Peters, Mark Neumann, Mohit Iyyer, Matt Gardner, Christopher Clark, Kenton Lee, and Luke Zettlemoyer. 2018. Deep contextualized word representations. In *Proceedings of the 2018 Conference of the North American Chapter of the Association for Computational Linguistics: Human Language Technologies, Volume 1 (Long Papers)*, pages 2227–2237, New Orleans, Louisiana. Association for Computational Linguistics.

Van-Minh Pho, Thibault André, Anne-Laure Ligozat, Brigitte Grau, Gabriel Illouz, and Thomas François. 2014. Multiple choice question corpus analysis for distractor characterization. In *Proceedings of the Ninth International Conference on Language Resources and Evaluation (LREC'14)*.

Juan Pino and Maxine Eskenazi. 2009. Semi-automatic generation of cloze question distractors effect of students' l1. In *International Workshop on Speech and Language Technology in Education*.

Juan Pino, Michael Heilman, and Maxine Eskenazi. 2008. A selection strategy to improve cloze question quality. In *Proceedings of the Workshop on Intelligent Tutoring Systems for Ill-Defined Domains. 9th International Conference on Intelligent Tutoring Systems, Montreal, Canada*, pages 22–32.

Simon Smith, PVS Avinesh, and Adam Kilgarriff. 2010. Gap-fill tests for language learners: Corpus-driven item generation. In *Proceedings of ICON-2010: 8th International Conference on Natural Language Processing*, pages 1–6. Macmillan Publishers.

Katherine Stasaski and Marti A Hearst. 2017. Multiple choice question generation utilizing an ontology. In *Proceedings of the 12th Workshop on Innovative Use of NLP for Building Educational Applications*, pages 303–312.

Eiichiro Sumita, Fumiaki Sugaya, and Seiichi Yamamoto. 2005. Measuring non-native speakers' proficiency of english by using a test with automatically-generated fill-in-the-blank questions. In *Proceedings of the second workshop on Building Educational Applications Using NLP*, pages 61–68.

Yuni Susanti, Takenobu Tokunaga, Hitoshi Nishikawa, and Hiroyuki Obari. 2018. Automatic distractor generation for multiple-choice english vocabulary questions. *Research and Practice in Technology Enhanced Learning*, 13(1):15.

Chak Yan Yeung, John SY Lee, and Benjamin K Tsou. 2019. Difficulty-aware distractor generation for gap-fill items. In *Proceedings of the The 17th Annual Workshop of the Australasian Language Technology Association*, pages 159–164.

Torsten Zesch and Oren Melamud. 2014. Automatic generation of challenging distractors using context-sensitive inference rules. In *Proceedings of the Ninth Workshop on Innovative Use of NLP for Building Educational Applications*, pages 143–148.

A   Supplemental Material

A.1   Dataset

There are some problematic words in the dataset, such as 'testing, test', 'find s', 'find ed' in MCD-SENT/MCDPARA candidate words. There are also some extra spaces (or non-breaking spaces) at the start or end of words. To keep the words the same as what the annotators saw, we only remove leading/trailing white space, and replace non-breaking spaces with ordinary spaces. By comparing the percentages of the circumstances where spaces are included in the string before/after tokenization, we find the percentage of extra spaces presented in Table 7. The vocabulary size after tokenization is presented in Table 8.

%	headword(c)	c	headword(d)	d
MCDSENT	0	0	0.0168	0.0332
MCDPARA	0.0160	0.0307	0.0364	0.0622

Table 7: Percentage of extra spaces (excluding those that are in the middle of words), where headword(c) denotes headword of correct answer, and d denotes distractor candidates of inflected forms. .

	headword(c)	c	headword(d)	d
MCDSENT	2571	2731	3514	11423
MCDPARA	2683	4174	3582	13749

Table 8: Vocabulary sizes.

A.2   Distractor Annotation

The software tool suggested distractor candidates based on the following priority ranking:

1. It is in a proprietary dictionary.

2. It has the same part-of-speech (POS) as the correct answer (if POS data is available) and satisfies 1.

3. It is part of a proprietary learnable word list for the language learning course under consideration, and satisfies 2.

4. It is in the same course as the correct answer and satisfies 3.

5. It is in the same proprietary study material bundle as the correct answer and satisfies 4.

6. It is in the previous or same study material as the correct answer and satisfies 5.

7. It is in the same study material as the correct answer and satisfies 6.

8. It is in the same NGSL frequency word list band as the correct answer and satisfies 7.

9. It is not used as a distractor for another word with the same task type in the same material at the time that the distractor list for quality assurance (QA) is loaded, and satisfies 8.

A.3   Context Position

Sometimes the blank resides at the start or end of the context, counts of which are shown in Table 9. The percentage when there is only one sentence as context in MCDPARA is 0.894%.

%	sent start	sent end	para start	para end
FB1	3.058	0.005	-	-
FB3	2.640	0.342	18.272	22.165

Table 9: Position of the candidates, where "sent" denotes sentence and "para" denotes paragraph. "para start" mean that the sentence containing the blank is at the beginning of the paragraph.

A.4   Correlations of Features and Annotations

The Spearman correlations for these features are presented in Table 10. The overall correlations are mostly close to zero, so we explore how the relationships vary for different ranges of feature values below. Nonetheless, we can make certain observations about the correlations:

- Length difference has a weak negative correlation with annotations, which implies that the probability of a candidate being selected decreases when the absolute value of word length difference between the candidate and correct answer increases. The same conclusion can be drawn with headword pairs although the correlation is weaker.

- Embedding similarity has a very weak correlation (even perhaps none) with the annotations. However, the correlation for headwords is slightly negative while that for inflected forms is slightly positive, suggesting that annotators tend to select distractors with different lemmas than the correct answer, but similar inflected forms.

- Candidate frequency also has a very weak correlation with annotations (negative for headwords and positive for inflected forms). Since the feature is the negative log frequency rank, a distractor with a rare headword but more common inflected form is more likely to be selected, at least for MCDSENT.

feature	MCDSENT		MCDPARA	
	head	infl	head	infl
length difference	-0.116	-0.171	-0.145	-0.173
embedding similarity	-0.018	0.026	-0.014	0.016
candidate frequency	-0.057	0.113	-0.062	0.028
freq. rank difference	-0.048	-0.161	-0.033	-0.091

Table 10: Spearman correlations with T/F choices, where "head" denotes headword pairs, and "infl" denotes inflected form pairs.

- Frequency rank difference has a weak negative correlation with annotations, and this trend is more significant with the inflected form pair. This implies that annotators tend to select distractors in the same frequency range as the correct answers.

The correlations are not very large in absolute terms, however we found that there were stronger relationships for particular ranges of these feature values and we explore this in the next section.

A.5 Label-Specific Feature Histograms

Figure 5 shows histograms of the feature values for each label on headword pairs.

A.6 Results Tuned Based on F1

We report our results tuned based on F1 in Table 11 and 12.

A.7 Supplement for Analysis

The example for MCDPARA is as below, and two sets of its distractors are shown in Figure 6.

- MCDPARA: A few years have passed since the Great Tohoku Earthquake occurred. It has been extremely costly to rebuild the damaged areas from scratch, with well over $200 billion dollars provided for reconstruction. However, the **availability** of these funds has been limited. However, a large portion of the money has been kept away from the victims due to a system which favors construction companies....

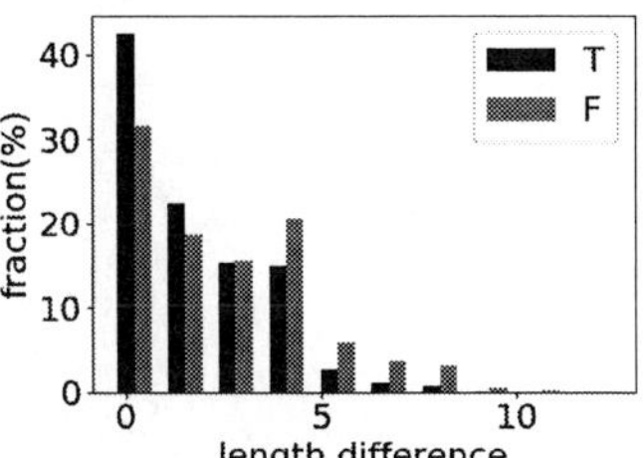
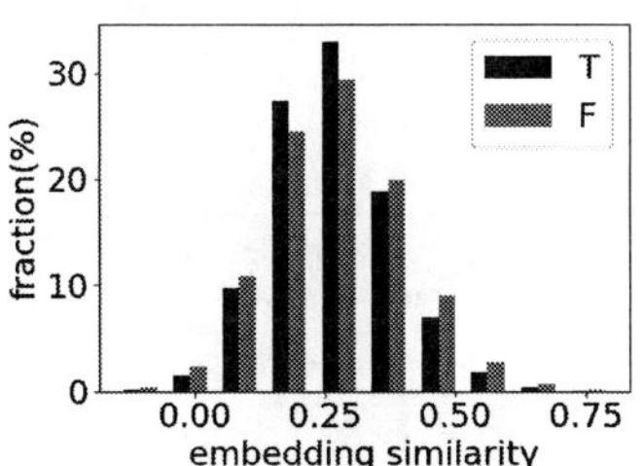
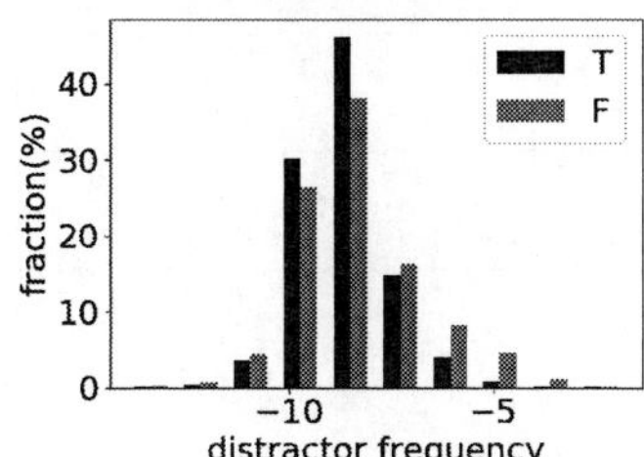
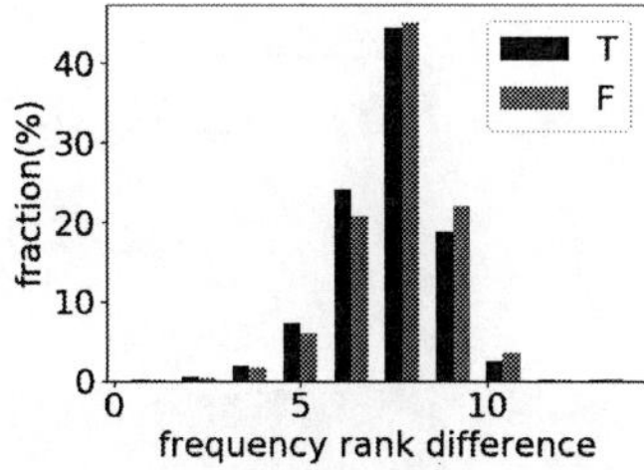

Figure 5: Label-normalized feature histograms for MCDSENT (headword pairs).

model	variant	development set				test set				BERT	features	best epoch	threshold
		precision	recall	F1	AUPR	precision	recall	F1	AUPR				
baseline		15.4	100	26.7	-	13.3	100	23.5	-	-	-	-	-
M_{feat}		33.3	64.8	44.0	35.1	23.2	59.1	33.3	25.0	none	yes	26	0.2
		42.1	67.0	**51.7**	45.4	31.5	57.4	40.7	32.3	base	yes	26	0.2
		41.3	67.1	51.1	**46.7**	32.4	56.6	**41.2**	**33.9**	large	yes	25	0.3
M_{ELMo}	none	49.0	79.1	60.5	58.5	46.5	75.7	57.6	53.9	-	no	6	0.3
	gru+c	49.7	77.6	60.6	54.1	46.1	73.3	56.7	53.5	-	no	3	0.4
	all	52.9	75.8	62.3	60.4	48.0	75.9	58.8	57.6	-	no	2	0.4
	none	51.0	84.0	63.4	63.1	47.7	81.4	60.1	60.6	large	yes	3	0.3
	gru+c	56.9	72.3	63.7	59.1	50.6	75.9	**60.8**	58.6	large	yes	5	0.4
	all	53.5	80.8	**64.4**	**63.4**	50.8	75.5	**60.8**	**59.6**	large	yes	3	0.4
M_{BERT}		48.8	85.5	62.1	56.6	43.8	82.8	57.3	51.5	base	no	4	0.2
		49.6	80.8	61.5	59.1	45.2	79.7	57.7	54.9	large	no	3	0.3
		51.5	84.2	**63.9**	61.7	46.0	78.6	58.0	55.0	base	yes	6	0.2
		51.4	81.1	62.9	**64.7**	46.4	79.8	**58.7**	**57.5**	large	yes	6	0.2

Table 11: Results for MCDSENT tuned based on F1.

model	development set				test set				BERT	features	best epoch	threshold
	precision	recall	F1	AUPR	precision	recall	F1	AUPR				
baseline	7.3	100	13.5	-	6.6	100	12.4	-	-	-	-	-
M_{feat}	17.1	53.1	25.9	15.9	15.6	51.3	23.9	15.0	-	yes	14	0.1
	19.5	63.0	29.8	20.4	17.6	61.0	22.3	**18.6**	base	yes	22	0.1
	20.4	63.1	**30.8**	**22.3**	16.7	62.7	**26.4**	**18.6**	large	yes	25	0.1
M_{ELMo}	35.2	55.4	43.1	37.0	31.2	54.6	39.8	33.9	-	no	5	0.3
	40.2	61.3	**48.5**	**43.8**	34.1	59.4	**43.3**	35.2	large	yes	5	0.3
$M_{ELMo}(\ell)$	28.7	72.9	41.2	33.8	25.7	71.3	37.7	30.3	-	no	2	0.2
	36.2	67.3	47.1	40.8	31.0	65.6	42.1	**37.3**	large	yes	7	0.3
M_{BERT}	35.8	64.2	46.0	39.3	28.9	64.3	39.9	34.5	base	no	5	0.2
	35.2	62.1	45.0	38.3	26.9	60.5	37.3	29.3	large	no	6	0.1
	44.3	55.4	49.3	**47.3**	34.6	56.2	42.8	36.7	base	yes	2	0.3
	37.8	63.3	47.4	44.0	32.7	66.1	**43.7**	**38.1**	large	yes	3	0.2
$M_{BERT}(\ell)$	34.0	64.3	44.5	36.7	29.6	62.1	40.1	32.1	base	no	5	0.2
	43.3	57.5	**49.4**	45.4	33.3	60.9	43.1	35.8	base	yes	3	0.3

Table 12: Results for MCDPARA tuned based on F1.

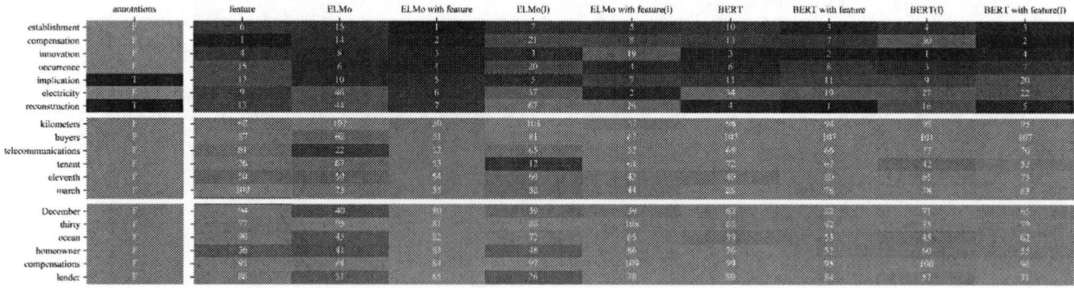

Figure 6: Ranks for distractor candidates of MCDPARA question "However, the **availability** of these funds has been limited." along with annotations.

Assisting Undergraduate Students in Writing Spanish Methodology Sections

Samuel González-López
Technological University of Nogales
Nogales, Sonora, México
sgonzalez@utnogales.edu.mx

Steven Bethard
University of Arizona
Tucson, Arizona, USA
bethard@email.arizona.edu

Aurelio López-López
National Institute of Astrophysics, Optics and Electronics
Tonantzintla, Puebla, México
allopez@inaoep.mx

Abstract

In undergraduate theses, a good methodology section should describe the series of steps that were followed in performing the research. To assist students in this task, we develop machine-learning models and an app that uses them to provide feedback while students write. We construct an annotated corpus that identifies sentences representing methodological steps and labels when a methodology contains a logical sequence of such steps. We train machine-learning models based on language modeling and lexical features that can identify sentences representing methodological steps with 0.939 f-measure, and identify methodology sections containing a logical sequence of steps with an accuracy of 87%. We incorporate these models into a Microsoft Office Add-in, and show that students who improved their methodologies according to the model feedback received better grades on their methodologies.

1 Introduction

In the Mexican higher education system, most undergraduate students write a thesis (*tesis de licenciatura*) before graduation. The academic advisor and the student are typically both involved. Throughout the process, the advisor spends time reviewing the draft that the student is building and gradually offering suggestions. This process becomes a cycle until the document meets established standards and/or institutional guidelines. This cycle is often slow due to the required changes in the structure of the thesis. One of the key components of such a thesis is a methodology section, which contains the steps and procedures used to develop the research. A methodology is supposed to provide a step-by-step explanation of the aspects necessary to understand and replicate the research including the techniques and procedures employed, the type of research, the population studied, the data sample, the collection instruments, the data selection process, the validation instrument, and the statistical analysis process (Allen, 1976).

Natural language processing techniques have the potential to assist students in writing such methodologies, as several aspects of good methodologies are visible from lexical and orthographic features of the text. A good methodology should have phrases or sentences that represent a series of steps, which may be written in a numbered list or in prose with sequential connectives like *next*. Steps in a methodology section should have a predicate that represents the action of that step, like *analyze* or *design*. And the list of steps should be in a logical order, e.g., an *explore* step should typically appear before (not after) an *implement* step. Good methodology sections should of course have much more beyond these simple features, but any methodology section that is missing these basic components is clearly in need of revision.

We thus focus on designing machine-learning models to detect and evaluate the quality of such steps in a Spanish-language student-written methodology section, and on incorporating such models into an interactive application that gives students feedback on their writing. Our contributions are the following:

- We annotate a small corpus of methodology sections drawn from Spanish information technology theses for the presence of steps and their logical order.
- We design a model to detect sentences that represent methodological steps, incorporating language model and verb taxonomy features, achieving 0.939 f-measure.

Proceedings of the 15th Workshop on Innovative Use of NLP for Building Educational Applications, pages 115–123
July 10, 2020. ©2020 Association for Computational Linguistics

- We design a model to identify when a methodology has a logical sequence of steps, incorporating language model and content word features, achieving an accuracy of 87%.
- We incorporate the models into an Add-In for Microsoft Word, and measure how the application's feedback improves student writing.

2 Background

There is a long history of natural language processing research on interactive systems that assist student writing. Essay scoring has been a popular topic, with techniques ranging from syntactic and discourse analysis (Burstein and Chodorow, 1999), to list-wise learning-to-rank (Chen and He, 2013), to recurrent neural networks (Taghipour and Ng, 2016). Yet the goal of such work is very different from ours, as we aim not to assign an overall score, but rather to provide detailed feedback on aspects of a good methodology that are present or absent from the draft.

Intelligent tutoring systems have been developed for a wide range of topics, including mechanical systems (Di Eugenio et al., 2002), qualitative physics (Litman and Silliman, 2004), learning a new language (Wang and Seneff, 2007), and introductory computer science (Fossati, 2008). As we focus on assisting students in writing thesis methodology sections, the most relevant prior work focuses on analysis of essays. ETS Criterion (Attali, 2004) uses features like n-gram frequency and syntactic analysis to provide feedback for grammatical errors, discourse structure, and undesirable stylistic features. The SAT system (Andersen et al., 2013) combines lexical and grammatical properties with a perceptron learner to provide detailed sentence-by-sentence feedback about possible lexical and grammatical errors. Revision Assistant (Woods et al., 2017) uses logistic regression over lexical and grammatical features to provide feedback on how individual sentences influence rubric-specific formative scores. All of these systems aim at general types of feedback, not the specific feedback needed for methodology sections.

Other related work touches on issues of logical organization. Barzilay and Lapata (2008) propose training sentence ordering models to differentiate between the original order of a well-written text and a permuted sentence order. Cui et al. (2018) continue in this paradigm, training an encoder-decoder network to read a series of sentences and reorder them for better coherence. Our goal is not to reorder a student's sentences, but to provide more detailed feedback on whether the right structures (e.g., steps) are present in the methodology. More relevant work is Persing et al. (2010), which combines lexical heuristics with sequence alignment models to score the organization of an essay. However, they provide only an overall score, and do not integrate this into any intelligent tutoring system.

A final major difference between our work and prior work is that all the work above focused on the English language, while we provide feedback for Spanish-language theses.

3 Data

A collection was created using the ColTyPi[1] site. This site includes Spanish-language theses within the Information Technologies subject area. The graduate level is composed of Doctoral and Master theses. The Undergraduate level is composed of Bachelor and Advanced College-level Technician (TSU) theses. All theses and research proposals in the collection have been reviewed at some point by a review committee.

3.1 Guidelines

A four-page guide was provided to the annotators with the instructions for labeling and a brief description of the elements to identify. Annotators marked each sentence (or text segment) that represented a step in a series of steps. For each step, annotators marked the main predicate (typically a verb). Finally, annotators judged whether or not the steps of the methodology represented a logical sequence.The guide included three examples for the annotators, the first one detailed a methodology that accomplished a series of steps and a logical sequence, the second example only met a series of steps, and the third example didn't show any feature. The annotators did not have access to the academic corresponding to each methodology. Figure 1 shows an annotated example.

3.2 Annotation

From ColTyPi, 160 methodologies were downloaded, 40 at the PhD level, 60 at the Master level, 40 at the Bachelor level, and 20 at the TSU level. Two professors in the computer area with experience in reviewing graduate and undergraduate

---

[1]We used, `http://coltypi.org/`

Para desarrollar el trabajo propuesto se siguió un conjunto de pasos para asegurar el cumplimiento de cada uno de los objetivos presentados. A continuación se enumeran las necesidades superadas en el desarrollo de la investigación:

1. Recopilación bibliográfica y análisis detallado de los acercamientos de desambiguación existentes.

2. *Caracterización* de las familias de lenguajes y su relación con el lenguaje español.

3. *Seleccionar* el idioma que se empleará como lenguaje meta en los textos paralelos.

4. *Comparar* y *aplicar* diversas herramientas de alineación a nivel de palabras sobre el corpus elegido.

5. *Analizar* diccionarios monolingües y bilingües disponibles.

6. *Diseñar* un algoritmo para la adquisición de etiquetas de sentidos extraídas de la alineación resultante.

To develop the proposed work, a set of steps was followed to ensure each of the objectives presented. Below are the tasks involved in this research:

1.Bibliographic compilation and detailed analysis of existing disambiguation approaches.

2.*Characterize* language families and their relationship with the Spanish language.

3. *Select* the language to be used as the target language in parallel texts.

4. *Compare* and *apply* various alignment tools at the word level on the chosen corpus.

5. *Analyze* monolingual and bilingual dictionaries available.

6. *Design* an algorithm for the acquisition of labels of senses extracted from the resulting alignment.

Figure 1: Part of a Spanish methodology tagged by the annotators (Spanish original above, English translation below). The series of steps is shaded in gray, the verbs identified are in italics, and the annotators marked this methodology as "Yes" for the presence of logical sequence.

student theses, were recruited as annotators. Both annotators tagged 160 methodology sections, and inter-annotator agreement was measured. For the two information extraction tasks, identifying steps and identifying predicates, inter-annotator agreement was measured with F-score following Hripcsak and Rothschild (2005). For logical sequence, which is a binary per-methodology judgment, inter-annotator agreement was measured with Cohen's Kappa (Landis and Koch, 1977). The annotators achieved 0.90 F-score on identifying steps, 0.89 F-score on identifying predicates, and 0.46 Kappa (moderate agreement) on judging logical sequence. Identifying the logical sequence was a complicated task for the annotators since the objective was that a whole methodology evidenced a logical sequence concerning the verbs used. For instance, in the first steps of the methodology, the student should use verbs like "identify" or "explore" and verbs like "implement" or "install" at the end of the methodology.

The annotated data was divided up for experiments. Only annotations that both annotators agreed on were considered. For the methodological step extraction task, we selected 300 sentences annotated as representing a step, and 100 sentences annotated as not representing a step, with the sentences selected to cover both graduate and undergraduate levels. For the logical sequence detection task, we selected 50 complete methodologies anno-

tated as having a logical sequence and 50 annotated as not having a logical sequence.

4 Model: step identification

The model for identifying which sentences represent steps (StepID) is a logistic regression[2] that takes a sentence as input, and predicts whether that sentence is a methodology step or not. The model considers the five types of features described in the following sections.

4.1 Language model features

To measure how well the words in a Methodology match the typical sequence of words in a good Methodology, we turn to language modeling techniques. We expected to capture facts like that the presence of verbs "Select', "Analyze" or "Compare" at the beginning of sentences is probably describing a series of steps. We preprocessed all sentences by extracting lemmas using FreeLing.[3] Afterwards, two language models were built, the first (TM) with tokens (words, numbers, punctuation marks) and the second (GM) with grammatical classes. These language models were built only on the sentences labeled as positive, i.e., on sentences that should be examples of good token/grammatical

---

[2]We used the implementation in Weka 3.6.13, `https://www.cs.waikato.ac.nz/ml/weka/`

[3]FreeLing4.1,`http://nlp.lsi.upc.edu/freeling/`

class sequences. We used the SRILM[4] toolkit with 4-grams and Kneser-Ney smoothing.[5] To generate these features for the 300 positive sentences on which the language models were trained, we used 10-fold cross-validation, so as not to overestimate the language model probabilities. The 100 negative sentences were also processed separately, again with a 10-fold cross-validation.Perplexity values from the language models were used as features. This component contributed 2 features to the StepID classifier.

4.2 Sentence location features

A methodology can begin immediately with sequence of steps, or there may be a brief introduction before the steps appear. Thus, location within the methodology may be a predictive feature. We identified whether the sentence under consideration is in the first third, second third, or final third of the methodology. This component contributed 3 features to the StepID classifier.

4.3 Verb taxonomy features

This component captures the type of the verbs used in the series of steps. We use a taxonomy based on the cyclical nature of engineering education (CNEE; Fernandez-Sanchez et al., 2012), structured in four successive levels. Categories of verbs include Knowledge and Comprehension, Application and Analysis, System Design, Engineering Creation. In addition, we added a category to identify verbs related to the writing process, as part of the steps to conclude the thesis.

We considered three ways of identifying such verb categories in sentences.

CNEE+Stem Each verb in the sentence is stemmed, and compared against the 54 verbs of the CNEE taxonomy.

CNEE+FastText The 54 verbs in the CNEE taxonomy are expanded to 540 verbs by taking the 10 most similar words according to pretrained word vectors from FastText (Bojanowski et al., 2016)[6]. Each verb in the sentence is compared against these 540 verbs.

CNEE+Manual An expert annotator manually labeled each verb with an appropriate one of the five categories from the CNEE taxonomy.

For CNEE+Stem and CNEE+FastText, only the first verb category found is included as a feature[7]. This component contributed 5 features to the StepID classifier.

4.4 Sequencing element features

The online writing lab at Purdue University[8] identifies a category of words designed "to show sequence" that includes words like *first*, *second*, *next*, *then*, *after*. We coupled the words from this category with a simple pattern to identify bullet points or numbered items to produce a rule that identifies whether such sequencing elements are present in the text. This component contributed 1 feature to the StepID classifier.

5 Model: logical sequence detection

The model for detecting logical sequence (LogicSeq) is a multilayer perceptron, with a single hidden layer of size two plus the number of features (Weka's a layer specifier), that takes an entire methodology as input, and predicts whether it contains a logical sequence of steps or not. The model considers the features described in the following section.

5.1 Language model features

We again incorporate language models to measure how sequences of terms are used in well-written methodologies. This component includes the same GM and TM features as Section 4.1, except trained on the 100 positive and negative methodologies, rather than on individual sentences. We also include a third language model that considers only the nouns and verbs (NV) of the sentences of the methodology. Each token is followed by its part of speech in the language model input. The goal is to focus on just the words most likely to express methodological steps – *characterize*, *select*, *compare*, *analyze*, *design*, etc. – without restricting the analysis to a specific lexicon of words.

We considered bigrams and/or 4-grams for the GM, TM, and NV features. This component contributed either 3 features to the LogicSeq classifier, or 6 features when both bigrams and 4-grams were used.

---

[4]SRILM 1.7.3, http://www.speech.sri.com/projects/srilm/

[5]In preliminary experiments, we also tried using the TheanoLM toolkit, but performance was lower than SRILM.

[6]https://fasttext.cc/

[7]In preliminary experiments, we also tried using all verb categories, but this did not improve performance.

[8]https://owl.purdue.edu/

TM	GM	Loc	CNEE+Stem	CNEE+FastText	CNEE+Manual	Precision	Recall	F
✓						0.808	0.953	0.875
	✓					0.816	0.947	0.877
✓	✓					0.834	0.953	0.890
✓	✓	✓				0.843	0.947	0.892
✓	✓	✓	✓			0.901	0.937	0.918
✓	✓	✓		✓		0.912	0.967	**0.939**
✓	✓	✓			✓	0.949	0.983	0.966

Table 1: 10-fold cross-validation performance on the "is this a methodological step" classification task.

GM bigram	TM bigram	NV bigram	GM 4-gram	TM 4-gram	NV 4-gram	Accuracy
✓						76 %
	✓					72 %
		✓				63 %
✓	✓	✓				77 %
			✓	✓	✓	79 %
✓	✓	✓	✓	✓	✓	**87 %**

Table 2: 10-fold cross-validation performance on the "is there a logical sequence " classification task.

6 StepID and LogicSeq results

Both classifiers were evaluated using 10-fold cross-validation on their respective parts of our annotated corpus.

Table 1 shows the performance of the step identification model in terms of precision, recall, and F-score for detecting steps. Including all proposed features proposed yields 0.918 when stemming is used to find verbs and 0.939 when FastText is used instead of stemming. Using the human-annotated verb features yields 0.966, suggesting that performance could be further improved with a better lexicon mapping technique.

Table 2 shows the performance of the logical sequence detection model. The best model used both bigrams and 4-grams of all three language-model features, and achieved an accuracy of 87%.

We thus find that despite our modest-sized data

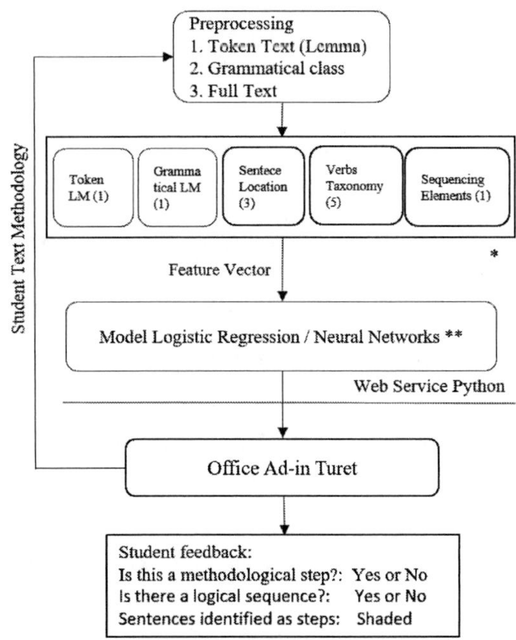

Figure 2: System architecture for TURET. *StepID used all features; LogicSeq used only LM features. **StepID used logistic regression; LogicSeq used neural networks.

sets, accurate models based on language-model features can be trained to detect methodological steps in a thesis and identify whether those steps appear in a logical order. In the next section, we move from the intrinsic evaluation of our models on the annotated dataset to an extrinsic evaluation in a user study.

7 Pilot test

We designed and performed a pilot test to assess the impact of using an application focused on the two models created, StepID and LogicSeq. The goal is to evaluate these models in an environment where students interact with the models while writing. Our main research question is: What elements incorporated in the developed methods will have a positive impact on the student's final document?

7.1 User interface

We first developed an Office add-in that could apply the StepID and LogicSeq models to a document while students were writing it. We chose to implement the app as an Office add-in as it allowed students to work in a writing environment they were already very familiar with: Microsoft Word. The software developed, Tutor Revisor de Tesis

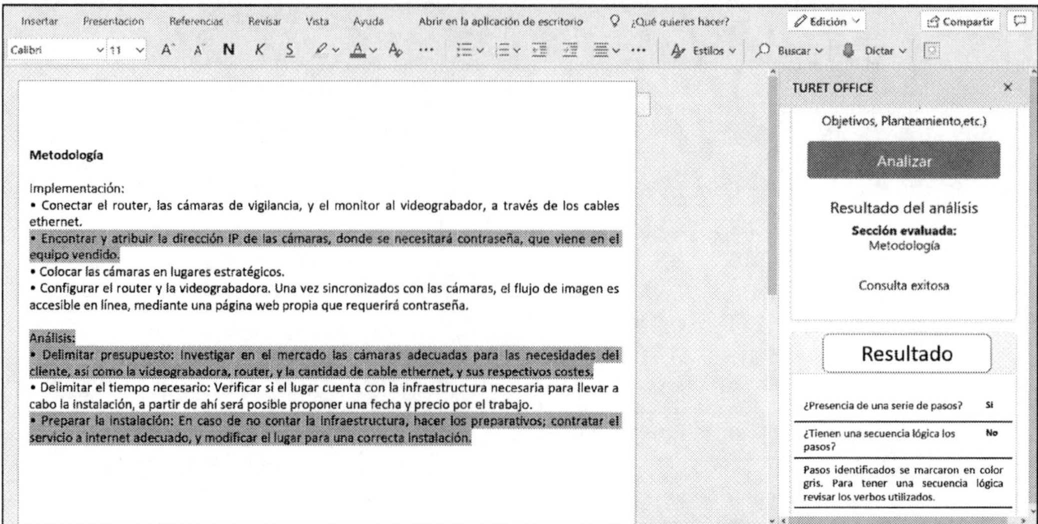

Figure 3: Application interface embedded in Office Ad-in

(TURET), was embedded in the Microsoft Word processor through a component developed in the Azure platform for Office Add-ins. As part of this development, we had to re-implement the StepID and LogicSeq algorithms using Scikit-learn, but reused the same language model features created with the SRILM toolkit. Figure 2 shows the architecture of the system. In the first stage the preprocessing was done sentence by sentence to compute eleven features established in the StepId method. For the LogicSeq method the entire methodology was processed to extract six features.

Figure 3 shows an example methodology open in Microsoft Word with TURET enabled. The methodology written by the student is shown on the left side. After clicking, sentences that are identified as being part of a series of steps are marked, and the student is also sent binary feedback indicating whether the methodology shows a series of steps and/or a logical sequence. Notice that the methodology shows seven steps, but the method only detects 3 of them as valid. This is most likely because words like *implementation* and *connect* are not generally appropriate at the beginning of a methodology. Thus, this example shows an absence of a logical sequence. The system correctly predicts this, as shown in through the *No* in the feedback frame.

7.2 Experimental design

The pilot test was conducted with two groups of 20 (for a total of 40) undergraduate computer science students. Each student received an introduction explaining how to use the TURET application. Then the student was provided with a problem statement related to a computer science project and was asked to write a methodology that provides a solution. Students were encouraged to try to achieve positive feedback from the system on two aspects: that the methodology had a logical sequence and that there was evidence of a series of steps. Students had access to the application for 1 month and were expected to use TURET at least twice (i.e., on a first draft and a final draft) but could freely use the application more frequently if desired.

We also included a control group of 20 undergraduate computer science students who did not use TURET, but still used Microsoft Word to write a methodology in response to the same problem statements.

To validate the quality of the documents generated by both the TURET students and the control students, a teacher experienced in grading undergraduate theses evaluated both the first and the final draft. Each methodology received a rating on a scale of 1 to 10, where 10 is the best. The teacher was not informed about the use of the TURET application; they graded the methodologies as they would. Of the total number of students who started the pilot test, only 35 completed the entire process.

7.3 Statistical analysis

A multiple regression analysis was made on the results obtained from the evaluation of the method-

Factor	Coefficients	P-values
Intercept	7.5552	0.0001
N-Steps	-0.1421	0.1263
Steps?	0.2652	0.6946
Logical Sequence?	1.2237	0.0096

Table 3: Coefficients of different final draft factors when predicting the final grade of a student.

Items	Coefficients	P-values
Intercept	0.7768	0.0231
N-Steps	-0.3066	0.0097
Steps?	1.0103	0.0342
Logical Sequence?	0.6342	0.1270

Table 4: Coefficients of different (Final - Draft) factors when predicting the change in grade between Draft and Final (i.e., the Final - Draft grade).

ologies, with the teacher's grade of the final draft as the dependent variable and the following factors measured on their final draft:

N-Steps A non-negative integer representing the number of sentences of each methodology that the StepId model recognized as methodological steps.

Steps? A binary value, with a value of 1 when the StepId model recognized at least one sentence as a methodological step, or a value of 0 if there was no such sentence.

Logical Sequence? A binary value, with a value of 1 when the LogicSeq model recognized the methodology as having a logical sequence, and a value of 0 otherwise.

Table 3 shows that when predicting the grade assigned to a student's final draft, the LogicSeq model's prediction is a statistically significant predictor: drafts judged to have a logical sequence were on average score 1.2237 higher than the other drafts.

We also explored a multiple regression designed to test how much changes in a student's writing predicted changes in their grade. Instead of considering only the final draft, as above, we consider the difference between the initial and the final for all factors as well as the dependent variable. We thus re-define the factors as follows.

N-Steps An integer representing the increase in number of sentences recognized as methodological steps by the StepId model when moving from the draft to the final document.

Steps? An integer, with a value of 1 when the StepId model found no steps in the draft but at least one in the final, a value of 0 when the number of steps identified by StepId was unchanged between draft and final, and a value of -1 when the StepId model found at least one step in the draft but none in the final.

Logical Sequence? An integer, with a value of 1 when the LogicSeq model found no logical

sequence in the draft but found one in the final, a value of 0 when there was no change in the prediction of the LogicSeq model between draft and final, and a value of -1 when the LogicSeq model found a logical sequence in the draft but none in the final.

Table 4 shows that when predicting how much a student's grade will improve from draft to final, the change in the number of steps identified by StepId is a statistically significant predictor. Students that went from having no steps to having one or more steps on average scored 1.0103 better than students with no change. Interestingly, having many steps was not necessarily a good thing: for each additional step, students on average lost 0.3066 from their score. This suggests that students who added too many more steps to their drafts were penalized for doing so.

Finally, we compared the TURET group of students against the control group of students. On the 20 problem statements that were common to the TURET and control groups, the TURET students on average scored 7.85, while the control students scored 6.8. The difference is significant ($p = .041139$) according to a t-test for two independent means (two tailed).

7.4 Satisfaction survey

To assess the opinion of the experimental group on using the TURET Office Add-in, a satisfaction survey based on the Technology Acceptance Model (Davis et al., 1989) was conducted. Students were asked about the usefulness, ease of use, adaptability and, their intention to use the system. For example, the "usefulness" questions were: Does the system improve your methodology? Did the system improve the performance of your learning? In general, do you think that the system was an advantage for your learning to write arguments? As another example, the "ease of use" questions were: Was learning to use the system easy for you? Was the process

Measure	Score
Usefulness	4.54
Ease of use	4.85
Adaptability	4.67
Intention to use	4.50

Table 5: Satisfaction survey results TAM

of using the system clear and understandable?. In general, do you think the system was easy to use?

Student answers were based on a five-point Likert scale ranging from 1 ("Strongly disagree") to 5 ("Strongly agree"), and the scores across each category of question were averaged. Table 5 shows that students rated the application above 4 points ("Agree") for all aspects. The highest score was 4.85 on ease of use, which we attribute to the use of a Microsoft Word Add-in, which takes advantage of students' already existing familiarity with Microsoft Word.

We also collected free-form comments from the students. Their biggest complaint was that TURET works only in the online version of Microsoft Office (since it must communicate with a server), and they would have liked to use it in offline mode.

8 Discussion

We have demonstrated that with a small amount of training data, several carefully engineered features, and standard supervised classification algorithms, we can construct models that can reliably (0.939 F) detect the presence of steps in student-written Spanish methodology sections, and reliably (87% accuracy) determine whether those steps are presented in a logical order. We have also shown that incorporating these models into an Office Add-in for Microsoft Word resulted in a system that students found useful and easy to use, and that the detections of the models were predictive of teacher-assigned essay grades.

There are some limitations to our study. First, because of the success of our simple models, we did not investigate more complex recent models like BERT (Devlin et al., 2019). Such models might yield improved predictive performance but at a significant additional computational cost. Second, the amount of data that we annotated was small, as it required a high level of expertise in the reviewing of Spanish-language methodology sections. (We relied on Spanish-speaking professors in computer science.) It would be good to expand the size of the dataset, but we take the high levels of performance of the models, and the fact that they make useful predictions on the unseen student-generated methodologies of the pilot test, as an indication that the dataset is already useful in its current size. Finally, the pilot study was a controlled experiment, where specific problem statements were given as prompts. It would be interesting to measure the utility of the application for students writing their own theses.

In the future, we would like to explore integrating other types of writing feedback into the TURET Office Add-in, since students found its feedback about methodology steps both intuitive and helpful. Though we focused on methodology sections in this article, our vision is a set of models that can provide useful feedback for all sections of a Spanish-language student thesis.

References

George R. Allen. 1976. *The Graduate Students' Guide to Theses and Dissertations: A Practical Manual for Writing and Research*, volume 1. Jossey-Bass Inc., Publishers, 615 Montgomery Street, San Francisco.

Øistein E. Andersen, Helen Yannakoudakis, Fiona Barker, and Tim Parish. 2013. Developing and testing a self-assessment and tutoring system. In *Proceedings of the Eighth Workshop on Innovative Use of NLP for Building Educational Applications*, pages 32–41, Atlanta, Georgia. Association for Computational Linguistics.

Yigal Attali. 2004. Exploring the feedback and revision features of criterion. *Journal of Second Language Writing*, 14:191–205.

Regina Barzilay and Mirella Lapata. 2008. Modeling local coherence: An entity-based approach. *Computational Linguistics*, 34(1):1–34.

Piotr Bojanowski, Edouard Grave, Armand Joulin, and Tomas Mikolov. 2016. Enriching word vectors with subword information. *arXiv preprint arXiv:1607.04606*.

Jill Burstein and Martin Chodorow. 1999. Automated essay scoring for nonnative English speakers. In *Computer Mediated Language Assessment and Evaluation in Natural Language Processing*.

Hongbo Chen and Ben He. 2013. Automated essay scoring by maximizing human-machine agreement. In *Proceedings of the 2013 Conference on Empirical Methods in Natural Language Processing*, pages 1741–1752, Seattle, Washington, USA. Association for Computational Linguistics.

Baiyun Cui, Yingming Li, Ming Chen, and Zhongfei Zhang. 2018. Deep attentive sentence ordering network. In *Proceedings of the 2018 Conference on Empirical Methods in Natural Language Processing*, pages 4340–4349, Brussels, Belgium. Association for Computational Linguistics.

Fred D. Davis, Richard P. Bagozzi, and Paul R. Warshaw. 1989. User acceptance of computer technology: A comparison of two theoretical models. *Management Science*, 35(8):982–1003.

Jacob Devlin, Ming-Wei Chang, Kenton Lee, and Kristina Toutanova. 2019. BERT: Pre-training of deep bidirectional transformers for language understanding. In *Proceedings of the 2019 Conference of the North American Chapter of the Association for Computational Linguistics: Human Language Technologies, Volume 1 (Long and Short Papers)*, pages 4171–4186, Minneapolis, Minnesota. Association for Computational Linguistics.

Barbara Di Eugenio, Michael Glass, and Michael Trolio. 2002. The DIAG experiments: Natural language generation for intelligent tutoring systems. In *Proceedings of the International Natural Language Generation Conference*, pages 120–127, Harriman, New York, USA. Association for Computational Linguistics.

Pilar Fernandez-Sanchez, Angel Salaverría, and Enrique Mandado. 2012. Taxonomía de los niveles del aprendizaje de la ingeniería y su implementación mediante herramientas informáticas. In *X Congreso de Tecnologías Aplicadas en la Enseñanza de la Electrónica*, pages 522–527.

Davide Fossati. 2008. The role of positive feedback in Intelligent Tutoring Systems. In *Proceedings of the ACL-08: HLT Student Research Workshop*, pages 31–36, Columbus, Ohio. Association for Computational Linguistics.

George Hripcsak and Adam S. Rothschild. 2005. Agreement, the f-measure, and reliability in information retrieval. *Journal of the American Medical Informatics Association*, 12(3):296–298.

J. Richard Landis and Gary G. Koch. 1977. The measurement of observer agreement for categorical data. *Biometrics*, 33(1):159–174.

Diane J. Litman and Scott Silliman. 2004. ITSPOKE: An intelligent tutoring spoken dialogue system. In *Demonstration Papers at HLT-NAACL 2004*, pages 5–8, Boston, Massachusetts, USA. Association for Computational Linguistics.

Isaac Persing, Alan Davis, and Vincent Ng. 2010. Modeling organization in student essays. In *Proceedings of the 2010 Conference on Empirical Methods in Natural Language Processing*, pages 229–239, Cambridge, MA. Association for Computational Linguistics.

Kaveh Taghipour and Hwee Tou Ng. 2016. A neural approach to automated essay scoring. In *Proceedings of the 2016 Conference on Empirical Methods in Natural Language Processing*, pages 1882–1891, Austin, Texas. Association for Computational Linguistics.

Chao Wang and Stephanie Seneff. 2007. Automatic assessment of student translations for foreign language tutoring. In *Human Language Technologies 2007: The Conference of the North American Chapter of the Association for Computational Linguistics; Proceedings of the Main Conference*, pages 468–475, Rochester, New York. Association for Computational Linguistics.

Bronwyn Woods, David Adamson, Shayne Miel, and Elijah Mayfield. 2017. Formative essay feedback using predictive scoring models. In *Proceedings of the 23rd ACM SIGKDD International Conference on Knowledge Discovery and Data Mining*, KDD '17, page 2071–2080, New York, NY, USA. Association for Computing Machinery.

Applications of Natural Language Processing in Bilingual Language Teaching: An Indonesian-English Case Study

Zara Maxwell-Smith[1]   Ben Foley[2]   Simón González Ochoa[1]   Hanna Suominen[1,3−4]

1. The Australian National University / Canberra, ACT, Australia
2. University of Queensland / Brisbane, QLD, Australia
3. Data61/Commonwealth Scientific and Industrial Research Organisation / Canberra, ACT, Australia
4. University of Turku / Turku, Finland

`Zara.Maxwell-Smith@anu.edu.au, b.foley@uq.edu.au, Simon.Gonzalez@anu.edu.au, Hanna.Suominen@anu.edu.au`

Abstract

Multilingual corpora are difficult to compile and a classroom setting adds pedagogy to the mix of factors which make this data so rich and problematic to classify. In this paper, we set out methodological considerations of using automated speech recognition to build a corpus of teacher speech in an Indonesian language classroom. Our preliminary results (64% word error rate) suggest these tools have the potential to speed data collection in this context. We provide practical examples of our data structure, details of our piloted computer-assisted processes, and fine-grained error analysis. Our study is informed and directed by genuine research questions and discussion in both the education and computational linguistics fields. We highlight some of the benefits and risks of using these emerging technologies to analyze the complex work of language teachers and in education more generally.

1 Introduction

Using quantitative methods to understand language learning and teaching is difficult work as limitations in the recording, transcribing, and analyzing of data continue to constrain the size of datasets. It is not surprising then, that quantitative studies looking at *second language*[1] *acquisition* have been critiqued for their low statistical power (Plonsky, 2013). Usage-based analyses of teacher corpora are an important next stage in understanding language acquisition (Ellis, 2017). Given the magnitude of worldwide investment in *L2 teaching and learning*, drawing on developments in automated methods of compiling this kind of speech data is timely.

Consequently, we sought to address the following main research question in this paper: How can *automated speech recognition* (ASR) be adapted for this use? More specifically, i) How well do these speech-to-text tools perform on this type of data? and ii) How do these tools and datasets relate to the overall purpose of opening a window into the practice of language teachers? Such an endeavor requires careful consideration of how ASR models are built, and what the underlying training data and desired output of such models might be. In this paper we use the term *ASR model* to refer to statistical models used to map speech sequences and sounds to respective text sequences (Jurafsky and Martin, 2009, pp. 38, 286, 287).

Our study is drawn from a project investigating the teaching of *Indonesian*. Data was collected from a tertiary Indonesian language program at an Australian university. A single teacher's speech was recorded throughout one semester of a second-year language program. In investigating Indonesian language teaching, ideally various instances of linguistic features and non-standard Indonesian would be annotated to allow for analyzing various topics, including, for instance, the comprehensibility of teachers' speech, movement between the L2 and assumed *first language* (L1), representations of regional Indonesian languages, and non-standard varieties and loanwords. Yet, the tools tend to restrict the data structures for annotating the audio. As an example from the conclusions of this paper, the classification of data as belonging to the L2 (Indonesian) or the L1 (*English*) quickly emerged as a very significant issue.

The paper is organized as follows: We begin by presenting an overview of related work in transcription and ASR before describing our methodological approach, with subsections on bilingual and classroom teacher data. This is followed by a more detailed description of our materials and methods to train and evaluate ASR models. Finally, we present experimental results of our machine transcription, discuss them, and conclude the study.

---

[1]a.k.a. target language or L2

Proceedings of the 15th Workshop on Innovative Use of NLP for Building Educational Applications, pages 124–134
July 10, 2020. ©2020 Association for Computational Linguistics

2   Background

Transcription is a complex task traditionally seen by linguists from the perspective of linguistic theory and documentation of complex language structures and phenomena. Linguists and their research teams become extremely familiar with their data during the process of transcribing, and their publications usually make reference to data-specific guidelines developed for their transcription teams (BNC-Consortium, 2007). Often these are adapted from generic guidelines or rules for annotating language which aim to record the "most basic transcription information: the words and who they were spoken by, the division of the stream of speech into turns and intonation units, the truncation of intonation units and words, intonation contours, medium and long pauses, laughter, and uncertain hearings or indecipherable words" (Du Bois et al., 1993). Most teams use sophisticated software tools, which provide a method for rich interlinear annotation of speech data by humans.[2] These annotations allow linguists to record more than 'just' the words used in human communication, but obviously cannot represent all characteristics of the audio data.

Acknowledging the *time constraints* and *subjectivity* or *bias* that enter the transcription process as transcription guidelines are developed is important. The purpose of these guidelines — namely, to create uniformity of practice from individual, and teams of transcribers — may not be achievable (Hovy and Lavid, 2010). In fact, experiments looking at the subjectivity of transcription led Lapadat and Lindsay (1998) to conclude that "the choices researchers make about transcription enact the theories they hold and constrain the interpretations they draw from their educational practice". Moreover, a transcription survey carried out by the *Centre of Excellence for the Dynamics of Language, Transcription Acceleration Project* (CoEDL TAP) team documented a significant variety in the way linguists go about transcribing their data. The survey also found that each minute of data takes, on average, 39 minutes for a linguist to transcribe, creating the well-known 'transcription bottleneck' (Durantin, 2017).

Advances in ASR and other *natural language processing* (NLP) bring researchers closer to overcoming this bottleneck, but many open challenges remain (Hirschberg and Manning, 2015). ASR tools can help by providing a first-pass hypothesis of audio for languages with large datasets to train the underlying models (Google, 2019; Nuance, 2019).[3] However, financial and ethical restrictions may prevent a study from using these off-the-shelf systems and cloud computing services.[4] Existing solutions may also have insufficient coverage of the domain-specific language used by speakers or not support a given L2.

Recognizing the potential benefit that integrating ASR tools into a linguist's workflow could have, the CoEDL TAP team has been building *Elpis* (Foley et al., 2018), an accessible interface for researchers to use the powerful but complex *Kaldi ASR toolkit*.[5] According to Gaida et al. (2014) "Compared to the other recognizers, the outstanding performance of Kaldi can be seen as a revolution in open-source [ASR] technology". This project constitutes an early use of the Elpis pipeline to prepare training data, ready for Kaldi to build ASR models, which can then be used to "infer" a hypothesis for un-transcribed audio.

The *interdisciplinary work* involved in this project shines a spotlight on the limitations on the type of data used by ASR systems; human transcribers often face difficult decisions as to what should and what should not be recorded in the training data.[6] Since bias and error may multiply in ASR models and create unreliable and undesirable outcomes, sharing the best practices and having transparent processes for creating training and evaluation data and protocols is of utmost importance (Hovy and Lavid, 2010). ASR trained on carefully compiled data can then be scientifically tested and variations to the training data analysed for their impact (Baur et al., 2018).

3   Methodological Approach

Our methodological considerations addressed the following: which ASR tool to use, how to prepare training data for this tool, and how to best manage the bias of the training data inherent in all transcription processes. Kaldi's orthographic transcription

---

[2]e.g., ELAN, Transana, and FLEx (last accessed on 4 December 2019)

[3]E.g., Google's Cloud Speech-to-Text and Nuance's ASR Self-Service support 120 languages and 86 languages/dialects, respectively (last accessed on 4 December 2019).

[4]E.g., purchasing a license for all participating teachers and obtaining each participant's informed consent for their speech data to be saved on a cloud owned by a private corporation, possibly using them to develop their ASR and other commercial products, may be infeasible or questionable.

[5]last accessed on 4 December 2019

[6]See our examples below for illustration.

capabilities and Elpis' processing and output of time-aligned ELAN files were a good fit with the broader research goals in lexical analysis, including dispersion analysis.

In general, we took a pragmatic approach to managing the loss of data from audio recordings, viewing information such as rising intonation[7] as something that was unnecessary to our lexical focus and which could be added later if the data were used for different research purposes. We were able to minimize some loss using a tier structure in the ELAN training data and this allowed us to maintain syntax relationships and other information used by Kaldi in the data.

Entwined in the issue of data loss, was the management of subjectivity in transcription. Indonesian and English native speakers, linguists, and an Indonesian language teacher worked together to transcribe our training data and we used extended discussions of specific samples to develop our transcription guidelines, including some discussions with our teacher participant. Meanwhile the tier structure allowed consideration of the teacher's behavior from an alternative framework discussed below; that is, translanguaging.

3.1 Transcription Decisions with Bilingual Data

Turell and Moyer (2009) argue that "transcription is already a first step in interpretation and analysis" and add that the complexity of the task inevitably increases when more than one language is at play: as the number of lexical items, morphemes, pragmatic strategies, and countless other linguistic possibilities increase, a transcriber must consider multiple possible 'first step' interpretations of their data.

In our data, the teacher used Australian English and Indonesian, the target language. Target languages are often understood as abstract and definable entities (Pennycook, 2016) used by imagined communities of native speakers (Norton, 2001). This is problematic as it hides the complexity and variation of natural languages, especially for Indonesian which exists in a highly diverse linguistic ecosystem; in Indonesian, complex concepts of social relationships play out in its variation across different speaking situations (Djenar, 2006, 2008; Morgan, 2011; Djenar and Ewing, 2015). Indonesian teachers, consciously or not, participate in and

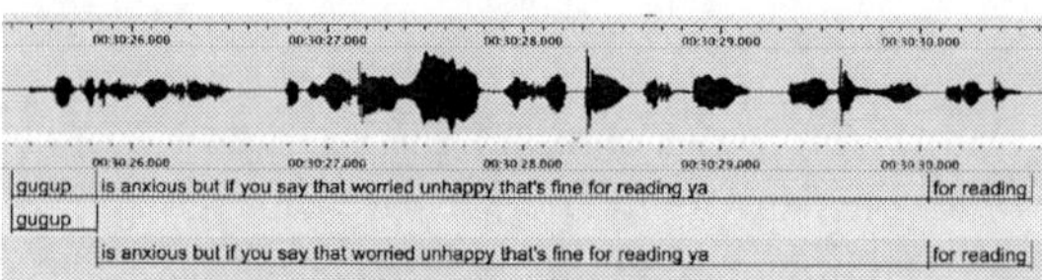

Figure 1: Community of Practice shared repertoire: 'reading'

negotiate the politics of ethnic diversity and variation in urban and rural Indonesia (Goebel, 2010, 2014). Furthermore, Indonesian could be considered diglossic, with two varieties of the language in use in everyday situations (Sneddon, 2003).

In our case study interview, the teacher explicitly acknowledged the diglossic nature of Indonesian and expressed the desire and intention to include *Colloquial Jakartan Indonesian* (CJI) in lessons as a speaking and listening target for students, while also stating that the written resources given to students focused more on the standardized or high variety of Indonesian. The teacher's intentions were consistent with the training data, which contained numerous CJI lexical items[8] and standard Indonesian. While not encountered in our small training dataset, our transcribers considered multiple English varieties due to the diverse English speaking experience of our teacher participant.

In addition to diglossic Indonesian and one variety of English, the teacher also used language consistent with the *Community of Practice* (CofP) framework, which, according to Wenger (1998, p. 76), involves a) mutual engagement, b) a joint negotiated enterprise, and c) a shared repertoire of negotiable resources accumulated over time. The teacher used language, or a repertoire, developed by the class through their interaction as a CofP. For example, the word 'reading' (Figure 1) was repurposed by the teacher participant to refer to a program-specific activity, assessment, and skillset that does not match with a general understanding/definition of this word in Australian English; it has become shorthand, or jargon, for something like a 'reading task'.

Thus far in this paper, we have relied on a presumption that it is desirable and theoretically sound to categorize teacher's speech into different languages. Such categorization rests on theorizing that languages are discrete entities and that teachers and students 'code-switch' — or alternate —

---

[7]which linguists often transcribe through special characters

[8]e.g., according to Sneddon (2006), 'gitu', 'dong', 'nggak' are from CJI

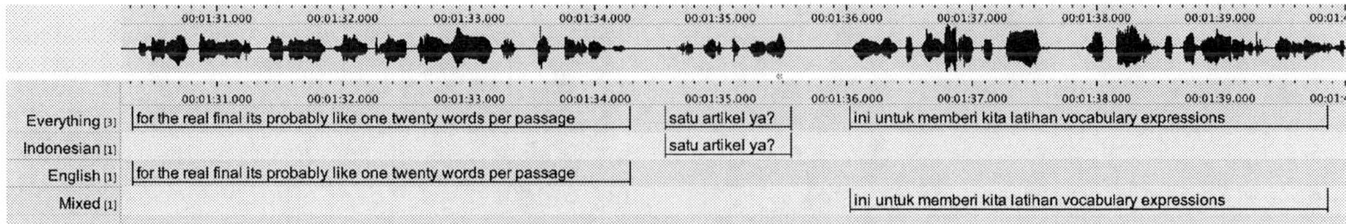

Figure 2: ELAN tier structure

"between two languages or dialects of the same language within the same conversation" (Boztepe, 2003). Recent discussions of an alternative framework — *translanguaging* (Garcia and Wei, 2014) — propose that multilinguals employ only one, expanded repertoire of linguistic features. This repertoire may contain two or more languages which are officially and externally recognized as distinct systems, but according to translanguaging theory, the distinction between the systems is not internally valid.

By using several ELAN tiers to create parallel structures for storing data (Figure 2), we balanced technological requirements without taking a particular stance in relation to translanguaging nor the internal mechanisms of bilinguals. The uppermost 'Everything' tier included all orthographical annotations for the data. The next two tiers contained data, which according to various phonological, syntactical, and morphological factors were separated by our transcription team into Indonesian and English according to a code-switch paradigm. Finally, we also created a tier labeled 'Mixed' to contain annotations, which were difficult to separate.

While some researchers battle with technologies to represent very different orthographies[9], we worked with two languages that are both written in the Roman alphabet. This presented some challenges of its own. Some words, for example, 'status' *(status)* and 'level' *(level)*, were spelled identically in both languages; meanwhile, names could have been represented in a number of different ways. Our decisions to use a certain orthography in training data impacted statistical relationships between words and phonemes in the ASR models. We chose to approximate all names in the Indonesian orthography as these proper nouns are somewhat language independent.[10] For example, our 'Indonesianized' class list included 'Jorj' (George), 'Shantel' (Chantelle), and 'Medi' (Maddy). This

decision allowed us to maintain the names within both Indonesian and English sentences, however, it did require manual creation of a phonemic map for that lexical item.[11] Similarly, we used only the Indonesian phonemic map for 'status' and 'level' as our participant's English incorporated Indonesian phonological characteristics (accent), and our intention was to strengthen our Indonesian computational model.

Decisions about orthography and tier allocations were very difficult and we made them only after extensive discussion in our transcription team. In some cases, within word changes between the typical Indonesian phonology and English phonology occurred. For example, in one segment, the teacher produced the first vowel of 'status' as [eɪ] (as in 'bait'), an English phoneme, but finished the word with the Indonesian /u/ (similar to 'book'). Even with a common set of characters used for bilingual data, the decisions taken developing training data had to be clearly documented and their impact considered in the ASR evaluation.

3.2 Toward Interpreting Teacher Speech

The complex bilingual transcription process outlined above was further complicated by the transcriber's interpretation of the educational setting. Given the conceivable criticism of a given teachers' professional practice made possible through the creation of corpora, we carefully considered the impacts of this scrutiny while developing our transcription guidelines and sought to minimize unfair or inaccurate treatment of teacher data. We also wish to proclaim the limitations of corpus data in this setting.

Although a full description and examination of these issues is beyond the scope of this paper, we identified some pertinent methodological implications of our own data structure. First, the task of analyzing the teacher's speech is likely to be over-simplified into binary L1 versus L2 catego-

---

[9](e.g., Halai (2007) for Urdu and English)

[10]They were also annotated in all tiers when they occurred alone.

[11]See Section 4 below.

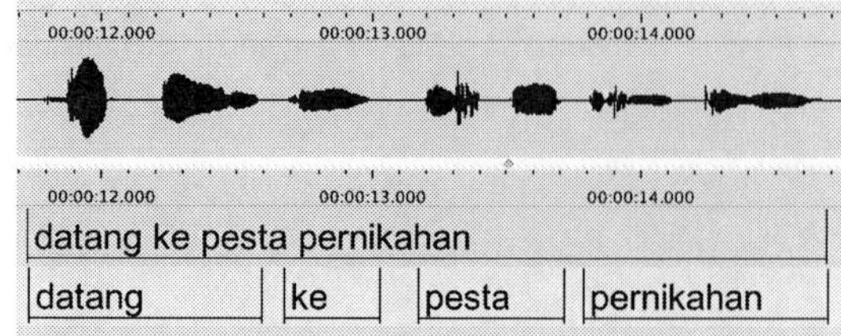

Figure 3: Treatment of pauses in teacher speech

rization of teacher's speech. The aforementioned methodological difficulties of teasing apart speech data and the questionable validity of delimiting languages raised by the translanguaging framework were central to our transcription guidelines. We also note that pauses in the teacher's language and other easily overlooked phenomena might skew the time counted towards a given language (Figure 3). We assessed that L2 was vulnerable to this skewing as the teacher extended pauses between words unfamiliar to the students, thus expanding the time counted as L2 speech. Conversely, cutting the L2 use apart when a teacher paused removed between-word-time from a cumulative L2 count and artificially shortened the time spent in the language.

Second, the goal of modifying sociolinguistic norms which brings people to language classrooms precipitated a level of variance and unpredictability unusual in other speech contexts as students learn and progress in their acquisition. We viewed variation in teacher speech from a pedagogically 'generous' perspective; for example, unusual linguistic forms were interpreted in line with research on language simplification (Saito and Poeteren, 2012; O Dela Rosa and Arguelles, 2016) or identity work with students (Norton and Toohey, 2011). However, a transcriber might note that in the Australian second language teaching setting, teachers often have less than 'native' proficiency in either the L2 or classroom L1. A proficiency-focused transcriber could be particularly sensitive to the teacher's productions of loanwords.[12] Thus, a transcriber's own perception of proficiency and speech errors, as well as their knowledge of, and stance on, pedagogical approaches are implicated in the interpretation of teacher speech.

With so many possible interpretations, asking the teacher to comment on or transcribe their own data

might seem useful. However, the intent of a teacher in using specific linguistic features is likely to be highly complex, as well as difficult to ascertain as this work is often the result of internally reasoned, impromptu responses to student feedback (Borko et al., 1990). With these features put together over thousands, possibly millions of teaching decisions each lesson, we were cautious in our asking our teacher participant to recall or explain what they were doing in retrospect. We noted that any disparity in teacher intention and the recorded data, or inability to recall the purpose of specific interactions, language choices and other behaviors may create an air of scrutiny which could skew resulting interpretation (Gangneux and Docherty, 2018).

Ensuring that teachers, their work, and their decisions are not misrepresented or misunderstood was important to us. We emphasized and are urging caution in the use of corpora to assess teacher practice until methodological questions have received prolonged and rigorous attention across a wide-range of datasets, including at the minimum different L1 and L2, teachers, pedagogical styles, and teaching situations.

4   Materials and Methods

The audio data was recorded in a second year tertiary Indonesian language program at an Australian university (Ethics Approval No. 2017/889 of the *Australian National University* Human Research Committee for the Speech Recognition; Building Datasets from Indonesian Language Classrooms and Resources protocol). The teacher, who was recorded over the course of one semester, grew up using Indonesian in school and public places, and a regional language at home. A semester of over 32 hours of class was recorded.[13]

The teacher wore a head-mounted microphone and wireless bodypack linked to a ZOOM recorder set to record 44.1 kHz, 36-bit WAV format audio. Because students were not the target of the study, the microphone settings were optimized to exclude their voices. Three lessons of approximately 50 minutes were chosen for transcription as training and test data for the ASR. The lessons were selected to contain a range of content, instructional styles, and activities. The remaining audio recordings were held out from training and testing.[14]

---

[12]E.g., the Indonesian loanword 'kelas' (class) might be interpreted as English should it not meet a transcriber's personal threshold for an Indonesian production.

[13]Excluded classes in which formal assessments took place, an introductory class, and some lesson segments where technical problems resulted in loss of data.

[14]They were kept in reserve for future experiments and anal-

Model	Training tier[a]	Tokens in training	Languages	n-gram	WER[b]	WER full set[c]	Correct	Long text spans	
								Words	Text spans
Bilingual_1G	*Everything* tier	6194	English Indonesian Mixed	1	77% (56/73)	117% (117/100)	38/100	4 3	2 1
Bilingual_3G	*Everything* tier	6194	English Indonesian Mixed	3	89% (65/73)	133% (133/100)	34/100	3	2
Indonesian_3G	*Indonesian* tier	3377	Indonesian	3	64% (23/36)	134% (134/100)	22/100[d] 22/51[e]	4 3	1 1

[a] See Figure 2 for tier structure
[b] Results when testing only with words found in training data
[c] Results including training words and testing words not found in training data
[d] In the full test set
[e] Indonesian and non-language specific words in the test set

Table 1: *Word Error Rates* (WER) from 3 ASR Models

PRAAT auto-segmentation with settings at the minimum pitch of 70 Hz, silence threshold of -50 Db, and minimum silent interval of 0.25 was used to segment the data. Segments were then manually edited to remove remnant student voices and extreme modality sounds[15] to avoid confusing the Kaldi acoustic training. Care was taken to find the boundaries between speech sounds and discriminate between the languages used, with challenging sections examined in PRAAT by the transcription team. Transcription was completed in ELAN and initially all teacher speech was transcribed on one tier before being expanded onto other tiers (see Figure 2).

To use the Kaldi toolkit, a lexicon with each word's phonemic representation was required. Due to the bilingual dataset in this study, we built a lexicon with consistent *grapheme-to-phoneme* (G2P) mapping across two orthographies. Our lexicon was built by adding missing English words to the *Carnegie Melon University* (CMU) Pronunciation Dictionary. Although the pronunciations of this dictionary are based on American English, it was the best available match with our teacher participant. We then merged this lexicon with an Indonesian lexicon, which was built using Elpis functionalities.[16] The tools used the regular G2P mapping in Indonesian to generate a pronunciation dictionary based on the orthographical representation of each word.

We trained three models (Table 1) on two lessons selected from the semester of teaching. We then used the three models to automatically transcribe a 100-word[17] test subset of data from a third lesson. We used the *word error rate* (WER)[18] as the primary evaluation measure in this analysis.

The two bilingual models, which were trained on all parts of the audio recordings, are referred to as bilingual models for ease of reference. However, it should be noted that there was nothing binary in these models:[19] Bilingual_1G and Bilingual_3G were each a single model, where 1G and 3G refer to n-grams.[20] We chose the unigram and trigram models to assess the importance of word sequences.

5 Preliminary Results from Automated Speech Recognition and Their Analysis

The WER of three models was from 64% to 89% (Table 1). This was large compared with those reported by major commercial ASR transcription services; however, this comparison requires interrogation.

The WER of the large commercial services is typically related monolingual tasks, usually on English data, and outside the classroom context. In a monolingual Spanish classroom environment, an impressively small WER of 10% was reported using a tailored, commercial ASR system with test data of two 50-minute university lectures and one 50-minute seminar with 10–16 year-old students (Iglesias et al., 2016). In contrast, for monolin-

---

yses.

[15]e.g. laughter, outbreaths, unintelligible whispers

[16]incl. the Indonesianised names

[17]duration of approx. 1 minute

[18]i.e., the number of deleted, inserted, and substituted words, divided by the total number of words

[19]No differentiation was made by the Kaldi toolkit between languages.

[20]i.e., a sequence of n words

gual US English-speaking teachers' speech, a WER from 44% to 100% was reported for five ASR systems, which were free of cost to use and required no additional supervised learning to train the ASR model (Nathaniel et al., 2015).

In our results, we analyzed teacher speech phenomena, such as emphasized articulation. For example, an instance of 'sma', an acronym for a senior high school produced as the Indonesian names of the letters, [es em ah] was hyper-articulated. Our Bilingual_3G and Indonesian_3G models produced reasonable approximations: 'ah sma aha' and 'hasan aha', respectively. Given the variation this sort of phenomena introduced into lexical items, teacher speech characteristics seem likely to have impacted our ASR performance.

ASR performance degrades in multilingual settings, but a range of techniques for reducing WER are available (see Yilmaz et al. (2016); Nakayama et al. (2018); van der Westhuizen and Niesler (2019); Yue et al. (2019)). Many of these studies note their shortage of training data and some report success in using training data from high resource languages to work with low resource languages. For example, Biswas et al. (2018) experimented with a new South African soap opera corpus in which five languages were present and found that the incorporation of monolingual, out-of-domain training data reduced their WER. Working with the same corpus, Biswas et al. (2019) first trained bilingual systems and a unified five-lingual system, and then experimented with adding convolutional neural network layers to these models. Overall they achieved WERs ranging from 43% to 64% for paired languages and from 26% to 78% for single languages.

While performance between different language pairs might not be suitable for comparison due to the interplay of language typologies interacting in distinctive ways, WERs from codeswitch bilingual data were more similar to our WER, especially given our small amount of training data. Yeong and Tan (2014) studied Indonesian, Iban, and Malay codeswitching in written work, however, to the best of our knowledge, our work was the first work on spoken Indonesian–English data.

WER rates were useful in relating our results with the overall progress being made in ASR, but given our goal to expedite human transcription, for us, it was more fruitful to analyze the number and length of correctly recognized text spans in the

ASR-based transcription. We theorized that these tools could begin to change workflow or decrease cognitive load for human transcribers by generating a draft transcript for revision.

The two 4-word and one 3-word correct text spans produced by our Bilingual_1G model would probably be the most useful in speeding transcription (Table 1). However, the preliminary results produced by the Indonesian_3G model were comparable to the two bilingual models. This was impressive given that nearly 50% of the test data was in English. Supposing a research interest in only the Indonesian spoken by the teacher, or the use of an English language model for the other data, the Indonesian model could reasonably be assessed as scoring 22 correct words from the 51 Indonesian words in the test data.

Proceeding to a more detailed study of the performance of the models, we undertook an error analysis to elucidate the type of errors occurring. We analyzed them as segments, from multiple perspectives (Figure 4). There was a high incidence of resyllabification[21] in the machine transcription, as words were split, concatenated with the preceding or succeeding word(s), a middle consonant was omitted, and/or an initial consonant was omitted. For example, 'perguruan' in the reference transcript and 'per keren' by ASR accumulated three errors: resyllabification and two counts of substitution.[22] Another example is, 'it' in the reference transcript produced as 'old' in the ASR output. This error was coded for a vowel change and consonant change.[23]

Given the small test set, using this error analysis, we made the tentative note that the Bilingual_3G model seemed slightly less likely to make errors of insertion and deletion, indicating that the errors were perhaps less 'disruptive' than the errors in the other models. Thus, despite the model's worse overall performance, it might improve rapidly with more training data.[24]

6 Discussion

As our principal result, we concluded that Kaldi, in conjunction with the Elpis interface, can expedite the transcription of teacher corpora. The time taken to transcribe speech can be extreme; in our project,

---

[21] word split

[22] consonant g > k and vowel change monophthong > diphthong

[23] monophthong > diphthong and t > d, respectively

[24] Our analysis of the Indonesian excluded all English words, reducing the test sample significantly.

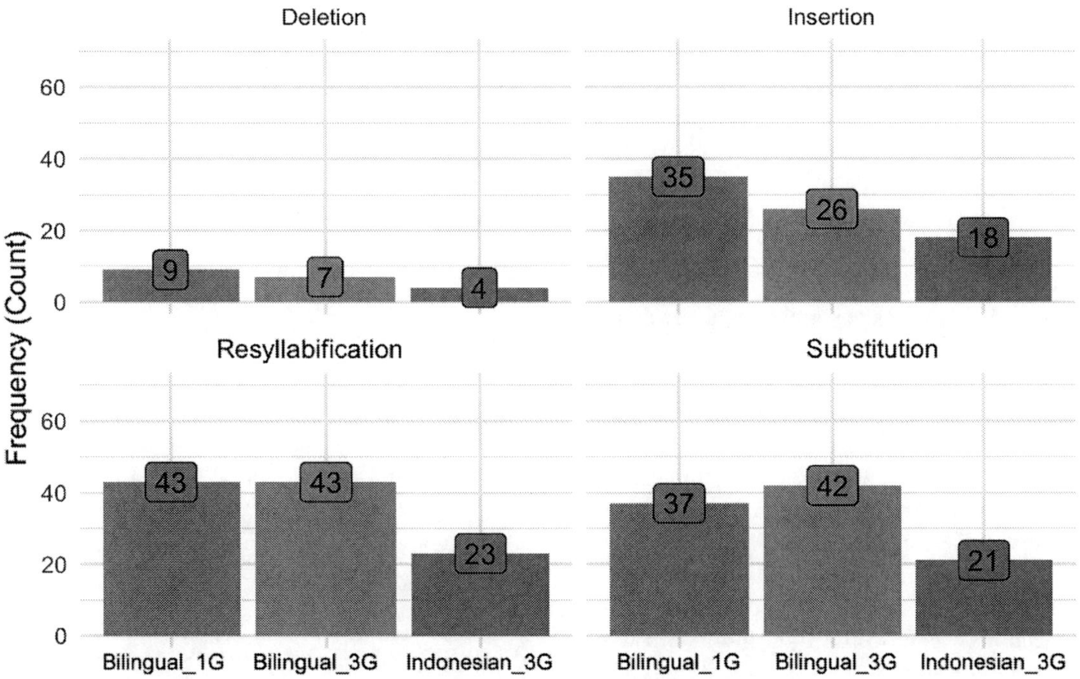

Figure 4: Segment analysis showing the frequency of error types at the phonemic level

transcribers spent months familiarizing themselves with the participants speech and setting up extensive transcription guidelines. Our final 51 minutes of test data took approximately $1,024$ minutes[25] to transcribe.[26] However, the use of Kaldi and Elpis was also time-consuming and required significant training and expertise. The continued development of Elpis may make the tool more viable for ASR-assisted transcription in research.

Our detailed discussion of methodological issues arising during human transcription of training data cannot prescribe a solution for all language teacher corpora; as Helm and Dooly (2017, p. 170) say of their own methodology paper examining the transcription of online language classroom data, their methods necessarily reflect "the research questions and the situated context of the study". However, we do hope to provide a baseline of discussion for those developing training datasets with this kind of complex speech. Similarly to Helm and Dooly (2017, p. 181), we hope to "highlight how we can try to be reflexive and critical in our research practices, increasing the transparency and accountability of our work and opening it up for discussion with others". This is especially pertinent as we de-

velop machine learning-based technologies, which often lack transparency and trustworthiness (Pynadath et al., 2018).

Beyond the goals of this study, our findings contribute to expanding bodies of research into the use of ASR with small datasets (Gonzalez et al., 2018), in educational and classroom settings, as well as ASR of multilingual data. Our results gave some indication that while developing an initial (small) training dataset, using a simpler unigram model with less lexical information is better. Of course, ASR could be enhanced with a larger training dataset and supplementary text corpora from teaching resources.

Data loss was inevitable when we converted enacted classroom interactional phenomena into the linear, rather two-dimensional written format of orthographic transcription. This loss of complexity causes us to raise a cautionary flag; datasets produced through these methods can be used to support teacher reflection on their practice, but should never be taken as the entirety of a teacher's work and metrics derived from them should be viewed with a careful understanding of how much they reduce the complexity of the phenomena they record. Losing the context of data is not an "obscure problem apparent to a few philosophers focused on cy-

---

[25]i.e., 17 hours

[26]i.e., the turnaround of about 1:20

bernetics" (Bornakke and Due, 2018, p. 1). In this paper, we highlight the importance of decisions about 'what data to lose' when transcribing, making tactical decisions that are justified by research questions (Gangneux and Docherty, 2018), and how transcription bias can be multiplied in unknown ways by computational processes.

Investments are necessary to convert the tools we used to a useable workflow for practicing teachers. Elpis is likely to make significant headway in this area, but the complex nature of transcribing bilingual teaching data requires specialized skills. Training teachers to do this work seems a useful area of technological investment in languages education. It could incorporate established uses of teacher corpora for teacher training and professional development with new goals of elucidating the language input teachers provide in the classroom. Teachers who transcribe a small training dataset of their own speech may gain deep insight into their own language use. Using ASR to accelerate transcription could lead to teachers having the capacity to build larger datasets, analyze their own teaching, and thereby progress their practice. Given the workload issues often associated with teaching, asking teachers to transcribe their own lessons may be unrealistic in the initial development of this tool but could be more appropriate in teacher training settings where it could be included as part of their studies. Engaging with concerns in education about the use of teaching technologies as performance management tools (Page, 2017; Tolofari, 2005), this tool in teachers' hands could advance action research and protect teachers from it being used as a supervision/performance management tool.

7   Conclusion

Having trained and applied ASR in the form of Kaldi and Elpis to a dataset of carefully prepared Indonesian language teaching data, it is clear that the applicability of these technologies is limited with such a small set of training data. Yet, further investigation and development toward the goal of expedited transcription is warranted because of the virtuous cycle of ASR-assisted human-workflow.

The limitations and risks of these technologies must be considered if we hope to use them to gain real insight into the practice of language teachers. However, it is crucial that education is not excluded from technological advances. Empirical information about teacher practice for teachers, curriculum writers, educational researchers, and policy makers could be used to inform and advance the education sector the same way as these computational advancements are already routinely used in industry and other sectors.

Acknowledgments

We gratefully acknowledge the contribution of anonymous reviewers, colleagues, and study participant to this paper.

References

Claudia Baur, Andrew Caines, Cathy Chua, Johanna Gerlach, Mengjie Qian, Manny Rayner, Martin Russell, Helmer Strik, and Xizi Wei. 2018. Overview of the 2018 spoken call shared task. In *Interspeech 2018*, pages 2354–2358.

Astik Biswas, Ewald van der Westhuizen, Thomas Niesler, and Febe de Wet. 2018. Improving asr for code-switched speech in under-resourced languages using out-of-domain data. In *SLTU 2018*, pages 122–126.

Astik Biswas, Emre Yilmaz, Febe de Wet, Ewald van der Westhuizen, and Thomas Niesler. 2019. Semi-supervised acoustic model training for five-lingual code-switched asr. In *Interspeech 2019*.

BNC-Consortium. 2007. *Reference Guide for the British National Corpus (XML Edition)*.

Hilda Borko, Carol Livingston, and Richard J. Shavelson. 1990. Teachers' thinking about instruction. *Remedial and Special Education*, 11(6):40–49.

Tobias Bornakke and Brian L. Due. 2018. Big–thick blending: A method for mixing analytical insights from big and thick data sources. *Big Data & Society*, 5(1).

Erman Boztepe. 2003. Issues in code-switching: Competing theories and models. *Issues in CS: Competing Theories and Models*, 3(2).

Dwi Noverini Djenar. 2006. Patterns and variation of address terms in colloquial indonesian. *Australian Review of Applied Linguistics*, 29(2):22–22.

Dwi Noverini Djenar. 2008. Which self? pronominal choice, modernity, and self-categorizations. *International Journal of the Sociology of Language*, 189:31–54.

Dwi Noverini Djenar and Michael C. Ewing. 2015. Language varieties and youthful involvement in indonesian fiction. *Language and Literature*, 24(2):108–128.

John W. Du Bois, Stephan Schuetze-Coburn, Susanna Cumming, and Danae Paolino. 1993. Outline of discourse transcription. In Jane A. Edwards and Martin D. Lampert, editors, *Talking data: Transcription and coding in discourse research*, pages 45–89. NJ: Erlbaum, Hillsdale.

Gautier Durantin. 2017. Early results from survey exploring transcription processes.

Nick C. Ellis. 2017. Cognition, corpora, and computing: Triangulating research in usage-based language learning. *Language learning*, 67(1):40–65.

Ben Foley, Josh Arnold, Gautier Durantin, T. Mark Ellison, Daan van Esch, Scott Heath, Nicholas Lambourne, Zara Maxwell-Smith, Ola Olsson, Aninda Saha, Nay San, Hywel Stoakes, and Janet Wiles. 2018. Building speech recognition systems for language documentation: The coedl endangered language pipeline and inference system (elpis). In *The 6th International Workshop on Spoken Language Technologies for Under-Resourced Languages*.

Christian Gaida, Patrick Lange, Rico Petrick, Patrick Proba, Ahmad Malatawy, and David Suendermann-Oeft. 2014. Comparing open-source speech recognition toolkits. In *NLPCS 2014 : 11th International Workshop on Natural Language Processing and Cognitive Science*.

Justine Gangneux and Stevie Docherty. 2018. At close quarters: Combatting facebook design, features and temporalities in social research. *Big Data & Society*, 5(2).

Ofelia Garcia and Li Wei. 2014. *Translanguaging: Language, Bilingualism and Education*. Palgrave Macmillan, New York.

Zane Goebel. 2010. Identity and social conduct in a transient multilingual setting. *Language in Society*, 39(02):203–240.

Zane Goebel. 2014. Doing leadership through sign-switching in the indonesian bureaucracy. *Journal of Linguistic Anthropology*, 24(2):193–215.

Simòn Gonzalez, Catherine E. Travis, James Grama, Danielle Barth, and Sunkulp Ananthanarayan. 2018. Recursive forced alignment: A test on a minority language. In *17th Speech Science and Technology Conference*.

Google. 2019. Google cloud speech-to-text api language support.

Nelofer Halai. 2007. Making use of bilingual interview data: Some experiences from the field. *The Qualitative Report*, 12(3):344–355.

Francesca Helm and Melinda Dooly. 2017. Challenges in transcribing multimodal data: A case study. *Language Learning & Technology*, 21(1):166–185.

Julia Hirschberg and Christopher D. Manning. 2015. Advances in natural language processing. *Science*, 349(6245):261–266.

Eduard Hovy and Julia Lavid. 2010. Towards a 'science' of corpus annotation: A new methodological challenge for corpus. *International Journal of Translation*, 22(1):13–36.

Ana Iglesias, Javier Jimenèz, Pablo Revuelta, and Lourdes Moreno. 2016. Avoiding communication barriers in the classroom: the apeinta project. *Interactive Learning Environments*, 24(4):829–843.

Daniel Jurafsky and James H. Martin. 2009. *Speech and Language Processing (2nd Edition)*. Prentice-Hall, Inc, Upper Saddle River, NJ, USA.

Judith C. Lapadat and Anne C. Lindsay. 1998. Examining transcription: A theory-laden methodology. Report, Social Sciences and Humanities Research Council of Canada, Ottawa (Ontario).

Anne-Marie Morgan. 2011. Me, myself, i: exploring conceptions of self and others in indonesian names and pronouns with early learners. *Babel*, 45(2-3):26.

Sahoko Nakayama, Andros Tjandra, Sakriani Sakti, and Satoshi Nakamura. 2018. Speech chain for semi-supervised learning of japanese-english code-switching asr and tts. In *2018 IEEE Spoken Language Technology Workshop (SLT)*, pages 182–189.

Blanchard Nathaniel, Michael Brady, Andrew M. Olney, Marci Glaus, Xiaoyi Sun, Martin Nystrand, Borhan Samei, Sean Kelly, and Sidney D'Mello. 2015. A study of automatic speech recognition in noisy classroom environments for automated dialog analysis. In *Artificial Intelligence in Education*, pages 23–33, Cham. Springer International Publishing.

Bonny Norton. 2001. Non-participation, imagined communities and the language classroom. In M Breen, editor, *Learner contributions to language learning: New directions in research*, pages 159–171. Cascadilla Press.

Bonny Norton and Kelleen Toohey. 2011. Identity, language learning, and social change. *Language Teaching*, 44(4):412–446.

Nuance. 2019. Nuance recognizer language availability.

John Paul O Dela Rosa and Diana C. Arguelles. 2016. Do modification and interaction work? – a critical review of literature on the role of foreigner talk in second language acquisition. *i-Manager's Journal on English Language Teaching*, 6(3):46–60.

Damien Page. 2017. Conceptualising the surveillance of teachers. *British Journal of Sociology of Education*, 38(7):991–1006.

Alastair Pennycook. 2016. Posthumanist applied linguistics. *Applied Linguistics*, 39(4):445–461.

Luke Plonsky. 2013. Study quality in sla: An assessment of designs, analyses, and reporting practices in quantitative l2 research. *Studies in Second Language Acquisition*, 35(4):655–687.

David V. Pynadath, Michael J. Barnes, Ning. Wang, and Jessie Y.C. Chen. 2018. Transparency communication for machine learning in human-automation interaction. In J. Zhou and F. Chen, editors, *Human and Machine Learning*, pages 75–90. Springer, Cham.

Kazuya Saito and Kim van Poeteren. 2012. Pronunciation-specific adjustment strategies for intelligibility in l2 teacher talk: results and implications of a questionnaire study. *Language Awareness*, 21(4):369–385.

James N. Sneddon. 2003. Diglossia in indonesian. *Bijdragen tot de taal-, land- en volkenkunde / Journal of the Humanities and Social Sciences of Southeast Asia*, 159(4):519–549.

James N. Sneddon. 2006. *Colloquial Jakartan Indonesian*, volume 581. Pacific Linguistics, Research School of Pacific and Asian Studies, Australian National University, Canberra.

Sowaribi Tolofari. 2005. New public management and education. *Policy Futures in Education*, 3(1):75–89.

Maria Teresa Turell and Melissa G. Moyer. 2009. Transcription. In Li Wei and Melissa Moyer, editors, *The Blackwell Guide to Research Methods in Bilingualism and Multilingualism*, book section 11. Blackwell Publishing Ltd, Carlton, Australia.

Etienne Wenger. 1998. *Communities of Practice: Learning, Meaning, and Identity*. Cambridge University Press, Cambridge.

Ewald van der Westhuizen and Thomas R Niesler. 2019. Synthesised bigrams using word embeddings for code-switched asr of four south african language pairs. *Computer Speech & Language*, 54:151–175.

Yin-Lai Yeong and Tien-Ping Tan. 2014. Language identification of code switching sentences and multilingual sentences of under-resourced languages by using multi structural word information. In *Interspeech 2014*, pages 3052–3055.

Emre Yilmaz, Henk van den Heuvel, and David Van Leeuwen. 2016. Investigating bilingual deep neural networks for automatic speech recognition of code-switching frisian speech. In *5th Workshop on Spoken Language Technology for Under-resourced Languages, SLTU 2016*, volume 81, pages 159–166.

Xianghu Yue, Grandee Lee, Emre Yilmaz, Fang Deng, and Haizhou Li. 2019. End-to-end code-switching asr for low-resourced language pairs. In *IEEE ASRU Workshop 2019*.

Appendices

A Code Versions

This study used custom scripts for data preparation, along with the Elpis and Kaldi software projects to train and apply ASR models.

Elpis is a wrapper for the Kaldi speech recognition toolkit. At the time of the study, Kaldi was at version 5.5.

The version of Elpis used was v0.3 of the kaldi_helpers code. The current version of Elpis can be accessed at github.com/CoEDL/elpis. DOI: 10.5281/zenodo.3833887

We have released the data preparation scripts under Apache License Version 2.0. These scripts handled the generation of pronunciation lexicons required by Kaldi, and the preparation of audio files for inferencing. The scripts can be downloaded by following the respective DOIs. Version 0.1 of kaldi-helpers-pron-lexicon was used to identify and make pronunciations for English and Indonesian words. DOI: 10.5281/zenodo.3835586. A script, released as kaldi-helpers-segment-infer v0.1, was written to segment long audio into shorter segments as required by Elpis v0.3. DOI: 10.5281/zenodo.3834016

An empirical investigation of neural methods for content scoring of science explanations

Brian Riordan[1], Sarah Bichler[2], Allison Bradford[2], Jennifer King Chen[2],
Korah Wiley[2], Libby Gerard[2], Marcia C. Linn[2]
[1]ETS
[2]University of California-Berkeley

Abstract

With the widespread adoption of the Next Generation Science Standards (NGSS), science teachers and online learning environments face the challenge of evaluating students' integration of different dimensions of science learning. Recent advances in representation learning in natural language processing have proven effective across many natural language processing tasks, but a rigorous evaluation of the relative merits of these methods for scoring complex constructed response formative assessments has not previously been carried out. We present a detailed empirical investigation of feature-based, recurrent neural network, and pre-trained transformer models on scoring content in real-world formative assessment data. We demonstrate that recent neural methods can rival or exceed the performance of feature-based methods. We also provide evidence that different classes of neural models take advantage of different learning cues, and pre-trained transformer models may be more robust to spurious, dataset-specific learning cues, better reflecting scoring rubrics.

1 Introduction

The Next Generation Science Standards (NGSS) call for the integration of three dimensions of science learning: disciplinary core ideas (DCIs), cross-cutting concepts (CCCs), and science and engineering practices (SEPs) (NGSS Lead States, 2013). Science teachers can promote knowledge integration of these dimensions using constructed response (CR) formative assessments to help their students build on productive ideas, fill in knowledge gaps, and reconcile conflicting ideas. However, the time burden associated with reading and scoring student responses to CR assessment items often leads to delays in evaluating student ideas. Such delays potentially make subsequent instructional interventions less impactful on student learning. Effective automated methods to score student responses to NGSS-aligned CR assessment items hold the potential to allow teachers to provide instruction that addresses students' developing understandings in a more efficient and timely manner and can increase the amount of time teachers have to focus on classroom instruction and provide targeted student support.

In this study, we describe a set of CR formative assessment items that call for students to express and integrate ideas across multiple dimensions of the NGSS. We collected student responses to each item in multiple middle school science classrooms and trained models to automatically score the content of responses with respect to a set of rubrics. This study explores the effectiveness of three classes of models for content scoring of science explanations with complex rubrics: feature-based models, recurrent neural networks, and pre-trained transformer networks. Specifically, we investigate the following questions:

(1) What is the relative effectiveness of automated content scoring models from different model classes on scoring science explanations for both (a) holistic knowledge integration and (b) NGSS dimensions?

(2) Do highly accurate model classes capture similar or different aspects of scoring rubrics?

2 Methods

2.1 Background

We focus on constructed response (CR) items for formative assessments during science units for middle school students accessed via an online classroom system (Gerard and Linn, 2016; Linn et al., 2014). In past research, items that assessed NGSS performance expectations (PEs) were scored with a single knowledge integration (KI) rubric (Liu

Proceedings of the 15th Workshop on Innovative Use of NLP for Building Educational Applications, pages 135–144
July 10, 2020. ©2020 Association for Computational Linguistics

et al., 2016). KI involves a process of building on and strengthening science understanding by incorporating new ideas and sorting out alternative perspectives using evidence. The KI rubric used to score student short essays rewards students for linking evidence to claims and for adding multiple evidence-claim links to their explanations (Linn and Eylon, 2011). In this study, we develop items that solicit student reasoning about two or more NGSS dimensions of DCIs, CCCs, and SEPs. We score each item for KI and NGSS "subscores" relating to the DCIs, CCCs, and practices.

3 Scoring item and rubric design

In this section we describe the design of the CR items that comprise the datasets for the content scoring models. The CR items formatively assess student understanding of multiple NGSS dimensions, namely, using SEPs while demonstrating integrated understanding of DCIs and CCCs.

We designed formative assessment items and associated rubrics for four units currently used in the online classroom system: Musical Instruments (MI), Photosynthesis and Cellular Respiration (PS), Solar Ovens (SO), and Thermodynamics Challenge (TC).

Musical Instruments and the Physics of Sound Waves (MI). The Musical Instruments unit engages students in testing and refining their ideas about the properties of sound waves (wavelength, frequency, amplitude, and pitch) and guides them in applying what they learn to design and build their own instrument, a water xylophone. The CR item we designed aligns with the NGSS PE MS-PS4-2 PE and assesses students' understanding of the relationship of pitch and frequency (DCI) and the characteristics of a sound wave when transmitted through different materials (CCC). Students are prompted to distinguish how the pitch of the sound made by tapping a full glass of water compares to the pitch made by tapping an empty glass. In their answer, they are asked to explain why they think the pitch of the sound waves generated by striking the two glasses will be the same or different.

Photosynthesis and Cellular Respiration (PS). This unit engages students in exploring the processes of photosynthesis and cellular respiration by interacting with dynamic models at the molecular level. We designed a CR item that aligns with NGSS performance expectation MS-LS1-6 that asks students to express an integrated explanation of how photosynthesis supports the survival of both plants and animals. This item explicitly solicits students' ideas related to the CCC of matter cycling (i.e. change) and energy flow (i.e. movement): "Write an energy story below to explain your ideas about how animals get and use energy from the sun to survive. Be sure to explain how energy and matter move AND how energy and matter change." Successful responses demonstrate proficiency in the SEP of constructing a scientific argument and reflect the synthesis of the DCIs and CCCs.

Solar Ovens (SO). The Solar Ovens unit asks students to collect evidence to agree or disagree with a claim made by a fictional peer about the functioning of a solar oven. Students work with an interactive model where they explore how different variables such as the size and capacity of a solar oven affect the transformation of energy from the sun. We designed a CR item that addresses NGSS PE MS-PS3-3 and assesses students for both the CCC of energy transfer and transformation and the SEP of analyzing and interpreting data. After working with the interactive model, students respond to the CR item with the prompt: "Explain why David's claim is correct or incorrect using the evidence you collected from the model. Be sure to discuss how the movement of energy causes one solar oven to heat up faster than the other."

Thermodynamics Challenge (TC). The Thermodynamics Challenge unit asks students to determine the best material for insulating a cold beverage using an online experimentation model. We designed a CR item that aligns with the NGSS PE MS-PS3-3 and assesses student performance proficiency with the targeted DCIs in the PE, understanding of the SEP of planning and carrying out an investigation, and the integration of both of these to construct a coherent and valid explanation. The CR item prompts students to explain the rationale behind their experiment plans with the model, using both key conceptual ideas as well as their understanding of experimentation as a scientific practice: "Explain WHY the experiments you [plan to test] are the most important ones for giving you evidence to write your report. Be sure to use your knowledge of insulators, conductors, and heat energy transfer to discuss the tests you chose as well as the ones you didn't choose."

We designed three scoring rubrics for each item corresponding to two "subscores" representing the degree to which the written responses expressed

PE-specific ideas, concepts, and practices and one KI score that represents how the responses integrated these elements.

NGSS subscore rubrics. To evaluate the written responses for the presence of the DCIs, CCCs, and SEPs, we designed subscore rubrics for two of the three dimensions (Table 1). Specifically, we synthesized the ideas, concepts, and practices described in the "evidence statement" documents of each targeted performance expectation to develop the evaluation criteria. We assigned each response a score on a scale of 1 to 3, corresponding to the absence, partial presence, or complete presence of the ideas, concepts, or practices.

KI score rubrics. The ideas targeted by the KI scoring rubrics aligned with subsets of the ideas described in the evidence statements. For example, the KI scoring rubrics for the Photosynthesis item evaluated written responses for the presence and linkage of five science ideas related to energy and matter transformation during photosynthesis. KI rubrics used a scale of 1 to 5.

3.1 Data collection

Participants were middle school students from 11 schools. Students engaged in the science units and contributed written responses to the CR items as part of pre- and post-tests. Across schools, 44% of students received free or reduced price lunch and 77% were non-white.

All items were scored by two researchers using the item-specific subscore and KI and rubrics described above. To ensure coding consistency, both researchers coded at least 10% of the items individually and resolved any disagreements through discussion. After the inter-rater reliability reached greater than 0.90, all of the remaining items were coded by one researcher (cf. the procedure in Liu et al. (2016))[1].

Table 2 displays the dataset sizes and mean words per response for the KI scores and NGSS subscores, and Figure 1 depicts the respective score distributions. Among the holistic KI scores, the highest score of 5 had relatively fewer responses than other score levels. By examining the shape of the distributions of scores across the NGSS subscores, we can see that students' expression of different aspects of NGSS performance expectations differed across items. For the Musical Instruments

---

[1]Datasets are not publicly available because of the IRB-approved consent procedure for participants (minors) in this research.

Item	PE	DCI	CCC	SEP
Musical Instruments	MS-PS4-2	•	•	
Photosynthesis	MS-LS1-6	•	•	
Solar Ovens	MS-PS3-3		•	•
Thermodynamics Challenge	MS-PS3-3	•		•

Table 1: NGSS performance expectations (PE) and targeted components: disciplinary core idea (DCI), cross-cutting concept (CCC), and science and engineering practices (SEP) targeted by each item.

Item	Type	Responses	Mean words per response
MI	KI	1306	25.40
PS	KI	1411	54.57
SO	KI	1740	31.87
TC	KI	994	31.73
MI	CCC DCI	1306	25.40
PS	CCC DCI	553	70.40
SO	SEP: eng CCC: sci	605	32.62
TC	SEP: exp DCI: sci	583	31.43

Table 2: Descriptive statistics for each item's dataset.

and Photosynthesis items, students expressed the disciplinary core ideas less than the cross-cutting concepts. For both the Solar Ovens and Thermodynamics Challenge items, students often did not explicitly articulate science concepts. The Thermodynamics Challenge item was particularly challenging, as many students did not express the targeted science or experimentation concepts.

3.2 Content scoring models

Content scoring models were built for each item and score type (knowledge integration and two NGSS dimensions). Models for each score type were trained independently on data for each item. In this way, the three models for an item formed different "perspectives" on the content of each response. Human-scored training data for the NGSS dimension models comprised either a subset of or overlapped with the training data for the KI models.

The models were trained to predict an ordinal score from each response's text, without access to expert-authored model responses or data augmentation. This type of "instance-based" model (cf. Horbach and Zesch (2019)) is effective when model responses are not available and can score responses of any length without additional modeling

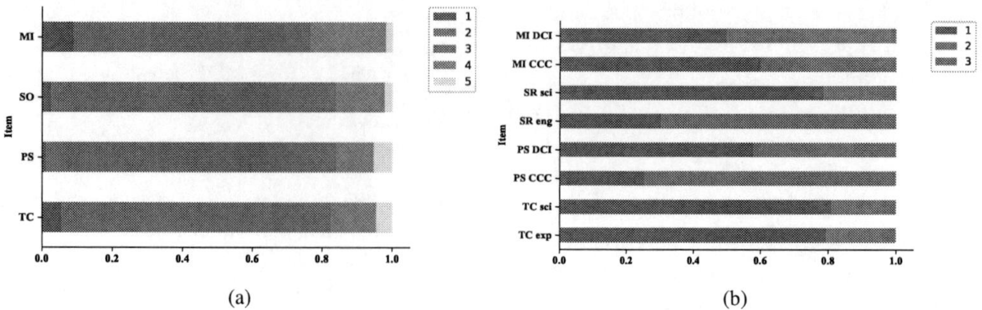

Figure 1: Score distributions for (a) knowledge integration scores and (b) NGSS subscores.

complexity. As we focus on content scoring, the models do not consider grammatical or usage errors that do not relate to the content of each response.

The feature-based model is a nonlinear support vector regression (SVR) model. The model is trained on a feature set of binarized word n-grams with n in $\{1, 2\}$.

The RNN model uses a simple architecture with pre-trained word embeddings and pooling of hidden states. Pre-trained word embeddings are processed by a bidirectional GRU encoder. The hidden states of the GRU are aggregated by a max pooling mechanism (Shen et al., 2018). The output of the encoder is aggregated in a fully-connected feedforward layer with sigmoid activation that computes a scalar output for the predicted score. Despite its simplicity, this architecture has achieved state-of-the-art performance on benchmark content scoring datasets (Riordan et al., 2019).

For the pre-trained transformer model, we used a standard instance of the BERT model (Devlin et al., 2019). BERT is a bidirectional transformer model trained on the tasks of masked token prediction and next sentence prediction across very large corpora (BooksCorpus and English Wikipedia). During training, a special token '[CLS]' is added to the beginning of each input sequence. To make predictions, the learned representation for this token is processed by an additional layer with nonlinear activation, outputting a score prediction. The model was 'fine-tuned' by training the additional layer's weights on each item's dataset.

3.3 Data preparation, model training, and hyperparameter optimization

SVR model. The SVR models used an RBF kernel. Hyperparameters C and *gamma* were tuned on the validation sets and were optimized by root mean squared error.

RNN model. Word tokens were embedded with GloVe 100 dimension vectors (Pennington et al., 2014) and fine-tuned during training. Word tokens that were not found in the embeddings vocabulary were mapped to a randomly initialized UNK embedding. On conversion to tensors, responses were padded to the same length in a batch; these padding tokens are masked out during model training. Prior to training, responses were scaled to [0, 1] to form the input to the networks. The scaled scores were converted back to their original range for evaluation.

The GRUs were 1 layer with a hidden state of size 250. The RNN models were trained with a mean squared error loss. For this investigation, the RNN was optimized with RMSProp with ρ of 0.9, learning rate 0.001, batch size 32, and gradient clipping (10.0). We used an exponential moving average of the model's weights for training (decay rate = 0.999) (Adhikari et al., 2019). In the tuning phase, models were trained for 50 epochs.

Pretrained transformer model. We used the *bert-base-uncased* pre-trained model (Wolf et al., 2019) and the Adam optimizer. On the Photosynthesis dataset, due to memory requirements, training required a batch size of 8; all other datasets were trained with a batch size 16. The learning rate was tuned individually for each dataset with a grid of {2e-5, 3e-5, 5e-5}. Matching the RNN model, an exponential moving average over the model's weights was employed during training. Hyperparameters were tuned for 20 epochs.

For all experiments, we trained models with 10-fold cross validation with train/validation/test splits, evaluating on pooled (concatenated) predictions across folds. We split the data into 80% train, 10% validation, and 10% test. For hyperparameter tuning, we trained on each train split and evaluated performance on the validation split, retaining

Item	Model	Corr	QWK	MSE	Sig.
MI	SVR	0.7804	0.7045	0.3298	
	RNN	0.7989	0.7642	0.3058	
	PT	**0.8134**	**0.7733**	**0.2956**	
PS	SVR	0.8296	0.7851	0.2098	R
	RNN	0.8215	0.7550	0.2285	
	PT	**0.8459**	**0.8246**	**0.1997**	S,R
SO	SVR	0.7491	0.6690	0.2737	
	RNN	0.7612	0.7116	0.2619	
	PT	**0.7691**	**0.7127**	**0.2608**	S,R
TC	SVR	0.6856	0.6156	0.4777	
	RNN	0.7106	0.6732	0.4465	S
	PT	**0.7286**	**0.6791**	**0.4266**	S

Table 3: Human-machine agreement for Knowledge Integration (KI) score models. QWK = quadratic-weighed kappa, MSE = mean squared error. SVR = support vector regression, RNN = recurrent neural network, PT = pre-trained Transformer. *Sig.* = significance by bootstrap replicability analysis; see main text for details.

Item	Sub-score	Model	Corr	QWK	MSE	Sig.
MI	CCC	SVR	.7008	.6314	.3185	
		RNN	.7685	.7322	.2561	S
		PT	**.7730**	**.7542**	**.2557**	S
MI	DCI	SVR	.7505	.7110	.1261	
		RNN	.7908	.7392	.1088	
		PT	**.8230**	**.7970**	**.0953**	
PS	CCC	SVR	.6992	.6050	.3102	
		RNN	**.7379**	**.7187**	**.2772**	
		PT	.7188	.6607	.2997	S
PS	DCI	SVR	.7410	.6956	.2245	
		RNN	.7795	.7471	.1955	
		PT	**.8044**	**.7701**	**.1826**	
SO	eng	SVR	.6957	.5915	.2684	
		RNN	.7484	.7112	.2503	
		PT	**.7662**	**.7263**	**.2428**	S
SO	sci	SVR	.5789	.4770	.1744	
		RNN	**.6872**	.5408	**.1623**	
		PT	.6480	**.6038**	.1834	
TC	exp	SVR	.5323	.4705	.1926	
		RNN	.5916	.4675	.1724	
		PT	**.6067**	**.5445**	**.1661**	
TC	sci	SVR	.5038	.0000	.2262	
		RNN	.5090	.3897	.1835	S
		PT	**.5303**	**.4182**	**.1779**	S

Table 4: Human-machine agreement for NGSS subscore models. *Sig.* = significance by bootstrap replicability analysis; see main text.

the predictions from the best performance across epochs and the epoch on which that performance was observed. We pooled the predictions from all folds on the validation sets, evaluated performance, and selected the best-performing configuration of hyperparameters. For final model training, we trained models on combined train and validation splits, again with 10-fold cross-validation, to the median best epoch across folds from the hyperparameter tuning phase. Final performance was evaluated on the pooled predictions from the test splits. This training and evaluation procedure improves the stability of estimates of performance during both the tuning and final testing phases and makes use of more data for training and evaluating the final models, providing better estimates of model performance.

3.4 Evaluation metrics

To evaluate the agreement of human scores and machine scores, we report Pearson's correlation, quadratic weighted kappa (QWK), and mean squared error (MSE). QWK is a measure of agreement that ranges between 0 and 1 and is motivated by accounting for chance agreement (Fleiss and Cohen, 1973). Correlation and MSE are computed over real-valued model predictions, while QWK is computed over rounded predictions.

4 Results

4.1 Human-machine agreement

The models for the KI scores showed mostly good agreement with human scores (Table 3). QWK for the Musical Instruments, Photosynthesis, and Solar Ovens items was substantially higher than the standard 0.7 recommended for human-machine agreement in real-word automated scoring applications (Williamson et al., 2012).

For NGSS subscore models (Table 4), those with more balanced score distributions (cf. Figure 1) showed good human-machine agreement, while the models trained on the most skewed data distributions showed lower levels of human-machine agreement. Specifically, Solar Ovens-Science and the Thermodynamics Challenge subscore models were trained on data where about 80% of responses had the lowest score. Each of these models' agreement with the human-scored data was relatively low and significantly below the 0.7 QWK threshold.

Across both KI score models and NGSS subscore models, the pre-trained transformer models showed higher human-machine agreement than both the SVR and RNN models in almost all cases. On the KI score datasets, the performance improvement from the PT models was relatively modest, except for the Photosynthesis dataset, where a larger improvement was observed. On the NGSS sub-score datasets, the improvement from the PT models was often larger. This may be the result of stronger representations from the pretrained models compensating from the smaller training dataset sizes. At the same time, RNN models also performed well on data-impoverished datasets such as Photosynthesis-CCC and Solar Ovens-science.

The cross-validation training and evaluation procedure employed here poses a challenge to statistically estimating the strengths of the differences between methods since the folds are not independent. Here we employ replicability analysis for multiple comparisons (Reichart et al., 2018; Dror et al., 2017). We use bootstrap-based significance testing on each fold for the final model on each dataset and then perform *K-Bonferonni* replicability analysis. We define significance as rejecting the null hypothesis of no difference for at least half of the folds. The results of these hypothesis tests are shown in Tables 3 and 4. For example, S indicates the model in that row (PT) performed significantly better than the $\underline{S}$VR model (similarly for the $\underline{R}$NN models). Although this hypothesis testing framework is conservative, the results support the conclusion that the pre-trained transformer models' performance was strong.

5 Error analysis

In this section, we explore the differences in the two neural models (RNN and PT) in more detail by looking at patterns of errors. We focus on instance-level saliency maps – gradient-based methods that identify the importance of tokens to the model by examining the gradient of the loss. For each dataset, we sample 100 responses and generate saliency maps for each. We use the *simple gradient* method (Simonyan et al., 2014) via AllenNLP (Wallace et al., 2019). The item developers manually analyzed the generated saliency maps for each response and model.

We analyzed two sets of cases:

1. One neural model accurately predicted the human score while the other did not. How do the error patterns in these cases illustrate how the models each learned differently from the training data?

2. Both models incorrectly predicted the human

score, and moreover predicted the same incorrect score. Do the models make the wrong prediction for the same or different reasons?

In the following, due to space constraints, we focus on error analysis for the scoring model for the Musical Instruments knowledge integration dataset.

One correct, one incorrect. Cases where one model accurately predicted the human score while the other did not illuminated several differences in the two neural models.

The RNN model tended to ignore or de-emphasize some keywords, while overemphasizing high frequency and function words. For example, Figure 2a shows a simple example where the RNN fails to emphasize the keyword *pitch*. The BERT model accurately registers this word as salient, and predicts the correct score. Similarly, in Figure 2b, the RNN misses the keyphrase *full glass* while the BERT model catches it. In Figure 2c, the RNN spuriously treats the function words *when* and *you* as salient and over-predicts the score.

For its part, the BERT model may de-emphasize many high frequency words but at the same time may regard discourse markers as salient. An example is in Figure 3a, where the BERT model emphasizes *because since*, and this may in part help the model reach the correct prediction.

If the BERT model is able to better learn important keywords (while ignoring more function words), it may sometimes "overlearn" the importance of those tokens, leading to over-prediction of scores. There are several examples where the model uses the word piece *##brate* to overpredict a score (Figure 3b).

Both incorrect with the same prediction. In many cases, the models made the same incorrect predictions for different reasons. An example is Figure 3c, where the RNN emphasizes *deeper* and *dense* while the BERT model focuses on *because* and *cup*. Overall, the same differences in the models identified above held for these cases of making the same incorrect prediction.

In general, although there was some variability across models, both models correctly identified the keywords necessary for scoring responses correctly, leading to good human-machine agreement. The RNN model may be more sensitive to tokens that are good indicators of the score in the training data (either high or low) but not in language in general, such as high frequency and function words, while

148053 score=3 prediction=2
the pitch gets a lot lower
148053 score=3 prediction=3
[CLS] the pitch gets a lot lower [SEP]

(a)

207529 score=3 prediction=2
The tap of a full glass is more low pitched and an empty glass is more
high pitched because there is no bellow
207529 score=3 prediction=3
[CLS] the tap of a full glass is more low pitched and an empty glass is
more high pitched because there is no bell ##ow [SEP]

(b)

147925 score=2 prediction=3
When you tap on a full glass the pitch stays the same as if you were
tapping on an empty glass because you are still tapping on a glass that
is going to make a high pitched sound no matter if it is full or not .
147925 score=2 prediction=2
[CLS] when you tap on a full glass the pitch stays the same as if you
were tapping on an empty glass because you are still tapping on a glass
that is going to make a high pitched sound no matter if it is full or not
. [SEP]

(c)

Figure 2: Error analysis: RNN model trends. In each example, the RNN model's saliency map appears on *top*.

237142 score=3 prediction=2
The pitch of the tapped full glass is lower than the pitch of the tapped
empty glass because since there is water inside you are not going to be
able to hear it as much .
237142 score=3 prediction=3
[CLS] the pitch of the tapped full glass is lower than the pitch of the
tapped empty glass because since there is water inside you are not going
to be able to hear it as much . [SEP]

(a)

148661 score=3 prediction=3
The one taht is full will vibrate less so it will be higher than the one
that is empty .
148661 score=3 prediction=4
[CLS] the one ta ##ht is full will vi ##brate less so it will be higher
than the one that is empty . [SEP]

(b)

176754 score=4 prediction=3
the cup with water has a deeper sound because its changing through
the dense water but the cup with no water stays the same because the
sound wave does n't have to go through anything or change anything .
176754 score=4 prediction=3
[CLS] the cup with water has a deeper sound because its changing
through the dense water but the cup with no water stays the same
because the sound wave doesn ' t have to go through anything or change
anything . [SEP]

(c)

Figure 3: Error analysis: Pre-trained transformer model trends. In each example, the pre-trained transformer
model's saliency map appears on the *bottom*.

BERT's pre-training regime may equip it to reduce any reliance on such tokens.

Notably, however, while the models usually made good use of keyword evidence to arrive at correct scores, when the models made inaccurate predictions, it was often because the response had the right vocabulary but the wrong science. For example, in the Musical Instruments item, a response might contain *pitch*, *lower*, *density*, and *vibrations*, but the response might attribute the lower pitch to the empty glass. At least two issues were observed in cases of model mis-prediction: (1) students used anaphoric *it* to refer to key concepts (e.g., *full glass* or *empty glass*), but the models do not incorporate anaphora resolution capabilities; (2) models fail to associate the right keywords with the right concepts, in the way that human raters did.

6 Related work

The task of automated content scoring has recently gained more attention (Kumar et al., 2017; Riordan et al., 2017; Burrows et al., 2015; Shermis, 2015). Our work is similar to Mizumoto et al. (2019), who developed a multi-task neural model for assigning an overall holistic score as well as content-based analytic subscores. We leave a multi-task formulation of our application setting for future work.

Sung et al. (2019) demonstrated state-of-the-art performance for similarity-based content scoring on the SemEval benchmark dataset (Dzikovska et al., 2016). In this work, we use pre-trained transformer models for instance-based content scoring (cf. Horbach and Zesch (2019)). That is, we use whole responses as training data and fine-tune pre-trained representations for response tokens on the content score prediction task.

Recently, methods have been introduced to incorporate "saliency" directly into the model training process (Ghaeini et al., 2019). The current work focuses on interpreting the predictions of models trained without additional annotations (for an overview of interpretability in NLP, see Belinkov and Glass (2019). Exploring the contribution of augmented datasets and training algorithms is future work. To our knowledge, our work is the first to to explore the relevance of the saliency in the predictions of neural methods for the content scoring task.

7 Conclusion

We described a set of constructed response items for middle-school science curricula that simultaneously assess students on expression of NGSS Disciplineary Core Ideas (DCIs), Cross-Cutting Concepts (CCCs), and Science and Engineering Practices (SEPs), and the integrative linkages between each, as part of engaging in scientific explanations and argumentation. We demonstrated that human and automated scoring of such CRs for the NGSS dimensions (via independent subscores) and the integration of knowledge (via Knowledge Integration scores) is feasible. We demonstrated that automated scoring can be developed with promising accuracy.

Comparing feature-based, RNN, and pre-trained transformer models on these datasets, we observed that the pre-trained transformer models obtained higher rates of human-machine agreement on most holistic KI score and NGSS subscore datasets. While the RNN models were often competitive with the pre-trained transformer models, an analysis of the different kinds of errors made by each model type indicated that the pre-trained transformer models may be more robust to strong dataset-specific, but spurious, cues to score prediction.

Results showed that, in the formative setting targeted by the online science learning environment used in this study, students often scored at the lowest levels of all three rubrics, which increased skewness in the datasets and likely contributed to reduced model accuracy. Future research will explore more robust methods for learning scoring models from less data in formative settings, especially from highly skewed score distributions, while continuing to provide accurate scoring.

Our findings demonstrate the ability to both develop and automatically score NGSS-aligned CR assessment items. With further refinement, we can provide teachers with both the instructional and technological assistance they need to effectively and efficiently support their students to demonstrate the multidimensional science learning called for by the NGSS.

Acknowledgments

We thank Aoife Cahill for many useful discussions and three anonymous reviewers, Beata Beigman Klebanov, Debanjan Ghosh, and Nitin Madnani for helpful comments. This material is based upon work supported by the National Science Foundation under Grant No. 1812660. Any opinions, findings, and conclusions or recommendations expressed in this material are those of the author(s) and do not necessarily reflect the views of the National Science Foundation.

References

Ashutosh Adhikari, Achyudh Ram, Raphael Tang, and Jimmy Lin. 2019. Rethinking Complex Neural Network Architectures for Document Classification. In *Proceedings of the 2019 Conference of the North American Chapter of the Association for Computational Linguistics: Human Language Technologies (NAACL-HLT)*.

Yonatan Belinkov and James Glass. 2019. Analysis Methods in Neural Language Processing: A Survey. *Transactions of the Association for Computational Linguistics*.

Steven Burrows, Iryna Gurevych, and Benno Stein. 2015. The Eras and Trends of Automatic Short Answer Grading. *International Journal of Artificial Intelligence in Education*, 25(1):60–117.

Jacob Devlin, Ming-Wei Chang, Kenton Lee, and Kristina Toutanova. 2019. BERT: Pre-training of Deep Bidirectional Transformers for Language Understanding. In *Proceedings of the 2019 Conference of the North American Chapter of the Association for Computational Linguistics: Human Language Technologies (NAACL-HLT)*.

Rotem Dror, Gili Baumer, Marina Bogomolov, and Roi Reichart. 2017. Replicability Analysis for Natural Language Processing: Testing Significance with Multiple Datasets. *Transactions of the Association for Computational Linguistics*, 5:471–486.

Myroslava O. Dzikovska, Rodney D. Nielsen, and Claudia Leacock. 2016. The joint student response analysis and recognizing textual entailment challenge: making sense of student responses in educational applications. *Language Resources and Evaluation*, 50(1):67–93.

Joseph L. Fleiss and Jacob Cohen. 1973. The equivalence of weighted kappa and the intraclass correlation coefficient as measures of reliability. *Educational and psychological measurement*, 33(3):613–619.

Libby F. Gerard and Marcia C. Linn. 2016. Using Automated Scores of Student Essays to Support Teacher Guidance in Classroom Inquiry. *Journal of Science Teacher Education*, 27(1):111–129.

Reza Ghaeini, Xiaoli Z. Fern, Hamed Shahbazi, and Prasad Tadepalli. 2019. Saliency Learning: Teaching the Model Where to Pay Attention. In *Proceedings of the 2019 Conference of the North American Chapter of the Association for Computational Linguistics: Human Language Technologies (NAACL-HLT)*.

Andrea Horbach and Torsten Zesch. 2019. The influence of variance in learner answers on automatic content scoring. *Frontiers in Education*, 4:28.

Sachin Kumar, Soumen Chakrabarti, and Shourya Roy. 2017. Earth Mover's Distance Pooling over Siamese LSTMs for Automatic Short Answer Grading. In *International Joint Conference on Artificial Intelligence (IJCAI)*.

Marcia C. Linn and Bat-Sheva Eylon. 2011. *Science Learning and Instruction: Taking Advantage of Technology to Promote Knowledge Integration*. Routledge, New York.

Marcia C. Linn, Libby Gerard, Kihyun Ryoo, Kevin McElhaney, Ou Lydia Liu, and Anna N Rafferty. 2014. Computer-guided inquiry to improve science learning. *Science*, 344(6180):155–156.

Ou Lydia Liu, Joseph A. Rios, Michael Heilman, Libby Gerard, and Marcia C. Linn. 2016. Validation of Automated Scoring of Science Assessments. *Journal of Research in Science Teaching*, 53(2):215–233.

Tomoya Mizumoto, Hiroki Ouchi, Yoriko Isobe, Paul Reisert, Ryo Nagata, Satoshi Sekine, and Kentaro Inui. 2019. Analytic Score Prediction and Justification Identification in Automated Short Answer Scoring. In *14th Workshop on Innovative Use of NLP for Building Educational Applications (BEA@ACL)*.

NGSS Lead States. 2013. *Next Generation Science Standards: For States, By States*. The National Academies Press, Washington, D.C.

Jeffrey Pennington, Richard Socher, and Christopher Manning. 2014. Glove: Global Vectors for Word Representation. In *Proceedings of the 2014 Conference on Empirical Methods in Natural Language Processing (EMNLP)*.

Roi Reichart, Rotem Dror, Gili Baumer, and Segev Shlomov. 2018. The Hitchhiker's Guide to Testing Statistical Significance in Natural Language Processing. In *Proceedings of the 56th Annual Meeting of the Association for Computational Linguistics (ACL)*.

Brian Riordan, Michael Flor, and Robert Pugh. 2019. How to account for mispellings: Quantifying the benefit of character representations in neural content scoring models. In *Proceedings of the 14th Workshop on Innovative Use of NLP for Building Educational Applications (BEA@ACL)*.

Brian Riordan, Andrea Horbach, Aoife Cahill, Torsten Zesch, and Chong Min Lee. 2017. Investigating neural architectures for short answer scoring. In *12th Workshop on Innovative Use of NLP for Building Educational Applications (BEA@EMNLP)*.

Dinghan Shen, Guoyin Wang, Wenlin Wang, Martin Renqiang Min, Qinliang Su, Yizhe Zhang, Chunyuan Li, Ricardo Henao, and Lawrence Carin. 2018. Baseline Needs More Love: On Simple Word-Embedding-Based Models and Associated Pooling Mechanisms. In *Proceedings of the 56th Annual Meeting of the Association for Computational Linguistics (ACL)*.

Mark D Shermis. 2015. Contrasting state-of-the-art in the machine scoring of short-form constructed responses. *Educational Assessment*, 20(1).

Karen Simonyan, Andrea Vedaldi, and Andrew Zisserman. 2014. Deep Inside Convolutional Networks: Visualising Image Classification Models and Saliency Maps. In *International Conference on Learning Representations (ICLR)*.

Chul Sung, Tejas I. Dhamecha, and Nirmal Mukhi. 2019. Improving Short Answer Grading Using Transformer-Based Pre-training. In *Proceedings of the 20th International Conference on Artificial Intelligence in Education (AIED)*.

Eric Wallace, Jens Tuyls, Junlin Wang, Sanjay Subramanian, Matthew Gardner, and Sameer Singh. 2019. AllenNLP Interpret: A Framework for Explaining Predictions of NLP Models. In *Proceedings of the 2019 Conference on Empirical Methods in Natural Language Processing (EMNLP)*.

David M. Williamson, Xiaoming Xi, and F. Jay Breyer. 2012. A framework for evaluation and use of automated scoring. *Educational measurement: issues and practice*, 31(1):2–13.

Thomas Wolf, Lysandre Debut, Victor Sanh, Julien Chaumond, Clement Delangue, Anthony Moi, Pierric Cistac, Tim Rault, R'emi Louf, Morgan Funtowicz, and Jamie Brew. 2019. HuggingFace's Transformers: State-of-the-art Natural Language Processing. *ArXiv*, abs/1910.03771.

An Exploratory Study of Argumentative Writing by Young Students: A Transformer-based Approach

Debanjan Ghosh, Beata Beigman Klebanov, Yi Song

Educational Testing Service

dghosh,bbeigmanklebanov,ysong@ets.org

Abstract

We present a computational exploration of argument critique writing by young students. Middle school students were asked to criticize an argument presented in the prompt, focusing on identifying and explaining the reasoning flaws. This task resembles an established college-level argument critique task. Lexical and discourse features that utilize detailed domain knowledge to identify critiques exist for the college task but do not perform well on the young students data. Instead, transformer-based architecture (e.g., BERT) fine-tuned on a large corpus of critique essays from the college task performs much better (over 20% improvement in F1 score). Analysis of the performance of various configurations of the system suggests that while children's writing does not exhibit the standard discourse structure of an argumentative essay, it does share basic local sequential structures with the more mature writers.

1 Introduction

Argument and logic are essential in academic writing as they enhance the critical thinking capacities of students. Argumentation requires systematic reasoning and the skill of using relevant examples to craft a support for one's point of view (Walton, 1996). In recent times, the surge in AI-informed scoring systems has made it possible to assess writing skills using automated systems. Recent research suggests the possibility of argumentation-aware automated essay scoring systems (Stab and Gurevych, 2017b).

Most of the current work on computational analysis of argumentative writing in educational context focuses on automatically identifying the argument structures (e.g., argument components and their relations) in the essays (Stab and Gurevych, 2017a; Persing and Ng, 2016; Nguyen and Litman, 2016) and by predicting essay scores from features derived from the structures (e.g., the number of claims and premises and the number of supported claims) (Ghosh et al., 2016). Related research has also addressed the problem of scoring a particular dimension of essay quality, such as relevance to the prompt (Persing and Ng, 2014), opinions and their targets (Farra et al., 2015), argument strength (Persing and Ng, 2015), among others.

While argument mining literature has addressed the educational context, it has so far mainly focused on analyzing college-level writing. For instance, Nguyen and Litman (2018) investigated argument structures in TOEFL11 corpus (Blanchard et al., 2013); Beigman Klebanov et al. (2017) and Persing and Ng (2015) analyzed writing of university students; Stab and Gurevych (2017b) used data from "essayforum.com", where college entrance examination is the largest forum. Computational analysis of arguments in young students' writing has not yet been done, to the best of our knowledge. Writing quality in essays by young writers has been addressed (Deane, 2014; Attali and Powers, 2008; Attali and Burstein, 2006), but identification of arguments was not part of these studies.

In this paper, we present a novel learning-and-assessment context where middle school students were asked to criticize an argument presented in the prompt, focusing on identifying and explaining the reasoning flaws. Using a relatively small pilot data collected for this task, our aim here is to automatically identify good argument critiques in the young students' writing, with the twin goals of (a) exploring the characteristics of young students' writing for this task, and (b) in view of potential scoring and feedback applications. We start with describing and exemplifying the data, as well as the argument critique annotation we performed on it (section 2). Experiments and results are pre-

145

Proceedings of the 15th Workshop on Innovative Use of NLP for Building Educational Applications, pages 145–150
July 10, 2020. ©2020 Association for Computational Linguistics

Dear Editor,

Advertising aimed at children under 12 should be allowed for several reasons.

First, one family in my neighbourhood sits down and watches TV together almost every evening. The whole family learns a lot, which shows that advertising for children is always a good thing because it brings families together.

Second, research shows that children can't remember commercials well anyway, so they can't be doing kids any harm.

Finally, the arguments against advertising aren't very effective. Some countries banned ads because kids thought the ads were funny. But that's not a good reason. Think about it: the advertising industry spends billions of dollars a year on ads for children. They wouldn't spend all the money if the ads weren't doing some good. Let's not hurt children by stopping a good thing.

If anyone doesn't like children's ads, the advertisers should just try to make them more interesting. The ads are allowed to be shown on TV, so they shouldn't be banned.

Table 1: The prompt of the argument critique task.

sented in section 3, followed by a discussion in section 4.

2 Dataset and Annotation

The data used in this study was collected as part of a pilot of a scenario-based assessment of argumentation skills with about 900 middle school students (Song et al., 2017).[1] Students engaged in a sequence of steps in which they researched and reflected on whether advertising to children under the age of twelve should be banned. The test consists of four tasks; we use the responses to Task 3 in which students are asked to review a letter to the editor and evaluate problems in the letter's *reasoning* or use of *evidence* (see Table 1).

Students were expected to produce a written critique of the arguments, demonstrating their ability to identify and explain problems in the reasoning or use of evidence. For example, the first excerpt below shows a well-articulated critique of the hasty generalization problem in the prompt:

(1) Just because it brings one family together to learn does not mean that it will bring all families together to learn.

(2) The first one about the family in your neighborhood is more like an opinion, not actual information from the article.

[1]The data was collected under the ETS CBAL (Cognitively Based Assessment of, for, and as Learning) Initiative.

(3) Their claims are badly writtin [sic] and have no good arguments. They need to support their claims with SOLID evidence and only claim arguments that can be undecicive [sic].

However, many students had difficulty explaining the reasoning flaws clearly. In the second excerpt, the student thought that an argument from the family in the neighborhood is not strong, but did not demonstrate an understanding of a weak generalization in his explanation. Other common problems included students summarizing the prompt without criticizing, or providing a generic critique that does not adhere to the particulars of the prompt (excerpt (3)).

The goal of the argument critique annotation (described next) was to identify where in a response *good* critiques are made, such as the one in the first excerpt.

Annotation of Critiques: We identified 11 valid critiques of the arguments in the letter. These critiques included: (1) overgeneralizing from a single example; (2) example irrelevant to the argument; (3) example misrepresenting what actually happened; (4) misrepresenting the goal of making advertisements; (5) misunderstanding the problem; (6) neglecting potential side effects of allowing advertising aimed at children; (7) making a wrong argument from sign; (8) argument contradicting authoritative evidence; (9) argument contradicting one's own experience; (10) making a circular argument; (11) making contradictory claims. All sentences containing any material belonging to a valid critique were marked and henceforth denoted as Arg; the rest are denoted as $NoArg$. Three annotators were employed to annotate the sentences to mark them as $Arg/NoArg$. We computed κ between each pair of annotators based on the annotation of 50 essays. Inter-annotator agreement for this sentence-level $Arg/NoArg$ classification for each pair of annotators was 0.714, 0.714, and 0.811, respectively resulting in an average κ of 0.746.

Descriptive statistics: We split the data into *training* (585 response critiques) and *test* (252 response critiques). The *training* partition has 2,220 sentences (515 Arg; 1,705 $NoArg$; average number of words per sentence is 11 (std = 8.03)); *test* contains 973 sentences.

3 Experiments and Results

3.1 Baseline

In this writing task, young students were asked to analyze the given prompt, focusing on identifying and explaining its reasoning flaws. This task is similar to a well-established task for college students previously discussed in the literature (Beigman Klebanov et al., 2017). Compared to the college task, the prompt for children appears to have more obvious reasoning errors. The tasks also differ in the types of responses they elicit. While the college task elicits a full essay-length response, the current critique task elicits a shorter, less formal response.

As our baseline, we evaluate the features that were reported as being effective for identifying argument critiques in the context of the college task. Beigman Klebanov et al. (2017) described a logistic regression classifier with two types of features:

- features capturing discourse **structure**, since it was found that argument critiques tended to occupy certain consistent discourse roles that are common in argumentative essays (such as the SUPPORT, rather than THESIS or BACKGROUND roles), as well as have a tendency to participate in roles that receive a lot of elaboration, such as a SUPPORT sentence following or preceding another SUPPORT sentence, or a CONCLUSION sentence followed by another sentence in the same role.

- features capturing **content**, based on hybrid word and POS ngrams (see Beigman Klebanov et al. (2017) for more detail).

Table 2 shows the results, with each of the two subsets of features separately and together. Clearly, the classifier performs quite poorly for detecting Arg sentences in children's data. Secondly, it seems that whatever performance is achieved is due to the content features, while the structural features fail to detect Arg. Thus, the well-organized nature of the mature writing, where essays have identifiable discourse elements such as THESIS, MAIN CLAIM, SUPPORT, CONCLUSION (Burstein et al., 2003), does not seem to carry over to young students' less formal writing.

3.2 Our system

As the training dataset is relatively small, we leverage pre-trained language models that are

Features	Category	Precision	Recall	F1
Content	$NoArg$	0.851	0.946	0.896
	Arg	0.611	0.338	0.436
Structure	$NoArg$	0.799	1.00	0.889
	Arg	0	0	0
Structure + Content	$NoArg$	0.852	0.940	0.894
	Arg	0.591	0.349	0.439

Table 2: Performance of baseline features. "Structure" corresponds to the *dr_pn* feature set, "Content" corresponds to the *1-3gr ppos* feature set, both from Beigman Klebanov et al. (2017).

shown to be effective in various NLP applications. Particularly, we focus on BERT (Devlin et al., 2018), a bi-directional transformer (Vaswani et al., 2017) based architecture that has produced excellent performance on argumentation tasks such as argument component and relation identification (Chakrabarty et al., 2019) and argument clustering (Reimers et al., 2019). The BERT model is initially trained over a 3.3 billion word English corpus on two tasks: (1) given a sentence containing multiple masked words predict the identity of a particular masked word, and (2) given two sentences, predict whether they are adjacent. The BERT model exploits a multi-head attention operation to compute context-sensitive representations for each token in a sentence. During its training, a special token "[CLS]" is added to the beginning of each training utterance. During evaluation, the learned representation for this "[CLS]" token is processed by an additional layer with nonlinear activation. A standard pre-trained BERT model can be used for transfer learning when the model is "fine-tuned" during training, i.e., on the classification data of Arg and $NoArg$ sentences (i.e., *training* partition) or by first fine-tuning the BERT language-model itself on a large unsupervised corpus from a partially relevant domain, such as a corpus of writings from advanced students and then again fine-tuned on the classification data. In both the cases, BERT makes predictions via the "[CLS]" token.

Fine-tuning on classification data: We first fine-tune a pre-trained BERT model (the "bert-base-uncased" version) with the *training* data. During training the class weights are proportional to the numbers of Arg and $NoArg$ instances. Unless stated otherwise we kept the following parameters throughout in the experiments: we utilize a batch size of 16 instances, learning_rate of 3e-5, warmup_proportion 0.1, and the Adam optimizer.

Experiment	Category	Precision	Recall	F1
BERT$_{bl}$	$NoArg$	0.884	0.913	0.898
	Arg	0.603	0.523	0.560
BERT$_{pair}$	$NoArg$	0.892	0.934	0.913
	Arg	**0.681**	0.556	0.612
BERT$_{bl+lm}$	$NoArg$	0.907	0.898	0.902
	Arg	0.610	0.636	0.623
BERT$_{pair+lm}$	$NoArg$	0.929	0.871	0.900
	Arg	0.592	**0.740**	**0.658**

Table 3: Performance of BERT transformer, various configurations. Rows 1, 2 present results of BERT fine-tuning with *training* data only; rows 3, 4 present the effect of additional language model fine-tuning. Highest scores are **bold**.

Hyperparameters were tuned for only five epochs. This experiment is denoted as BERT$_{bl}$ in Table 3. We observe that the F1 score for Arg is 56%, resulting in a 12% absolute improvement in F1 score over the structure+content features (Table 2). This confirms that BERT is able to perform well even after fine-tuning with a relatively small training corpus with default parameters.

In the next step, we re-utilize the same pre-trained BERT model while transforming the *training* instances to *paired* sentence instances, where the first sentence is the candidate Arg or $NoArg$ sentence and the second sentence of the pair is the immediate next sentence in the essay. For instance, for the first example in section 2, "Just because ... to learn", now the instance also contains the subsequent sentence:

> <Just because ... to learn.>,<Second, children can't remember commercials anyway, so they can't be doing any harm," says the letter.>

A special token "FINAL_SENTENCE" is used when the candidate Arg or $NoArg$ sentence is the last sentence in the essay. This modification of the data representation might help the BERT model for two reasons. First, pairing of the candidate sentence and the next one will encourage the model to more directly utilize the next sentence prediction task. Secondly, since multi-sentence same-discourse-role elaboration was found to be common in Beigman Klebanov et al. (2017) data, BERT may exploit such sequential structures if they at all exist in our data. This is model BERT$_{pair}$ in Table 3. With the paired-sentences transformation of the instances the F1 improves to 61.2%, a boost of 5% over BERT$_{bl}$.

Fine-tuning with a large essay corpus: It has been shown in related research (Chakrabarty et al., 2019) that transfer learning by fine-tuning on a domain-specific corpus using a supervised learning objective can boost performance. We used a large proprietary corpus of college-level argument critique essays similar to those analyzed by Beigman Klebanov et al. (2017). This corpus consists of 351,363 unannotated essays, where an average essay contains 16 sentences, resulting in a corpus of 5.64 million sentences. We fine-tune the pre-trained BERT language model on this large corpus for five epochs and then again fine-tune it with the *training* partition (BERT$_{bl+lm}$). Likewise, BERT$_{pair+lm}$ represents the model after pre-trained BERT language model is fine-tuned with the large corpus and then again fine-tuned with the paired instances of *training*. We observe that fine-tuning the language model improves F1 to 62.3% whereas BERT$_{pair+lm}$ results in the highest F1 of 65.8%, around 5% higher than BERT$_{pair}$ and over 20% higher than the feature-based model.

4 Discussion

The difference in F1 between BERT$_{bl}$, BERT$_{bl+lm}$, and BERT$_{pairs+lm}$ is almost exclusively in recall – they have comparable precision at about 0.6, with recall of 0.52, 0.64, and 0.74, respectively. Partitioning out 10% of the *training* data for a *development* set, we found that BERT$_{bl+lm}$ detected 13 more Arg sentences than BERT$_{bl}$ in the development data. These fell into two **sequential** patterns: (a) the sentence is followed by another that further develops the critique (7 cases) – see excerpts (4) and (5) below; (b) the sentence is the final sentence in the response (6 cases); excerpt (6).

(4) They werent made to be appealing to adults. They only need kids to want the product, and beg their parents for it.

(5) Finally, is spending billions of dollars on something that has no point a good thing? There are many arguements that all this money is just going to waste, and it could be used on more important things.

(6) I say this because in an article I found out that children do remember advertisements that they have seen before.

Our interpretation of this finding is that BERT$_{bl+lm}$ captured organizational elements in children's writing that *are* similar to adult patterns. Beigman Klebanov et al. (2017) found that adult writers often reiterate a previously stated critique in an extended CONCLUSION and spread critiques across consecutive SUPPORT sentences. Thus, even though alignment of critiques with "standard" discourse elements such as CONCLUSION and SUPPORT is not recognizable in children's writing (as witnessed by the failure of the structural features to detect critiques), some **basic local sequential patterns** do exist, and they are sufficiently similar to the ones in adult writing that a system with its language model tuned on adult critique writing can capitalize on this knowledge.

Interestingly, $BERT_{pairs}$ learned similar sequential patterns – indeed 7 of the 13 sentences gained by $BERT_{bl+lm}$ over $BERT_{bl}$ are also recalled by $BERT_{pairs}$. This further reinforces the conclusion that young writers exhibit certain local sequential patterns of discourse organization that they share with mature argument critique writers.

5 Conclusion and Future Work

We present a computational exploration of argument critiques written by middle school children. A feature set designed for *college-level* critique writing has poor recall of critiques when trained on children's data; a pre-trained BERT model fine-tuned on children's data does better by 18%. When BERT's language model is additionally fine-tuned on a large corpus of *college* critique essays, recall improves by further 20%, suggesting the existence of *some* similarity between young and mature writers. Performance analysis suggests that BERT capitalized on certain sequential patterns in critique writing; a larger study examining patterns of argumentation in children's data is needed to confirm the hypothesis. In future, we plan to fine-tune our models on auxiliary dataset, such as the convincing argument dataset from Habernal and Gurevych (2016).

References

Yigal Attali and Jill Burstein. 2006. Automated essay scoring with e-rater v.2. *The Journal of Technology, Learning and Assessment*, 4(3).

Yigal Attali and Don Powers. 2008. A developmental writing scale. *ETS Research Report Series*, 2008(1):i–59.

Beata Beigman Klebanov, Binod Gyawali, and Yi Song. 2017. Detecting Good Arguments in a Non-Topic-Specific Way: An Oxymoron? In *Proceedings of the 55th Annual Meeting of the Association for Computational Linguistics (Volume 2: Short Papers)*, pages 244–249, Vancouver, Canada. Association for Computational Linguistics.

Daniel Blanchard, Joel Tetreault, Derrick Higgins, Aoife Cahill, and Martin Chodorow. 2013. Toefl11: A corpus of non-native english. *ETS Research Report Series*, 2013(2):i–15.

Jill Burstein, Daniel Marcu, and Kevin Knight. 2003. Finding the WRITE Stuff: Automatic Identification of Discourse Structure in Student Essays. *IEEE Intelligent Systems*, 18(1):32–39.

Tuhin Chakrabarty, Christopher Hidey, Smaranda Muresan, Kathleen Mckeown, and Alyssa Hwang. 2019. Ampersand: Argument mining for persuasive online discussions. In *Proceedings of the 2019 Conference on Empirical Methods in Natural Language Processing and the 9th International Joint Conference on Natural Language Processing (EMNLP-IJCNLP)*, pages 2926–2936.

Paul Deane. 2014. Using writing process and product features to assess writing quality and explore how those features relate to other literacy tasks. *ETS Research Report Series*, 2014(1):1–23.

Jacob Devlin, Ming-Wei Chang, Kenton Lee, and Kristina Toutanova. 2018. Bert: Pre-training of deep bidirectional transformers for language understanding. *arXiv preprint arXiv:1810.04805*.

Noura Farra, Swapna Somasundaran, and Jill Burstein. 2015. Scoring persuasive essays using opinions and their targets. In *Proceedings of the Workshop on Innovative Use of NLP for Building Educational Applications*, pages 64–74.

Debanjan Ghosh, Aquila Khanam, Yubo Han, and Smaranda Muresan. 2016. Coarse-grained argumentation features for scoring persuasive essays. In *Proceedings of the 54th Annual Meeting of the Association for Computational Linguistics (Volume 2: Short Papers)*, pages 549–554, Berlin, Germany. Association for Computational Linguistics.

Ivan Habernal and Iryna Gurevych. 2016. Which argument is more convincing? analyzing and predicting convincingness of web arguments using bidirectional lstm. In *Proceedings of the 54th Annual Meeting of the Association for Computational Linguistics (Volume 1: Long Papers)*, pages 1589–1599.

Huy Nguyen and Diane Litman. 2016. Context-aware argumentative relation mining. In *Proceedings of the 54th Annual Meeting of the Association for Computational Linguistics (Volume 1: Long Papers)*, pages 1127–1137.

Huy V Nguyen and Diane J Litman. 2018. Argument mining for improving the automated scoring of persuasive essays. In *Thirty-Second AAAI Conference on Artificial Intelligence*.

Isaac Persing and Vincent Ng. 2014. Modeling prompt adherence in student essays. In *Proceedings of the 52nd Annual Meeting of the Association for Computational Linguistics (Volume 1: Long Papers)*, pages 1534–1543.

Isaac Persing and Vincent Ng. 2015. Modeling argument strength in student essays. In *Proceedings of the 53rd Annual Meeting of the Association for Computational Linguistics and the 7th International Joint Conference on Natural Language Processing (Volume 1: Long Papers)*, pages 543–552.

Isaac Persing and Vincent Ng. 2016. End-to-end argumentation mining in student essays. In *Proceedings of the 2016 Conference of the North American Chapter of the Association for Computational Linguistics: Human Language Technologies*, pages 1384–1394.

Nils Reimers, Benjamin Schiller, Tilman Beck, Johannes Daxenberger, Christian Stab, and Iryna Gurevych. 2019. Classification and clustering of arguments with contextualized word embeddings. *arXiv preprint arXiv:1906.09821*.

Yi Song, Paul Deane, and Mary Fowles. 2017. Examining students' ability to critique arguments and exploring the implications for assessment and instruction. *ETS Research Report Series*, 2017(16):1–12.

Christian Stab and Iryna Gurevych. 2017a. Parsing argumentation structures in persuasive essays. *Computational Linguistics*, 43(3):619–659.

Christian Stab and Iryna Gurevych. 2017b. Recognizing insufficiently supported arguments in argumentative essays. In *Proceedings of the 15th Conference of the European Chapter of the Association for Computational Linguistics: Volume 1, Long Papers*, pages 980–990, Valencia, Spain. Association for Computational Linguistics.

Ashish Vaswani, Noam Shazeer, Niki Parmar, Jakob Uszkoreit, Llion Jones, Aidan N Gomez, Łukasz Kaiser, and Illia Polosukhin. 2017. Attention is all you need. In *Advances in neural information processing systems*, pages 5998–6008.

Douglas N Walton. 1996. *Argumentation schemes for presumptive reasoning*. Psychology Press.

Should You Fine-Tune BERT for Automated Essay Scoring?

Elijah Mayfield and **Alan W Black**
Language Technologies Institute
Carnegie Mellon University
elijah@cmu.edu, awb@cs.cmu.edu

Abstract

Most natural language processing research now recommends large Transformer-based models with fine-tuning for supervised classification tasks; older strategies like bag-of-words features and linear models have fallen out of favor. Here we investigate whether, in automated essay scoring (AES) research, deep neural models are an appropriate technological choice. We find that fine-tuning BERT produces similar performance to classical models at significant additional cost. We argue that while state-of-the-art strategies do match existing best results, they come with opportunity costs in computational resources. We conclude with a review of promising areas for research on student essays where the unique characteristics of Transformers may provide benefits over classical methods to justify the costs.

1 Introduction

Automated essay scoring (AES) mimics the judgment of educators evaluating the quality of student writing. Originally used for summative purposes in standardized testing and the GRE (Chen et al., 2016), these systems are now frequently found in classrooms (Wilson and Roscoe, 2019), typically enabled by training data scored on reliable rubrics to give consistent and clear goals for writers (Reddy and Andrade, 2010).

More broadly, the natural language processing (NLP) research community in recent years has been dominated by deep neural network research, in particular, the Transformer architecture popularized by BERT (Devlin et al., 2019). These models use large volumes of existing text data to pre-train multilayer neural networks with context-sensitive meaning of, and relations between, words. The models, which often consist of over 100 million parameters, are then fine-tuned to a specific new labeled dataset and used for classification, generation, or structured prediction.

Research in AES, though, has tended to prioritize simpler models, usually multivariate regression using a small set of justifiable variables chosen by psychometricians (Attali and Burstein, 2004). This produces models that retain direct mappings between variables and recognizable characteristics of writing, like coherence or lexical sophistication (Yannakoudakis and Briscoe, 2012; Vajjala, 2018). In psychometrics more generally, this focus on features as valid "constructs" leans on a rigorous and well-defined set of principles (Attali, 2013). This approach is at odds with Transformer-based research, and so our core question for this work is: for AES specifically, is a move to deep neural models worth the cost?

The chief technical contribution of this work is to measure results for BERT when fine-tuned for AES. In section 3 we describe an experimental setup with multiple levels of technical difficulty from bag-of-words models to fine-tuned Transformers, and in section 5 we show that the approaches perform similarly. In AES, human interrater reliability creates a ceiling for scoring model accuracy. While Transformers match state-of-the-art accuracy, they do so with significant tradeoffs; we show that this includes a slowdown in training time of up to 100x. Our data shows that these Transformer models improve on N-gram baselines by no more than 5%. Given this result, in section 6 we describe areas of contemporary research on Transformers that show both promising early results and a potential alignment to educational pedagogy beyond reliable scoring.

2 Background

In AES, student essays are scored either on a single holistic scale, or analytically following a rubric that breaks out subscores based on "traits." These scores are almost always integer-valued, and almost universally have fewer than 10 possible score points, though some research has used scales with

151

Proceedings of the 15ᵗʰ Workshop on Innovative Use of NLP for Building Educational Applications, pages 151–162
July 10, 2020. ©2020 Association for Computational Linguistics

as many as 60 points (Shermis, 2014). In most contexts, students respond to "prompts," a specific writing activity with predefined content. Work in natural language processing and speech evaluation has used advanced features like discourse coherence (Wang et al., 2013) and argument extraction (Nguyen and Litman, 2018); for proficient writers in professional settings, automated scaffolds like grammatical error detection and correction also exist (Ng et al., 2014).

Natural language processing has historically used n-gram bag-of-words features to predict labels for documents. These were the standard representation of text data for decades and are still in widespread use (Jurafsky and Martin, 2014). In the last decade, the field moved to word *embeddings*, where words are represented not as a single feature but as dense vectors learned from large unsupervised corpora. While early approaches to dense representations using latent semantic analysis have been a major part of the literature on AES (Foltz et al., 2000; Miller, 2003), these were corpus-specific representations. In contrast, recent work is general-purpose, resulting in off-the-shelf representations like GloVe (Pennington et al., 2014). This allows similar words to have approximately similar representations, effectively managing lexical sparsity.

But the greatest recent innovation has been *contextual* word embeddings, based on deep neural networks and in particular, Transformers. Rather than encoding a word's semantics as a static vector, these models adjust the representation of words based on their context in new documents. With multiple layers and sophisticated *attention mechanisms* (Bahdanau et al., 2015), these newer models have outperformed the state-of-the-art on numerous tasks, and are currently the most accurate models on a very wide range of tasks (Vaswani et al., 2017; Dai et al., 2019). The most popular architecture, BERT, produces a 768-dimensional final embedding based on a network with over 100 million total parameters in 12 layers; pre-trained models are available for open source use (Devlin et al., 2019).

For document classification, BERT is "fine-tuned" by adding a final layer at the end of the Transformer architecture, with one output neuron per class label. When learning from a new set of labeled training data, BERT evaluates the training set multiple times (each pass is called an *epoch*).

A loss function, propagating backward to the network, allows the model to learn relationships between the class labels in the new data and the contextual meaning of the words in the text. A learning rate determines the amount of change to a model's parameters. Extensive results have shown that careful control of the learning rate in a *curriculum* can produce an effective fine-tuning process (Smith, 2018). While remarkably effective, our community is only just beginning to identify exactly what is *learned* in this process; research in "BERT-ology" is ongoing (Kovaleva et al., 2019; Jawahar et al., 2019; Tenney et al., 2019).

These neural models are just starting to be used in machine learning for AES, especially as an intermediate representation for automated essay feedback (Fiacco et al., 2019; Nadeem et al., 2019). End-to-end neural AES models are in their infancy and have only seen exploratory studies like Rodriguez et al. (2019); to our knowledge, no commercial vendor yet uses Transformers as the representation for high-stakes automated scoring.

3 NLP for Automated Essay Scoring

To date, there are no best practices on fine-tuning Transformers for AES; in this section we present options. We begin with a classical baseline of traditional bag-of-words approaches and non-contextual word embeddings, used with Naïve Bayes and logistic regression classifiers, respectively. We then describe three curriculum learning options for fine-tuning BERT using AES data based on broader best practices. We end with two approaches based on BERT but without fine-tuning, with reduced hardware requirements.

3.1 Bag-of-Words Representations

The simplest features for document classification tasks, "bag-of-words," extracts surface N-grams of length 1-2 with "one-hot" binary values indicating presence or absence in a document. In prior AES results, this representation is surprisingly effective, and can be improved with simple extensions: N-grams based on part-of-speech tags (of length 2-3) to capture syntax independent of content, and character-level N-grams of length 3-4, to provide robustness to misspellings (Woods et al., 2017; Riordan et al., 2019). This high-dimensional representation typically has a cutoff threshold where rare tokens are excluded: in our implementation, we exclude N-grams without at least 5 occurrences in training data. Even after this reduction, this is a sparse feature space with thousands of dimensions. For learning with bag-of-words, we use a Naïve Bayes classifier with Laplace smoothing from Scikit-learn (Pedregosa et al., 2011), with part-of-speech tagging from SpaCy (Honnibal and Montani, 2017).

3.2 Word Embeddings

A more modern representation of text uses word-level embeddings. This produces a vector, typically of up to 300 dimensions, representing each word in a document. In our implementation, we represent each document as the term-frequency-weighted mean of word-level embedding vectors from GloVe (Pennington et al., 2014). Unlike one-hot bag-of-words features, embeddings have dense real-valued features and Naïve Bayes models are inappropriate; we instead train a logistic regression classifier with the LibLinear solver (Fan et al., 2008) and L2 regularization from Scikit-learn.

3.3 Fine-Tuning BERT

Moving to neural models, we fine-tune an uncased BERT model using the Fast.ai library. This library's visibility to first-time users of deep learning and accessible online learning materials[1] mean their default choices are the most accessible route for practitioners.

Fast.ai recomends use of *cyclical* learning rate curricula for fine-tuning. In this policy, an upper and lower bound on learning rates are established. lr_{max} is a hyperparameter defining the maximum learning rate in one epoch of learning. In cyclical learning, the learning rate for fine-tuning begins at the lower bound, rises to the upper bound, then descends back to the lower bound. A high learning rate midway through training acts as regularization, allowing the model to avoid overfitting and avoiding local optima. Lower learning rates at the beginning and end of cycles allow for optimization within a local optimum, giving the model an opportunity to discover fine-grained new information again. In our work, we set $lr_{max} = 0.00001$. A lower bound is then derived from the upper bound, $lr_{min} = 0.04 * lr_{max}$; this again is default behavior in the Fast.ai library.

We assess three different curricula for cyclical learning rates, visualized in Figure 1. In the default approach, a maximum learning rate is set and

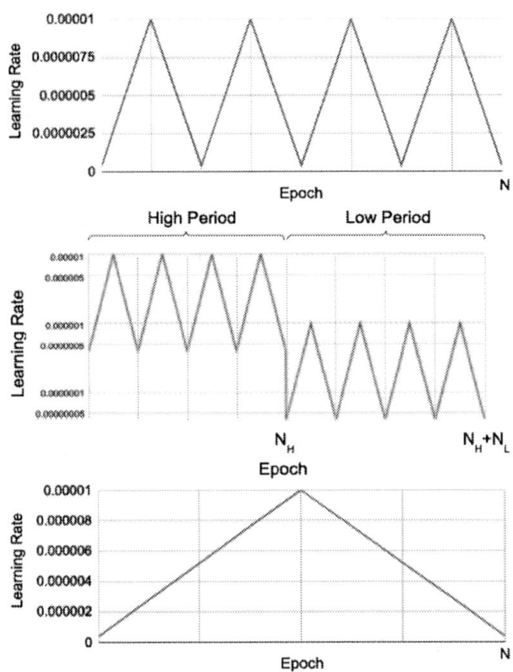

Figure 1: Illustration of cyclical (top), two-period cyclical (middle, log y-scale), and 1-cycle (bottom) learning rate curricula over N epochs.

cycles are repeated until reaching a threshold; for a halting criterion, we measure validation set accuracy. Because of noise in deep learning training, halting at *any* decrease can lead to premature stops; it is preferable to allow some occasional, small drop in performance. In our implementation we halt when accuracy on a validation set, measured in quadratic weighted kappa, decreases by over 0.01. In the second, "two-rate" approach (Smith, 2018), we follow this algorithm, but when we would halt, we instead backtrack by one epoch to a saved version of the network and restart training with a learning rate of 1×10^{-6} (one order of magnitude smaller). Finally, in the "1-cycle" policy, training is condensed into a single rise-and-fall pattern, spread over N epochs. Defining the exact training time N is a hyperparameter tuned on validation data. Finally, while BERT is optimized for sentence encoding, it is able to process documents up to 512 words long. In our data, we truncate a small number of essays longer than this maximum, mostly in ASAP dataset #2.

3.4 Feature Extraction from BERT

Fine-tuning is computationally expensive and can only run on GPU-enabled devices. Many prac-

---

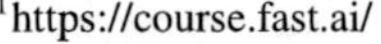

[1]https://course.fast.ai/

titioners in low-resource settings may not have access to appropriate cloud computing environments for these techniques. Previous work has described a compromise approach for using Transformer models without fine-tuning. In Peters et al. (2019), the authors describe a new pipeline. Document texts are processed with an untuned BERT model; the final activations from network on the [CLS] token are then used directly as contextual word embeddings. This 768-dimensional feature vector represents the full document, and is used as inputs for a linear classifier. In the education context, a similar approach was described in Nadeem et al. (2019) as a baseline for evaluation of language-learner essays. This process allows us to use the world knowledge embedded in BERT without requiring fine-tuning of the model itself, and without need for GPUs at training or prediction time. For our work, we train a logistic regression classifier as described in Section 3.2.

3.5 DistilBERT

Recent work has highlighted the extreme carbon costs of full Transformer fine-tuning (Strubell et al., 2019) and the desire for Transformer-based prediction on-device without access to cloud compute. In response to these concerns, Sanh et al. (2019) introduce DistilBERT, which they argue is equivalent to BERT in most practical aspects while reducing parameter size by 40% to 66 million, and decreasing model inference time by 60%. This is accomplished using a distillation method (Hinton et al., 2015) in which a new, smaller "student" network is trained to reproduce the behavior of a pretrained "teacher" network. Once the smaller model is pretrained, interacting with it for the purposes of fine-tuning is identical to interacting with BERT directly. DistilBERT is intended for use cases where compute resources are a constraint, sacrificing a small amount of accuracy for a drastic shrinking of network size. Because of this intended use case, we only present results for DistilBERT with the "1-cycle" learning rate policy, which is drastically faster to fine-tune.

4 Experiments

To test the overall impact of fine-tuning in the AES domain, we use five datasets from the ASAP competition, jointly hosted by the Hewlett Foundation and Kaggle.com (Shermis, 2014). This set of essay prompts was the subject of intense public attention and scrutiny in 2012 and its public release has shaped the discourse on AES ever since. For our experiments, we use the original, deanonymized data from Shermis and Hamner (2012); an anonymized version of these datasets is available online[2]. In all cases, human inter-rater reliability (IRR) is an approximate upper bound on performance, but reliability above human IRR is possible, as all models are trained on *resolved* scores that represent two scores plus a resolution process for disagreements between annotators.

We focus our analysis on the five datasets that most closely resemble standard AES rubrics, discarding three datasets - prompts #1, 7, and 8 - with a scale of 10 or more possible points. Results on these datasets are not representative of overall performance and can skew reported results due to rubric idiosyncrasies, making comparison to other published work impossible (see for example (Alikaniotis et al., 2016), which groups 60-point and 4-point rubrics into a single dataset and therefore produced correlations that cannot be aligned to results from any other published work). Prompts 2-6 are scored on smaller rubric scales with 4-6 points, and are thus generalizable to more AES contexts. Note that nevertheless, each dataset has its own idiosyncrasies; for instance, essays in dataset #5 were written by younger students in 7th and 8th grade, while dataset #4 contains writing from high school seniors; datasets #3 and 4 were responses to specific texts while others were open-ended; and scores in dataset #2 was actually scored on two separate traits, the second of which is often discarded in followup work (as it is here). Our work here does not specifically isolate effects of these differences that would lead to discrepancies in performance or in modeling behavior.

4.1 Metrics and Baselines

For measuring reliability of automated assessments, we use a variant of Cohen's κ, with quadratic weights for "near-miss" predictions on an ordinal scale (QWK). This metric is standard in the AES community (Williamson et al., 2012). High-stakes testing organizations differ on exact cutoffs for acceptable performance, but threshold values between 0.6 and 0.8 QWK are typically used as a floor for testing purposes; human reliability below this threshold is generally not fit for summative student assessment.

---

[2] https://www.kaggle.com/c/asap-aes

In addition to measuring reliability, we also measure training and prediction time, in seconds. As this work seeks to evaluate the practical trade-offs of the move to deep neural methods, this is an important secondary metric. For all experiments, training was performed on Google Colab Pro cloud servers with 32 GB of RAM and an NVideo Tesla P100 GPGPU.

We compare the results of BERT against several previously published benchmarks and results.

- Human IRR as initially reported in the Hewlett Foundation study (Shermis, 2014).

- Industry best performance, as reported by eight commercial vendors and one open-source research team in the initial release of the ASAP study. (Shermis, 2014).

- An early deep learning approach using a combination CNN+LSTM architecture that outperformed most reported results at that time (Taghipour and Ng, 2016).

- Two recent results using traditional non-neural models: Woods et al. (2017), which uses n-gram features in an ordinal logistic regression, and Cozma et al. (2018), which uses a mix of string kernels and word2vec embeddings in a support vector regression.

- Rodriguez et al. (2019), the one previously-published work that attempts AES with a variety of pretrained neural models, including BERT and the similar XLNet (Yang et al., 2019), with numerous alternate configurations and training methods. We report their result with a baseline BERT fine-tuning process, as well as their best-tuned model after extensive optimization.

4.2 Experimental Setup

Following past publications, we train a separate model on each dataset, and evaluate all dataset-specific models using 5-fold cross-validation. Each of the five datasets contains approximately 1,800 essays, resulting in folds of 360 essays each. Additionally, for measuring loss when fine-tuning BERT, we hold out an additional 20% of each training fold as a validation set, meaning that each fold has approximately 1,150 essays used for training and 300 essays used for validation. We

report mean QWK across the five folds. For measurement of training and prediction time, we report the sum of training time across all five folds and all datasets. For slow-running feature extraction, like N-gram part-of-speech features and word embedding-based features, we tag each sentence in the dataset only once and cache the results, rather than re-tagging each sentence on each fold. Finally, for models where distinguishing extraction from training time is meaningful, we present those times separately.

5 Results

5.1 Accuracy Evaluation

Our primary results are presented in Table 1. We find, broadly, that all approaches to machine learning replicate human-level IRR as measured by QWK. Nearly eight years after the publication of the original study, no published results have exceeded vendor performance on three of the five prompt datasets; in all cases, a naive N-gram approach underperforms the state-of-the-art in industry and academia by 0.03-0.06 QWK.

Of particular note is the low performance of GloVe embeddings relative to either neural or N-gram representations. This is surprising: while word embeddings are less popular now than deep neural methods, they still perform well on a wide range of tasks (Baroni et al., 2014). Few publications have noted this negative result for GloVe in the AES domain; only Dong et al. (2017) uses GloVe as the primary representation of ASAP texts in an LSTM model, reporting lower QWK results than any baseline we presented here. One simple explanation for this may be that individual keywords matter a great deal for model performance. It is well established that vocabulary-based approaches are effective in AES tasks (Higgins et al., 2014) and the lack of access to specific word-based features may hinder semantic vector representation. Indeed, only one competitive recent paper on AES uses non-contextual word vectors: Cozma et al. (2018). In this implementation, they do use word2vec, but rather than use word embeddings directly they first cluster words into a set of 500 "embedding clusters." Words that appear in texts are then counted in the feature vector as the centroid of that cluster - in effect, creating a 500-dimensional bag-of-words model.

Our results would suggest that fine-tuning with BERT also reaches approximately the same level

Table 1: Performance on each of ASAP datasets 2-6, in QWK. The final row shows the gap in QWK between the best neural model and the N-gram baseline.

Model	2	3	4	5	6
Human IRR	.80	.77	.85	.74	.74
Hewlett	**.74**	**.75**	.82	**.83**	.78
Taghipour	.69	.69	.81	.81	.82
Woods	.71	.71	.81	.82	**.83**
Cozma	.73	.68	**.83**	**.83**	**.83**
Rodriguez (BERT)	.68	.72	.80	.81	.81
Rodriguez (best)	.70	.72	.82	.82	.82
N-Grams	.71	.71	.78	.80	.79
Embeddings	.42	.41	.60	.49	.36
BERT-CLR	.66	.70	.80	.80	.79
BERT-1CYC	.64	.71	.82	.81	.79
BERT Features	.61	.59	.75	.75	.74
DistilBERT	.65	.70	.82	.81	.79
N-Gram Gap	-.05	.00	.04	.01	.00

Table 2: Cumulative experiment runtime, in seconds, of feature extraction (F), model training (T), and predicting on test sets (P), for ASAP datasets 2-6 with 5-fold cross-validation. Models with 1-cycle fine-tuning are measured at 5 epochs.

Model	F	T	P	Total
Embeddings	93	6	1	100
N-Grams	82	27	2	111
BERT Features	213	10	1	224
DistilBERT	1,972	108		2,080
BERT-1CYC	2,956	192		3,148
BERT-CLR	11,309	210		11,519

of performance as other methods, slightly underperforming previous published results. This is likely an underestimate, due to the complexity of hyperparameter optimization and curriculum learning for Transformers. Rodriguez et al. (2019) demonstrate that it is, in fact, possible to improve the performance of neural models to more closely approach (but not exceed) the state-of-the-art using neural models. Sophisticated approaches like gradual unfreezing, discriminative fine-tuning, or greater parameterization through newer deep learning models in their work consistently produces improvements of 0.01-0.02 QWK compared to the default BERT implementation. But this result emphasizes our concern: we do not claim our results are the best that could be achieved with BERT fine-tuning. We are, in fact, confident that they can be improved through optimization. What the results demonstrate instead is that the ceiling of results for AES tasks lessens the value of that intensive optimization effort.

5.2 Runtime Evaluation

Our secondary evaluation of models is based on training time and resource usage; those results are reported in Table 2. Here, we see that deep learning approaches on GPU-enabled cloud compute produce an approximately 30-100 fold increase in end-to-end training time compared to a naive approach. In fact, this understates the gap, as approximately 75% of feature extraction and model training time in the naive approach is due to part-of-

speech tagging rather than learning. Using BERT features as inputs to a linear classifier is an interesting compromise option, producing slightly lower performance on these datasets but with only a 2x slowdown at training time, all in feature extraction, and potentially retaining some of the semantic knowledge of the full BERT model. Further investigation should test whether additional features for intermediate layers, as explored in Peters et al. (2019), is merited for AES.

We can look at this gap in training runtime more closely in Figure 2. Essays in the prompt 2 dataset are longer persuasive essays and are on average 378 words long, while datasets 3-6 correspond to shorter, source-based content knowledge prompts and are on average 98-152 words long. The need for truncation in dataset #2 for BERT, but not for other approaches, may explain the underperformance of the model in that dataset. Additionally, differences across datasets highlight two key differences for fine-tuning a BERT model:

- Training time increases linearly with number of epochs and with average document length. As seen in Figure 2, this leads to a longer training for the longer essays of dataset 2, nearly as long as the other datasets combined.

- Performance converges on human inter-rater reliability more quickly for short content-based prompts, and performance begins to decrease due to overfitting in as few as 4 epochs. By comparison, in the longer, persuasive arguments of dataset 2, very small performance gains on held-out data continued even at the end of our experiments.

Figure 2 also presents results for DistilBERT. Our work verifies prior published claims of speed

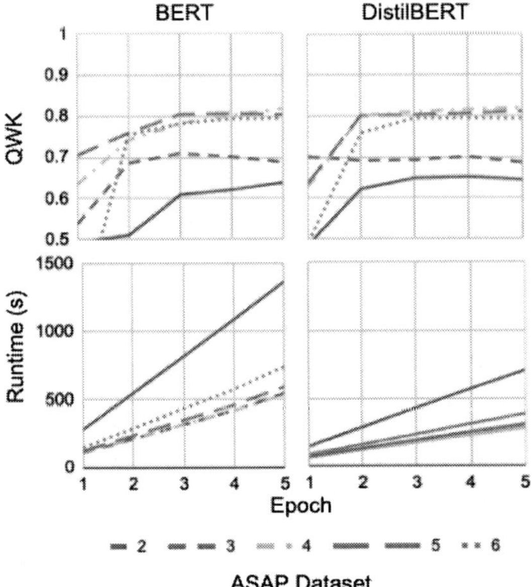

Figure 2: QWK (top) and training time (bottom, in seconds) and for 5-fold cross-validation of 1-cycle neural fine-tuning on ASAP datasets 2-6, for BERT (left) and DistilBERT (right).

improvements both in fine-tuning and at prediction time, relative to the baseline BERT model: training time was reduced by 33% and prediction time was reduced by 44%. This still represents at least a 20x increase in runtime relative to N-gram baselines both for training and prediction.

6 Discussion

For scoring essays with reliably scored, prompt-specific training sets, both classical and neural approaches produce similar reliability, at approximately identical levels to human inter-rater reliability. There is a substantial increase in technical overhead required to implement Transformers and fine-tune them to reach this performance, with minimal gain compared to baselines. The policy lesson for NLP researchers is that using deep learning for scoring alone is unlikely to be justifiable, given the slowdowns at both training and inference time, and the additional hardware requirements. For scoring, at least, Transformer architectures are a hammer in search of a nail.

But it's hardly the case that automated writing evaluation is limited to scoring. In this section we cover major open topics for technical researchers in AES to explore, focusing on areas where neural models have proven strengths above baselines in other domains. We prioritize three major areas: *domain transfer*, *style*, and *fairness*. In each we cite specific past work that indicates a plausible path forward for research.

6.1 Domain Transfer

A major challenge in AES is the inability of prompt-specific models to generalize to new essay topics (Attali et al., 2010; Lee, 2016). Collection of new prompt-specific training sets, with reliable scores, continues to be one of the major stumbling blocks to expansion of AES systems in curricula (Woods et al., 2017). Relatively few researchers have made progress on generic essay scoring: Phandi et al. (2015) introduces a Bayesian regression approach that extracts N-gram features then capitalizes on correlated features across prompts. Jin et al. (2018) shows promising prompt-independent results using an LSTM architecture with surface and part-of-speech N-gram inputs, underperforming prompt-specific models by relatively small margins across all ASAP datasets. But in implementations, much of the work of practitioners is based on workarounds for prompt-specific models; Wilson et al. (2019), for instance, describes psychometric techniques for measuring generic writing ability across a small sample of known prompts.

While Transformers *are* sensitive to the data they were pretrained on, they are well-suited to transfer tasks in mostly unseen domains, as evidenced by part-of-speech tagging for historical texts (Han and Eisenstein, 2019), sentiment classification on out-of-domain reviews (Myagmar et al., 2019), and question answering in new contexts (Houlsby et al., 2019). This last result is promising for content-based short essay prompts, in particular. Our field's open challenge in scoring is to train AES models that can meaningfully evaluate short response texts for correctness based on world knowledge and domain transfer, rather than memorizing the vocabulary of correct, in-domain answers. Promising early results show that relevant world knowledge is *already* embedded in BERT's pretrained model (Petroni et al., 2019). This means that BERT opens up a potentially tractable path to success that was simply not possible with N-gram models.

6.2 Style and Voice

Skepticism toward AES in the classroom comes from rhetoric and composition scholars, who express concerns about its role in writing pedagogy (NCTE, 2013; Warner, 2018). Indeed, the relatively "solved" nature of summative scoring that we highlight here is of particular concern to these experts, noting the high correlation between scores and features like word count (Perelman, 2014).

Modern classroom use of AES beyond high-stakes scoring, like *Project Essay Grade* (Wilson and Roscoe, 2019) or Turnitin *Revision Assistant* (Mayfield and Butler, 2018), makes claims of supporting student agency and growth; here, adapting to writer individuality is a major current gap. Dixon-Román et al. (2019) raises a host of questions about these topics specifically in the context of AES, asking how algorithmic intervention can produce strong writers rather than merely good essays: *"revision, as adjudicated by the platform, is [...] a re-direction toward the predetermined shape of the ideal written form [...] a puzzle-doer recursively consulting the image on the puzzle-box, not that of author returning to their words to make them more lucid, descriptive, or forceful."*

This critique is valid: research on machine translation, for instance, has shown that writer style is not preserved across languages (Rabinovich et al., 2017). There is uncharted territory for AES to adapt to individual writer styles and give feedback based on *individual* writing rather than prompt-specific exemplars. Natural language understanding researchers now argue that *"...style is formed by a complex combination of different stylistic factors"* (Kang and Hovy, 2019); Style-specific natural language generation has shown promise in other domains (Hu et al., 2017; Prabhumoye et al., 2018) and has been extended not just to individual preferences but also to overlapping identities based on attitudes like sentiment and personal attributes like gender (Subramanian et al.). Early work suggests that style-specific models *do* see major improvements when shifting to high-dimensionality Transformer architectures (Keskar et al., 2019). This topic bridges an important gap: for assessment, research has shown that "authorial voice" has measurable outcomes on writing impact (Matsuda and Tardy, 2007), while individual expression is central to decades of pedagogy (Elbow, 1987). Moving the field toward individual expression and away from prompt-specific datasets may be a path to lending legitimacy to AES, and Transformers may be the technical leap necessary to make these tasks work.

6.3 Fairness

Years ago, researchers suggested that demographic bias is worth checking in AES systems (Williamson et al., 2012). But years later, the field has primarily reported fairness experiments on simulated data, and shared toolkits for measuring bias, rather than results on real-world AES implementations or high-stakes data (Madnani et al., 2017; Loukina et al., 2019).

Prompted by social scientists (Noble, 2018), NLP researchers have seen a renaissance of fairness research based on the flaws in default implementations of Transformers (Bolukbasi et al., 2016; Zhao et al., 2017, 2018). These works typicallly seek to reduce the amplification of bias in pretrained models, starting with easy-to-measure proof that demographic bias can be "removed" from word embedding spaces. But iterating on inputs to algorithmic classifiers – precisely the intended use case of formative eeedback for writers! – can reduce the efficacy of "de-biasing" (Liu et al., 2018; Dwork and Ilvento, 2019). More recent research has shown that bias may simply be masked by these approaches, rather than resolved (Gonen and Goldberg, 2019).

What these questions offer, though, is a wellspring of new and innovative technical research. Developers of learning analytics software, including AES, are currently encouraged to focus on scalable experimental evidence of efficacy for learning outcomes (Saxberg, 2017), rather than focus on specific racial or gender bias, or other equity outcomes that are more difficult to achieve through engineering. But Transformer architectures are nuanced enough to capture immense world knowledge, producing a rapid increase in explainability in NLP (Rogers et al., 2020).

Meanwhile, in the field of learning analytics, a burgeoning new field of fairness studies are learning how to investigate these issues in algorithmic educational systems (Mayfield et al., 2019; Holstein and Doroudi, 2019). Outside of technology applications but in writing assessment more broadly, fairness is also a rich topic with a history of literature to learn from (Poe and Elliot, 2019). Researchers at the intersection of *both* these fields have an enormous open opportunity to better understand AES in the context fairness, using the latest tools not just to build reliable scoring but to advance social change.

References

Dimitrios Alikaniotis, Helen Yannakoudakis, and Marek Rei. 2016. Automatic text scoring using neural networks. In *Proceedings of the Association for Computational Linguistics*, pages 715–725.

Yigal Attali. 2013. Validity and reliability of automated essay scoring. *Handbook of automated essay evaluation: Current applications and new directions*, page 181.

Yigal Attali, Brent Bridgeman, and Catherine Trapani. 2010. Performance of a generic approach in automated essay scoring. *The Journal of Technology, Learning and Assessment*, 10(3).

Yigal Attali and Jill Burstein. 2004. Automated essay scoring with e-rater® v. 2.0. *ETS Research Report Series*, (2).

Dzmitry Bahdanau, Kyunghyun Cho, and Yoshua Bengio. 2015. Neural machine translation by jointly learning to align and translate. In *Proceedings of the International Conference on Learning Representations*.

Marco Baroni, Georgiana Dinu, and Germán Kruszewski. 2014. Don't count, predict! a systematic comparison of context-counting vs. context-predicting semantic vectors. In *Proceedings of the Association for Computational Linguistics*, pages 238–247.

Tolga Bolukbasi, Kai-Wei Chang, James Y Zou, Venkatesh Saligrama, and Adam T Kalai. 2016. Man is to computer programmer as woman is to homemaker? debiasing word embeddings. In D. D. Lee, M. Sugiyama, U. V. Luxburg, I. Guyon, and R. Garnett, editors, *Advances in Neural Information Processing Systems 29*, pages 4349–4357. Curran Associates, Inc.

Jing Chen, James H Fife, Isaac I Bejar, and André A Rupp. 2016. Building e-rater® scoring models using machine learning methods. *ETS Research Report Series*, 2016(1):1–12.

Mădălina Cozma, Andrei Butnaru, and Radu Tudor Ionescu. 2018. Automated essay scoring with string kernels and word embeddings. In *Proceedings of the Association for Computational Linguistics*.

Zihang Dai, Zhilin Yang, Yiming Yang, William W Cohen, Jaime Carbonell, Quoc V Le, and Ruslan Salakhutdinov. 2019. Transformer-xl: Attentive language models beyond a fixed-length context. In *Proceedings of the Association for Computational Linguistics*.

Jacob Devlin, Ming-Wei Chang, Kenton Lee, and Kristina Toutanova. 2019. Bert: Pre-training of deep bidirectional transformers for language understanding. In *Proceedings of the NAACL HLT Conference*.

Ezekiel Dixon-Román, T. Philip Nichols, and Ama Nyame-Mensah. 2019. The racializing forces of/in ai educational technologies. *Learning, Media & Technology Special Issue on AI and Education: Critical Perspectives and Alternative Futures*.

Fei Dong, Yue Zhang, and Jie Yang. 2017. Attention-based recurrent convolutional neural network for automatic essay scoring. In *Proceedings of the Conference on Computational Natural Language Learning*, pages 153–162.

Cynthia Dwork and Christina Ilvento. 2019. Fairness under composition. In *Innovations in Theoretical Computer Science Conference*. Schloss Dagstuhl-Leibniz-Zentrum fuer Informatik.

Peter Elbow. 1987. Closing my eyes as i speak: An argument for ignoring audience. *College English*, 49(1):50–69.

Rong-En Fan, Kai-Wei Chang, Cho-Jui Hsieh, Xiang-Rui Wang, and Chih-Jen Lin. 2008. Liblinear: A library for large linear classification. *Journal of Machine Learning Research*, 9(Aug):1871–1874.

James Fiacco, Elena Cotos, and Carolyn Rosé. 2019. Towards enabling feedback on rhetorical structure with neural sequence models. In *Proceedings of the International Conference on Learning Analytics & Knowledge*, pages 310–319. ACM.

Peter W Foltz, Sara Gilliam, and Scott Kendall. 2000. Supporting content-based feedback in on-line writing evaluation with lsa. *Interactive Learning Environments*, 8(2):111–127.

Hila Gonen and Yoav Goldberg. 2019. Lipstick on a pig: Debiasing methods cover up systematic gender biases in word embeddings but do not remove them. *Proceedings of the Association for Computational Linguistics*.

Xiaochuang Han and Jacob Eisenstein. 2019. Unsupervised domain adaptation of contextualized embeddings: A case study in early modern english. *arXiv preprint arXiv:1904.02817*.

Derrick Higgins, Chris Brew, Michael Heilman, Ramon Ziai, Lei Chen, Aoife Cahill, Michael Flor, Nitin Madnani, Joel Tetreault, Daniel Blanchard, et al. 2014. Is getting the right answer just about choosing the right words? the role of syntactically-informed features in short answer scoring. *arXiv preprint arXiv:1403.0801*.

Geoffrey Hinton, Oriol Vinyals, and Jeff Dean. 2015. Distilling the knowledge in a neural network. *stat*, 1050:9.

Kenneth Holstein and Shayan Doroudi. 2019. Fairness and equity in learning analytics systems (fairlak). in. In *Companion Proceedings of the International Learning Analytics & Knowledge Conference (LAK 2019)*.

Matthew Honnibal and Ines Montani. 2017. spacy 2: Natural language understanding with bloom embeddings, convolutional neural networks and incremental parsing.

Neil Houlsby, Andrei Giurgiu, Stanislaw Jastrzebski, Bruna Morrone, Quentin De Laroussilhe, Andrea Gesmundo, Mona Attariyan, and Sylvain Gelly. 2019. Parameter-efficient transfer learning for nlp. In *Proceedings of the International Conference on Machine Learning*, pages 2790–2799.

Zhiting Hu, Zichao Yang, Xiaodan Liang, Ruslan Salakhutdinov, and Eric P Xing. 2017. Toward controlled generation of text. In *Proceedings of the International Conference on Machine Learning*, pages 1587–1596.

Ganesh Jawahar, Benoît Sagot, and Djamé Seddah. 2019. What does bert learn about the structure of language? In *Proceedings of the Association for Computational Linguistics*, pages 3651–3657.

Cancan Jin, Ben He, Kai Hui, and Le Sun. 2018. Tdnn: a two-stage deep neural network for prompt-independent automated essay scoring. In *Proceedings of the Association for Computational Linguistics*, pages 1088–1097.

Dan Jurafsky and James H Martin. 2014. *Speech and language processing*, volume 3. Pearson London.

Dongyeop Kang and Eduard Hovy. 2019. xslue: A benchmark and analysis platform for cross-style language understanding and evaluation. *arXiv preprint arXiv:1911.03663*.

Nitish Shirish Keskar, Bryan McCann, Lav R Varshney, Caiming Xiong, and Richard Socher. 2019. Ctrl: A conditional transformer language model for controllable generation. *arXiv preprint arXiv:1909.05858*.

Olga Kovaleva, Alexey Romanov, Anna Rogers, and Anna Rumshisky. 2019. Revealing the dark secrets of bert. In *Proceedings of Empirical Methods in Natural Language Processing*, volume 1, pages 2465–2475.

Yong-Won Lee. 2016. Investigating the feasibility of generic scoring models of e-rater for toefl ibt independent writing tasks. *English Language Teaching*, 71.

Lydia T Liu, Sarah Dean, Esther Rolf, Max Simchowitz, and Moritz Hardt. 2018. Delayed impact of fair machine learning. In *Proceedings of the International Conference on Machine Learning*.

Anastassia Loukina, Nitin Madnani, and Klaus Zechner. 2019. The many dimensions of algorithmic fairness in educational applications. In *Proceedings of the ACL Workshop on Innovative Use of NLP for Building Educational Applications*.

Nitin Madnani, Anastassia Loukina, Alina von Davier, Jill Burstein, and Aoife Cahill. 2017. Building better open-source tools to support fairness in automated scoring. In *Proceedings of the ACL Workshop on Ethics in Natural Language Processing*, pages 41–52.

Paul Kei Matsuda and Christine M Tardy. 2007. Voice in academic writing: The rhetorical construction of author identity in blind manuscript review. *English for Specific Purposes*, 26(2):235–249.

Elijah Mayfield and Stephanie Butler. 2018. Districtwide implementations outperform isolated use of automated feedback in high school writing. In *Proceedings of the International Conference of the Learning Sciences (Industry and Commercial Track)*.

Elijah Mayfield, Michael Madaio, Shrimai Prabhumoye, David Gerritsen, Brittany McLaughlin, Ezekiel Dixon-Román, and Alan W Black. 2019. Equity beyond bias in language technologies for education. In *Proceedings of ACL Workshop on Innovative Use of NLP for Building Educational Applications*.

Tristan Miller. 2003. Essay assessment with latent semantic analysis. *Journal of Educational Computing Research*, 29(4):495–512.

Batsergelen Myagmar, Jie Li, and Shigetomo Kimura. 2019. Transferable high-level representations of bert for cross-domain sentiment classification. In *Proceedings on the International Conference on Artificial Intelligence (ICAI)*, pages 135–141.

Farah Nadeem, Huy Nguyen, Yang Liu, and Mari Ostendorf. 2019. Automated essay scoring with discourse-aware neural models. In *Proceedings of the ACL Workshop on Innovative Use of NLP for Building Educational Applications*, pages 484–493.

NCTE. 2013. Position statement on machine scoring. *National Council of Teachers of English*. Accessed 2019-09-24.

Hwee Tou Ng, Siew Mei Wu, Ted Briscoe, Christian Hadiwinoto, Raymond Hendy Susanto, and Christopher Bryant. 2014. The conll-2014 shared task on grammatical error correction. In *Proceedings of the Conference on Computational Natural Language Learning: Shared Task*, pages 1–14.

Huy V Nguyen and Diane J Litman. 2018. Argument mining for improving the automated scoring of persuasive essays. In *Proceedings of the AAAI Conference on Artificial Intelligence*.

Safiya Umoja Noble. 2018. *Algorithms of oppression: How search engines reinforce racism*. NYU Press.

Fabian Pedregosa, Gaël Varoquaux, Alexandre Gramfort, Vincent Michel, Bertrand Thirion, Olivier Grisel, Mathieu Blondel, Peter Prettenhofer, Ron Weiss, Vincent Dubourg, et al. 2011. Scikit-learn:

Machine learning in python. *Journal of Machine Learning Research*, 12(Oct):2825–2830.

Jeffrey Pennington, Richard Socher, and Christopher Manning. 2014. Glove: Global vectors for word representation. In *Proceedings of Empirical Methods in Natural Language Processing*, pages 1532–1543.

Les Perelman. 2014. When "the state of the art" is counting words. *Assessing Writing*, 21:104–111.

Matthew E Peters, Sebastian Ruder, and Noah A Smith. 2019. To tune or not to tune? adapting pretrained representations to diverse tasks. In *Proceedings of the Workshop on Representation Learning for NLP (RepL4NLP-2019)*, pages 7–14.

Fabio Petroni, Tim Rocktäschel, Sebastian Riedel, Patrick Lewis, Anton Bakhtin, Yuxiang Wu, and Alexander Miller. 2019. Language models as knowledge bases? In *Proceedings of Empirical Methods in Natural Language Processing*, pages 2463–2473.

Peter Phandi, Kian Ming A Chai, and Hwee Tou Ng. 2015. Flexible domain adaptation for automated essay scoring using correlated linear regression. In *Proceedings of Empirical Methods in Natural Language Processing*, pages 431–439.

Mya Poe and Norbert Elliot. 2019. Evidence of fairness: Twenty-five years of research in assessing writing. *Assessing Writing*, 42:100418.

Shrimai Prabhumoye, Yulia Tsvetkov, Ruslan Salakhutdinov, and Alan W Black. 2018. Style transfer through back-translation. In *Proceedings of the Association for Computational Linguistics*, pages 866–876.

Ella Rabinovich, Raj Nath Patel, Shachar Mirkin, Lucia Specia, and Shuly Wintner. 2017. Personalized machine translation: Preserving original author traits. In *Proceedings of the European Chapter of the Association for Computational Linguistics*, pages 1074–1084.

Y Malini Reddy and Heidi Andrade. 2010. A review of rubric use in higher education. *Assessment & evaluation in higher education*, 35(4):435–448.

Brian Riordan, Michael Flor, and Robert Pugh. 2019. How to account for mispellings: Quantifying the benefit of character representations in neural content scoring models. In *Proceedings of the ACL Workshop on Innovative Use of NLP for Building Educational Applications*, pages 116–126.

Pedro Uria Rodriguez, Amir Jafari, and Christopher M Ormerod. 2019. Language models and automated essay scoring. *arXiv preprint arXiv:1909.09482*.

Anna Rogers, Olga Kovaleva, and Anna Rumshisky. 2020. A primer in bertology: What we know about how bert works. *arXiv preprint arXiv:2002.12327*.

Victor Sanh, Lysandre Debut, Julien Chaumond, and Thomas Wolf. 2019. Distilbert, a distilled version of bert: smaller, faster, cheaper and lighter. *arXiv preprint arXiv:1910.01108*.

Bror Saxberg. 2017. Learning engineering: the art of applying learning science at scale. In *Proceedings of the ACM Conference on Learning@ Scale*. ACM.

Mark D Shermis. 2014. State-of-the-art automated essay scoring: Competition, results, and future directions from a united states demonstration. *Assessing Writing*, 20:53–76.

Mark D Shermis and Ben Hamner. 2012. Contrasting state-of-the-art automated scoring of essays: Analysis. In *Annual national council on measurement in education meeting*, pages 14–16.

Leslie N Smith. 2018. A disciplined approach to neural network hyper-parameters: Part 1–learning rate, batch size, momentum, and weight decay. *arXiv preprint arXiv:1803.09820*.

Emma Strubell, Ananya Ganesh, and Andrew McCallum. 2019. Energy and policy considerations for deep learning in nlp. *Proceedings of the Association for Computational Linguistics*.

Sandeep Subramanian, Guillaume Lample, Eric Michael Smith, Ludovic Denoyer, Marc'Aurelio Ranzato, and Y-Lan Boureau. Multiple-attribute text style transfer. *Age*, 18(24):65.

Kaveh Taghipour and Hwee Tou Ng. 2016. A neural approach to automated essay scoring. In *Proceedings of Empirical Methods in Natural Language Processing*, pages 1882–1891.

Ian Tenney, Dipanjan Das, and Ellie Pavlick. 2019. Bert rediscovers the classical nlp pipeline. In *Proceedings of the Association for Computational Linguistics*.

Sowmya Vajjala. 2018. Automated assessment of non-native learner essays: Investigating the role of linguistic features. *International Journal of Artificial Intelligence in Education*, 28(1):79–105.

Ashish Vaswani, Noam Shazeer, Niki Parmar, Jakob Uszkoreit, Llion Jones, Aidan N Gomez, Łukasz Kaiser, and Illia Polosukhin. 2017. Attention is all you need. In *Advances in neural information processing systems*, pages 5998–6008.

Xinhao Wang, Keelan Evanini, and Klaus Zechner. 2013. Coherence modeling for the automated assessment of spontaneous spoken responses. In *Proceedings of the North American chapter of the Association for Computational Linguistics: Human language technologies*, pages 814–819.

John Warner. 2018. *Why They Can't Write: Killing the Five-Paragraph Essay and Other Necessities*. JHU Press.

David M Williamson, Xiaoming Xi, and F Jay Breyer. 2012. A framework for evaluation and use of automated scoring. *Educational measurement: issues and practice*, 31(1):2–13.

Joshua Wilson, Dandan Chen, Micheal P Sandbank, and Michael Hebert. 2019. Generalizability of automated scores of writing quality in grades 3–5. *Journal of Educational Psychology*, 111(4):619.

Joshua Wilson and Rod D Roscoe. 2019. Automated writing evaluation and feedback: Multiple metrics of efficacy. *Journal of Educational Computing Research*.

Bronwyn Woods, David Adamson, Shayne Miel, and Elijah Mayfield. 2017. Formative essay feedback using predictive scoring models. In *Proceedings of ACM Conference on Knowledge Discovery and Data Mining*, pages 2071–2080. ACM.

Zhilin Yang, Zihang Dai, Yiming Yang, Jaime Carbonell, Russ R Salakhutdinov, and Quoc V Le. 2019. Xlnet: Generalized autoregressive pretraining for language understanding. In *Advances in neural information processing systems*, pages 5754–5764.

Helen Yannakoudakis and Ted Briscoe. 2012. Modeling coherence in esol learner texts. In *Proceedings of the ACL Workshop on Building Educational Applications Using NLP*, pages 33–43. Association for Computational Linguistics.

Jieyu Zhao, Tianlu Wang, Mark Yatskar, Vicente Ordonez, and Kai-Wei Chang. 2017. Men also like shopping: Reducing gender bias amplification using corpus-level constraints. In *Proceedings of Empirical Methods in Natural Language Processing*, pages 2979–2989.

Jieyu Zhao, Yichao Zhou, Zeyu Li, Wei Wang, and Kai-Wei Chang. 2018. Learning gender-neutral word embeddings. In *Proceedings of Empirical Methods in Natural Language Processing*, pages 4847–4853.

GECToR – Grammatical Error Correction: Tag, Not Rewrite

Kostiantyn Omelianchuk   Vitaliy Atrasevych[*]   Artem Chernodub[*]   Oleksandr Skurzhanskyi[*]

Grammarly

{firstname.lastname}@grammarly.com

Abstract

In this paper, we present a simple and efficient GEC sequence tagger using a Transformer encoder. Our system is pre-trained on synthetic data and then fine-tuned in two stages: first on errorful corpora, and second on a combination of errorful and error-free parallel corpora. We design custom token-level transformations to map input tokens to target corrections. Our best single-model/ensemble GEC tagger achieves an $F_{0.5}$ of 65.3/66.5 on CoNLL-2014 (test) and $F_{0.5}$ of 72.4/73.6 on BEA-2019 (test). Its inference speed is up to 10 times as fast as a Transformer-based seq2seq GEC system. The code and trained models are publicly available[1].

1 Introduction

Neural Machine Translation (NMT)-based approaches (Sennrich et al., 2016a) have become the preferred method for the task of Grammatical Error Correction (GEC)[2]. In this formulation, errorful sentences correspond to the source language, and error-free sentences correspond to the target language. Recently, Transformer-based (Vaswani et al., 2017) sequence-to-sequence (seq2seq) models have achieved state-of-the-art performance on standard GEC benchmarks (Bryant et al., 2019). Now the focus of research has shifted more towards generating synthetic data for pretraining the Transformer-NMT-based GEC systems (Grundkiewicz et al., 2019; Kiyono et al., 2019). NMT-based GEC systems suffer from several issues which make them inconvenient for real world deployment: (i) slow inference speed, (ii) demand for

large amounts of training data and (iii) interpretability and explainability; they require additional functionality to explain corrections, e.g., grammatical error type classification (Bryant et al., 2017).

In this paper, we deal with the aforementioned issues by simplifying the task from sequence generation to sequence tagging. Our GEC sequence tagging system consists of three training stages: pretraining on synthetic data, fine-tuning on an errorful parallel corpus, and finally, fine-tuning on a combination of errorful and error-free parallel corpora.

Related work. LaserTagger (Malmi et al., 2019) combines a BERT encoder with an autoregressive Transformer decoder to predict three main edit operations: keeping a token, deleting a token, and adding a phrase before a token. In contrast, in our system, the decoder is a softmax layer. PIE (Awasthi et al., 2019) is an iterative sequence tagging GEC system that predicts token-level edit operations. While their approach is the most similar to ours, our work differs from theirs as described in our contributions below:

1.   We develop custom g-transformations: token-level edits to perform (g)rammatical error corrections. Predicting g-transformations instead of regular tokens improves the generalization of our GEC sequence tagging system.

2. We decompose the fine-tuning stage into two stages: fine-tuning on errorful-only sentences and further fine-tuning on a small, high-quality dataset containing both errorful and error-free sentences.

3. We achieve superior performance by incorporating a pre-trained Transformer encoder in our GEC sequence tagging system. In our experiments, encoders from XLNet and RoBERTa outperform three other cutting-edge Transformer encoders (ALBERT, BERT, and GPT-2).

---

[*]Authors contributed equally to this work, names are given in an alphabetical order.

[1]https://github.com/grammarly/gector

[2]http://nlpprogress.com/english/ grammatical_error_correction.html (Accessed 1 April 2020).

Proceedings of the 15th Workshop on Innovative Use of NLP for Building Educational Applications, pages 163–170
July 10, 2020. ©2020 Association for Computational Linguistics

Dataset	# sentences	% errorful sentences	Training stage
PIE-synthetic	9,000,000	100.0%	I
Lang-8	947,344	52.5%	II
NUCLE	56,958	38.0%	II
FCE	34,490	62.4%	II
W&I+LOCNESS	34,304	67.3%	II, III

Table 1: Training datasets. Training stage I is pretraining on synthetic data. Training stages II and III are for fine-tuning.

2 Datasets

Table 1 describes the finer details of datasets used for different training stages.

Synthetic data. For pretraining stage I, we use 9M parallel sentences with synthetically generated grammatical errors (Awasthi et al., 2019)[3].

Training data. We use the following datasets for fine-tuning stages II and III: National University of Singapore Corpus of Learner English (NUCLE)[4] (Dahlmeier et al., 2013), Lang-8 Corpus of Learner English (Lang-8)[5] (Tajiri et al., 2012), FCE dataset[6] (Yannakoudakis et al., 2011), the publicly available part of the Cambridge Learner Corpus (Nicholls, 2003) and Write & Improve + LOCNESS Corpus (Bryant et al., 2019)[7].

Evaluation data. We report results on CoNLL-2014 test set (Ng et al., 2014) evaluated by official M^2 scorer (Dahlmeier and Ng, 2012), and on BEA-2019 dev and test sets evaluated by ERRANT (Bryant et al., 2017).

3 Token-level transformations

We developed custom token-level transformations $T(x_i)$ to recover the target text by applying them to the source tokens $(x_1 \ldots x_N)$. Transformations increase the coverage of grammatical error corrections for limited output vocabulary size for the most common grammatical errors, such as *Spelling*, *Noun Number*, *Subject-Verb Agreement* and *Verb Form* (Yuan, 2017, p. 28).

The edit space which corresponds to our default tag vocabulary size = 5000 consists of 4971

---

[3]https://github.com/awasthiabhijeet/PIE/tree/master/errorify

[4]https://www.comp.nus.edu.sg/~nlp/corpora.html

[5]https://sites.google.com/site/naistlang8corpora

[6]https://ilexir.co.uk/datasets/index.html

[7]https://www.cl.cam.ac.uk/research/nl/bea2019st/data/wi+locness_v2.1.bea19.tar.gz

---

basic transformations (token-independent KEEP, DELETE and 1167 token-dependent APPEND, 3802 REPLACE) and 29 token-independent *g-transformations*.

Basic transformations perform the most common token-level edit operations, such as: keep the current token unchanged (tag *$KEEP*), delete current token (tag *$DELETE*), append new token t_1 next to the current token x_i (tag *$APPEND_t_1*) or replace the current token x_i with another token t_2 (tag *$REPLACE_t_2*).

g-transformations perform task-specific operations such as: change the case of the current token (*CASE* tags), merge the current token and the next token into a single one (*MERGE* tags) and split the current token into two new tokens (*SPLIT* tags). Moreover, tags from *NOUN NUMBER* and *VERB FORM* transformations encode grammatical properties for tokens. For instance, these transformations include conversion of singular nouns to plurals and vice versa or even change the form of regular/irregular verbs to express a different number or tense.

To obtain the transformation suffix for the *VERB_FORM* tag, we use the verb conjugation dictionary[8]. For convenience, it was converted into the following format: $token_0\_token_1 : tag_0\_tag_1$ (e.g., $go\_goes : VB\_VBZ$). This means that there is a transition from $word_0$ and $word_1$ to the respective tags. The transition is unidirectional, so if there exists a reverse transition, it is presented separately.

The experimental comparison of covering capabilities for our token-level transformations is in Table 2. All transformation types with examples are listed in Appendix, Table 9.

Preprocessing. To approach the task as a sequence tagging problem we need to convert each target sentence from training/evaluation sets into a sequence of tags where each tag is mapped to a single source token. Below is a brief description of our 3-step preprocessing algorithm for color-coded sentence pair from Table 3:

Step 1). Map each token from source sentence to subsequence of tokens from target sentence. [A $\mapsto$ A], [ten $\mapsto$ ten, -], [years $\mapsto$ year, -], [old $\mapsto$ old], [go $\mapsto$ goes, to], [school $\mapsto$ school, .].

---

[8]https://github.com/gutfeeling/word_forms/blob/master/word_forms/en-verbs.txt

Tag vocab. size	Transformations	
	Basic transf.	All transf.
100	60.4%	79.7%
1000	76.4%	92.9%
5000	89.5%	98.1%
10000	93.5%	100.0%

Table 2: Share of covered grammatical errors in CoNLL-2014 for basic transformations only (KEEP, DELETE, APPEND, REPLACE) and for all transformations w.r.t. tag vocabulary's size. In our work, we set the default tag vocabulary size = 5000 as a heuristical compromise between coverage and model size.

For this purpose, we first detect the minimal spans of tokens which define differences between source tokens $(x_1 \ldots x_N)$ and target tokens $(y_1 \ldots y_M)$. Thus, such a span is a pair of selected source tokens and corresponding target tokens. We can't use these span-based alignments, because we need to get tags on the token level. So then, for each source token x_i, $1 \leq i \leq N$ we search for best-fitting subsequence $\Upsilon_i = (y_{j_1} \ldots y_{j_2})$, $1 \leq j_1 \leq j_2 \leq M$ of target tokens by minimizing the modified Levenshtein distance (which takes into account that successful g-transformation is equal to zero distance).

Step 2). For each mapping in the list, find token-level transformations which convert source token to the target subsequence: [A ↦ A]: $KEEP, [ten ↦ ten, -]: $KEEP, $MERGE_HYPHEN, [years ↦ year, -]: $NOUN_NUMBER_SINGULAR, $MERGE_HYPHEN], [old ↦ old]: $KEEP, [go ↦ goes, to]: $VERB_FORM_VB_VBZ, $APPEND_to, [school ↦ school, .]: $KEEP, $APPEND_{.}].

Step 3). Leave only one transformation for each source token: A ⇔ $KEEP, ten ⇔ $MERGE_HYPHEN, years ⇔ $NOUN_NUMBER_SINGULAR, old ⇔ $KEEP, go ⇔ $VERB_FORM_VB_VBZ, school ⇔ $APPEND_{.}.

The iterative sequence tagging approach adds a constraint because we can use only a single tag for each token. In case of multiple transformations we take the first transformation that is not a $KEEP tag. For more details, please, see the preprocessing script in our repository[9].

4 Tagging model architecture

Our GEC sequence tagging model is an encoder made up of pretrained BERT-like transformer

---

[9]https://github.com/grammarly/gector

Iteration #	Sentence's evolution	# corr.
Orig. sent	A ten years old boy go school	-
Iteration 1	A ten-years old boy **goes** school	2
Iteration 2	A ten-**year**-old boy goes **to** school	5
Iteration 3	A ten-year-old boy goes to school.	6

Table 3: Example of iterative correction process where GEC tagging system is sequentially applied at each iteration. Cumulative number of corrections is given for each iteration. Corrections are in bold.

stacked with two linear layers with softmax layers on the top. We always use cased pretrained transformers in their Base configurations. Tokenization depends on the particular transformer's design: BPE (Sennrich et al., 2016b) is used in RoBERTa, WordPiece (Schuster and Nakajima, 2012) in BERT and SentencePiece (Kudo and Richardson, 2018) in XLNet. To process the information at the token-level, we take the first subword per token from the encoder's representation, which is then forwarded to subsequent linear layers, which are responsible for error detection and error tagging, respectively.

5 Iterative sequence tagging approach

To correct the text, for each input token x_i, $1 \leq i \leq N$ from the source sequence $(x_1 \ldots x_N)$, we predict the tag-encoded token-level transformation $T(x_i)$ described in Section 3. These predicted tag-encoded transformations are then applied to the sentence to get the modified sentence.

Since some corrections in a sentence may depend on others, applying GEC sequence tagger only once may not be enough to fully correct the sentence. Therefore, we use the iterative correction approach from (Awasthi et al., 2019): we use the GEC sequence tagger to tag the now modified sequence, and apply the corresponding transformations on the new tags, which changes the sentence further (see an example in Table 3). Usually, the number of corrections decreases with each successive iteration, and most of the corrections are done during the first two iterations (Table 4). Limiting the number of iterations speeds up the overall pipeline while trading off qualitative performance.

Iteration #	P	R	$F_{0.5}$	# corr.
Iteration 1	72.3	38.6	61.5	787
Iteration 2	73.7	41.1	63.6	934
Iteration 3	74.0	41.5	64.0	956
Iteration 4	73.9	41.5	64.0	958

Table 4: Cumulative number of corrections and corresponding scores on CoNLL-2014 (test) w.r.t. number of iterations for our best single model.

Training stage #	CoNLL-2014 (test)			BEA-2019 (dev)		
	P	R	$F_{0.5}$	P	R	$F_{0.5}$
Stage I.	55.4	35.9	49.9	37.0	23.6	33.2
Stage II.	64.4	46.3	59.7	46.4	37.9	44.4
Stage III.	66.7	**49.9**	62.5	52.6	**43.0**	50.3
Inf. tweaks	**77.5**	40.2	**65.3**	**66.0**	33.8	**55.5**

Table 5: Performance of GECToR (XLNet) after each training stage and inference tweaks.

6 Experiments

Training stages. We have 3 training stages (details of data usage are in Table 1):

I Pre-training on synthetic errorful sentences as in (Awasthi et al., 2019).

II Fine-tuning on errorful-only sentences.

III Fine-tuning on subset of errorful and error-free sentences as in (Kiyono et al., 2019).

We found that having two fine-tuning stages with and without error-free sentences is crucial for performance (Table 5).

All our models were trained by Adam optimizer (Kingma and Ba, 2015) with default hyperparameters. Early stopping was used; stopping criteria was 3 epochs of 10K updates each without improvement. We set batch size=256 for pre-training stage I (20 epochs) and batch size=128 for fine-tuning stages II and III (2-3 epochs each). We also observed that freezing the encoder's weights for the first 2 epochs on training stages I-II and using a batch size greater than 64 improves the convergence and leads to better GEC performance.

Encoders from pretrained transformers. We fine-tuned BERT (Devlin et al., 2019), RoBERTa (Liu et al., 2019), GPT-2 (Radford et al., 2019), XLNet (Yang et al., 2019), and ALBERT (Lan et al., 2019) with the same hyperparameters setup. We also added LSTM with randomly initialized embeddings ($dim = 300$) as a baseline. As follows from Table 6, encoders from fine-tuned Transformers significantly outperform LSTMs. BERT, RoBERTa and XLNet encoders perform better than

GPT-2 and ALBERT, so we used them only in our next experiments. All models were trained out-of-the-box[10] which seems to not work well for GPT-2. We hypothesize that encoders from Transformers which were pretrained as a part of the entire encoder-decoder pipeline are less useful for GECToR.

Encoder	CoNLL-2014 (test)			BEA-2019 (dev)		
	P	R	$F_{0.5}$	P	R	$F_{0.5}$
LSTM	51.6	15.3	35.0	-	-	-
ALBERT	59.5	31.0	50.3	43.8	22.3	36.7
BERT	65.6	36.9	56.8	48.3	29.0	42.6
GPT-2	61.0	6.3	22.2	44.5	5.0	17.2
RoBERTa	**67.5**	38.3	**58.6**	**50.3**	30.5	**44.5**
XLNet	64.6	**42.6**	58.5	47.1	**34.2**	43.8

Table 6: Varying encoders from pretrained Transformers in our sequence labeling system. Training was done on data from training stage II only.

Tweaking the inference. We forced the model to perform more precise corrections by introducing two inference hyperparameters (see Appendix, Table 11), hyperparameter values were found by random search on BEA-dev.

First, we added a permanent positive *confidence bias* to the probability of \$KEEP tag which is responsible for not changing the source token. Second, we added a sentence-level *minimum error probability* threshold for the output of the error detection layer. This increased precision by trading off recall and achieved better $F_{0.5}$ scores (Table 5).

Finally, our best single-model, GECToR (XLNet) achieves $F_{0.5} = 65.3$ on CoNLL-2014 (test) and $F_{0.5} = 72.4$ on BEA-2019 (test). Best ensemble model, GECToR (BERT + RoBERTa + XLNet) where we simply average output probabilities from 3 single models achieves $F_{0.5} = 66.5$ on CoNLL-2014 (test) and $F_{0.5} = 73.6$ on BEA-2019 (test), correspondingly (Table 7).

Speed comparison. We measured the model's average inference time on NVIDIA Tesla V100 on batch size 128. For sequence tagging we don't need to predict corrections one-by-one as in autoregressive transformer decoders, so inference is naturally parallelizable and therefore runs many times faster. Our sequence tagger's inference speed is up to 10 times as fast as the state-of-the-art Transformer from Zhao et al. (2019), beam size=12 (Table 8).

---

[10] https://huggingface.co/transformers/

GEC system	Ens.	CoNLL-2014 (test)			BEA-2019 (test)		
		P	**R**	**F$_{0.5}$**	**P**	**R**	**F$_{0.5}$**
Zhao et al. (2019)		67.7	40.6	59.8	-	-	-
Awasthi et al. (2019)		66.1	43.0	59.7	-	-	-
Kiyono et al. (2019)		67.9	**44.1**	61.3	65.5	**59.4**	64.2
Zhao et al. (2019)	✓	74.1	36.3	61.3	-	-	-
Awasthi et al. (2019)	✓	68.3	43.2	61.2	-	-	-
Kiyono et al. (2019)	✓	72.4	**46.1**	65.0	74.7	56.7	70.2
Kantor et al. (2019)	✓	-	-	-	78.3	58.0	73.2
GECToR (BERT)		72.1	42.0	63.0	71.5	55.7	67.6
GECToR (RoBERTa)		73.9	41.5	64.0	77.2	55.1	71.5
GECToR (XLNet)		**77.5**	40.1	**65.3**	79.2	53.9	**72.4**
GECToR (RoBERTa + XLNet)	✓	76.6	42.3	66.0	79.4	57.2	**73.7**
GECToR (BERT + RoBERTa + XLNet)	✓	**78.2**	41.5	**66.5**	78.9	**58.2**	73.6

Table 7: Comparison of single models and ensembles. The M^2 score for CoNLL-2014 (test) and ERRANT for the BEA-2019 (test) are reported. In ensembles we simply average output probabilities from single models.

GEC system	Time (sec)
Transformer-NMT, beam size = 12	4.35
Transformer-NMT, beam size = 4	1.25
Transformer-NMT, beam size = 1	0.71
GECToR (XLNet), 5 iterations	0.40
GECToR (XLNet), 1 iteration	0.20

Table 8: Inference time for NVIDIA Tesla V100 on CoNLL-2014 (test), single model, batch size=128.

7 Conclusions

We show that a faster, simpler, and more efficient GEC system can be developed using a sequence tagging approach, an encoder from a pretrained Transformer, custom transformations and 3-stage training.

Our best single-model/ensemble GEC tagger achieves an $F_{0.5}$ of 65.3/66.5 on CoNLL-2014 (test) and $F_{0.5}$ of 72.4/73.6 on BEA-2019 (test). We achieve state-of-the-art results for the GEC task with an inference speed up to 10 times as fast as Transformer-based seq2seq systems.

8 Acknowledgements

This research was supported by Grammarly. We thank our colleagues Vipul Raheja, Oleksiy Syvokon, Andrey Gryshchuk and our ex-colleague Maria Nadejde who provided insight and expertise that greatly helped to make this paper better. We would also like to show our gratitude to Abhijeet Awasthi and Roman Grundkiewicz for their support in providing data and answering related questions. We also thank 3 anonymous reviewers for their contribution.

References

Abhijeet Awasthi, Sunita Sarawagi, Rasna Goyal, Sabyasachi Ghosh, and Vihari Piratla. 2019. Parallel iterative edit models for local sequence transduction. In *Proceedings of the 2019 Conference on Empirical Methods in Natural Language Processing and the 9th International Joint Conference on Natural Language Processing (EMNLP-IJCNLP)*, pages 4260–4270, Hong Kong, China. Association for Computational Linguistics.

Christopher Bryant, Mariano Felice, Øistein E. Andersen, and Ted Briscoe. 2019. The BEA-2019 shared task on grammatical error correction. In *Proceedings of the Fourteenth Workshop on Innovative Use of NLP for Building Educational Applications*, pages 52–75, Florence, Italy. Association for Computational Linguistics.

Christopher Bryant, Mariano Felice, and Ted Briscoe. 2017. Automatic annotation and evaluation of error types for grammatical error correction. In *Proceedings of the 55th Annual Meeting of the Association for Computational Linguistics (Volume 1: Long Papers)*, pages 793–805, Vancouver, Canada. Association for Computational Linguistics.

Daniel Dahlmeier and Hwee Tou Ng. 2012. Better evaluation for grammatical error correction. In *Proceedings of the 2012 Conference of the North American Chapter of the Association for Computational Linguistics: Human Language Technologies*, pages 568–572. Association for Computational Linguistics.

Daniel Dahlmeier, Hwee Tou Ng, and Siew Mei Wu. 2013. Building a large annotated corpus of learner english: The nus corpus of learner english. In *Proceedings of the eighth workshop on innovative use of NLP for building educational applications*, pages 22–31.

Jacob Devlin, Ming-Wei Chang, Kenton Lee, and Kristina Toutanova. 2019. BERT: Pre-training of deep bidirectional transformers for language understanding. In *Proceedings of the 2019 Conference of the North American Chapter of the Association for Computational Linguistics: Human Language Technologies, Volume 1 (Long and Short Papers)*, pages 4171–4186, Minneapolis, Minnesota. Association for Computational Linguistics.

Roman Grundkiewicz, Marcin Junczys-Dowmunt, and Kenneth Heafield. 2019. Neural grammatical error correction systems with unsupervised pre-training on synthetic data. In *Proceedings of the Fourteenth Workshop on Innovative Use of NLP for Building Educational Applications*, pages 252–263.

Yoav Kantor, Yoav Katz, Leshem Choshen, Edo Cohen-Karlik, Naftali Liberman, Assaf Toledo, Amir Menczel, and Noam Slonim. 2019. Learning to combine grammatical error corrections. In *Proceedings of the Fourteenth Workshop on Innovative Use of NLP for Building Educational Applications*, pages 139–148, Florence, Italy. Association for Computational Linguistics.

Diederik P Kingma and Jimmy Ba. 2015. Adam (2014), a method for stochastic optimization. In *Proceedings of the 3rd International Conference on Learning Representations (ICLR), arXiv preprint arXiv*, volume 1412.

Shun Kiyono, Jun Suzuki, Masato Mita, Tomoya Mizumoto, and Kentaro Inui. 2019. An empirical study of incorporating pseudo data into grammatical error correction. In *Proceedings of the 2019 Conference on Empirical Methods in Natural Language Processing and the 9th International Joint Conference on Natural Language Processing (EMNLP-IJCNLP)*, pages 1236–1242, Hong Kong, China. Association for Computational Linguistics.

Taku Kudo and John Richardson. 2018. SentencePiece: A simple and language independent subword tokenizer and detokenizer for neural text processing. In *Proceedings of the 2018 Conference on Empirical Methods in Natural Language Processing: System Demonstrations*, pages 66–71, Brussels, Belgium. Association for Computational Linguistics.

Zhenzhong Lan, Mingda Chen, Sebastian Goodman, Kevin Gimpel, Piyush Sharma, and Radu Soricut. 2019. Albert: A lite bert for self-supervised learning of language representations. *arXiv preprint arXiv:1909.11942*.

Yinhan Liu, Myle Ott, Naman Goyal, Jingfei Du, Mandar Joshi, Danqi Chen, Omer Levy, Mike Lewis, Luke Zettlemoyer, and Veselin Stoyanov. 2019. Roberta: A robustly optimized bert pretraining approach. *arXiv preprint arXiv:1907.11692*.

Eric Malmi, Sebastian Krause, Sascha Rothe, Daniil Mirylenka, and Aliaksei Severyn. 2019. Encode, tag, realize: High-precision text editing. In *Proceedings of the 2019 Conference on Empirical Methods in Natural Language Processing and the 9th International Joint Conference on Natural Language Processing (EMNLP-IJCNLP)*, pages 5054–5065, Hong Kong, China. Association for Computational Linguistics.

Hwee Tou Ng, Siew Mei Wu, Ted Briscoe, Christian Hadiwinoto, Raymond Hendy Susanto, and Christopher Bryant. 2014. The conll-2014 shared task on grammatical error correction. In *Proceedings of the Eighteenth Conference on Computational Natural Language Learning: Shared Task*, pages 1–14.

Diane Nicholls. 2003. The cambridge learner corpus: Error coding and analysis for lexicography and elt. In *Proceedings of the Corpus Linguistics 2003 conference*, volume 16, pages 572–581.

Alec Radford, Jeffrey Wu, Rewon Child, David Luan, Dario Amodei, and Ilya Sutskever. 2019. Language models are unsupervised multitask learners. *OpenAI Blog*, 1(8):9.

Mike Schuster and Kaisuke Nakajima. 2012. Japanese and korean voice search. In *2012 IEEE International Conference on Acoustics, Speech and Signal Processing (ICASSP)*, pages 5149–5152. IEEE.

Rico Sennrich, Barry Haddow, and Alexandra Birch. 2016a. Edinburgh neural machine translation systems for WMT 16. In *Proceedings of the First Conference on Machine Translation: Volume 2, Shared Task Papers*, pages 371–376, Berlin, Germany. Association for Computational Linguistics.

Rico Sennrich, Barry Haddow, and Alexandra Birch. 2016b. Neural machine translation of rare words with subword units. In *Proceedings of the 54th Annual Meeting of the Association for Computational Linguistics (Volume 1: Long Papers)*, pages 1715–1725, Berlin, Germany. Association for Computational Linguistics.

Toshikazu Tajiri, Mamoru Komachi, and Yuji Matsumoto. 2012. Tense and aspect error correction for esl learners using global context. In *Proceedings of the 50th Annual Meeting of the Association for Computational Linguistics: Short Papers-Volume 2*, pages 198–202. Association for Computational Linguistics.

Ashish Vaswani, Noam Shazeer, Niki Parmar, Jakob Uszkoreit, Llion Jones, Aidan N Gomez, Łukasz Kaiser, and Illia Polosukhin. 2017. Attention is all you need. In *Advances in neural information processing systems*, pages 5998–6008.

Zhilin Yang, Zihang Dai, Yiming Yang, Jaime Carbonell, Russ R Salakhutdinov, and Quoc V Le. 2019. Xlnet: Generalized autoregressive pretraining for language understanding. In *Advances in neural information processing systems*, pages 5754–5764.

Helen Yannakoudakis, Ted Briscoe, and Ben Medlock. 2011. A new dataset and method for automatically grading esol texts. In *Proceedings of the 49th Annual Meeting of the Association for Computational Linguistics: Human Language Technologies-Volume 1*, pages 180–189. Association for Computational Linguistics.

Zheng Yuan. 2017. Grammatical error correction in non-native english. Technical report, University of Cambridge, Computer Laboratory.

Wei Zhao, Liang Wang, Kewei Shen, Ruoyu Jia, and Jingming Liu. 2019. Improving grammatical error correction via pre-training a copy-augmented architecture with unlabeled data. In *Proceedings of the 2019 Conference of the North American Chapter of the Association for Computational Linguistics: Human Language Technologies, Volume 1 (Long and Short Papers)*, pages 156–165, Minneapolis, Minnesota. Association for Computational Linguistics.

A Appendix

id	Core transformation	Transformation suffix	Tag	Example
basic-1	KEEP	∅	$KEEP	…many people want to travel during the summer …
basic-2	DELETE	∅	$DELETE	…not sure if you are {you ⇒ ∅} gifting …
basic-3	REPLACE	a	$REPLACE_a	…the bride wears {**the** ⇒ **a**} white dress …
…	…	…	…	…
basic-3804	REPLACE	cause	$REPLACE_cause	…hope it does not {**make** ⇒ **cause**} any trouble …
basic-3805	APPEND	for	$APPEND_for	…he is {**waiting** ⇒ **waiting for**} your reply …
…	…	…	…	
basic-4971	APPEND	know	$APPEND_know	…I {**don't** ⇒ **don't know**} which to choose…
g-1	CASE	CAPITAL	$CASE_CAPITAL	…surveillance is on the {**internet** ⇒ **Internet**} …
g-2	CASE	CAPITAL_1	$CASE_CAPITAL_1	…I want to buy an {**iphone** ⇒ **iPhone**} …
g-3	CASE	LOWER	$CASE_LOWER	…advancement in {**Medical** ⇒ **medical**} technology …
g-4	CASE	UPPER	$CASE_UPPER	…the {**it** ⇒ **IT**} department is concerned that…
g-5	MERGE	SPACE	$MERGE_SPACE	…insert a special kind of gene {**in to** ⇒ **into**} the cell …
g-6	MERGE	HYPHEN	$MERGE_HYPHEN	…and needs {**in depth** ⇒ **in-depth**} search …
g-7	SPLIT	HYPHEN	$SPLIT_HYPHEN	…support us for a {**long-run** ⇒ **long run**} …
g-8	NOUN_NUMBER	SINGULAR	$NOUN_NUMBER_SINGULAR	…a place to live for their {**citizen** ⇒ **citizens**}
g-9	NOUN_NUMBER	PLURAL	$NOUN_NUMBER_PLURAL	…carrier of this {**diseases** ⇒ **disease**} …
g-10	VERB FORM	VB_VBZ	$VERB_FORM_VB_VBZ	…going through this {**make** ⇒ **makes**} me feel …
g-11	VERB FORM	VB_VBN	$VERB_FORM_VB_VBN	…to discuss what {**happen** ⇒ **happened**} in fall …
g-12	VERB FORM	VB_VBD	$VERB_FORM_VB_VBD	…she sighed and {**draw** ⇒ **drew**} her …
g-13	VERB FORM	VB_VBG	$VERB_FORM_VB_VBG	…shown success in {**prevent** ⇒ **preventing**} such …
g-14	VERB FORM	VB_VBZ	$VERB_FORM_VB_VBZ	…a small percentage of people {**goes** ⇒ **go**} by bike …
g-15	VERB FORM	VBZ_VBN	$VERB_FORM_VBZ_VBN	…development has {**pushes** ⇒ **pushed**} countries to …
g-16	VERB FORM	VBZ_VBD	$VERB_FORM_VBZ_VBD	…he {**drinks** ⇒ **drank**} a lot of beer last night …
g-17	VERB FORM	VBZ_VBG	$VERB_FORM_VBZ_VBG	…couldn't stop {**thinks** ⇒ **thinking**} about it …
g-18	VERB FORM	VBN_VB	$VERB_FORM_VBN_VB	…going to {**depended** ⇒ **depend**} on who is hiring …
g-19	VERB FORM	VBN_VBZ	$VERB_FORM_VBN_VBZ	…yet he goes and {**eaten** ⇒ **eats**} more melons …
g-20	VERB FORM	VBN_VBD	$VERB_FORM_VBN_VBD	…he {**driven** ⇒ **drove**} to the bus stop and …
g-21	VERB FORM	VBN_VBG	$VERB_FORM_VBN_VBG	…don't want you fainting and {**broken** ⇒ **breaking**} …
g-22	VERB FORM	VBD_VB	$VERB_FORM_VBD_VB	…each of these items will {**fell** ⇒ **fall**} in price …
g-23	VERB FORM	VBD_VBZ	$VERB_FORM_VBD_VBZ	…the lake {**froze** ⇒ **freezes**} every year …
g-24	VERB FORM	VBD_VBN	$VERB_FORM_VBD_VBN	…he has been went {**went** ⇒ **gone**} since last week …
g-25	VERB FORM	VBD_VBG	$VERB_FORM_VBD_VBG	…talked her into {**gave** ⇒ **giving**} me the whole day …
g-26	VERB FORM	VBG_VB	$VERB_FORM_VBG_VB	…free time, I just {**enjoying** ⇒ **enjoy**} being outdoors …
g-27	VERB FORM	VBG_VBZ	$VERB_FORM_VBG_VBZ	…there still {**existing** ⇒ **exists**} many inevitable factors …
g-28	VERB FORM	VBG_VBN	$VERB_FORM_VBG_VBN	…people are afraid of being {**tracking** ⇒ **tracked**} …
g-29	VERB FORM	VBG_VBD	$VERB_FORM_VBG_VBD	…there was no {**mistook** ⇒ **mistaking**} his sincerity …

Table 9: List of token-level transformations (section 3). We denote a tag which defines a token-level transformation as concatenation of two parts: a *core transformation* and a *transformation suffix*.

Training stage #	CoNLL-2014 (test)			BEA-2019 (dev)		
	P	R	$F_{0.5}$	P	R	$F_{0.5}$
Stage I.	57.8	33.0	50.2	40.8	22.1	34.9
Stage II.	68.1	42.6	60.8	51.6	33.8	46.7
Stage III.	68.8	**47.1**	63.0	54.2	**41.0**	50.9
Inf. tweaks	**73.9**	41.5	**64.0**	**62.3**	35.1	**54.0**

Table 10: Performance of GECToR (RoBERTa) after each training stage and inference tweaks. Results are given in addition to results for our best single model, GECToR (XLNet) which are given in Table 5.

System name	Confidence bias	Minimum error probability
GECToR (BERT)	0.10	0.41
GECToR (RoBERTa)	0.20	0.50
GECToR (XLNet)	0.35	0.66
GECToR (RoBERTa + XLNet)	0.24	0.45
GECToR (BERT + RoBERTa + XLNet)	0.16	0.40

Table 11: Inference tweaking values which were found by random search on BEA-dev.

Interpreting Neural CWI Classifiers' Weights as Vocabulary Size

Yo Ehara

Shizuoka Institute of Science and Technology / 2200-2, Toyosawa, Fukuroi, Shizuoka, Japan.
`ehara.yo@sist.ac.jp`

Abstract

Complex Word Identification (CWI) is a task for the identification of words that are challenging for second-language learners to read. Even though the use of neural classifiers is now common in CWI, the interpretation of their parameters remains difficult. This paper analyzes neural CWI classifiers and shows that some of their parameters can be interpreted as vocabulary size. We present a novel formalization of vocabulary size measurement methods that are practiced in the applied linguistics field as a kind of neural classifier. We also contribute to building a novel dataset for validating vocabulary testing and readability via crowdsourcing.

1 Introduction

The readability of second-language learners has attracted great interest in studies in the field of natural language processing (NLP) (Beinborn et al., 2014; Pavlick and Callison-Burch, 2016). As NLP mainly addresses automatic editing of texts, readability assessment studies in this field have focused on identifying complex parts by assuming that the words identified are eventually simplified so that learners can read them. To this end, complex word identification (CWI) (Paetzold and Specia, 2016; Yimam et al., 2018) tasks have been studied extensively. Recently, a personalized CWI task has been proposed, where the goal of the task is to predict whether a word is complex for each learner in a personalized manner (Paetzold and Specia, 2017; Lee and Yeung, 2018). Neural models are also employed in these studies and have achieved excellent performance.

The weights, or parameters, of a personalized high-performance neural CWI, obviously include information on how to measure the word difficulty and learner ability from a variety of features. If such information could be extracted from the model in a form that is easy to interpret, it would not only

be use (Hoshino, 2009; Ehara et al., 2012, 2013, 2014; Sakaguchi et al., 2013; Ehara et al., 2016, 2018; Ehara, 2019). To this end, this paper proposes a method for interpreting the weights of personalized neural CWI models. Let us suppose that we have a corpus and that its word frequency ranking reflects its word difficulty. Using our method, a word's difficulty can be interpreted as the *frequency rank* of the word in the corpus and a learner's ability can be interpreted as the *vocabulary size* with respect to the corpus, i.e., the number of words known to the learner when counted in a descending order of frequency in the corpus.

Our key idea is to compare CWI studies with *vocabulary testing* studies in applied linguistics (Nation, 2006; Laufer and Ravenhorst-Kalovski, 2010). Second-language vocabulary is extensive and occupies most of the time spent in learning a language. Vocabulary testing studies focus on measuring each learner's second language vocabulary quickly. One of the major findings of these studies is that a learner needs to "know" at least from 95% to 98% of the tokens in a target text to read. Here, to measure if a learner "knows" a word, vocabulary testing studies use the learner's vocabulary size and word frequency ranking of a balanced corpus. Hence, by formalizing the measurement method used in vocabulary testing studies as a neural personalized CWI, we can interpret neural personalized CWI models' weights as vocabulary size and word frequency ranking.

Our contributions are summarized as follows:

1. To predict whether a learner knows a word through the use of a vocabulary test result in hand, vocabulary size-based methods were previously used for vocabulary testing. We show that this method can represent a special case of typical neural CWI classifiers that take a specific set of features as input. Furthermore, we theoretically propose novel methods that enable the weights of certain neural classifiers

Proceedings of the 15th Workshop on Innovative Use of NLP for Building Educational Applications, pages 171–176
July 10, 2020. ©2020 Association for Computational Linguistics

to become explainable on the basis of the vocabulary size of a learner.

2. To validate the proposed models, we want a dataset in which each learner/test-taker takes both vocabulary and reading comprehension tests. To this end, we build a novel dataset and make it publicly available.

2 Related Work

2.1 Vocabulary size-based testing

Vocabulary size-based testing studies (Nation, 2006; Laufer and Ravenhorst-Kalovski, 2010) measure the vocabulary size of second-language learners. Assuming that all learners memorize words in the same order, i.e., that the difficulty of words is identical for each learner, all words are ranked in one dimension using this method. Subsequently, it is determined whether or not a learner knows a target word by checking if the vocabulary size of the learner is greater than the easiness *rank* of the word.

The vocabulary size-based method can be formalized as follows. Let us consider the case in which we have J learners $\{l_1, l_2, \ldots, l_j, \ldots, l_J\}$ and I words $\{v_1, v_2, \ldots, v_i, \ldots, v_I\}$. j is the index of the learners and i is the index of the words. When there is no ambiguity, we denote word v_i as word i and learner l_j as learner j, for the sake of simplicity. We write the *rank* of word v_i as r_i and the vocabulary *size* of learner l_j as s_j. Then, to determine whether learner l_j knows word v_i, the following decision function f is used:

$$f(l_j, v_i) = s_j - r_i \tag{1}$$

Interpretting Eq. 1 is simple: if $f(l_j, v_i) \geq 0$, then learner l_j knows word v_i; if $f(l_j, v_i) < 0$, then learner l_j does not know word v_i.

The performance of Eq. 1 depends solely on how to determine the vocabulary size of learner l_j, s_j, and the easiness rank of word v_i, r_i. As several methods have previously been proposed to estimate this, we describe them in the following subsections.

2.1.1 Measuring rank of word v_i

Easiness *rank*s of words are important in vocabulary size-based testing. To this end, word frequency rankings from a balanced corpus, especially the British National Corpus (BNC Consortium, 2007), are used: the more frequent words in the corpus are ranked higher and considered to be easier. Some previous studies in the field manually adjust the BNC word frequency rankings to make them compatible with language teachers' intuitions. BNC collects British English. Recent studies also take into account word frequency obtained from the Corpus of Contemporary American (COCA) English (Davies, 2009) by simply adding the word frequencies of both corpora in order to obtain a word frequency ranking.

2.1.2 Measuring the vocabulary size of learner l_j

An intuitive and simple method for measuring the vocabulary size of learner l_j is as follows. First, we randomly sample some words from a large vocabulary sample of the target language. Second, we test whether learner l_j knows each of the sampled words and identify the ratio of words known to the learner. Third, we estimate the learner's vocabulary size as the ratio $\times$ the number of correctly answered questions.

This is how the Vocabulary Size Test (Beglar and Nation, 2007) works. Using the frequency ranking of $20,000$ words from the BNC corpus, the words are first split into 20 levels, with each level consisting of $1,000$ words. It is assumed that the $1,000$ words grouped in the same level have similar difficulty. Then, from the $1,000$ words at each level, 5 words are carefully sampled and a vocabulary test is built that consists of 100 words in total. Finally, the number of words that learner l_j correctly answered $\times$ 200 is estimated to be the vocabulary size of learner l_j. This simple method was later validated by a study from another independent group (Beglar, 2010) and is widely accepted.

Examples of the Vocabulary Size Test are publicly available (Nation, 2007). Each question asks learners taking the test to choose the correct answer by selecting one of the four offered options that has the same meaning as one of the underlined words in the question. It should be noted that, in the Vocabulary Size Test, each word is placed in a sentence to disambiguate the usage of each word and each option can directly be replaced with the underlined part without the need to grammatically rewrite the sentence, e.g., for singular/plural differences. Although a typical criticism of vocabulary tests relates to the fact that they do not take contexts into account, each question in the Vocabulary Size Test is specifically designed to account for such criticism by asking the meaning of a word within a sentence.

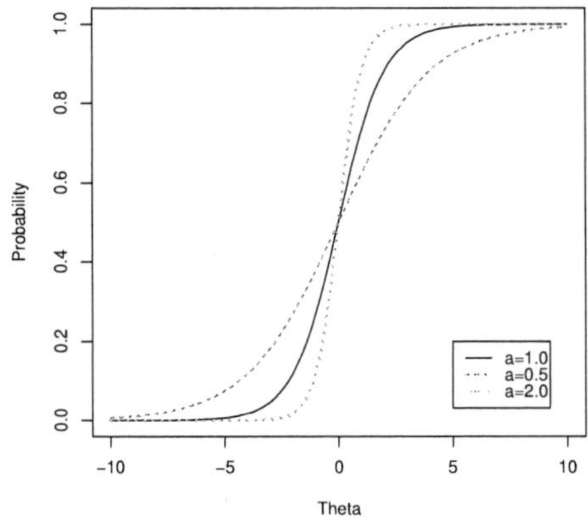

Figure 1: Probability against θ when changing the value of a.

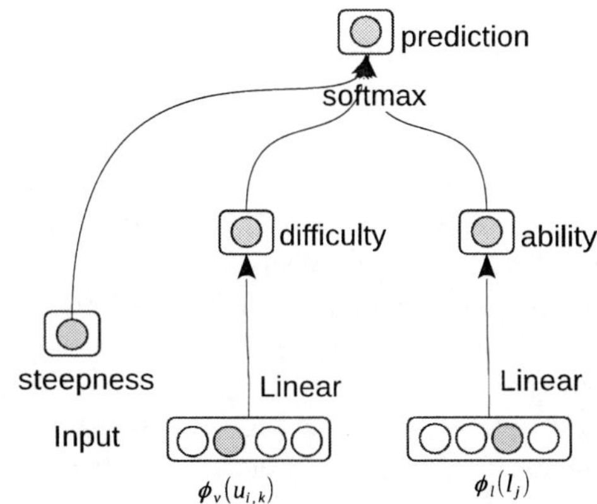

Figure 2: Neural network illustration of a vocabulary size-based prediction.

3 Proposed Formulation

The following notations are used. We have J learners $\{l_1, l_2, \ldots, l_j, \ldots, l_J\}$ and I words $\{v_1, v_2, \ldots, v_i, \ldots, v_I\}$. j is the index of the learners and i is the index of the words. When there is no ambiguity, we denote word v_i as word i and learner l_j as learner j, for the sake of simplicity. Let K_i be the number of occurrences of word v_i. While we do not use in our experiments, for generality, we explicitly write the index for each of the occurrences, i.e., k. Let $u_{i,k}$ be the k-th occurrence of word v_i in the text. Let b_j be the ability of learner j and let $d_{i,k}$ be the difficulty of the k-th occurrence of word v_i.

A dichotomous decision using a neural network-based formulation is typically modeled using a probabilistic formulation. Let $y_{j,i,k}$ be a binary random variable that takes 1 if learner l_j knows the k-th occurrence of word v_i, otherwise it takes 0. Subsequently, it is typical to use a function that maps a real number to the $[0, 1]$ range so that the real number can be interpreted as a probability. To this end, typically σ is the logistic sigmoid function, i.e., $\sigma(x) = \frac{1}{\exp(-x)+1}$ is used. Then, the probability that learner l_j knows the k-th occurrence of word v_i, namely, $u_{i,k}$, can be modeled as in Eq. 2.

$$p(y_{i,k,j} = 1|u_{i,k}, l_j) = \sigma(a(b_j - d_{i,k})) \qquad (2)$$

Qualitative characteristics of Eq. 2 are explained as follows. Let $\theta = a(b_j - d_{i,k})$. The logistic sigmoid function maps an arbitrary real number to the $[0, 1]$ range and makes it possible to interpret the real number as a probability. Here, θ is mapped to the range. As θ increases, the larger the probability becomes. We can see that $a > 0$ is the parameter that determines the steepness of the slope. A large a results in a steep slope. When a is large enough, 4.0 for example, numerically, the function is very close to the *identity* function that returns 0 if $\theta < 0$ and 1 if $\theta \geq 0$.

Probability in a dichotomous classification is most ambiguous when it takes 0.5. By focusing on the point the vertical line takes 0.5, we can see that the sign of $b_j - d_{i,k}$ determines whether or not the probability is larger than 0.5.

3.1 Vocabulary size-based classification as neural classification

These characteristics of Eq. 2 enable it to express the decision function employed in the previous vocabulary size-based decision function Eq. 1 as its special case. Let us consider the case when a is large and the curve is very steep, say $a = 10$, for example. Then, by setting $b_j = s_j$ and $d_{i,k} = r_i$ for all k for word v_i, the decision about whether learner j knows the k-th occurrence of word v_i in Eq. 1 is virtually identical to that of Eq. 2. In this manner, the previous vocabulary size-based decision functions for whether learner l_j knows word v_i in applied linguistics can be converted to a neural network-based classifier and vice versa.

We can see that there exists a *freedom* in the parameters. In the above example, we can achieve the same setting by setting $b_j = 0.1s_j$, $d_{i,k} = 0.1r_i$ and $a = 100$. In this way, the same vocabulary size classification can be achieved by different parameter values.

This freedom in terms of parameters is the key for conversion: by setting an appropriate a, we can convert neural classifier parameters as each learner's vocabulary size and the rank of each word.

3.2 Rewriting parameters

While b_j and $d_{i,k}$ are parameters, we rewrite them using one-hot vectors that are widely used to describe neural network-based models. Let us introduce two types of feature functions: ϕ_l and ϕ_v. The former returns the feature vector of learner l_j, and the latter returns the feature vector of the k-th occurrence of word v_i, $u_{i,k}$.

Then, the ability and difficulty parameters of Eq. 2 can be written as the inner product of a weight vector and a feature vector. Let us introduce $\mathbf{w}_l$ as the weight vector for ϕ_l. Let $\mathbf{h}$ be a function that returns the one-hot representation of the augment. We write $\mathbf{h}_l(l_j)$ to denote a function that returns J-dimensional one-hot vector, where only the j-th element is 1 while the other elements are 0. Then, we can rewrite b_j as the inner product of the weight vector and the one-hot vector as $b_j = \mathbf{w}_l^\top \mathbf{h}_l(l_j)$.

In the same way, $d_{i,k}$ can be rewritten as the inner product of its weight vector and feature vector. Being reminded that K_i denotes the number of occurrences of word v_i, we consider a very long $\sum_{i=1}^{I} K_i$-dimensional one-hot vector $\mathbf{h}_v(u_{i,k})$, where only one element that corresponds to the k-th element of word v_i is 1 and all other elements are 0. Then, by introducing a weight vector $\mathbf{w}_v$ that has the same dimension with $\mathbf{h}_v(u_{i,k})$, we can rewrite $d_{i,k}$ as $d_{i,k} = \mathbf{w}_v^\top \mathbf{h}_v(u_{i,k})$. Using these expressions, Eq. 2 can be illustrated using a typical neural network illustration as in Fig. 2.

Overall, the equation using one-hot vector representation can be described as follows:

$$
\begin{aligned}
&p(y_{i,k,j} = 1 | u_{i,k}, l_j) \\
&= \sigma(a(\mathbf{w}_l^\top \mathbf{h}_l(l_j) - \mathbf{w}_v^\top \mathbf{h}_v(u_{i,k})))
\end{aligned} \tag{3}
$$

3.3 Weights as learner vocabulary sizes and word frequency ranks

Eq. 3 provides us with a hint to convert neural classifier weights into vocabulary sizes and word frequency rankings. To this end, we can do the following. First, we use Eq. 3 to estimate parameters: a, $\mathbf{w}_l$, and $\mathbf{w}_v$. Typically, for a binary classification setting using the logistic sigmoid function, cross-entropy loss is chosen as the loss function. We use $L(a, \mathbf{w}_l, \mathbf{w}_v)$ to denote the sum of the cross-entropy loss function for each of the following: all data, all learners, and all occurrences of all words.

From a, $\mathbf{w}_l$ and $\mathbf{w}_v$, we can estimate the frequency rank of word v_i as follows: $a\mathbf{w}_v^\top \mathbf{h}_v(u_{i,k})$. Hence, by comparing the estimate with the observed ranking value r_i of word v_i, we can also tune all parameters. We can simply employ $R(a, \mathbf{w}_v) = \sum_{i=1}^{I} \sum_{k=1}^{K_i} ||a\mathbf{w}_v^\top \mathbf{h}_v(u_{i,k}) - r_i||^2$ for a loss function that measures how distant the estimated rank and the observed rank are. Of course, we can compare $a\mathbf{w}_l^\top \mathbf{h}_l(l_j)$ and s_j, the observed vocabulary size of learner l_j. However, since the observed vocabulary size of each learner is usually much more inaccurate than the ranking of a word, we do not use this term. As ranks usually take large values but never larger than 1, we can use the logarithm of the rank of word v_i for r_i instead of its raw values.

3.4 Proposed Model

Practically, it is important to note that the one-hot vector $\mathbf{h}_v(u_{i,k})$ in L and R functions can be replaced with any feature vector of $u_{i,k}$ or with the k-th occurrence of word v_i. In our experiments, we simply used this replacement.

We propose the following minimization problem that simultaneously tunes both parameters. We let the parameter $\gamma \in [0, 1]$ be the parameter that tunes the two loss functions, namely, L and R. Note that, as the optimal value of a is different for term L and for term R, we modeled the two terms separately: a_1 and a_2, respectively. Since most of Eq. 4 consists of continuous functions, then Eq. 4 can easily be optimized as a neural classifier using a typical deep learning framework, such as **PyTorch**.

$$
\min_{a_1, a_2, \mathbf{w}_l, \mathbf{w}_v} \gamma L(a_1, \mathbf{w}_l, \mathbf{w}_v) + (1 - \gamma) R(a_2, \mathbf{w}_v) \tag{4}
$$

For the input, we prepare the vocabulary test results of J learners, the vocabulary feature function $\mathbf{h}$, and the vocabulary ranking r_i. By preparing these data for input, we can train the model through estimating the $\mathbf{w}$ parameters by minimizing $Eq.$ 4. The tuning of the γ value can be conducted using validation data that are disjointed from both the training and test data. Or, γ can also be tuned by jointly minimizing γ with other parameters in Eq. 4. Finally, in the test phase, using the trained parameter a_1 and $\mathbf{w}_l$ – we can estimate learner l_j's vocabulary size as $a_1\mathbf{w}_l^\top \mathbf{h}_l(l_j)$. Using the trained parameter a_2, $\mathbf{w}_v$, we can estimate the rank of the first occurrence of a new word v_i, which did not appear in the training data, as $a_2 \mathbf{w}_v^\top \mathbf{h}_v(u_{i,1})$.

4 Dataset

4.1 Description

To evaluate Eq. 4, we need a real dataset that covers both vocabulary size and reading comprehension tests, assuming that the text coverage hypothesis of 98% holds true. To our knowledge, there is no such dataset widely available. There are certain existing vocabulary test result datasets, such as (Ehara, 2018), as well as many reading comprehension test result datasets - however; we could not find a dataset in which a second-language learner subject is asked to provide both vocabulary size and reading comprehension test results.

To this end, this paper provides such a dataset. Following (Ehara, 2018), we used the Lancers crowdsourcing service to collect 55 vocabulary test results as well as answers to 1 long and 1 short reading comprehension question from 100 learners. We paid around 5 USD for each participant. In comparison to the dataset by (Ehara, 2018), the number of vocabulary test questions was reduced so that subjects would have enough time to solve the reading comprehension test. For the vocabulary test part, we used the Vocabulary Size Test (Beglar and Nation, 2007). The reading comprehension questions were taken from the sample set of the questions in the Appendix section in (Laufer and Ravenhorst-Kalovski, 2010). The correct options for these questions are on a website that can also be reached from the description of (Laufer and Ravenhorst-Kalovski, 2010) [1].

In the same manner as (Ehara, 2018), all participants were required to have ever taken the Test of English for International Communication (TOEIC) test provided by English Testing Services (ETS) and to write scores on a self-report basis. This requirement filters out learners who have never studied English seriously but try to participate for economical merits.

In the dataset, each line describes all the responses from a learner. The first columns, which contain the term TOEIC in their headings, provide TOEIC scores and dates. Then, the 55 vocabulary testing questions follow. The columns that start with "l" denote the responses on the long reading

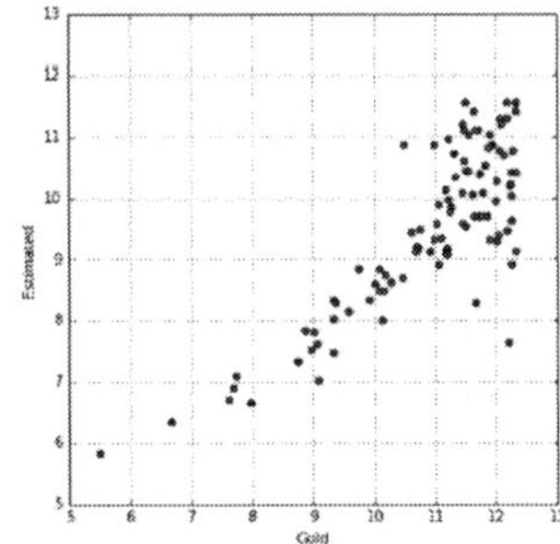

Figure 3: Estimated LFRs against Gold LFRs.

comprehension test and those with "s" denote the responses on the short one.

4.2 Preliminary Experiments

Finally, we show preliminary experiments by using our dataset. We used 33 words from the dataset, i.e., 3,300 responses. Hereafter, we simply denote the logarithm of frequency ranks in a descending order as "LFR". For r_i, we used the LFR of the BNC corpus (BNC Consortium, 2007). For features of $\mathbf{h}_v$, we used the logarithm of the frequency of the COCA corpus (Davies, 2009). We obtained parameters by optimizing the minimization parameters Eq. 4. Then, for 100 words *disjoint from the 33 training words*, we plotted the estimated LFR values against the gold LFR values in Fig. 3. We can easily see that they have a good correlation. The Spearman's correlation coefficient for Fig. 3 was 0.70, which can be construed as a strong correlation (Taylor, 1990).

5 Conclusions

In this paper, we theoretically showed that previous vocabulary size-based classifiers can be seen as a special case of a neural classifier. We also built a dataset necessary for this evaluation and made it publicly available in the form of an attached dataset. Future work include more detailed experiments on language learners' second language vocabularies.

Acknowledgments

This work was supported by JST ACT-I Grant Number JPMJPR18U8 and JSPS KAKENHI Grant Number JP18K18118. We used the AI Bridging Cloud Infrastructure (ABCI) by the National Institute of Advanced Industrial Science and Technology (AIST), Japan. We thank anonymous reviewers for their insightful and constructive comments.

---

[1]For more detailed information for the dataset, refer to `http://yoehara.com/vocabulary-prediction/`.

References

David Beglar. 2010. A Rasch-based validation of the Vocabulary Size Test. *Language Testing*, 27(1):101–118.

David Beglar and Paul Nation. 2007. A vocabulary size test. *The Language Teacher*, 31(7):9–13.

Lisa Beinborn, Torsten Zesch, and Iryna Gurevych. 2014. Predicting the Difficulty of Language Proficiency Tests. *Transactions of the Association for Computational Linguistics*, 2:517–530.

The BNC Consortium. 2007. *The British National Corpus, version 3 (BNC XML Edition)*.

Mark Davies. 2009. The 385+ million word corpus of contemporary american english (1990–2008+): Design, architecture, and linguistic insights. *International journal of corpus linguistics*, 14(2):159–190.

Yo Ehara. 2018. Building an English Vocabulary Knowledge Dataset of Japanese English-as-a-Second-Language Learners Using Crowdsourcing. In *Proc. of LREC*.

Yo Ehara. 2019. Neural rasch model: How word embeddings affect to word difficulty? In *Proc. of the 16th International Conference of the Pacific Association for Computational Linguistics (PACLING)*.

Yo Ehara, Yukino Baba, Masao Utiyama, and Eiichiro Sumita. 2016. Assessing Translation Ability through Vocabulary Ability Assessment. In *Proc. of IJCAI*.

Yo Ehara, Yusuke Miyao, Hidekazu Oiwa, Issei Sato, and Hiroshi Nakagawa. 2014. Formalizing Word Sampling for Vocabulary Prediction as Graph-based Active Learning. In *Proc. of EMNLP*, pages 1374–1384.

Yo Ehara, Issei Sato, Hidekazu Oiwa, and Hiroshi Nakagawa. 2012. Mining Words in the Minds of Second Language Learners: Learner-Specific Word Difficulty. In *Proceedings of COLING 2012*, pages 799–814, Mumbai, India. The COLING 2012 Organizing Committee.

Yo Ehara, Issei Sato, Hidekazu Oiwa, and Hiroshi Nakagawa. 2018. Mining words in the minds of second language learners for learner-specific word difficulty. *Journal of Information Processing*, 26:267–275.

Yo Ehara, Nobuyuki Shimizu, Takashi Ninomiya, and Hiroshi Nakagawa. 2013. Personalized Reading Support for Second-language Web Documents. *ACM Trans. Intell. Syst. Technol.*, 4(2):31:1–31:19.

Ayako Hoshino. 2009. *Automatic Question Generation for Language Testing and its Evaluation Criteria*. Ph.D. thesis, Graduate School of Interdisciplinary Information Studies, The University of Tokyo.

Batia Laufer and Geke C. Ravenhorst-Kalovski. 2010. Lexical Threshold Revisited: Lexical Text Coverage, Learners' Vocabulary Size and Reading Comprehension. *Reading in a Foreign Language*, 22(1):15–30.

John Lee and Chak Yan Yeung. 2018. Personalizing lexical simplification. In *Proceedings of the 27th International Conference on Computational Linguistics*, pages 224–232, Santa Fe, New Mexico, USA. Association for Computational Linguistics.

I. Nation. 2006. How Large a Vocabulary is Needed For Reading and Listening? *Canadian Modern Language Review*, 63(1):59–82.

I. Nation. 2007. Vocabulary size test. https://www.wgtn.ac.nz/lals/about/staff/paul-nation#vocab-tests.

Gustavo Paetzold and Lucia Specia. 2016. Collecting and Exploring Everyday Language for Predicting Psycholinguistic Properties of Words. In *Proceedings of COLING 2016, the 26th International Conference on Computational Linguistics: Technical Papers*, pages 1669–1679, Osaka, Japan. The COLING 2016 Organizing Committee.

Gustavo Paetzold and Lucia Specia. 2017. Lexical Simplification with Neural Ranking. In *Proc. of EACL*, pages 34–40, Valencia, Spain.

Ellie Pavlick and Chris Callison-Burch. 2016. Simple PPDB: A Paraphrase Database for Simplification. In *Proceedings of the 54th Annual Meeting of the Association for Computational Linguistics (Volume 2: Short Papers)*, pages 143–148, Berlin, Germany. Association for Computational Linguistics.

Keisuke Sakaguchi, Yuki Arase, and Mamoru Komachi. 2013. Discriminative Approach to Fill-in-the-Blank Quiz Generation for Language Learners. In *Proc. of the 51st Annual Meeting of the Association for Computational Linguistics (Volume 2: Short Papers)*, pages 238–242, Sofia, Bulgaria. Association for Computational Linguistics.

Richard Taylor. 1990. Interpretation of the correlation coefficient: a basic review. *Journal of diagnostic medical sonography*, 6(1):35–39.

Seid Muhie Yimam, Chris Biemann, Shervin Malmasi, Gustavo H. Paetzold, Lucia Specia, Sanja Štajner, Anaïs Tack, and Marcos Zampieri. 2018. A Report on the Complex Word Identification Shared Task 2018. *arXiv:1804.09132 [cs]*. ArXiv: 1804.09132.

Automated Scoring of Clinical Expressive Language Evaluation Tasks

Yiyi Wang[†], Emily Prud'hommeaux[†], Meysam Asgari[‡], and Jill Dolata[‡]
[†] Boston College, Chestnut Hill MA, USA
[‡] Oregon Health & Science University, Portland OR, USA
{wangdil,prudhome}@bc.edu, {asgari,dolataj}@ohsu.edu

Abstract

Many clinical assessment instruments used to diagnose language impairments in children include a task in which the subject must formulate a sentence to describe an image using a specific target word. Because producing sentences in this way requires the speaker to integrate syntactic and semantic knowledge in a complex manner, responses are typically evaluated on several different dimensions of appropriateness yielding a single composite score for each response. In this paper, we present a dataset consisting of non-clinically elicited responses for three related sentence formulation tasks, and we propose an approach for automatically evaluating their appropriateness. Using neural machine translation, we generate correct-incorrect sentence pairs to serve as synthetic data in order to increase the amount and diversity of training data for our scoring model. Our scoring model uses transfer learning to facilitate automatic sentence appropriateness evaluation. We further compare custom word embeddings with pre-trained contextualized embeddings serving as features for our scoring model. We find that transfer learning improves scoring accuracy, particularly when using pre-trained contextualized embeddings.

1 Introduction

It is estimated that between 5% and 10% of the pediatric population will experience a speech or language impairment (Norbury et al., 2016; Rosenbaum and Simon, 2016). Diagnosing these impairments is complex, requiring the integration of structured assessments, medical history, and clinical observation, and there is evidence that language impairments are frequently misdiagnosed and underdiagnosed (Conti-Ramsden et al., 2006; Grimm and Schulz, 2014; Rosenbaum and Simon, 2016). As a result, there is a need for tools and technologies that can support efficient and remote screening for language impairment. However, developing methods for automatically scoring the subtests used to diagnose language disorders can be challenging because of the very limited amount of labeled data available for these subtests from these special populations.

In this paper, we focus on a task we have adapted from the Formulated Sentences (FS) subtest of the Clinical Evaluation of Language Fundamentals 4 (CELF-4), one of the most widely used language diagnostic instruments in the United States (Semel et al., 2003). In the CELF-4 Formulated Sentences task, a child is presented with a target word and an image, and must use that word in a sentence about that image. Poor performance on this subtest is strongly correlated with expressive language impairments. Responses are scored on a scale from 0 to 2; a sentence assigned a score of 2 must correctly use the target word, be a complete and grammatically correct sentence, and relate to the content and activities shown in the image. Reliable manual scoring can be difficult and time-consuming because of the large of number of factors that must be considered. This degree of subjectivity, together with the task's important role in identifying expressive language impairments, make automatic scoring of the formulated sentences subtest particularly worthwhile.

This paper makes the following contributions:

- We present a new data set of non-clinically elicited formulated sentence task responses, annotated for appropriateness evaluation (scores: 0, 1, and 2), which can be used as a benchmark and as a data source for future automated scoring of clinically elicited responses. The dataset includes 2160 sentences from three related sentence formulation tasks (Section 3).

Proceedings of the 15th Workshop on Innovative Use of NLP for Building Educational Applications, pages 177–185
July 10, 2020. ©2020 Association for Computational Linguistics

- We develop a neural machine translation model trained on second language learner data and generate two artificial datasets for training the formulated sentences scoring classifier.

- We demonstrate that our transfer learning model has benefits for scoring formulated sentences.

- We systematically compare the use of custom task-specific embeddings and pre-trained generic contextualized embeddings for scoring formulated sentences.

2   Related Work

Scoring formulated sentences in terms of syntactic correctness can be analogous to the more common task of Grammatical Error Detection (GED), in which points are deducted for each grammatical error detected in a sentence or text. The state-of-the-art approaches to GED use a supervised neural sequence labeling setup to detect errors trained on artificial data (Rei 2017; Kasewa et al. 2018). Performance on this task can generally benefit from using a large size of high-quality training data, but collecting large quantities of such data is expensive.

Data augmentation can increase the amount and diversity of training data, provide additional information about the representations of sentences, and improve performance on the GED task. The current state-of-the-art GED trains on artificially generated data produced via error induction. One traditional way is to use the patterns learned from annotated learner corpora and apply them to grammatically correct text to generate specific type of errors, such as noun errors (Brockett et al., 2006) and article errors (Rozovskaya and Roth, 2010). More recently, artificial training data is typically generated by using machine translation, where the source text is error-free text and the target is ungrammatical text (Rei 2017).

Deploying vectorized representation of word and sentence is now a ubiquitous technique in most NLP tasks. Incorporating word embeddings as features can provide another possible solution in low-resource scenarios. The current state of the art GED is achieved by using BERT embeddings to capture the contextual information. Bell et al. (2019) compare using ELMo, BERT and Flair embeddings on several publicly available GED datasets, and propose an approach to effectively integrate such representations to detect grammatical errors.

Our work is inspired by this prior research on using machine translation to generate artificial data and comparing the influence of task-specific versus generic embeddings. Although these methods are typically trained on second language learners' data in essay writing tasks, our goal is to seek a general representation of the syntactic and semantic representation of a single sentence in a constrained domain by children who are L1 speakers but may have deficits in expressive language. Given the very limited amount of clinical data, however, we make the assumption that the types of errors language learners make can be leveraged to evaluate formulated sentences responses, an assumption that will be empirically validated in future work with our clinical dataset.

3   Data

In this section, we describe the non-clinical formulated sentences dataset we have collected, as well as two other publicly accessible datasets, MS-COCO (Lin et al., 2014) and FCE (Yannakoudakis et al., 2011), which we use to train embeddings and generate artificial training data.

Formulated Sentences (FS) Dataset   Using our own stimuli designed to mimic the properties of the CELF-4 Formulated Sentences (FS) stimuli, we collected 2160 sentences from Amazon Mechanical Turk workers and scored the responses according to the published guidelines for the CELF-4 FS task, which rely on syntactic grammaticality and semantic appropriateness given the image. Each of the 24 numbered stimulus words was manually selected by a speech language pathologist in order to be comparable to the corresponding CELF-4 FS stimulus word in terms of part of speech, age of acquisition, and phonological complexity. The participants were recruited on Amazon Mechanical Turk (AMT) and directed to take the test within the online survey platform Qualtrics (Barnhoorn et al., 2015), as required by the affiliated university's Institutional Review Board.

Our FS data collection effort is composed of three sub-tasks:

- Task 1: Formulating sentences from an image and a target word. Participants view an image and a target word and write a sentence using that word to describe that image.

- Task 2: Formulating sentence from target word only (no image). Participants are asked to write a sentence that includes the target word.

- Task 3: Formulating sentences from an image only (no target word). Participants are asked to write a sentence description of the image in their own words.

Each participant was randomly assigned to take one of the three sub-tasks. The participant was instructed to view a sample stimulus and response and was then asked to take two trial stimuli to ensure they were familiarized with the test format and environment. Since there are intra-relationship between the three tasks, a participant was able to complete only one sub-task to avoid covariate effects. There were 30 participants for each task, with 24 stimuli in each test, resulting in 2160 sentences (24 stimuli * 3 tasks * 30 participants) included in the dataset.

The collected sentences were scored by four native speakers of English by giving a score of 0, 1, or 2. A score of 2 indicates that the sentence fully expresses the content of the image by using the given word without any grammatical errors. If there is one grammatical error, or the sentence only represents unimportant details of the image, the sentences is marked as 1. If there are two or more grammatical errors, or if the content is unrelated to the image, it is assigned a score of 0.

	2	1	0	Total
Task 1	511	52	157	720
Task 2	658	29	33	720
Task 3	370	123	27	720
All Tasks	1739	204	217	2160

Table 1: Score distribution in 3 tasks.

Each grader was assigned to evaluate 2 sub-tasks, and the average pairwise kappa between the graders was 0.625. When there was a disagreement between two graders, the third grader was recruited, and the final score was the majority of the three graders.

Integrating a target word into an image description requires more complicated linguistic competence than using the target word to make a sentence or having a free choice of vocabulary in describing an image. Therefore, Task 1 is considered to be more challenging than Task 2 or 3. As shown in Table 1 and Figure 2, there are significantly more sentences in Task 1 that are scored 0 or 1 than in

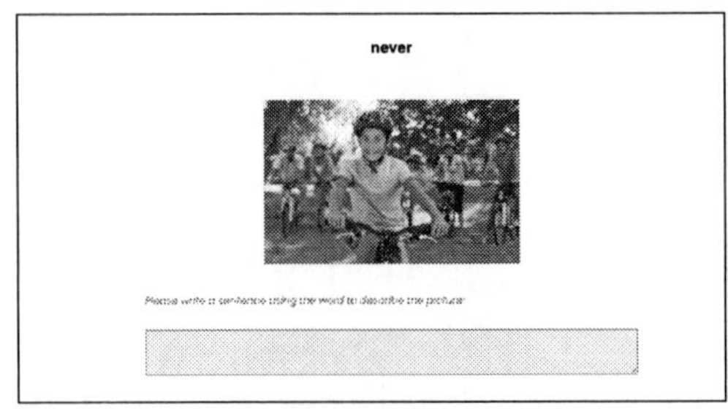

Figure 1: Example of the formulated sentence task (stimulus 3 of Task 1). For Task 2, only the target word "never" is displayed, and for Task 3 only the image is displayed.

Task	Score-0 sentences
1	*Boys are never driving the bicycle.*
	The boy has never let down his family.
	Run to cycle.
	The boy never driving the cycle.
	Three generation family on cycle ride in countryside.
	Never is a all boys cycle driving.
	Never give up the place.
	The boy doesn't ride his bike with the others, but he doesn't care.
2	*Never get compromised for a second option.*
3	*This boy active for bike.*
	The are cycling competition.
	The boy biking the cycle.

Table 2: Score-0 sentences for stimulus 3, target word "never", image shown in Figure 2.

Tasks 2 and 3. For example, for Stimulus 3 with target word "never" (shown in Figure 2), 8 sentences are assigned a score of 0 in Task 1, while only one sentence is given 0 in Task 2 and 3 sentences are marked as 0 in Task 3 (Table 2).

The final sentence-formulation dataset includes 5 columns: subject ID, task, stimulus, sentence and score. The participant's personal information is replaced by a randomly assigned 5-digit subject ID. The score distribution of the three tasks is summarized in Table 1 and the data is released for public access [1].

COCO COCO is a publicly released large-scale dataset for object detection, segmentation, and captioning (Lin et al., 2014). For each image, five hu-

---

[1] https://github.com/yiyiwang515/Automated-Scoring-of-Clinical-Expressive-Language-Evaluation-Tasks.git

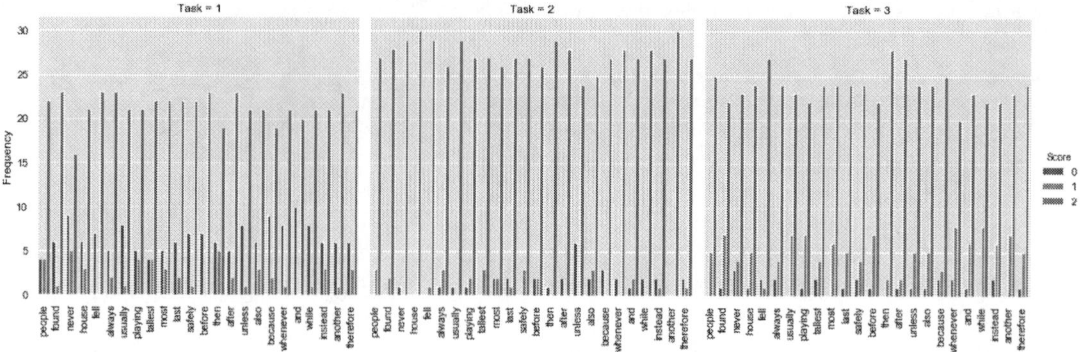

Figure 2: Score distribution for each stimulus in three tasks. Each stimulus is represented by its associated target word.

man generated captions were collected from AMT. In our work, we use the 2017 train dataset, which includes approximately 20k images with 600k captions. Since some of the captions were either empty or had likely incomplete sentences (fewer than 4 words), we exclude those captions resulting in a final dataset of 33,366 sentences.

The linguistic characteristics of COCO are analogous to our sentence formulation task regarding choice of lexicon, the use of syntactic structures, and the semantic context of the utterances. We therefore use COCO dataset for two purposes: (1) to train a task-specific Word2vec embedding to capture meaning-related and syntactic relationships; and (2) to use as score-2 source input to machine translation models that are trained to generate artificial errored (score-1 and score-0) sentences.

FCE First Certificate in English (FCE) (Yannakoudakis et al., 2011) is a publicly available dataset, including 1244 essays written by nonnative learners of English with different first language backgrounds. The FCE exam is used to assess English proficiency of upper-intermediate level learners. The essays are annotated by language assessment experts with types of errors and their corresponding corrections in XML. The original incorrect sentences in the essay and their corrected counterparts are extracted by sentence pairs. The sentences containing no errors or with a length (including punctuation) less than 5 are excluded from the final dataset used for training our models.

A label is added for each sentence. For all the correct sentences, label of 2 is added to mark the appropriateness of the sentence. A sentence with one error is assigned a label of 1, while a sentence with two or more errors is assigned a label of 0.

The final dataset includes 10799 correct sentences, 4810 sentences with one grammatical error, and 5989 sentences with two or more errors. The FCE data serves as training data for two neural machine translation models that we use to generate inappropriate (score-1 and score-0) sentences by taking appropriate (score-2) sentences as input.

4 Experiments

4.1 Sentence Embedding

Three types of sentence embeddings are used in this work: BERT, ELMo and Word2Vec embeddings (Devlin et al. 2018; Peters et al. 2017; Mikolov et al. 2013). For context sensitive embeddings BERT and ELMo, we use the publicly available pre-trained models. We trained a Word2cvec embedding on the 600,000 COCO captions.

BERT BERT can integrate information in raw corpora (BooksCorpus and English Wikipedia) while considering task-specific information contained in the target dataset. Kaneko and Komachi (2019) use BERT contextualized representation to achieve state-of-the-art results for word-based GED tasks. In addition to improving results in the GED task, BERT (Devlin et al., 2018) has been shown to be a powerful feature extractor for various other tasks. We employ BERT to generate pre-trained contextual representations. BERT pretrained embeddings have two versions. We use a lighter version of BERT which yields 768 dimensions for sentence embeddings. The DistilBERT is smaller but can roughly match the performance of using the full BERT (Sanh et al. 2019).

ELMo The ELMo pre-trained model we use is trained on the One Billion Word Benchmark corpus. The sentence representation is learned by a sequence labeler during training.

The BERT and ELMo models used here are trained on formal published writings, such as books and news articles. This is not a perfect domain or stylistic match for the evaluation of responses from the formulated sentences task. In order to better represent the linguistic nature of our task, we also train a task-specific Word2vec embedding.

Word2vec We train our Word2vec model using the Gensim Python library (Rehurek and Sojka, 2010). We use skip-grams to train a word embedding model with 300 dimensions, again using the COCO captions. Words occurring fewer than 5 times are filtered out, and the maximum distance between a target word and its surrounding content is set as 4. The number of threads used is 5. A sentence embedding is calculated as the mean of the component word embeddings. Since COCO captions share similar linguistic features with the sentence formulation tasks, this custom sentence embedding is expected to capture a richer linguistic representation of the task.

4.2 Data Augmentation

In our FS dataset, score-1 and score-0 sentences account for around 20% of the total number of sentences. Since most of the classification algorithms are sensitive to imbalance in predicting classes, such a dataset can bias the classification model towards score-2. In this case, a baseline majority-class classifier, which predicts score-2 for all the sentences, can achieve 0.8 accuracy (Table 1). The unbalanced nature of this data requires us to synthesize additional score-1 and score-0 sentences to increase the size and variety of training set.

We implement two LSTM machine translation models using OpenNMT (Klein et al., 2017). The score-2 (corrected) sentences from the FCE dataset are used as the source data, and the score-0 or score-1 (incorrect) sentences serve as the target data. For example, for the source-2 to target-1 (2-1) model, we trained the model on sentences pairs from FCE dataset containing only one grammatical error. The LSTM model is a two-layer bidirectional LSTM with 500 hidden units with a global attention layer. We set an early stop if the training accuracy score dropped consistently for 10 epochs. Similarly, we train another source-2 to target-0 (2-0) model with the same settings to generate score-0 sentences.

Having trained a NMT model, we then "trans-

late" 939 score-2 sentences from our formulated sentences dataset and convert the sentences into the same number of score-0/1 sentences by using the 2-0 and 2-1 machine translation models respectively. Eight hundred score-2 sentences were excluded for synthesizing data to reserve for testing. The final synthesized formulated sentence (SFS) dataset used for training includes 2817 sentences. The COCO captions used for training word embedding are further selected in this process serving as the error-free input. A large number of COCO captions are incomplete sentences with heavy noun phrases containing a long modifier. We remove such captions in final training set to preserve sentence-level grammaticality. For example, "Man in apron standing on front of oven with pans and bakeware" is excluded, because the root of the dependency parsing tree ("man") is not a verb. A subset of COCO captions containing 14017 sentences is selected using parse information extracted using the SpaCy library (Honnibal and Montani, 2017). The final synthesized COCO (SCOCO) dataset used for training includes 42051 sentences.

4.3 Transfer Learning

Transfer learning is a viable method for building NLP models in low-resource scenarios by leveraging data from other related sources. The two artificial data datasets, SFS and SCOCO, produced by applying machine translation to the FS dataset and the COCO captions, can provide a good basis for transfer learning (Section 4.2). We implement a Multilayer Perceptron model (MLP) by using Keras with tensorflow as the backend[2]. The MLP model has two hidden layers with five nodes in each layer and uses Relu as the activation function. The output layer has three nodes, corresponding to each score class with the softmax activation function. The categorical cross-entropy loss function is minimized, and stochastic gradient descent is used to learn the problem.

The two models are fit for 200 epochs on SFS and SCOCO datasets separately during training. We transfer the weights from the two standalone models to learn the initialize the weights for the formulated sentence evaluation tasks. The original FS data is split proportionally into a training and a test sets in terms of task, stimulus, and score distribution. The training set used for tuning the model includes 1160 sentences. The test set has

---

[2]https://github.com/keras-team/keras

1000 sentences, and the distribution of scores is presented in Table 3.

	Task 1	Task 2	Task 3	Total
2	235	303	262	800
1	25	14	61	100
0	70	15	15	100
Total	330	332	338	1000

Table 3: Score distribution in our formulated sentences test set.

		P	R	F1	Acc
BL1 Majority Class		0.80	0.80	0.80	0.80
BL2 Target Word		0.82	0.82	0.82	0.82
W2V	SFS	0.69	0.59	0.63	0.59
	SFS-FS	0.74	0.80	0.76	0.80
	SCOCO	0.67	0.70	0.68	0.70
	SCOCO-FS	0.72	0.73	0.72	0.73
ELMo	SFS	0.78	0.63	0.68	0.63
	SFS-FS	0.79	0.75	0.77	0.75
	SCOCO	0.77	0.72	0.74	0.72
	SCOCO-FS	0.80	0.79	0.79	0.79
BERT	SFS	0.80	0.78	0.77	0.78
	SFS-FS	0.76	0.85	0.81	0.85
	SCOCO	0.77	0.79	0.78	0.79
	SCOCO-FS	**0.82**	**0.85**	**0.83**	**0.85**

Table 4: Sentence evaluation precision, recall, F1 and accuracy on the full three-task test set.

5 Results

Table 4 presents the results of integrating contextual embeddings with and without transfer learning, evaluating all the three sentence formulation tasks together. The method of using transfer learning incorporating BERT contextual embeddings achieves the best performance in most of the cases, except for transferring from SFS with BERT (Figure 3(a)).

The experiments demonstrate a marginal increase in precision and substantial improvement in recall for the sentence formulation tasks. Although the three tasks all involve making sentences, each task tests different aspects of linguistic knowledge. Therefore it is more valuable to investigate the model performance on individual tasks, presented in Table 5.

On the test sets of Task 1 and Task 2, the best performing model is transferred SFS (Task 1: F1 = 0.81; Task 2: F1 = 0.92) with BERT. For Task 3, the best model is trained on the larger SCOCO dataset

(F1 = 0.82) with BERT embeddings. Task 2 and Task 3 have marginal improvement compared with the baseline. However, Task 1, which is the actual parallel to the CELF-4 Formulated Sentence task used to diagnose language impairments in children, shows a substantial improvement in performance. The improvement by incorporating BERT embedding achieves the best performance in all the three tasks individually.

These experiments demonstrate that transfer learning provides a beneficial addition for evaluating formulated sentence tasks. The language representations trained on a large general dataset allow the model to acquire a better representation of linguistic knowledge. Overall, we find that the model with transfer learning and BERT embeddings achieves the largest improvement across all three tasks.

6 Discussion

Transfer learning is generally used in situations in which the related task has more training data than the problem of interest, and the two tasks share similarities in structure. In this paper, we train an MLP model on two artificial datasets (SFS and SCOCO) and improve the performance of formulated sentence scoring task. The two datasets are similar in terms of lexicon variations, syntactic structures, and semantic expressions. They are generated by using the same machine translation models. The difference between these two sets is in the number of sentences contained. Since the number of correct sentences used for generated SCOCO is 14 times larger than that used to generated the SFS set, the final data of SCOCO is much larger than SFS.

Although the SCOCO dataset is larger, the best performance on both Task 1 and Task 2 is achieved by using transfer learning from in-domain SFS data. One of the similarities between the two tasks is the requirement of applying stimuli words in the generated sentences, whereas the test participants have a free choice of words in Task 3. This requirement influences the grading of the sentences. If the target word is not included in a sentence, no matter how grammatical the sentence is, it is marked with a label 0 in Task 1 and Task 2. For all the score-2 sentences in SFS, the target stimuli words are included; however this is not always the case in SCOCO. The lack of target word representation information in SCOCO may cause the transfer learning results to be inferior to the SFS model.

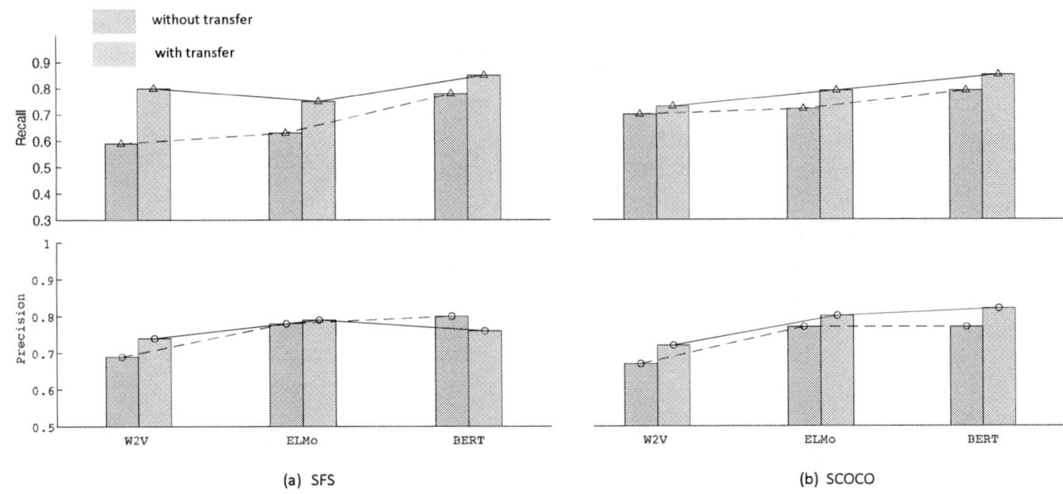

Figure 3: Precision and recall on full dataset using (a) SFS and (b) SCOCO with and without transfer learning.

		Task 1				Task 2				Task 3			
		P	R	F1	Acc	P	R	F1	Acc	P	R	F1	Acc
BL1 Majority Class		0.71	0.71	0.71	0.71	0.91	0.91	0.91	0.91	0.78	0.78	0.78	0.78
BL2 Target Word		0.77	0.77	0.77	0.77	0.92	0.92	0.92	0.92	0.78	0.78	0.78	0.78
W2V	SFS	0.66	0.63	0.64	0.63	0.84	0.43	0.56	0.43	0.69	0.71	0.70	0.71
	SFS-FS	0.71	0.75	0.71	0.75	0.84	0.86	0.85	0.86	0.75	0.78	0.73	0.78
	SCOCO	0.56	0.65	0.59	0.65	0.84	0.69	0.76	0.69	0.69	0.75	0.70	0.75
	SCOCO-FS	0.70	0.68	0.67	0.68	0.85	0.8	0.82	0.80	0.68	0.69	0.69	0.69
ELMo	SFS	0.75	0.68	0.71	0.68	0.89	0.54	0.65	0.54	0.78	0.67	0.71	0.67
	SFS-FS	0.77	0.76	0.76	0.76	0.88	0.71	0.78	0.71	0.81	0.79	0.79	0.79
	SCOCO	0.74	0.72	0.73	0.72	0.86	0.69	0.76	0.69	0.79	0.75	0.76	0.75
	SCOCO-FS	0.80	0.78	0.78	0.78	0.87	0.80	0.83	0.80	0.80	0.80	0.80	0.80
BERT	SFS	0.79	0.83	0.81	0.83	0.88	0.73	0.79	0.73	0.83	0.78	0.76	0.78
	SFS-FS	0.79	**0.85**	**0.81**	**0.85**	0.88	**0.92**	**0.90**	**0.92**	0.68	0.79	0.73	0.79
	SCOCO	0.78	0.77	0.76	0.77	0.86	0.80	0.83	0.80	0.76	0.79	0.76	0.79
	SCOCO-FS	**0.80**	0.82	0.80	0.82	**0.89**	0.91	0.90	0.91	**0.84**	**0.82**	**0.80**	**0.82**

Table 5: Sentence evaluation precision, recall, F1 and accuracy on individual tasks.

Embedding representations can capture underlying meanings and relationships. Different embeddings trained on distinct datasets may focus on particular aspects of linguistic and context information. We use two pre-trained contextual embedding and a customized embedding trained by using the COCO captions, which is much more similar to the data we intend to evaluate. The results show that BERT generally outperforms others in all tasks. Word2vec embeddings achieve results comparable to those of using BERT and outperform ELMo on Task 2. For the tasks involving sentence-level semantic meanings, however, its performance is inferior to the two contextualized representations.

The results we have presented here point the way to new approaches for automatically scoring tasks used in clinical diagnosis of language impairments, where labeled data for training models is typically scarce. In our future work, we will apply these models to data we are currently collecting from children with language disorders, autism spectrum disorder, ADHD, and typical development. Although there are differences between the populations studied (MTurk workers vs. children) and the modalities in which the responses were (written vs. spoken), our findings demonstrate the robustness of our methods even in the presence of domain or modality mismatch.

Acknowledgements

We thank Beth Calamé, Julie Bird, Kristin Hinton, Christine Yang, and Emily Fabius for their contributions to data collection and annotation. This work was supported in part by NIH NIDCD awards R01DC012033 and R21DC017000. Any opinions, findings, conclusions, or recommendations expressed in this publication are those of the authors and do not necessarily reflect the views of the NIH or NIDCD.

References

Jonathan S Barnhoorn, Erwin Haasnoot, Bruno R Bocanegra, and Henk van Steenbergen. 2015. Qrtengine: An easy solution for running online reaction time experiments using qualtrics. *Behavior research methods*, 47(4):918–929.

Samuel Bell, Helen Yannakoudakis, and Marek Rei. 2019. Context is key: Grammatical error detection with contextual word representations. *arXiv preprint arXiv:1906.06593*.

Chris Brockett, William B Dolan, and Michael Gamon. 2006. Correcting esl errors using phrasal smt techniques. In *Proceedings of the 21st International Conference on Computational Linguistics and the 44th annual meeting of the Association for Computational Linguistics*, pages 249–256. Association for Computational Linguistics.

Gina Conti-Ramsden, Zoë Simkin, and Nicola Botting. 2006. The prevalence of autistic spectrum disorders in adolescents with a history of specific language impairment (sli). *Journal of Child Psychology and Psychiatry*, 47(6):621–628.

Jacob Devlin, Ming-Wei Chang, Kenton Lee, and Kristina Toutanova. 2018. Bert: Pre-training of deep bidirectional transformers for language understanding. *arXiv preprint arXiv:1810.04805*.

Angela Grimm and Petra Schulz. 2014. Specific language impairment and early second language acquisition: the risk of over-and underdiagnosis. *Child Indicators Research*, 7(4):821–841.

Matthew Honnibal and Ines Montani. 2017. spaCy 2: Natural language understanding with Bloom embeddings, convolutional neural networks and incremental parsing. To appear.

Masahiro Kaneko and Mamoru Komachi. 2019. Multihead multi-layer attention to deep language representations for grammatical error detection. *arXiv preprint arXiv:1904.07334*.

Sudhanshu Kasewa, Pontus Stenetorp, and Sebastian Riedel. 2018. Wronging a right: Generating better errors to improve grammatical error detection.
In *Proceedings of the 2018 Conference on Empirical Methods in Natural Language Processing*, pages 4977–4983, Brussels, Belgium. Association for Computational Linguistics.

Guillaume Klein, Yoon Kim, Yuntian Deng, Jean Senellart, and Alexander Rush. 2017. OpenNMT: Opensource toolkit for neural machine translation. In *Proceedings of ACL 2017, System Demonstrations*, pages 67–72, Vancouver, Canada. Association for Computational Linguistics.

Tsung-Yi Lin, Michael Maire, Serge Belongie, James Hays, Pietro Perona, Deva Ramanan, Piotr Dollár, and C Lawrence Zitnick. 2014. Microsoft coco: Common objects in context. In *European conference on computer vision*, pages 740–755. Springer.

Tomas Mikolov, Kai Chen, Greg Corrado, and Jeffrey Dean. 2013. Efficient estimation of word representations in vector space. *arXiv preprint arXiv:1301.3781*.

Courtenay Frazier Norbury, Debbie Gooch, Charlotte Wray, Gillian Baird, Tony Charman, Emily Simonoff, George Vamvakas, and Andrew Pickles. 2016. The impact of nonverbal ability on prevalence and clinical presentation of language disorder: evidence from a population study. *Journal of Child Psychology and Psychiatry*, 57(11):1247–1257.

Matthew Peters, Waleed Ammar, Chandra Bhagavatula, and Russell Power. 2017. Semi-supervised sequence tagging with bidirectional language models. In *Proceedings of the 55th Annual Meeting of the Association for Computational Linguistics (Volume 1: Long Papers)*, pages 1756–1765, Vancouver, Canada. Association for Computational Linguistics.

Radim Rehurek and Petr Sojka. 2010. Software framework for topic modelling with large corpora. In *In Proceedings of the LREC 2010 Workshop on New Challenges for NLP Frameworks*. Citeseer.

Marek Rei. 2017. Semi-supervised multitask learning for sequence labeling. In *Proceedings of the 55th Annual Meeting of the Association for Computational Linguistics (Volume 1: Long Papers)*, pages 2121–2130, Vancouver, Canada. Association for Computational Linguistics.

Sara Rosenbaum and Patti Simon. 2016. *Speech and Language Disorders in Children: Implications for the Social Security Administration's Supplemental Security Income Program.* ERIC.

Alla Rozovskaya and Dan Roth. 2010. Generating confusion sets for context-sensitive error correction. In *Proceedings of the 2010 conference on empirical methods in natural language processing*, pages 961–970. Association for Computational Linguistics.

Victor Sanh, Lysandre Debut, Julien Chaumond, and Thomas Wolf. 2019. Distilbert, a distilled version of bert: smaller, faster, cheaper and lighter. *arXiv preprint arXiv:1910.01108*.

Eleanor Semel, Elizabeth Wiig, and Wayne Secord. 2003. *Clinical Evaluation of Language Fundamentals–Fouth Edition (CELF-4)*. NCS Pearson, Bloomington, MN.

Helen Yannakoudakis, Ted Briscoe, and Ben Medlock. 2011. A new dataset and method for automatically grading ESOL texts. In *Proceedings of the 49th Annual Meeting of the Association for Computational Linguistics: Human Language Technologies*, pages 180–189, Portland, Oregon, USA. Association for Computational Linguistics.

Context-based Automated Scoring of Complex Mathematical Responses

Aoife Cahill, James H. Fife, Brian Riordan, Avijit Vajpayee, and Dmytro Galochkin

acahill@ets.org, ejreed215@verizon.net,
{briordan, avajpayee, dgalochkin} @ets.org
ETS, Princeton, NJ 08541, USA

Abstract

The tasks of automatically scoring either textual or algebraic responses to mathematical questions have both been well-studied, albeit separately. In this paper we propose a method for automatically scoring responses that contain both text and algebraic expressions. Our method not only achieves high agreement with human raters, but also links explicitly to the scoring rubric – essentially providing explainable models and a way to potentially provide feedback to students in the future.

1 Introduction

In this paper we present work on automatically scoring student responses to constructed-response mathematics items where the response should contain both text and mathematical equations or expressions. Existing work on automated scoring of mathematics items has largely focused on items where either only text is required (c.f. related work on automated short-answer-scoring (Galhardi and Brancher, 2018; Burrows et al., 2015)) or only an expression or equation is required (Drijvers, 2018; Fife, 2017; Sangwin, 2004). This is the first work, to our knowledge, that attempts to automatically score responses that contain both.

Items that elicit such responses could be algebra, trigonometry, or calculus items that ask the student to solve a problem and/or provide an argument. Items at levels much below algebra most likely would not require the student to include an equation – at least one that requires an equation editor for proper entry – in the text, and items at a higher level might require the student to include abstract mathematical expressions that would themselves present automated scoring difficulties. These kinds of items are quite common on paper-and-pencil algebra exams. However, they are less common on computer-delivered exams, primarily because the technology of calling up an equation editor to insert equations in text is new and not generally used.

The challenge with automatically scoring these kinds of responses, in a construct-valid way, is that the system needs to be able to interpret the correctness of the equations and expressions *in the context of* the surrounding text.

Our goal is not just to achieve accurate scoring but to also have explainable models. Explainable models have a number of advantages including (i) giving users evidence that the models are fair and unbiased; (ii) the ability to leverage the models for feedback; and (iii) compliance with new laws, e.g. the General Data Protection Regulation (EU) 2016/679 (GDPR) which requires transparency and accountability of any form of automated processing of personal data. In this paper we present an approach that not only achieves high agreement with human raters, but also links explicitly to the scoring rubric – essentially providing explainable models and a way to potentially provide feedback to students in the future.

2 Data

In this paper we use data from 3 pilot-study items that elicited responses containing both textual explanations as well as equations and expressions. An example item is given in Figure 1, and a sample response (awarded 2 points on a 0-3 point scale) is given in Figure 2.[1] The pilot was administered as part of a larger project in four high schools located in various regions of the United States. The items assumed one year of algebra and involved writing solutions to algebra problems, similar to what a student would be expected to write on a paper-based classroom test. Responses were collected digitally;

---

[1]This item corresponds to Item 2 in our dataset. The scoring rubric is given in Appendix A.1.

Proceedings of the 15th Workshop on Innovative Use of NLP for Building Educational Applications, pages 186–192
July 10, 2020. ©2020 Association for Computational Linguistics

Explain, using words and equations, how
you would use the quadratic formula to
find two values of x for which

$$195 = -2x^2 + 40x.$$

You may also use the on-screen
calculator.

Figure 1: Sample item that elicits textual explanations as well as equations and mathematics.

$$x = \frac{-40 + \sqrt{40^2 - 4(-2)(-195)}}{2(-2)}$$

To solve this you must first put your
equation in standard form, which gives
you y=-2x+40x-195. You then plug your
a, b, and c values into the quadratic
formula. To start finding your x
value, you must first multiply all your
values in parentheses. You must then
simplify the square root you get from
multiplying. With your new equation,
you make two more equations, one adding
your simplified square root and one
subtracting it. The two answers you get
from those equations are your two values
of x.

Figure 2: Sample response to the item in Figure 1 (2-point response). The student has put the equation into standard form with a slight error. $-2x^2$ has become $-2x$; the student was not using the equation editor and could not type the exponent. The student does not explicitly give the values of a, b, and c, but correctly substitutes these values into the formula, so we may assume that the student has determined these values correctly. We may also assume that the student has corrected the missing exponent in the standard form. The student talks about "two answers" but only gives one root, however, so this response is worth 2 points.

students used an interface that included an optional equation editor. The responses were captured as text, with the equations captured as MathML enclosed in <math> tags. Two of the items involved quadratic functions, requiring the student to use the equation editor to properly format equations in their responses. Nonetheless, many students did not use the equation editor consistently. In fact only 60% of all students used the equation editor. Of all equations entered by the students, only 34% were entered via the equation editor since most of the students preferred to write simple equations as regular text.[2]

There were over 1,000 responses collected for each item, however some responses were blank

---

[2]This presents obvious challenges for automatically scoring the mathematical components of the responses, since the first step is to even identify them (see Section 3.2 for how we address this).

Item	Total	% 0	% 1	% 2	% 3
1	924	49.35	19.37	6.93	24.35
2	889	70.97	12.49	11.59	4.95
3	859	77.65	3.49	3.26	15.6

Table 1: Descriptive Statistics for the 3 items, including the total number of responses per item, as well as the percentage of responses at each score point.

and therefore not included in this study. Table 1 gives some descriptive statistics for the final data used in this study. Items 2 and 3 were somewhat difficult for this pilot student population, with 71% and 78% of students receiving a score of 0 for those items. All responses were scored by two trained raters; the quadratic-weighted kappa values for the human-human agreement on the three items ranged from 0.91 to 0.95, indicating that humans were able to agree very well on the assignment of scores.

3 Methods

3.1 Automatically scoring equations and expressions

We use m-rater, an automated scoring engine developed by Educational Testing Service (Fife, 2013, 2017) to automatically score the equations and mathematical expressions in our data. M-rater uses SymPy[3], an open-source computer algebra system, to determine if the student's response is mathematically equivalent to the intended response. M-rater can process standard mathematical format, with exponents, radical signs, fractions, and so forth. M-rater is a deterministic system, and as such has 100% accuracy, given well-formed input.

If, as in this study, the responses consist of a mixture of text and equations or mathematical expressions, m-rater can evaluate the correctness (or partial correctness) of the equations and expressions, but it cannot evaluate text.

3.2 Automatically identifying equations and expressions in text

While the students had access to an equation editor as part of the delivery platform, many did not use it consistently. This means that we cannot rely on the MathML encoding to identify all of the equations and mathematical expressions in the text. For example, a student may have wanted to enter the equation: $2x^2 - 40x + 195 = 0$. They may use the equation editor to enter the entire equation, or

---

[3]https://www.sympy.org/en/index.html

some of it (e.g. the piece after the = sign, or after the exponent expression), or none of it. This leads to construct-irrelevant variations in representations.

Therefore, we develop a regular-expression based system for automatically identifying equations and expressions in responses where all data from the equation editor has been rendered as plain text. Our processing includes the following assumptions which are appropriate for our dataset:

- Variables can only consist of single letters;

- We only detect simple functions (square root, absolute and very basic trigonometric functions);

- Equations containing line breaks are treated as two different equations.

We processed all responses to the three pilot items with this script and all identified equations and expressions were manually checked by a content expert. In almost all cases, the system correctly identified the equations or expressions. There were 9 incorrectly identified equations in total (out of 2,672). Mis-identifications were usually due to incorrect spacing in the equation – either too much space between characters in the equation or no space between the equation and subsequent text. A few students used the letter x to denote multiplication, which was read by the system as the variable x.

It is possible to convert the m-rater evaluations of the individual equations and expressions contained in a response into features. This is done by automatically extracting the equations and expressions and using m-rater to match each one to an element in the scoring rubric (also called concepts). These features encode a binary indicator of whether a particular concept is present or not in a response. Note that some concepts represent known or expected misconceptions in student responses. For example, the set of six binary features instantiated for each response to Item 2 are as follows: (i) has the equation been correctly transformed into standard form (rubric element 1); (ii) did the student answer a=2 (rubric element 2); (iii) did the student answer b=40 (rubric element 2); (iv) did the student answer c=195 (rubric element 2); (v) did the student find solution 1 (rubric element 3); (vi) did the student find solution 2 (rubric element 3).

3.3 Automatically scoring short texts for correctness

We use 4 approaches for automatically scoring short texts with mathematical expressions. The baseline system (LinReg_m) is an ordinary Linear Regression on the math features automatically extracted from m-rater evaluations and does not include any textual context. System 2 (SVR_{csw}) is a feature-based Support Vector Regressor (SVR) that encodes (1) key words and phrases (in the form of word ngrams); (2) character-ngrams as well as (3) key syntactic relationships in the text as binary features. Note that system 2 does not take any explicit math features into account, and the mathematical expressions are assumed to be captured through character level features. System 3 (SVR_{msw}) is a feature-based SVR taking into account both textual context (through word-ngrams and syntactic dependencies) as well as explicit math features, but no character-level ngrams. Our final system is a recurrent neural network (RNN) system. The RNN model uses pre-trained word embeddings encoded by a bidirectional gated recurrent unit (GRU). The hidden states of the GRU are aggregated by a max pooling mechanism (Shen et al., 2018). The output of the encoder is aggregated in a fully-connected feedforward layer with sigmoid activation to predict the score of the response. This architecture has achieved state-of-the-art performance on the ASAP-SAS benchmark dataset (Riordan et al., 2019). Additional information about steps to replicate the system can be found in the Appendix.

4 Experiments

We conduct a set of experiments to answer the following research questions:

1. How important is textual context for responses involving mathematical expressions with respect to automated scoring? (Comparing **Exp 0** and **Exp 1**)

2. Do character level features capture mathematical expressions? (**Exp 0**)

3. Can explainability be included in scoring models without severely compromising accuracy? (Comparing **Exp 0** to **Exp 1–3**)

For our baseline experiment (**Exp 0**), student responses are taken with all equations and expressions converted to plain text. For this experiment,

System	Item 1	Item 2	Item 3
$LinReg_m$	0.506	0.457	0.587
SVR_{csw}	0.870	0.789	0.933
SVR_{msw}	**0.897**	0.797	**0.935**
Word RNN	0.887	**0.835**	0.923

Table 2: Quadratically-weighted kappa results for **Exp 0** (plain text, no expression replacement)

System	Exp 1			Exp 2			Exp 3		
	Item 1	Item 2	Item 3	Item 1	Item 2	Item 3	Item 1	Item 2	Item 3
SVR_{msw}	0.888	0.783	0.897	0.891	0.776	0.889	0.894	0.781	0.894
SVR_{csw}	0.788	0.593	0.664	0.827	0.689	0.867	0.882	0.776	0.891
Word RNN	0.767	0.649	0.725	0.842	0.75	0.887	0.901	0.829	0.888

Table 3: Quadratically-weighted kappa results for explainability experiments

we use all 4 systems as described in Section 3.3. Subsequently, we perform 3 experiments where all expressions and equations (as identified by m-rater) are converted to pre-defined tokens with increasing degree of explainability:

Exp 1 All equations and expressions automatically identified and converted to a single token (@expression@)

Exp 2 All equations and expressions automatically identified and converted to one of @correct@ or @incorrect@. The correctness of an equation is determined automatically by matching against the scoring rubric using m-rater (see Section 3.1).

Exp 3 All equations and expressions automatically identified and converted to one of @correct_N@ or @incorrect@, where N indicates the set of concept numbers from the scoring rubric and is automatically identified using m-rater.

For each pair of system and response variant, we conduct a 10-fold nested cross validation experiment. We split our data into 80% train, 10% dev and 10% test. For each fold, we train on the train+dev portions and make predictions on the held-out test portion, having tuned the hyperparameters on the dev set. There are no overlapping test folds. For evaluation, we pool predictions on test sets from all folds and compute agreement statistics between the rater 1 score and the machine predictions.

5 Results

Table 2 gives the results of all models used for the baseline experiment where all responses are converted to plain text. Even without pre-processing the mathematical expressions, textual context is very important, as we see by the poor performance of the Linear Regression model on purely mathematical features ($LinReg_m$). It can also be seen that character level features, while partially capturing mathematical expressions, do not perform as well as the SVR model with explicit math features (comparing SVR_{csw} to SVR_{msw}). The difference, however, is not statistically significant for any item (details given in Appendix A.3). Another interesting result is that the RNN model without character level OR explicit math information performs well, being a close second to the SVR_{msw} model and the differences between them are not statistically significant.

Table 3 gives the results for the explainability experiments i.e. **Exp 1 to 3** where mathematical expressions and equations were pre-identified and replaced in the response text. Comparing these with the results for the experiment on the original text responses (Table 2), it can be seen that the replacement that includes the mappings to rubric concepts (**Exp 3**) not only increases explainability but is also competitive in performance to models with explicit math features but no expression replacement (outperforming them on Item 1). Models SVR_{csw} and WordRNN are not significantly different on any item for any of the 3 explainability experiments (**Exp 1 to 3**).

Coming back to our original research questions:

1. *How important is textual context for responses*

involving mathematical expressions with respect to automated scoring?

Context is important for automatically scoring responses that integrate text and algebraic information. Evaluating the mathematical expressions alone does not perform well (**Exp 0**). Additionally, **Exp 1** has no context for the mathematical expressions, and we see lower results for the system that still includes mathematical information as independent features, but out of context (SVR_{msw}), compared to systems that encode the mathematical information in some way *in context*.

2. *Do character level features capture mathematical expressions?*

Character level features certainly do capture a large portion of mathematical expressions. We see that in the **Exp 0** results, where there is no interpretation of the mathematical expressions, that systems perform almost as well as the systems that do explicit interpretation.

3. *Can explainability be included in scoring models without severely compromising accuracy?*

Yes, we can include model interpretability without compromising scoring accuracy. The differences between the best models from **Exp 0** and **Exp3** ranged from -0.004 to +0.041). By explicitly linking aspects of the rubric to each response, we yield interpretable models that perform comparably to systems without this interpretative layer. Although the overall results are lower, they are not statistically significantly lower.

6 Conclusion

To summarize, this work presented a hybrid scoring model using a deterministic system for evaluating the correctness (or partial correctness) of mathematical equations, in combination with text-based automated scoring systems for evaluating the appropriateness of the textual explanation of a response.

We contribute the following:

1. Systems that produce extremely high agreement between an automated system and human raters for the task of automatically scoring items that elicit both textual and algebraic components

2. A method for linking rubric information to the automated scoring system, resulting in an more interpretable model than one based purely on the raw response

Acknowledgments

We would like to thank the anonymous reviewers for their valuable comments and suggestions. We would also like to thank Michael Flor, Swapna Somasundaran and Beata Beigman-Klebanov for their helpful comments.

References

Ashutosh Adhikari, Achyudh Ram, Raphael Tang, and Jimmy Lin. 2019. Rethinking Complex Neural Network Architectures for Document Classification. In *Proceedings of the 2019 Conference of the North American Chapter of the Association for Computational Linguistics: Human Language Technologies, Volume 1 (Long and Short Papers)*, pages 4046–4051, Minneapolis, Minnesota. Association for Computational Linguistics.

Steven Burrows, Iryna Gurevych, and Benno Stein. 2015. The eras and trends of automatic short answer grading. *International Journal of Artificial Intelligence in Education*, 25(1):60–117.

Janez Demšar. 2006. Statistical comparisons of classifiers over multiple data sets. *Journal of Machine learning research*, 7(Jan):1–30.

Paul Drijvers. 2018. Digital assessment of mathematics: Opportunities, issues and criteria. *Mesure et évaluation en éducation*, 41(1):41–66.

James H Fife. 2013. Automated scoring of mathematics tasks in the Common Core era: Enhancements to m-rater in support of CBAL^{TM}, mathematics and the Common Core assessments . *ETS Research Report Series*, 2013(2):i–35.

James H Fife. 2017. The m-rater Engine: Introduction to the Automated Scoring of Mathematics Items. *Research Memorandum, ETS RM-17-02*, pages 10–24.

Lucas Busatta Galhardi and Jacques Duílio Brancher. 2018. Machine learning approach for automatic short answer grading: A systematic review. In *Ibero-American Conference on Artificial Intelligence*, pages 380–391. Springer.

Peter Nemenyi. 1963. Distribution-free multiple comparisons,(mimeographed).

Brian Riordan, Michael Flor, and Robert Pugh. 2019. How to account for mispellings: Quantifying the benefit of character representations in neural content scoring models. In *Proceedings of the 14th Workshop on Innovative Use of NLP for Building Educational Applications (BEA)*.

Chris Sangwin. 2004. Assessing mathematics automatically using computer algebra and the internet. *Teaching Mathematics and Its Applications: An International Journal of the IMA*, 23(1):1–14.

Dinghan Shen, Guoyin Wang, Wenlin Wang, Martin Renqiang Min, Qinliang Su, Yizhe Zhang, Chunyuan Li, Ricardo Henao, and Lawrence Carin. 2018. Baseline needs more love: On simple word-embedding-based models and associated pooling mechanisms. In *Proceedings of the 56th Annual Meeting of the Association for Computational Linguistics (Volume 1: Long Papers)*, pages 440–450, Melbourne, Australia. Association for Computational Linguistics.

Sudhir Varma and Richard Simon. 2006. Bias in error estimation when using cross-validation for model selection. *BMC bioinformatics*, 7(1):91.

A   Appendices

A.1   Scoring Rubric for Item 2

- 1 pt. for writing the equation as $2x^2 - 40x + 195 = 0$ or $-2x^2 + 40x - 195 = 0$. It's acceptable to just write the expression $2x^2 - 40x + 195 = 0$ or $-2x^2 + 40x - 195 = 0$. It's also acceptable to say something like "Move 195 to the other side of the equation" if they find the correct values for a, b, and c (with correct signs).

- 1 pt. for determining the values of a, b, and c. $a = 2$, $b = 40$, $c = 195$ OR $a = 2$, $b = 40$, $c = 195$ 0 pts. if they mix the values up (e.g., $a = 2$, $b = 40$, $c = 195$). 1 pt. if they implicitly complete this step by correctly substituting the correct values for a, b, and c into the quadratic formula in the next step.

- 1 pt. for substituting the values of a, b, and c into the quadratic formula and obtaining two solutions. Students do not need to simplify the answers. Students can write any equivalent expressions for the two values of x, including $x = \frac{40+\sqrt{40^2-4*2*195}}{2*2}$ and $x = \frac{40-\sqrt{40^2-4*2*195}}{2*2}$ OR $x = \frac{-40+\sqrt{40^2-4*-2*-195}}{2*-2}$ and $x = \frac{-40-\sqrt{40^2-4*-2*-195}}{2*-2}$. It's also acceptable for students to write $x = \frac{40\pm\sqrt{40^2-4*2*195}}{2*2}$ to mean both solutions. Or students may write that the two values of x are x = 11.5811... and x = 8.4188..., correct to at least one decimal place, provided they arrive at these numbers through the quadratic formula and not by solving the equation numerically.

- Max 2/3 for finding one correct solution.

- Max 2/3 for writing the two correct solutions with no explanation of where the values of a, b, and c come from.

- 1/3 if the student provides an outline of the solution without actually carrying out any of the steps.

A.2   Additional information for training the RNN model

The text is preprocessed with the spaCy tokenizer with some minor postprocessing to correct tokenization mistakes on noisy data. On conversion to tensors, responses are padded to the same length in a batch; these padding tokens are masked out during model training. Prior to training, responses are scaled to [0, 1] to form the input to the networks. The scaled scores are converted back to their original range for evaluation. Word tokens are embedded with GloVe 100 dimension vectors and fine-tuned during training. Word tokens not in the embeddings vocabulary are each assigned a unique randomly initialized vector. The GRUs were 1 layer with a hidden state of size 250. The network was trained with mean squared error loss. We optimized the network with RMSProp with hyperparameters set as follows: learning rate of 0.001, batch size of 32, and gradient clipping set to 10.0. An exponential moving average of the model's weights is used during training (Adhikari et al., 2019).

A.3   Additional details on significance testing of results

Although nested cross-validation gives a fairly unbiased estimate of true error as shown by Varma and Simon (2006), we performed statistical significance testing to pair-wise compare 4 models for **Exp 0: no expression replacement** and 2 models for **Exp 3: expressions replaced with incorrect/correct along with concept numbers**.

Friedman's test as suggested by Demšar (2006) is run to compare 6 models (corresponding to treatments) across multiple repeated measures (10 folds) for each item individually. Note that such a setup of comparing multiple models across 10 folds on a dataset has to be regarded as non-independent data as even though the test folds will be distinct, the training data for each fold may partially overlap. Hence Friedman's test is appropriate here to

	0_SVR_{csw}	0_SVR_{msw}	$0\_WordRNN$	3_SVR_{csw}	$3\_WordRNN$
0_LinReg_{m}	1 / 3	2 / 3	3 / 3	1 / 3	2 / 3
0_SVR_{csw}	-	0	0	0	0
0_SVR_{msw}		-	0	0	0
$0\_WordRNN$			-	1 / 3	0
3_SVR_{csw}				-	0

Table 4: Pair-wise Comparisons of Models with fraction of datasets with significant difference between models

test whether any pair of models are statistically different.

Following Friedman's test, we do pair-wise post-hoc testing through Nemenyi's test (Nemenyi, 1963). Note that this testing is per-item and we report the fraction of times the differences were significant in table 4.

Predicting the Difficulty and Response Time of Multiple Choice Questions Using Transfer Learning

Kang Xue[1]   Victoria Yaneva[2]   Christopher Runyon[2]   Peter Baldwin[2]

[1]Department of Educational Psychology, University of Georgia, Athens, USA
`KangXue@uga.edu`
[2]National Board of Medical Examiners, Philadelphia, USA
`{vyaneva, crunyon, pbaldwin}@nbme.org`

Abstract

This paper reports on whether transfer learning can improve the prediction of the difficulty and response time parameters for $\approx$ 18,000 multiple-choice questions from a high-stakes medical exam. The type of the signal that best predicts difficulty and response time is also explored, both in terms of representation abstraction and item component used as input (e.g., whole item, answer options only, etc.). The results indicate that, for our sample, transfer learning can improve the prediction of item difficulty when response time is used as an auxiliary task but not the other way around. In addition, difficulty was best predicted using signal from the item stem (the description of the clinical case), while all parts of the item were important for predicting the response time.

1   Introduction

The questions on standardized exams need to meet certain criteria for the exam to be considered fair and valid. For example, it is often desirable to collect measurement information across a range of examinee proficiencies but this requires that question difficulties span a similar range. Another consideration is the time required to answer each question: allocating too little time makes the exam speeded whereas allocating too much time makes it inefficient. Typically, difficulty and response time measures are needed before new questions can be used for scoring. Currently, these measures are obtained by presenting new questions alongside scored items on real exams; however, this process is time consuming and costly. To address this challenge, there is an emerging interest in predicting item parameters based on item text (Section 2). The goal of this application is to filter out items that should not be embedded in live exams—even as unscored items—because of their low probability of having the desired characteristics.

In practice, there may be situations where data are available for one item parameter but not for

another. For example, when a pen-and-paper test is being migrated to a computer-based test, response time measures to individual questions will not be among the historical pen-and-paper data whereas item difficulty measures will be. In this scenario, the only available response-time data would be those collected from the small sample of examinees who first piloted the computer-based test. Yet, since item characteristics like response time and difficulty are often related (e.g., more difficult items may require longer to solve), it is conceivable that information stored while learning to predict one parameter then could be used to improve the prediction of another. In this paper, we explore whether approaches from the field of transfer learning may be useful for improving item parameter modeling.

We hypothesize that transfer learning (TL) can improve the prediction of difficulty and response time parameters for a set of $\approx$18,000 multiple-choice questions (MCQs) from the United States Medical Licensing Examination (USMLE®). We present two sets of experiments, where learning to predict one parameter is used as an auxiliary task for the prediction of the other and vice versa. In addition to our interest in parameter modeling, we investigate the type of signal that best predicts difficulty and response time, which is done both in terms of exploring potential differences in the level of representation abstraction required to predict the two variables and in terms of the part of the item that contains information most relevant to each parameter. This is accomplished by extracting two levels of item representations, *embeddings* and *encodings*, from various parts of the MCQ (answer options only, question only, whole item). Predictions are compared to i) the predictions for each parameter *without* the use of an auxiliary task, and ii) a ZeroR baseline. The results from the transfer learning experiments show the usefulness and limitations of this approach for modeling item parameters with a view to practical scenarios where

Proceedings of the 15ᵗʰ Workshop on Innovative Use of NLP for Building Educational Applications, pages 193–197
July 10, 2020. ©2020 Association for Computational Linguistics

we have more data for one parameter. The results for the source of the signal suggest item writing strategies that may be adopted to manipulate specific item parameters.

2   Related Work

The majority of work related to predicting question difficulty has been done in the field of language learning (Huang et al., 2017; Beinborn et al., 2015; Loukina et al., 2016). Some exceptions include estimating difficulty for automatically generated questions by measuring the semantic similarity between the a given question and its associated answer options (Alsubait et al., 2013; Ha and Yaneva, 2018; Kurdi et al., 2016) and measuring the difficulty and discrimination parameters of questions used in e-learning exams (Benedetto et al., 2020). With regards to medical MCQs, previous work has shown modest but statistically significant improvements in predicting difficulty using a combination of linguistic features and embeddings (Ha et al., 2019) as well as predicting the probability that an item meets the difficulty and discriminatory power criteria for use in live exams (Yaneva et al., 2020).

The literature on response time prediction is rather limited and comes mainly from the field of educational testing. The range of predictors that have been explored includes item presentation position (Parshall et al., 1994), item content category (Parshall et al., 1994; Smith, 2000), the presence of a figure (Smith, 2000; Swanson et al., 2001), and item difficulty and discrimination (Halkitis et al., 1996; Smith, 2000). The only text-related feature used in these studies was word count. A more recent study by Baldwin et al. (2020) modeled the response time of medical MCQs using a broad range of linguistic features and embeddings (similar to Yaneva et al. (2019)) and showed that the predicted response times can be used to improve fairness by reducing the time intensity variance of exam forms.

To the best of our knowledge, the use of transfer learning for predicting MCQ parameters has not yet been investigated. The next sections present an initial exploration of this approach for a sample of medical MCQs.

3   Data

The data consists of $\approx$ 18,000 MCQs from a high-stakes medical licensing exam. An example of an MCQ is presented in Table 1. Let *stem* denote the part of the question that contains the description of

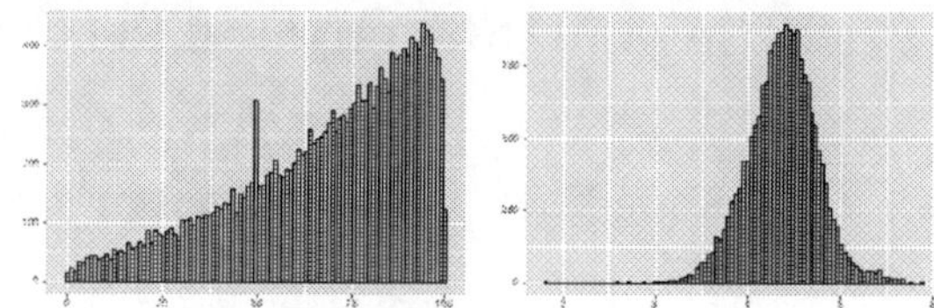

Figure 1: Distribution of the P-value (left) and log Response Time (right) variables

the clinical case and let *options* denote the possible answer choices. All items tested medical knowledge and were written by experienced item-writers following a set of guidelines stipulating adherence to a standard structure. All items were administered as (unscored) pretest items for six standard annual cycles between 2010 and 2015 and test-takers had no way of knowing which items were used for scoring and which were being pretested. All examinees were from accredited[1] medical schools in the USA and Canada and were taking the exam for the first time.

Here, the difficulty of an item is defined by the proportion of its responses that are correct. In the educational testing community this metric is commonly referred to as *P-value*. For example, a P-value of .67 means that the item was answered correctly by 67% of the examinees who saw that item. (Since greater P-values are associated with greater proportions of examinees responding correctly, P-value might be better described as a measure of item easiness than item difficulty.) Response Time is measured in seconds and represents the average amount of time it took all examinees who saw the item to answer it. The distribution of P-values and log Response Times for the data set is presented in Figure 1. The correlation between the two parameters for the set of items is .37.

4   Method

Three types of item text configurations were used as input: i) item stem, ii) item options, and iii) a combination of the stem and options (this combination was used both as a single vector and as two separate vectors). After preprocessing the raw text (tokenization, lemmatization and stopword removal), it was used to train an ELMo (Peters et al., 2018) model[2]. The model was trained with two

---

[1] Accredited by the Liaison Committee on Medical Education (LCME).

[2] Data pre-processing and feature extraction were implemented using the `PyTorch` and `Allennlp` libraries and the

A 55-year-old woman with small cell carcinoma of the lung is admitted to the hospital to undergo chemotherapy. Six days after treatment is started, she develops a temperature of 38C (100.4F). Physical examination shows no other abnormalities. Laboratory studies show a leukocyte count of 100/mm3 (5% segmented neutrophils and 95% lymphocytes). Which of the following is the most appropriate pharmacotherapy to increase this patient's leukocyte count?

(A) Darbepoetin   (B) Dexamethasone
(C) Filgrastim   (D) Interferon alfa
(E) Interleukin-2 (IL-2)   (F) Leucovorin

Table 1: An example of a practice item

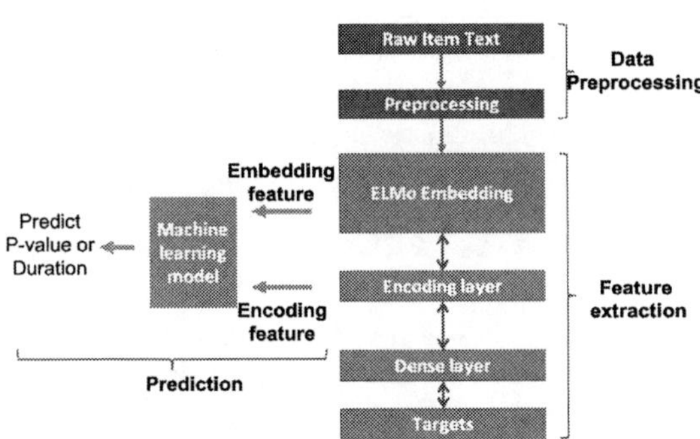

Figure 2: Diagram of the proposed methods.

ELMo types	Number of Parameter	Output dimension	Parameters updating
Small	13.6 million	128	Tuning
Middle	20.8 million	256	Tuning
Original	93.6 million	1024	Freezing

Table 2: ELMo architectures. Parameter tuning was performed for the Small and Middle models. When training the Original ELMo structure, the parameters were frozen (or not updated) because of the memory limitations (6GB) of our NVIDIA Tesla M60 GPU platform.

separate objectives: one was to predict P-value and the other one was to predict Response Time. To learn the sequential information from the ELMo embedding output, an encoding layer was added after the ELMo embedding layers (Figure 2). The encoding layer was constructed using a Bidirectional LSTM network (Graves et al., 2005). This layer allowed the extraction of encoding features, which captured more abstract information than the embeddings alone (the two are later compared). The encoding layer was followed by a dense layer in order to convert the feature vectors to the targets through a non-linear combination of the elements in the feature vectors.

As shown in Table 2, we used three different ELMo configurations (small, middle, and original), each with a different number of parameters. Since the number of parameters of these three ELMo structures was relatively large compared to the size of our item pool, we used the parameters pretrained on the 1 Billion Word Benchmark (Chelba et al., 2013) as the initialization.

Two modeling approaches were applied. The first approach (Method 1) used the pre-trained ELMo parameters as the initialization and trained on the MCQ data with the aim of predicting the item parameter of interest (either P-value or Response Time). In this scenario, the target variable used in the training procedure was the same as the target variable in the prediction part. The second approach (Method 2) also used the pre-trained ELMo parameters as the initialization but these were updated when training on the auxiliary task. In other words, if the target variable in the prediction part was P-value, then the target variable in the training part was Response Time and vice-versa. Since we are also interested in understanding the effects of different levels of abstraction on parameter prediction (as captured by the embeddings and encodings), we used linear regression (LR) to predict the item characteristics using the extracted features as input. The training set, the validation set and the testing set consisted of 12,000 samples, 3,000 samples, and 3,000 samples, respectively.

5 Results and Discussion

The results for the experiments are presented in Table 3. As can be seen, the models achieved a slight but significant RMSE decrease compared to the ZeroR baseline. In addition, Method 2 significantly improved the prediction of the Response Time variable (when predicting P-value is used as an auxiliary task) but this was not the case the other way around (predicting P-value with Response Time as an auxiliary task). A possible explanation for this result is the fact that the models were much better at predicting the Response Time component

prediction part was implemented using the `scikit-learn` library. The NVIDIA Tesla M60 GPU was used to accelerate the model training.

| | | P-value (M1) | | Resp. Time (M1) | | P-value (M2) | | Resp. Time (M2) | |
ELMo	Item component	Embed	Encod	Embed	Encod	Embed	Encod	Embed	Encod
Original	Stem	23.60	23.32	0.31	0.33	23.62	23.33	0.31	0.33
Original	Answer options	23.61	23.35	0.35	0.35	23.63	23.29	0.35	0.35
Original	Full Item	23.55	23.43	0.31	0.33	23.60	23.34	0.31	0.34
Original	Stem + Options	23.71	23.40	0.32	0.32	24.24	23.27	0.32	0.33
Average		23.61	23.38	0.32	0.33	23.77	23.31	0.32	0.34
Small	Stem	23.74	23.67	0.31	0.30	23.16*	23.20*	0.33	0.33
Small	Answer options	23.48	23.68	0.35	0.34	23.23*	23.31*	0.36	0.36
Small	Full Item	27.64	NA	0.31	0.30	23.20	23.23	0.38	0.70
Small	Stem + Options	23.71	23.71	0.30	0.29	23.04*	23.21*	0.34	0.33
Average		24.64	23.69	0.32	0.31	23.16	23.24	0.35	0.43
Middle	Stem	23.54	23.73	0.31	0.30	23.32	23.16*	0.32	0.36
Middle	Answer options	24.90	23.74	0.35	0.35	23.67	23.38*	0.37	0.37
Middle	Full Item	23.45	23.65	0.30	0.30	23.39	23.22*	0.32	0.33
Middle	Stem + Options	24.76	23.95	0.31	0.30	23.82	23.24*	0.33	0.37
Average		24.16	23.77	0.32	0.31	23.55	23.25	0.34	0.36
Total aver.		24.17	23.60	0.32	0.32	23.49	23.26	0.34	0.38
Baseline									
ZeroR		23.97		0.35					

Table 3: Results for P-value and Response Time using Method 1 (columns 3-4) and Method 2 (columns 5-6). The values represent the Root Mean Squared Error (RMSE) for each model obtained using linear regression. Values marked with * represent cases, where the use of Method 2 has resulted in a statistically significant improvement compared to Method 1 (95% Confidence Intervals). The best result in each column is marked in red.

compared to the ZeroR baseline and this knowledge successfully transferred into improving the P-value prediction. The gains in predicting the P-value on the other hand were much more modest, which may explain why they did not contribute to the prediction of Response Time. Another possible explanation could be that P-values were highly skewed whereas Response Times were normally distributed. It could be that the normalized distribution of the Response Time variable facilitates learning of better representations compared to the skewed distribution of the P-value variable. A direction for future work is to test this by normalizing both distributions.

Not all parts of the item were equally important for predicting the two parameters. Signal from the stem alone provided the best results for the P-value variable in Method 1 (23.32) and when P-value was used as an auxiliary task for predicting Response Time (0.31) in Method 2 (i.e., adding information from the answer options did not improve the result). By contrast, signal from the full item outperformed other configurations when the Response Time was predicted using Method 1 (0.29) and when Response Time was used as an auxiliary task for predicting the P-value (23.04). Therefore, the stem contained signal that was most relevant to the P-value variable, while the Response Time was best predicted using information from the entire item. This suggests that deliberating between the different answer options and reading the stem all have effects on the Response Time. However, the difficulty of the clinical case presented in the stem seems to have a stronger relation to the P-value than the difficulty attributed to choosing between the answer options. Using the stem and options content as two predictors (Stem + Options) had no significant effects but, on average, provided slightly more accurate results than the single predictor (Full Item). Finally, no clear pattern emerged with regards to the predictive utility of using embeddings vs. encodings or the embedding dimensions and weight tuning produced by training the three ELMo models (Small, Middle and Original).

These results represent a first step towards the exploration of transfer learning for item parameter prediction and may have implications for both parameter modeling and item writing.

6 Conclusion

This study investigated the use of transfer learning for predicting difficulty and Response Times for clinical MCQs. Both parameters were predicted with a small but statistically significant improvement over ZeroR. This prediction was further improved for P-value by using transfer learning. It was also shown that the item stem contained signal that was most relevant to the P-value variable, while the Response Time was best predicted using information from the entire item.

References

Tahani Alsubait, Bijan Parsia, and Ulrike Sattler. 2013. A similarity-based theory of controlling mcq difficulty. In *e-Learning and e-Technologies in Education (ICEEE), 2013 Second International Conference on*, pages 283–288. IEEE.

Peter Baldwin, Victoria Yaneva, Janet Mee, Brian E Clauser, and Le An Ha. 2020. Using natural language processing to predict item response times and improve test construction. *Journal of Educational Measurement*.

Lisa Beinborn, Torsten Zesch, and Iryna Gurevych. 2015. Candidate evaluation strategies for improved difficulty prediction of language tests. In *Proceedings of the Tenth Workshop on Innovative Use of NLP for Building Educational Applications*, pages 1–11.

Luca Benedetto, Andrea Cappelli, Roberto Turrin, and Paolo Cremonesi. 2020. R2de: a nlp approach to estimating irt parameters of newly generated questions. In *Proceedings of the Tenth International Conference on Learning Analytics & Knowledge*, pages 412–421.

Ciprian Chelba, Tomas Mikolov, Mike Schuster, Qi Ge, Thorsten Brants, Phillipp Koehn, and Tony Robinson. 2013. One billion word benchmark for measuring progress in statistical language modeling. *arXiv preprint arXiv:1312.3005*.

Alex Graves, Santiago Fernández, and Jürgen Schmidhuber. 2005. Bidirectional lstm networks for improved phoneme classification and recognition. In *International Conference on Artificial Neural Networks*, pages 799–804. Springer.

Le An Ha and Victoria Yaneva. 2018. Automatic distractor suggestion for multiple-choice tests using concept embeddings and information retrieval. In *Proceedings of the Thirteenth Workshop on Innovative Use of NLP for Building Educational Applications*, pages 389–398.

Le An Ha, Victoria Yaneva, Peter Baldwin, Janet Mee, et al. 2019. Predicting the difficulty of multiple choice questions in a high-stakes medical exam. In *Proceedings of the Fourteenth Workshop on Innovative Use of NLP for Building Educational Applications*, pages 11–20.

Perry N Halkitis et al. 1996. Estimating testing time: The effects of item characteristics on response latency.

Zhenya Huang, Qi Liu, Enhong Chen, Hongke Zhao, Mingyong Gao, Si Wei, Yu Su, and Guoping Hu. 2017. Question difficulty prediction for reading problems in standard tests. In *AAAI*, pages 1352–1359.

Ghader Kurdi, Bijan Parsia, and Uli Sattler. 2016. An experimental evaluation of automatically generated multiple choice questions from ontologies. In *OWL: Experiences And directions–reasoner evaluation*, pages 24–39. Springer.

Anastassia Loukina, Su-Youn Yoon, Jennifer Sakano, Youhua Wei, and Kathy Sheehan. 2016. Textual complexity as a predictor of difficulty of listening items in language proficiency tests. In *Proceedings of COLING 2016, the 26th International Conference on Computational Linguistics: Technical Papers*, pages 3245–3253.

Cynthia G Parshall et al. 1994. Response latency: An investigation into determinants of item-level timing.

Matthew E. Peters, Mark Neumann, Mohit Iyyer, Matt Gardner, Christopher Clark, Kenton Lee, and Luke Zettlemoyer. 2018. Deep contextualized word representations. In *Proc. of NAACL*.

Russell Winsor Smith. 2000. An exploratory analysis of item parameters and characteristics that influence item level response time.

David B Swanson, Susan M Case, Douglas R Ripkey, Brian E Clauser, and Matthew C Holtman. 2001. Relationships among item characteristics, examine characteristics, and response times on usmle step 1. *Academic Medicine*, 76(10):S114–S116.

Victoria Yaneva, Peter Baldwin, Janet Mee, et al. 2019. Predicting the difficulty of multiple choice questions in a high-stakes medical exam. In *Proceedings of the Fourteenth Workshop on Innovative Use of NLP for Building Educational Applications*, pages 11–20.

Victoria Yaneva, Le An Ha, Peter Baldwin, and Janet Mee. 2020. Predicting item survival for multiple choice questions in a high-stakesmedical exam. In *Proceedings of the 12th Conference on Language Resources and Evaluation (LREC 2020) , Marseille, 11–16 May 2020*, page 6814-6820.

A Comparative Study of Synthetic Data Generation Methods for Grammatical Error Correction

Maxwell White and Alla Rozovskaya
Department of Computer Science
Queens College, City University of New York
`maxwell.white94@qmail.cuny.edu, arozovskaya@qc.cuny.edu`

Abstract

Grammatical Error Correction (GEC) is concerned with correcting grammatical errors in written text. Current GEC systems, namely those leveraging statistical and neural machine translation, require large quantities of annotated training data, which can be expensive or impractical to obtain. This research compares techniques for generating synthetic data utilized by the two highest scoring submissions to the restricted and low-resource tracks in the BEA-2019 Shared Task on Grammatical Error Correction.

1 Introduction

Grammatical Error Correction (GEC) is the task of automatically correcting grammatical errors in written text. More recently, significant progress has been made, especially in English GEC, within the framework of statistical machine translation (SMT) and neural machine translation (NMT) approaches (Susanto et al., 2014; Yuan and Briscoe, 2016; Hoang et al., 2016; Chollampatt et al., 2016; Junczys-Dowmunt and Grundkiewicz, 2016; Mizumoto and Matsumoto, 2016; Jianshu et al., 2017; Chollampatt and Ng, 2018). The success of these approaches can be partially attributed to the availability of several large training sets.

In the most recent Building Educational Applications (BEA) 2019 Shared Task (Bryant et al., 2019), which continued the tradition of earlier GEC competitions (Dale et al., 2012; Ng et al., 2014), all of the 24 participating teams applied NMT and/or SMT approaches. One of the goals of BEA-2019 was to re-evaluate the field after a long hiatus, as recent GEC systems have become difficult to evaluate given a lack of standardised experimental settings: Although significant progress has been made since the end of the last CoNLL-2014 shared task, recent systems have

been trained, tuned and tested on different combinations of metrics and corpora. The BEA-2019 Shared Task also introduced a new dataset that represents a diverse cross-section of English language levels and domains (Bryant et al., 2019), and separate evaluation tracks, namely the *Restricted*, *Unrestricted* and *Low Resource* tracks. The Unrestricted track allowed the use of any resources; the Restricted track limited the use of learner corpora to those that are publicly available, while the Low Resource track significantly limited the use of annotated data, to encourage development of systems that do not rely on large quantities of human-annotated data.

The two top scoring systems in the Restricted and Low Resource tracks, UEDIN-MS (Grundkiewicz et al., 2019) and Kakao&Brain (Choe et al., 2019), outperformed the other teams by a large margin in both tracks; furthermore, both systems made use of artificial data for training their NMT systems, but they generated artificial data in different ways. Interestingly, in the Restricted Track, both of the systems scored on par, while in the Low Resource Track Kakao&Brain exhibited a larger gap in performance (a drop of more than 10 points compared to the Restricted track) vs. 4 points for UEDIN-MS. While both teams used the same model architecture, transformer-based neural machine translation (NMT) (Vaswani et al., 2017), in addition to the differences in the data generation methods, the systems used different training scenarios, hyperpameter values, and training corpora of native data.

The goal of this paper is to compare the techniques for generating synthetic data used by the UEDIN-MS and Kakao&Brain systems. The method used in the UEDIN-MS system utilizes confusion sets generated by a spellchecker, while the Kakao&Brain method relies on learner patterns extracted from a small annotated sample and

Proceedings of the 15th Workshop on Innovative Use of NLP for Building Educational Applications, pages 198–208
July 10, 2020. ©2020 Association for Computational Linguistics

on POS-based confusions. Henceforth, we refer to these as *Inverted Spellchecker* method and *Patterns+POS* method, respectively. To ensure a fair comparison of the methods, we control for the other variables, such as model choice, hyperparameters, and the choice of native data. We train NMT systems and evaluate our models on two learner corpora, the W&I+LOCNESS corpus introduced in BEA-2019, and the FCE corpus (Yannakoudakis et al., 2011). Using the automatic error type tool ERRANT (Bryant et al., 2017), we also show performance evaluation by error type on the two corpora.

The paper makes the following contributions: (1) we provide a fair comparison of two methods for generating synthetic parallel data for GEC, using two evaluation datasets; (2) we find that the two methods train different complementary systems and target different types of errors: while the Inverted Spellchecker approach is good at identifying spelling errors, the Patterns+POS approach is better at correcting errors relating to grammar, such as noun number, verb agreement, and verb tense; (3) overall, the Patterns+POS method exhibits stronger results, compared to the Inverted Spellchecker method in multiple training scenarios that include only synthetic parallel data, synthetic data augmented with in-domain learner data, and synthetic data augmented with out-of-domain learner data; (4) adding an off-the-shelf spellchecker is beneficial, and is especially helpful for the Patterns+POS approach.

In the next section, we discuss related work. Section 3 gives an overview of the W&I+LOCNESS and FCE learner datasets. Section 4 describes the error generation methods. Experiments are presented in section 5. Section 6 analyzes the results. Section 7 concludes the paper.

2 Related Work

Progress in English GEC Earlier GEC approaches focused on English as a Second Language Learners and made use of linear machine learning algorithms and developed classifiers for specific error types, such as articles, prepositions, or noun number (Gamon, 2010; Rozovskaya and Roth, 2010, 2014; Dahlmeier and Ng, 2012). The classifiers can be trained on native English data, learner data, or a combination thereof.

The CoNLL shared tasks on English grammar correction provided a first large annotated corpus

of learner data for training (NUCLE, (Ng et al., 2014)), as well as two test sets. All the data was produced by learners of English studying at the National University of Singapore (majority of which were native speakers of Chinese). The statistical machine translation approach was shown to be successful in the CoNLL-2014 competition for the first time (Junczys-Dowmunt and Grundkiewicz, 2014). Since then, the state-of-the-art results on the CoNLL datasets were obtained using SMT and NMT approaches. The systems are typically trained on a combination of NUCLE and the English part of the Lang-8 corpus (Mizumoto et al., 2012), even though the latter is known to contain noise, as it is only partially corrected.

Minimally-Supervised and Data-Augmented GEC There has been a lot of work on generating synthetic training data for GEC. The approaches can be broken down into those that attempt to make use of additional resources (e.g. Wikipedia edits) or noisify correct English data via artificial errors. Boyd (2018) augmented training data with edits extracted from Wikipedia revision history in German. The edits were classified and only those relating to GEC were kept. Wikipedia edits are extracted from the revision history using Wiki Edits (Grundkiewicz and Junczys-Dowmunt, 2014). The contribution of the resulting edits is demonstrated using a multilayer convolutional encoder-decoder neural network model that we also use in this work. Mizumoto et al. (2011) extracted a Japanese learners corpus from the revision log of Lang-8 (about 1 million sentences) and implemented a character-based machine-translation model.

The other approach of generating parallel data creates artificial errors in well-formed native data. This approach was shown to be effective within the classification framework (Rozovskaya and Roth, 2011; Dahlmeier and Ng, 2011; Felice and Yuan, 2014).

3 The Learner Datasets

We make use of two publicly-available datasets of learner texts for evaluation – the W&I+LOCNESS and the FCE – described below.

The BEA-2019 Shared Task introduced a new parallel corpus designed to represent a wide range of English proficiency levels. The W&I+LOCNESS corpus consists of hand-annotated data drawn from two sources. The Cambridge English Write & Improve (W&I) data

| | FCE (all) | W&I+LOCNESS | |
		Training	Dev
Type	%	%	%
ADJ	1.36	1.52	1.48
ADJ:FORM	0.28	0.24	0.21
ADV	1.94	1.51	1.51
CONJ	0.67	0.51	0.58
CONTR	0.32	0.30	0.39
DET	10.86	11.25	10.43
MORPH	1.90	1.85	2.07
NOUN	4.57	4.36	4.30
NOUN:INFL	0.50	0.12	0.13
NOUN:NUM	3.34	4.05	3.29
NOUN:POSS	0.51	0.60	0.87
ORTH	2.94	4.77	4.61
OTHER	13.26	12.76	12.84
PART	0.29	0.84	0.79
PREP	11.21	9.79	9.70
PRON	3.51	2.64	2.33
PUNCT	9.71	17.16	19.37
SPELL	9.59	3.74	5.07
UNK	3.13	2.59	2.24
VERB	7.01	5.86	5.27
VERB:FORM	3.55	3.56	3.09
VERB:INFL	0.19	0.04	0.07
VERB:SVA	1.52	2.23	1.94
VERB:TENSE	6.04	6.07	6.20
WO	1.82	1.64	1.25
Total Edits	52,671	63,683	7,632

Table 1: Error distributions by type.

comes from a web-based platform that provides feedback for non-native English students around the world to improve their writing. LOCNESS was compiled by researchers at the Centre for English Corpus Linguistics at the University of Louvain, and consists of essays written by native English students.

W&I+LOCNESS contains 3,700 texts, consisting of 43,169 sentences or 801,361 tokens. 34,308 sentences were made available for training and 4,384 for development.

To provide an additional benchmark for evaluation, we also evaluate on the test dataset from the FCE corpus (Yannakoudakis et al., 2011). The First Certificate in English (FCE) corpus is a subset of the Cambridge Learner Corpus (CLC) that contains 1,244 written answers to the FCE exam, which assesses English at an upper-intermediate level. FCE was originally annotated according to a different error type framework, but was re-annotated automatically using ERRANT for use in the shared task.

A breakdown of error types for the W&I+LOCNESS and FCE corpora can be seen in Table 1. The W&I+LOCNESS and the FCE datasets have a similar percentage of some of the most common errors: determiner, preposition, noun and noun number, verb, verb form, and verb tense. Two notable exceptions are punctuation errors (9.71% of all errors in the FCE corpus, and between 17.16% and 19.37% in the W&I+LOCNESS training and development data); and spelling errors; almost 10% of all errors in FCE, and between 3.74-5.05 in W&I+LOCNESS.

4 Synthetic Data Generation Methods

In this section, we describe the two methods to generate synthetic parallel data for training.

4.1 The Inverted Spellchecker Method

The method for generating unsupervised parallel data utilized in the system submitted by the UEDIN-MS team is characterized by usage of confusion sets extracted from a spellchecker. This artificial data is then used to pre-train a Transformer sequence-to-sequence model.

Noising method overview The Inverted Spellchecker method utilizes the Aspell spellchecker to generate a list of suggestions for a given word. Suggestions are sorted by weighted edit distance of the proposed word to the input word and the distance between their phonetic equivalents. The system then chooses the top 20 suggestions to act as the confusion set for the input word.

For each sentence, a number of words to change is determined based on the word error rate of the development data set. For each chosen word, one of the following operations is performed. With probability 0.7, the word is replaced with a word randomly chosen from the confusion set. With probability 0.1, the word is deleted. With probability 0.1, a random word is inserted. With probability 0.1, the word's position is swapped with an adjacent word. Additionally, the above operations are performed at the character level for 10% of words to introduce spelling errors. It should be emphasized that although the Inverted Spellchecker method uses confusion sets from a spellchecker, the idea of the method is to generate synthetic noisy data for training a general-purpose GEC system to correct various grammatical errors.

Training specifics The UEDIN-MS system generated parallel artificial data by applying the Inverted Spellchecker method to 100 million sentences sampled from the WMT News Crawl corpus. This data was used to pre-train transformer models in both the Restricted track and the Low-Resource track; the models differed primarily in the data sets used for fine-tuning.

In the Restricted track, all of the available annotated data from FCE, Lang-8, NUCLE, and W&I+LOCNESS train was used for fine-tuning. In the Low-Resource track, a subset of the WikiEd corpus was used. The WikiEd corpus consists of 56 million parallel sentences automatically extracted from Wikipedia revisions. The hand annotated W&I+LOCNESS training data was used as a seed corpus to select 2 million sentence pairs from the WikiEd corpus that best match the domain. These 2 million sentences were then used to fine-tune the models that were pre-trained on synthetic data.

4.2 The Patterns+POS Method

The Kakao&Brain system generates artificial data by introducing two noising scenarios: a token-based approach (patterns) and a type-based approach (POS). Similar to the UEDIN-MS system, artificial data is then used to pre-train a transformer model.

Noising method overview The method first uses a small learner sample from W&I+LOCNESS training data to extract error patterns, i.e. the edits that occurred and their frequency. Edit information is used to construct a dictionary of commonly-used edits. This dictionary is then used to generate noise by applying edits in reverse to grammatically correct sentences.

For any token in the native training data that is not found in the edit pattern dictionary, a type-based noising scenario is applied. In the type-based approach, noise is added based on parts-of-speech (POS). Here, only prepositions, nouns, and verbs are noisified, with probability 0.15 for an individual token, as follows: a noun may be replaced with its singular/plural version; a verb may be replaced with its morphological variant; a preposition may be replaced with another preposition.

Training specifics Artificial data for the Kakao&Brain system was generated by applying the Patterns+POS method to native English data from the Gutenberg dataset (Lahiri,

	Sentences	**Tokens**
News Crawl	2,060,499	50,000,109
W&I+L train	34,308	628,720
FCE-train	28,350	454,736
NUCLE	57,151	1,161,567
Lang-8	1,037,561	11,857,938
W&I+L dev	4,384	86,973
FCE-test	2,695	41,932

Table 2: Corpora statistics.

2014), the Tatoeba dataset[1], and the WikiText-103 dataset (Merity et al., 2016). The final pre-training data set was a collection of 45 million sentence pairs, with the noising approach applied multiple times to each dataset (1x Gutenberg, 12x Tatoeba, and 5x WikiText-103) to approximately balance data from each source. In both the Restricted track and the Low Resource track, these 45 million sentence pairs were used to pre-train weights. The respective systems for these tracks primarily differed in the data sets then used for additional training. In the Restricted track, all of the available annotated data from FCE, Lang-8, NUCLE, W&I+LOCNESS train was used in the training step. In the Low Resource track, training was done on a subset of 3 thousand sentences sampled from the W&I+LOCNESS development data.

5 Experiments

To compare the Inverted Spellchecker and Patterns+POS noising methods, we present a series of experiments that should provide evidence for the efficacy of the noising methods separate from the implementation of the systems as a whole.

5.1 Experimental Setup

We implement the approach described in Chollampatt and Ng (2018), which is a neural machine translation approach that uses Convolutional Encoder-Decoder Neural Network architecture (CNN). More specifically, we train a CNN model with reranking. We use the same hyperparameters specified by the authors in the paper. The reranking is performed using edit operations (EO) and language model (LM) (see the paper for more detail). We present results for an ensemble of four models trained with different initializations; results are averaged). We additionally attempted an

---

[1]https://tatoeba.org/eng/downloads

approach using a transformer architecture, but in preliminary results it did not outperform the CNN.

The language model (LM) is a 5-gram LM trained on the publicly available WMT News Crawl corpus (233 million sentences), using the KenLM toolkit (Heafield et al., 2013). We also use an off-the-shelf speller (Flor, 2012; Flor and Futagi, 2012) as a pre-processing step (prior to running the grammar correction system). We include results with and without the use of the speller.

Most of the experiments (except experiment 1, as shown below) are performed using 2 million sentences (50 million tokens) from the WMT News Crawl corpus. We use this data to create artificially noised source data with the noising techniques described above. For the Inverted Spellchecker method, we use the same error rate of 0.15 used by the authors in their original system (the error rate is chosen to simulate the error rate of the learner data). The same probabilities for word-level and character-level modifications are used as well (probability 0.7 to replace a token with another from the confusion set, and 0.1 each to delete, insert, or swap with an adjacent token). For the Patterns+POS method, we use a sample of 2,000 sentences from W&I+LOCNESS train for the token-based portion of the noising method. We also use the same error rates as the authors in their original system: probability 0.9 to apply an edit in reverse if it appears in the edit dictionary, and probability 0.10 to apply a POS-based noising scenario. For all models, the same 2,000 sentences from W&I+LOCNESS train are used to train the reranker.

All of the results are reported on the development section of the W&I+LOCNESS dataset and on the test section of the FCE corpus (the W&I+LOCNESS test data set has not been publicly released and the task participants were evaluated via CodaLab).

We address the following research questions:

- How do the two data generation methods compare on the FCE and W&I+LOCNESS evaluation datasets?
- How does the performance improve when the synthetically-generated parallel data is augmented with parallel learner data from in-domain and out-of-domain?
- How do the two methods perform on different error types?

Experiments vary by the sources of additional annotated learner data that were added to the artificially-generated data. Our goal in combining synthetic data with learner data is to evaluate to contribution of synthetic data (generated in different ways) in various scenarios with in-domain and out-domain learner data available. The additional *learner* training data comes from the publicly-available learner corpora of various sizes and various sources of data: the W&I+LOCNESS and the FCE training partitions (treated as in-domain for the respective evaluation datasets), the Lang-8 corpus (Mizumoto et al., 2012), and the NUCLE corpus from the CoNLL-2014 shared task (Dahlmeier et al., 2013) (both treated as out-of-domain for the two datasets). These learner corpora were also allowed for use in the Restricted track. Statistics for the amounts of data can be seen in Table 2.

The first experiment trains models on 50M tokens of artificial data generated by each noising method. The second experiment adds W&I+LOCNESS training data to the artificial data. Experiment 3 adds the FCE training set to the artificial data. In the fourth experiment, we add the entirety of the annotated training corpora (FCE, Lang-8, and NUCLE) consisting of 13.5 million tokens to the initial artificially-generated training set, excluding W&I+LOCNESS training dataset. Finally, the fifth experiment modifies the fourth by also including the W&I+LOCNESS training dataset.

Experiment 1: Artificial data only For the first experiment, only artificial data generated by either respective noising method is used to train models. The results can be viewed in Table 3.

Two observations can be made here. First, without adding the spellchecker, the Patterns+POS outperforms the Inverted Spellchecker method by more than 2 points on the W&I+LOCNESS corpus; however, on the FCE dataset, the Inverted Spellchecker method is superior (6 point difference). Since the Patterns+POS method uses data from W&I+LOCNESS train to generate a token edit dictionary, this may explain the relatively improved results of this method on in-domain W&I+LOCNESS evaluation data. To explore this hypothesis, we analyze these models' performance with respect to ERRANT error types in Section 6.

We also note that, when a spellchecker is added, performance is improved substantially for the Patterns+POS methods (5 and 7 points, respectively, on W&I+LOCNESS and FCE datasets). In con-

Noising method	W&I+L dev			FCE test		
	P	**R**	**F0.5**	**P**	**R**	**F0.5**
Inverted Spellchecker	30.55	10.71	22.29	39.88	13.65	28.81
Patterns+POS	33.93	12.24	25.05	32.43	10.05	22.43
Inverted Spellchecker*	30.12	11.85	23.02	40.72	15.87	31.01
Patterns+POS*	37.04	16.77	29.83	37.04	16.77	29.83

Table 3: Experiment 1 results: Ensemble of 4 models trained on 50 million tokens of artificial data and tuned with a sample of 2 thousand sentences from W&I+LOCNESS train (*speller applied during pre-processing).

Noising method	W&I+L dev			FCE test		
	P	**R**	**F0.5**	**P**	**R**	**F0.5**
Inverted Spellchecker	32.78	15.68	26.91	35.94	18.07	30.01
Patterns+POS	41.56	15.41	31.03	35.57	12.46	25.95
Inverted Spellchecker*	31.30	16.24	26.41	35.31	19.48	30.37
Patterns+POS*	42.96	20.00	34.94	41.55	19.94	34.15

Table 4: Experiment 1 results continued: Ensemble of 4 models trained on 500 million tokens of artificial data (*speller applied during pre-processing).

Noising method	W&I+L dev			FCE test		
	P	**R**	**F0.5**	**P**	**R**	**F0.5**
Inverted Spellchecker	39.63	19.50	32.85	39.25	19.26	32.50
Patterns+POS	42.57	22.07	35.90	38.88	18.84	32.06
Inverted Spellchecker*	38.45	20.71	32.83	38.89	21.13	33.29
Patterns+POS*	43.42	26.51	38.50	42.86	25.65	37.79

Table 5: Experiment 2 results: Ensemble of 4 models trained on 50 million tokens of artificial data with 600,000 tokens from W&I+LOCNESS train added (*speller applied during pre-processing).

Noising method	W&I+L dev			FCE test		
	P	**R**	**F0.5**	**P**	**R**	**F0.5**
Inverted Spellchecker	33.38	13.89	26.06	44.88	20.73	36.40
Patterns+POS	39.30	15.48	30.05	44.64	18.49	34.80
Inverted Spellchecker*	32.34	14.76	26.12	44.57	22.47	37.24
Patterns+POS*	40.51	19.54	33.35	47.09	23.68	39.32

Table 6: Experiment 3 results: Ensemble of 4 models trained on 50 million tokens of artificial data with 450,000 tokens from FCE train added (*speller applied during pre-processing).

Noising method	W&I+L dev			FCE test		
	P	**R**	**F0.5**	**P**	**R**	**F0.5**
Inverted Spellchecker	44.80	22.97	37.65	52.43	31.02	46.07
Patterns+POS	46.36	25.06	39.62	50.96	29.72	44.59
Inverted Spellchecker*	42.65	23.64	36.74	50.16	31.81	44.97
Patterns+POS*	45.78	28.13	40.68	50.44	32.69	45.50

Table 7: Experiment 4 results: Ensemble of 4 models trained on 50 million tokens of artificial data with 13.5 million tokens from FCE train, Lang-8, and NUCLE (*speller applied during pre-processing).

Noising method	W&I+L dev			FCE test		
	P	**R**	**F0.5**	**P**	**R**	**F0.5**
Inverted Spellchecker	46.76	26.34	40.48	50.02	31.94	44.93
Patterns+POS	48.35	28.01	42.22	50.31	30.16	44.38
Inverted Spellchecker*	44.75	27.42	39.73	48.43	33.15	44.34
Patterns+POS*	47.68	31.03	43.06	49.56	33.06	45.06

Table 8: Experiment 5 results: Ensemble of 4 models trained on 50 million tokens of artificial data with 14 million tokens of additional annotated data from W&I+LOCNESS, FCE train, Lang-8, and NUCLE (*speller applied during pre-processing).

trast, the Inverted Spellchecker method benefits by less than one point and by 2 points on the respective evaluation sets.

To gauge the effect of using a larger synthetic data set, we repeat experiment 1 with 500M tokens of synthetic data (approximately 20M sentences). Results can be viewed in Table 4. We note that the gap between the two methods increases by about 2 points on W&I+LOCNESS, with Patterns+POS outperforming the Inverted Spellchecker. Further, the Patterns+POS now also outperforms the Inverted Spellchecker method on FCE by 4 points (with a spellchecker added). It is worth noting that although both methods use 2,000 training sentences from W&I+LOCNESS for tuning, the Patterns+POS method also uses the 2,000 sentences to generate patterns, which seems to benefit more the W&I+LOCNESS data, compared to the FCE data.

Experiment 2: Adding W&I+LOCNESS training data In this experiment, W&I+LOCNESS training data (with the exception of 2,000 tokens used to train the reranker) is added to the 50 million native data. The results can be viewed in Table 5.

The addition of annotated learner data to the training impacts the performance of each noising method similarly, showing a significantly larger improvement evaluated on the in-domain W&I+LOCNESS dataset, compared to results of experiment 1. Both methods improve by almost 10 points, with and without a spellchecker is added. Further, although both methods make use of the in-domain training data, the Patterns+POS approach still outperforms the Inverted Spellchecker method. This suggests that the generated synthetic errors provide additional knowledge to the model that is not present in the learner parallel data.

Interestingly, on FCE, Patterns+POS shows a similar jump in performance compared to experiment 1, while improvements are more modest for the Inverted Spellchecker method. Overall, comparing the best results on FCE that include the spellchecker, the Inverted Spellchecker improves by 2 points, while the Patterns+POS method improves by 8 points.

Overall, adding in-domain training data for W&I+LOCNESS benefits the W&I+LOCNESS more than the FCE test set, and helps both synthetic data methods. Improvements are smaller when a spellchecker is added; the smallest improvements are attained on the FCE dataset. The Patterns+POS method is superior on both datasets.

Experiment 3: FCE training data added In this experiment, FCE training data is added to the 50 million artificial tokens for training. The results can be viewed in Table 6.

Compared to the addition of W&I+LOCNESS data in experiment 2, the addition of FCE data results in a larger improvement when evaluated on FCE test: 6 and 10 points (with a spellchecker added) for the Inverted SpellChecker and Patterns+POS, respectively. Improvements are modest on the W&I+LOCNESS dataset and very similar for the two methods (3-4 points). Here, as before, the Patterns+POS method outperforms the Inverted Spellchecker method on the W&I+LOCNESS dataset, and on FCE when the spellchecker is applied. In general, it can be seen that the Patterns+POS methods takes advantage of the 2,000 training sentences to a greater extent than the Inverted Spellchecker method. As a result, the Patterns+POS method is always superior on the in-domain W&I+LOCNESS data. However, the addition of a spellchecker is extremely helpful and substantially improves the performance of the method also on out-of-domain FCE data.

Experiment 4: Out-of-domain annotated training data added In experiment 4, all annotated data, with the exception of W&I+LOCNESS, is added. This experiment considers the effect of out-of-domain learner data (out-of-domain relative to the W&I+LOCNESS dataset). Results are in Table 7. Even though all of the datasets include ESL data and most of them contain student essays, we consider these data sets out-of-domain relative to the W&I+LOCNESS set since they contain texts written on a different set of topics and by learners of different proficiency levels .

Significant improvements over the previous experiments can be observed, due to the volume of additional data added. The Inverted Spellchecker method improves by 15 points on W&I+LOCNESS dev and 17 points on FCE test, compared to only using artificial data. The Patterns+POS method improves by 15 points on W&I+LOCNESS and 12 points on FCE test. We observe that the two methods are very close on FCE , while the Patterns+POS method still outperforms the Inverted Spellchecker method on W&I+Locness (by 2 and 4 points with and without the spellchecker added, respectively). This is interesting and suggests that the Patterns+POS method is especially useful when there is no in-domain training data available, even though large amounts of out-of-domain learner data are available. It should also be noted that adding a spellchecker does not improve Inverted Spellchecker models, while it is still useful for the Patterns+POS models.

Experiment 5: All annotated training data added In experiment 5, all available annotated data including the W&I+LOCNESS training data (approximately 14 million tokens) is added to the artificially generated data. Results can be viewed in Table 8. This model produces the best results on the W&I+LOCNESS data, improving by 3 points compared to experiment 4, while on the FCE dataset there is no additional improvement. The two methods perform similarly on the FCE test, and the Patterns+POS method outperforms the Inverted Spellchecker method on W&I+LOCNESS data.

6 Discussion and Error Analysis

Results in the previous section indicate that the Patterns+POS method outperforms the Inverted Spellchecker method on W&I+LOCNESS, both when used on its own, and when additional learner training data is available, with and without a spellchecker. on the FCE dataset, the Patterns+POS method is superior only when a spellchecker is added. In general, the Pat-

terns+POS method benefits more from the addition of a spellchecker in all experiments. Adding an off-the-shelf spellchecker to a GEC system is a common pre-processing step: a spellchecker is developed to specifically target spelling errors, so a GEC system, which is typically more complex, can focus on other language misuse. The greater gap in performance between the methods on W&I+LOCNESS, compared to FCE, can be attributed to the utilization of in-domain data as part of the Patterns+POS noising approach.

Evaluation by Error Type To examine the discrepancies in performance between the two noising methods across the two evaluation datasets, we present an evaluation of performance by ER-RANT error type. Type-based evaluation results for the top 10 most common error types for each respective evaluation dataset can be seen in Tables 9 and 10 (note that these results do not include the off-the-shelf spellchecker). The Inverted Spellchecker method significantly outperforms the Patterns+POS method on spelling errors on both datasets. As spelling errors make up approximately 10% of errors in the FCE test set (double the relative frequency of spelling errors in W&I+LOCNESS), this may explain the improved performance of the Inverted Spellchecker method when evaluated on FCE, compared to its own performance on W&I+LOCNESS.

In contrast, the Patterns+POS method outperforms the Inverted Spellchecker method on verb tense errors and noun number errors. This makes sense, since the POS-based confusion sets produce errors that reflect misuse of these grammatical categories. On the most common and notoriously difficult errors – articles and prepositions – the two methods exhibit similar performance. Finally, the Patterns+POS method outperforms the Inverted Spellchecker method by 25 points on punctuation errors on the W&I+LOCNESS data, but is outperformed by 2 points on FCE. This may be due to the fact that the Patterns+POS method utilizes in-domain data as part of its noising process.

Comparison with BEA-2019 results The highest score achieved on W&I+LOCNESS data is F0.5 43.49 (experiment 5), obtained by the Patterns+POS method with all of the annotated data added to training, combined with the spellchecker (see Table 8). The model that only uses 2,000 sentences for reranking and to generate the patterns table (experiment 1, Table 3) obtains a score of 28.06 on W&I+LOCNESS and 30.98 on

Type	Error count	%	Inverted Spellchecker			Pattern+POS		
			P	R	F0.5	P	R	F0.5
PUNCT	1478	19.81	42.72	12.72	28.87	43.16	26.69	38.13
OTHER	980	13.13	12.46	4.42	8.84	6.40	0.56	2.07
DET	796	10.67	36.02	12.41	25.98	33.33	13.63	25.53
PREP	740	9.92	27.66	6.25	16.37	22.07	7.50	15.54
VERB:TENSE	473	6.34	14.77	2.48	7.34	29.12	10.36	20.14
VERB	402	5.39	6.39	2.30	4.57	8.40	0.38	1.57
SPELL	387	5.19	64.96	58.01	63.37	16.62	2.00	6.69
ORTH	352	4.72	66.33	5.54	20.34	61.50	3.41	13.91
NOUN	328	4.40	5.41	4.04	4.95	7.91	0.91	3.12
NOUN:NUM	251	3.36	41.85	3.88	13.19	71.74	7.76	26.12
Overall	7461	100	27.30	10.24	20.37	31.54	12.39	23.87

Table 9: Type-based results on experiment 1 (50M tokens artificial data only) on W&I+LOCNESS Dev.

Type	Error count	%	Inverted Spellchecker			Pattern+POS		
			P	R	F0.5	P	R	F0.5
DET	625	13.74	52.79	15.04	35.12	47.81	15.16	33.12
OTHER	580	12.75	20.62	6.59	14.04	0.00	0.00	0.00
PREP	477	10.49	29.11	5.61	15.80	25.47	8.33	17.75
PUNCT	471	10.35	25.70	12.85	21.21	18.80	18.20	18.61
SPELL	452	9.94	67.15	52.16	63.36	25.10	3.15	10.33
VERB	243	5.34	9.22	2.68	6.09	6.62	0.31	1.29
VERB:TENSE	232	5.10	21.50	2.91	9.34	24.49	7.00	15.27
NOUN	202	4.44	8.97	5.95	7.82	5.42	0.75	2.39
NOUN:NUM	174	3.83	21.39	46.71	23.75	35.97	54.60	38.29
VERB:FORM	166	3.65	35.29	29.77	33.77	45.34	26.36	39.51
Overall	4549	100	36.26	12.88	26.51	29.74	10.02	21.26

Table 10: Type-based results on experiment 1 (50M tokens artificial data only) on FCE test.

FCE. Choe et al. (2019) report results of 53.00 and 52.79, respectively, which is likely due to the difference in amount of artificial data utilized. The UEDIN-MS system used the Inverted Spellchecker method to generate 100 million sentences of artificial data, while the Kakao&Brain system used the Pattern+POS method to generate 45 million sentences, while we used 2 million native sentences. We note, however, that our experiments using larger training sets (20 million sentences, shown in Table 4) suggest that our findings carry over to models trained on larger datasets.

7 Conclusions and Future Work

In this paper, we conduct a fair comparison of two methods for generating synthetic parallel data for grammatical error correction – using spellchecker-based confusion sets and using learner patterns and POS-based confusions. Our models are evaluated on two benchmark GEC English learner datasets. We show that the methods are better-suited for different types of language misuse. In general, the Patterns+POS methods demonstrated stronger performance than the Inverted Spellchecker methods.

For future work, we will investigate how these noising approaches complement each other. This can be done by training models on a mixture of synthetic data generated from both approaches independently, or by utilizing a hybrid noising method that combines the character-level perturbation method of the Inverted Spellchecker method with the Pattern+POS method in order to generate additional artificial spelling errors. We will also perform experiments with larger training sets. It would also be interesting to examine how these noising scenarios perform for languages other than English.

Acknowledgments

We thank the anonymous reviewers for their insightful comments. We thank Michael Flor for his help with running the ConSpel spellchecker on our data.

References

A. Boyd. 2018. Using wikipedia edits in low resource grammatical error correction. In *Proceedings of the 4th Workshop on Noisy User-generated Text (W-NUT*.

C. Bryant, M. Felice, Ø. Andersen, and T. Briscoe. 2019. The BEA-19 shared task on grammatical error correction. In *Proceedings of the ACL Workshop on Innovative Use of NLP for Building Educational Applications (BEA-19)*.

C. Bryant, M. Felice, and T. Briscoe. 2017. Automatic annotation and evaluation of error types for grammatical error correction. In *Proceedings of the 55th Annual Meeting of the Association for Computational Linguistics (Volume 1: Long Papers)*, pages 793–805, Vancouver, Canada. Association for Computational Linguistics.

Y. J. Choe, J. Ham, K. Park, and Y. Yoon. 2019. A neural grammatical error correction system built on better pre-training and sequential transfer learning . In *Proceedings of the ACL Workshop on Innovative Use of NLP for Building Educational Applications (BEA-19)*.

S. Chollampatt and H. T. Ng. 2018. A multilayer convolutional encoder-decoder neural network for grammatical error correction. In *Proceedings of the AAAI*. Association for the Advancement of Artificial Intelligence.

S. Chollampatt, K. Taghipour, and H. T. Ng. 2016. Neural network translation models for grammatical error correction. In *IJCAI*.

D. Dahlmeier and H. T. Ng. 2011. Grammatical error correction with alternating structure optimization. In *Proceedings of ACL*.

D. Dahlmeier and H. T. Ng. 2012. A beam-search decoder for grammatical error correction. In *Proceedings of EMNLP-CoNLL*.

D. Dahlmeier, H. T. Ng, and S. M. Wu. 2013. Building a large annotated corpus of learner english: The nus corpus of learner english. In *Proceedings of the Eighth Workshop on Innovative Use of NLP for Building Educational Applications*, pages 22–31, Atlanta, Georgia. Association for Computational Linguistics.

R. Dale, I. Anisimoff, and G. Narroway. 2012. A report on the preposition and determiner error correction shared task. In *Proceedings of the NAACL Workshop on Innovative Use of NLP for Building Educational Applications*.

M. Felice and Z. Yuan. 2014. Generating artificial errors for grammatical error correction. In *Proceedings of the Student Research Workshop at EACL*, Gothenburg, Sweden. Association for Computational Linguistics.

M. Flor. 2012. Four types of context for automatic spelling correction. *Traitement Automatique des Langues (TAL)*, 53(3):61–99.

M. Flor and Y. Futagi. 2012. On using context for automatic correction of non-word misspellings in student essays. In *Proceedings of the 7th Workshop on Innovative Use of NLP for Building Educational Applications*. Association for Computational Linguistics.

M. Gamon. 2010. Using mostly native data to correct errors in learners' writing. In *Proceedings of NAACL*.

R. Grundkiewicz and M. Junczys-Dowmunt. 2014. The Wiked error corpus: A corpus of corrective wikipedia edits and its application to grammatical error correction. In *Advances in Natural Language Processing – Lecture Notes in Computer Science*, volume 8686, pages 478–490. Springer.

R. Grundkiewicz, M. Junczys-Dowmunt, and K. Heafield. 2019. Neural grammatical error correction systems with unsupervised pre-training on synthetic data. In *Proceedings of the ACL Workshop on Innovative Use of NLP for Building Educational Applications (BEA-19)*.

K. Heafield, I. Pouzyrevsky, J. H. Clark, and P. Koehn. 2013. Scalable modified Kneser-Ney language model estimation. In *ACL*.

D.-T. Hoang, S. Chollampatt, and H.-T. Ng. 2016. Exploiting n-best hypotheses to improve an SMT approach to grammatical error correction. In *IJCAI*.

J. Jianshu, Q. Wang, K. Toutanova, Y. Gong, S. Truong, and Jianfeng J. Gao. 2017. A nested attention neural hybrid model for grammatical error correction. In *ACL*.

M. Junczys-Dowmunt and R. Grundkiewicz. 2014. The AMU system in the CoNLL-2014 shared task: Grammatical error correction by data-intensive and feature-rich statistical machine translation. In *Proceedings of the Eighteenth Conference on Computational Natural Language Learning: Shared Task*.

M. Junczys-Dowmunt and R. Grundkiewicz. 2016. Phrase-based machine translation is state-of-the-art for automatic grammatical error correction. In *EMNLP*.

S. Lahiri. 2014. Complexity of Word Collocation Networks: A Preliminary Structural Analysis. In *Proceedings of the Student Research Workshop at the 14th Conference of the European Chapter of the Association for Computational Linguistics*.

S. Merity, C. Xiong, J. Bradbury, and R. Socher. 2016. Pointer sentinel mixture models. *CoRR*, abs/1609.07843.

T. Mizumoto, Y. Hayashibe, M. Komachi, M. Nagata, and Y. Matsumoto. 2012. The effect of learner corpus size in grammatical error correction of esl writings. In *COLING*.

T. Mizumoto, M. Komachi, M. Nagata, and Y. Matsumoto. 2011. Mining revision log of language learning SNS for automated japanese error correction of second language learners. In *IJCNLP*.

T. Mizumoto and Y. Matsumoto. 2016. Discriminative reranking for grammatical error correction with statistical machine translation. In *NAACL*.

H. T. Ng, S. M. Wu, T. Briscoe, C. Hadiwinoto, R. H. Susanto, and C. Bryant. 2014. The conll-2014 shared task on grammatical error correction. In *Proceedings of the Eighteenth Conference on Computational Natural Language Learning: Shared Task*, pages 1–14, Baltimore, Maryland. Association for Computational Linguistics.

A. Rozovskaya and D. Roth. 2010. Training paradigms for correcting errors in grammar and usage. In *Proceedings of NAACL*.

A. Rozovskaya and D. Roth. 2011. Algorithm selection and model adaptation for ESL correction tasks. In *Proceedings of ACL*.

A. Rozovskaya and D. Roth. 2014. Building a State-of-the-Art Grammatical Error Correction System. In *Transactions of ACL*.

R. H. Susanto, P. Phandi, and H. T. Ng. 2014. System combination for grammatical error correction. In *EMNLP*.

A. Vaswani, N. Shazeer, N. Parmar, J. Uszkoreit, L. Jones, A. N. Gomez, Ł. Kaiser, and I. Polosukhin. 2017. 2017. Attention is all you need. *In I. Guyon, U. V. Luxburg, S. Bengio, H. Wallach, R. Fergus, S. Vishwanathan, and R. Garnett, editors, Advances in Neural Information Processing Systems*.

H. Yannakoudakis, T. Briscoe, and B. Medlock. 2011. A new dataset and method for automatically grading esol texts. In *Proceedings of the 49th Annual Meeting of the Association for Computational Linguistics: Human Language Technologies*, pages 180–189, Portland, Oregon, USA. Association for Computational Linguistics.

Z. Yuan and T. Briscoe. 2016. Grammatical error correction using neural machine translation. In *NAACL*.

Author Index

Association for Computational Linguistics
209 N. Eighth Street
Stroudsburg, Pennsylvania 18360

ISBN 978-1-7138-1382-8